CAMPAIGNS
OF THE
CIVIL WAR

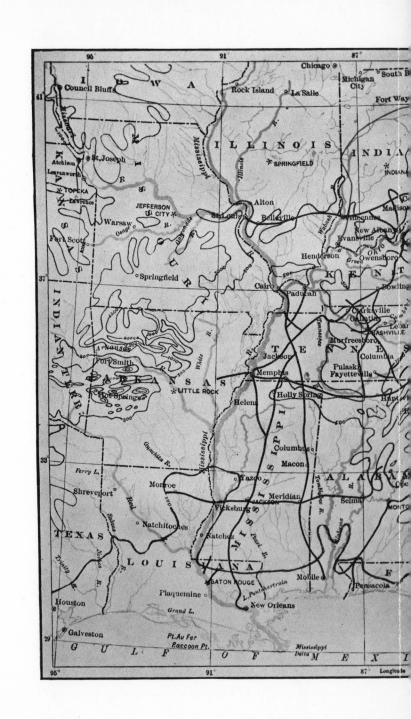

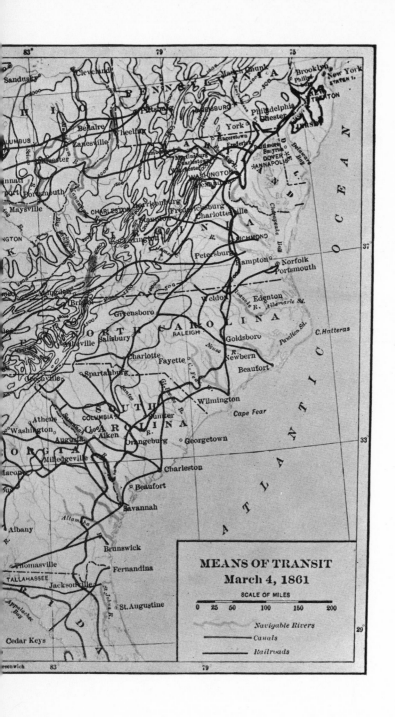

MEANS OF TRANSIT
March 4, 1861

SCALE OF MILES

0   25   50   100   150   200

Navigable Rivers
Canals
Railroads

CAMPAIGNS

OF THE

CIVIL WAR

BY

WALTER GEER

AUTHOR OF "NAPOLEON THE FIRST,"
"THE FRENCH REVOLUTION," ETC.

KONECKY&KONECKY

Konecky & Konecky
72 Ayers Point Rd.
Old Saybrook, CT 06475

ISBN: 1-56852-268-1

Printed and bound in the USA

FOREWORD

IT has been said that Fortune always favors the heaviest battalions, or, as Napoleon put it, that "Providence is always on the side of the last reserve." Military history shows no real exceptions to this axiom, that wars are won by superior strength — by weight of numbers, if the numbers are properly trained and supplied.

The North began the Civil War with all the advantages but two. Her white population outnumbered that of the South by four to one. She had the greater wealth, all the larger industries, the mineral fields, the shipbuilding yards, and all the navy there was. She had all the rank and file of the regular army and two-thirds of the officers.

On the other hand, the South had two advantages which nearly gave her the victory. She was much better fitted for military organization than the North: the great majority of her citizens were country people who could ride and march and shoot; and she had on her side by far the abler generals. The North produced some competent generals in the end — Grant, Sherman, Sheridan, Thomas, not to mention McClellan, Buell, and Rosecrans, who fell by the way. But the South had, in Lee and Stonewall Jackson, generals who have had few superiors in the art of war. If Jackson had been at the side of Lee at Gettysburg, the South would probably have won her independence. And Lee ranks with Alexander, Hannibal, Cæsar, Frederick, and Napoleon, as one of the six greatest captains of all the ages. It detracts nothing from his glory, that he, like Napoleon, finally fell under the accumulated weight of numbers.

Notwithstanding all of her many great advantages, however, the North was confronted by a serious problem. A hundred years before the outbreak of the Civil War, Chatham had said in the British Parliament: "Conquer a free population of three million souls? The thing is impossible!" This phrase has become an axiom in politics.

FOREWORD

The North faced the task of subduing five and a half million people in deadly earnest, with three and a half million slaves behind them to do the manual labor, while the whole adult white male population took the field. Was victory possible under these circumstances?

It is a popular fallacy that the Great War, which ended nearly a decade ago, superseded, so far as military interest goes, not only Napoleon's campaigns, but our own Civil War. This is not true. Marshal Foch put in practice the main principles that underlay the campaigns of Napoleon; and in the Civil War all the principal strategic and tactical developments of the Great War were foreshadowed: a half a century earlier, America had faced most of its problems and brilliantly solved them. While German staff officers have regarded the Civil War as a mere squabble of amateurs, the British Staff College, for two generations, has made a careful study of the battles of North and South, and the French General Staff has recently (1925) added the history of the American Civil War to the list of subjects studied at the École de Guerre. It is interesting to note, to what an extent technical matters in the earlier contest anticipated the later. In the combats of the Wilderness, the whole technique of trench warfare was foreshadowed; cavalry, for the first time, was used as mounted infantry; many of the modern weapons of war were originated; and the minor tactics on both sides were curiously like those of to-day.

The Civil War will always possess a fascination to the student of history, if for no other reason, because of the two great leaders it produced: Lee on the one side, and Lincoln on the other. To Lee can well be applied the epitaph of Bossuet on Turenne: " He could fight without anger, win without ambition, and triumph without vanity." Lincoln has already passed into legend, and no words can enhance his grandeur: he was one of the two or three greatest men ever born of Anglo-Saxon blood.

The Biblical saying, " Of making many books there is no end," well applies to works relating to the Civil War.

FOREWORD

There are histories, biographies, and memoirs, too numerous to mention. A list compiled in 1866 gives over six thousand titles, and this has been enormously increased in the sixty years which have elapsed since the close of the war. "Yet," says Major Steele, in his recent book, *American Campaigns,* — "yet, there is no single work that covers the whole war concisely and in a way to satisfy the military student."

It may seem presumptuous on the part of a civilian to undertake this task, but the writer is emboldened by the words of Arnold, in his *Lectures on Modern History,* where he says: "There must be a point up to which an unprofessional judgment on a professional subject may not only be competent, but of high authority. . . . The distinction seems to lie originally in the difference between the power of doing a thing and that of perceiving whether it is well done or not. . . . As to what is generally called strategy, . . . an unprofessional person may, without blame, speak or write on military subjects, and may judge of them sufficiently."

The object of the present book is to give a concise military narrative of the principal campaigns of the Civil War. A discussion of the political differences which brought on the great conflict lies entirely outside the scope of this work.

WALTER GEER

NEW YORK, September, 1926.

TABLE OF CONTENTS

MAPS

CAMPAIGNS
OF THE
CIVIL WAR

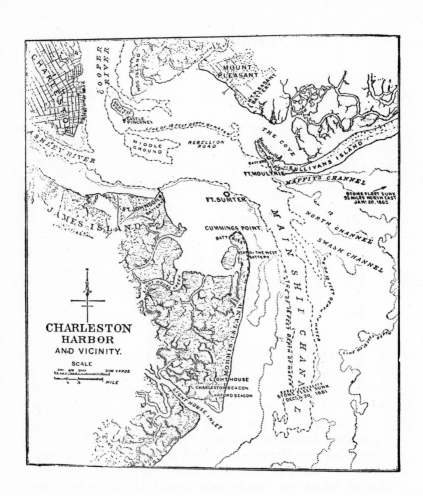

CHARLESTON
HARBOR
AND VICINITY.

SCALE

CAMPAIGNS *of the* CIVIL WAR

CHAPTER ONE

1861

FORT SUMTER

Election of Lincoln — Sentiment of the South — South Carolina Secedes from the Union — Anderson Moves to Fort Sumter — The State Constructs Batteries — The *Star of the West* Fired on — Envoys Sent to Washington — No Action Taken — Six More States Secede — The Confederacy Organized — Lincoln's Policy — Decision to Provision Sumter — The Fort Bombarded — Anderson Surrenders — Civil War Begins — Four More States Secede — The Theatre of War — Means of Transit — Obstacles to Overcome — General Strategy of the War — The Shenandoah Valley — Numbers of the Combatants — Advantages and Disadvantages on Both Sides — Command of the Sea — Southern Hopes of Foreign Intervention — Robert E. Lee — Stonewall Jackson — His Youth — West Point — Compared to Napoleon — The Mexican War — The Virginia Military Institute — His Study of Napoleon's Campaigns — Southern Aptitude for War — Superior Organization of the Confederate Army

DURING the first seventy years of the life of this Republic, from the adoption of the Constitution in 1789 to the outbreak of the Civil War in 1861, the control of the Government was almost continuously in the hands of the South. Of the first fifteen Presidents, eight were from that section of the country, and five of these Southern Presidents served for eight years apiece, while not one of the Northern Presidents was reelected. Moreover, throughout nearly all this period, the Southerners, with the help of their Northern allies, controlled one or both Houses of the Federal Congress; and the major part of the Justices of the Supreme Court of the United States were Southerners in every year of its existence. But, in 1860, there was a split in the Democratic

[3]

party, which had so long dominated the three branches of the Government, and the newly-formed Republican party was victorious at the polls. On the 6 November 1860, Abraham Lincoln was elected President of the United States.[1]

With the exception of some ballots cast for him in the western part of Virginia — now the State of West Virginia — Lincoln received no votes in the slave States. The great majority of the people of the South sincerely felt that they were in danger of persecution and disaster; that the North wished to ruin them. If the Southerners submitted tamely to Lincoln's election, they must expect to see slavery abolished from Delaware to Texas: only independence could save them. It was then that the Southern leaders finally determined to leave the Union.[2]

Since the founding of the government there had been a difference of opinion between the North and the South on the question of the constitutional position of the States within the Union. In the North, it was generally held that the Union was sovereign and the States part of it. In the South, the consensus of public opinion was just the opposite. Every man felt that his first allegiance was to his native State: to her, he owed not merely devotion, but life itself.

From the date of Mr. Lincoln's election, the intention of the people of South Carolina to secede from the Union was clearly shown, and on the 20 December the State formally took this action. The convention which passed the ordinance of secession at once appointed three commissioners, to proceed to Washington to treat with the United States Government for the delivery of the forts, arsenals, and other property of the Government within the limits of South Carolina.

It is impossible to imagine what reception these commissioners would have met at Washington, provided there had been no change in the situation at Charleston prior to their arrival at the capital. But on reaching Washington on the morning of the 27 December, they were confronted by a despatch from Charleston announcing that Major

[1] *Cf.* 6 Channing, 2.   [2] See 6 Channing, 250, 258, 264.

Anderson had transferred his command from Fort Moultrie to Fort Sumter.

Anderson, with two small companies, in all about one hundred officers and men, had been stationed at Fort Moultrie, on the north side of the harbor of Charleston. The two other forts, Castle Pinckney, a small work near the city, and Fort Sumter, erected on a ledge in the middle of the harbor, were not garrisoned. A captain of engineers, Foster,[3] was engaged in putting the latter fort in order for occupancy. Moultrie was commanded by sand hills at a distance of only 160 yards, and was untenable. On the other hand, Sumter was in the middle of the entrance to the harbor, more than a mile from Fort Moultrie on the north, and two-thirds of a mile from Cumming's Point on the south.

Early in December, Major Buell had been sent from Washington to Major Anderson, with verbal instructions, which were afterwards reduced to writing. Anderson was ordered to avoid any act which would tend to provoke aggression, but to hold the forts in the harbor, and, if attacked, to defend himself to the last extremity. On account of the smallness of his force, he was authorized to transfer his command, in case of any act of hostility, to the fort most capable of resistance. He was also authorized to take similar steps whenever he had " tangible evidence of a design to proceed to a hostile act." [4]

This " design," Anderson thought that he had discovered, and on the evening of the 26 December, with great skill and address, he transferred his command to Fort Sumter. There can be little question of the fact that he acted entirely within his orders, under the belief that the emergency had arisen which made it his duty to transfer his command to Sumter.[5]

That the authorities of South Carolina had not then any intention of attacking or seizing the forts seems to be proved by the presence in Washington of the commissioners sent to treat with the Government for their sur-

[3] Afterwards Major-General John G. Foster.
[4] See 1 Official Records, 89, 103, 117.
[5] See 1 Ropes, 39. Also, for the Southern point of view, 1 Davis, *Rise and Fall*, 216; Alexander, 9–11.

[5]

render. The commissioners were much excited on receipt of this news. After an interview with Mr. Floyd, the Secretary of War, who assured them that Anderson had violated the understanding given to the South Carolina representatives, they made an attack on the President, charging that the faith of the Government had been forfeited by Anderson's conduct. They further insisted that the President should immediately order the evacuation of Charleston Harbor by the United States forces.[6] After a very acrimonious correspondence with the President, the commissioners returned to Charleston at the beginning of January.

As soon as Anderson's removal to Fort Sumter became known, Governor Pickens seized Castle Pinckney and Fort Moultrie. He then proceeded to repair the damage which Anderson had done to Moultrie on evacuating it, and to put it in condition for use against Fort Sumter, should it become necessary. He also took possession of the arsenal in Charleston, and ordered the construction of batteries on Morris Island and Cumming's Point, so as to command the entrance of the harbor, and prevent reënforcements or provisions being sent to Fort Sumter by the Government. These steps were most certainly acts of war, and in fact were so regarded at the time by every one.[7]

When the news of these proceedings reached Washington, President Buchanan decided to reënforce Sumter at once. An unarmed steamer, the *Star of the West*, was chartered by the Government, and despatched to Charleston. When this vessel arrived at the entrance of the harbor, on the 9 January, it was fired on by the battery on Morris Island, and forced to retire without having reached Fort Sumter. The ship was hit twice, but no one was hurt. Anderson wrote Pickens that, unless this act were promptly disclaimed, he should treat it as an act of war, and the Governor replied the same day, assuming entire responsibility. Pickens stated further that he regarded the retention of Sumter by the United States forces as " an act of positive hostility." In order to clear up the situation, Anderson informed Pickens that he intended to send

---

[6] Buchanan, 182.   [7] 1 Ropes, 43.

an officer to Washington for further instructions. No objections were raised, and Lieutenant Talbot left the same evening.

On the 11 January, Pickens sent a formal demand, under a flag of truce, for the surrender of the fort. Anderson refused, but at the same time proposed to send another officer to Washington, accompanied by an envoy to be named by the Governor, to refer the matter to the President. Pickens assented, and appointed Mr. Hayne, the Attorney-General of the State. Anderson detailed Lieutenant Hall, and these envoys arrived in Washington on the 13 January.

In the meantime, a letter had been received at Washington from Anderson, stating that he had provisions sufficient to last him beyond the 4 March, and could hold the fort against any force which could be brought against him. The administration of Mr. Buchanan therefore allowed matters to drift until the end of its term of office. For this anomalous situation, Anderson himself was in part responsible. His position is stated in a letter written just before the attack on the fort in April: " Had I demanded reënforcements while Mr. Holt [8] was in the War Department, I know that he would have despatched them at all hazards. I did not ask them, because I knew that, the moment it should be known here that additional troops were coming, they would assault me, and thus inaugurate civil war. My policy . . . was to keep still, to preserve peace, to give time for the quieting of the excitement, . . . in the hope of avoiding bloodshed." [9]

While these events were taking place at Charleston, the other Cotton and Gulf States were not idle. In January, Georgia, Florida, Alabama, Mississippi and Louisiana seceded from the Union, and were followed by Texas on the first day of February. On the 8 February, the seven seceding States organized at Montgomery, Alabama, the Confederate States of America. A month later, they

[8] Mr. Floyd had resigned as Secretary of War on the 29 December, and had been succeeded by Joseph Holt, who, with the exception of Cass, was the only member of the Cabinet not in sympathy with the South.

[9] Crawford, *Genesis of the Civil War*, 290.

adopted a constitution very similar to that of the United States. Jefferson Davis, of Mississippi, was elected President, and Alexander H. Stephens, of Georgia, Vice-President of the new Confederacy. Both were able men, of large experience in public affairs.

In view of the critical situation of affairs, Mr. Hayne was advised, on reaching Washington, to postpone his demand for the surrender of Fort Sumter until the end of January. Then, after some exchange of letters, the Administration refused the demand, and Hayne left Washington on the 8 February. Before his departure, he telegraphed Governor Pickens the result of his mission, and the same day orders were issued for making the necessary preparations to bombard Fort Sumter. But this action was prevented for the moment by a resolution passed on the 12th by the Confederate Congress, giving the new Government charge of all questions between the several States and the United States Government. Under these circumstances the authorities of South Carolina reluctantly yielded the control of all military operations in Charleston Harbor to the new Confederate Government. Mr. Davis wrote Governor Pickens that he would send an engineer of " military skill " to take charge, and later advised him that General Beauregard had been selected for the position. That officer arrived at Charleston on the 3 March. The next day Abraham Lincoln was inaugurated President of the United States: the opportunity of taking Fort Sumter during Mr. Buchanan's administration had passed away.[10]

The policy of the new President was plainly declared in his Inaugural Address. " To the extent of my ability," he said, " I shall take care . . . that the laws of the Union be faithfully executed in all the States." And he closed with the words: " In your hands, my dissatisfied fellow-countrymen, and not in mine, is the momentous issue of civil war. The Government will not assail you. You can have no conflict without being yourselves the aggressors."

Few men in America, if any, have been the equals of

[10] 1 Ropes, 72.

Lincoln in political sagacity, and the calm, serious tone of warning which pervades the whole address shows the characteristic political ability of its author.[11]

One of the first questions considered by the Cabinet of President Lincoln was the problem of Fort Sumter. On the 29 March, a decision was finally reached, and Governor Pickens was officially informed, on the 8 April, that " an attempt will be made to supply Fort Sumter with provisions only; and if such attempt be not resisted, no effort to throw in men, arms or ammunition will be made without further notice." [12]

This message again shows the political sagacity of Mr. Lincoln. He unquestionably expected that resistance would be made, and he knew that nothing would more certainly arouse the national feeling of the North than an attack made upon Anderson and his little force.

On the 11 April, General Beauregard sent to Major Anderson a formal demand for the surrender of Fort Sumter, which was at once refused. At half-past four on the morning of the 12 April 1861 the Confederate batteries opened fire, and the bombardment continued without cessation until the next afternoon. An ineffective reply was made by the guns of the fort, until the supply of cartridges gave out. After gallantly defending the post for two days, Anderson accepted the honorable terms of surrender which were offered. On Sunday, the 14th, after saluting his flag with fifty guns, Major Anderson, with his command, was conveyed to the fleet waiting outside the bar, and sailed for New York.

It is remarkable how little we know of the inner thoughts of the great men of the world, and how different their actions often seem to their contemporaries and to historians half a century later. It is very difficult, at this point of time, to understand the mode of reasoning of the Southern leaders in deciding to force the issue of civil war. " A few men more or less at Sumter," writes Professor Channing, " and food for another month or so, would make little difference in the ultimate course of

[11] 1 Ropes, 74.   [12] 1 Official Records, 291; 6 Lincoln, 241.

events. But aggressive action on the part of the Confederates would at once bring on the crisis that true policy forbade." [13] The order to open fire on the fort was given, notwithstanding the fact that Anderson had told the Confederate officers who were sent to demand his surrender that he could not hold out for two days if he were not supplied with food.[14] One is amazed to-day at the lack of political vision shown by the Southern leaders. They little expected the explosion that was to follow!

The President's demand for troops, to enforce the laws, met with a prompt and angry refusal from the Border States. Virginia, Arkansas, Tennessee, and North Carolina promptly passed ordinances of secession, and joined the new Confederacy. Three other States — Maryland, Kentucky, and Missouri — were only kept in the Union by the power of the United States Government, and these States furnished many men to the Confederate armies.

Thus the lines were finally drawn. Twenty-two States remained united; opposed to them stood the eleven States which had seceded, and now constituted the Confederate States of America. After the people of Virginia ratified the ordinance of secession, on the 23 May the seat of the Confederate Government was transferred from Montgomery to Richmond, which continued to be the capital until the end of the war.

On land the theatre of the Civil War was bounded on the north by the Potomac, Ohio, and Missouri rivers; on the east and south, by the coasts of the Atlantic and the Gulf of Mexico; on the west, by the frontiers of Missouri, Arkansas, and Texas. With the exceptions of the battles of Antietam and Gettysburg, which were fought a short distance north of the Potomac, all the principal military operations took place within the limits mentioned.

The *terrain* thus bounded — approximately one million square miles — was widely diversified in its characteristics. The parallel ranges of the Appalachians, running from northeast to southwest, divided the region between the

[13] 6 Channing, 312.
[14] For a full discussion of this subject, see Stephenson's *Lincoln*, 446–447. Also, 6 Channing, 313, note.

coast and the Mississippi into two nearly equal parts. Within this area was comprised every variety of country — mountains, prairies, forests, swamps. The armies were forced to cope with every possible physical obstacle.[15]

The frontiers of the Confederacy were far apart. The coast washed by the Gulf of Mexico is 800 miles south of the Potomac; the Rio Grande, the river boundary of Texas, is 1700 miles west of Charleston on the Atlantic. Across this vast expanse of territory then ran but six continuous lines of railway.[16]

1. Richmond, Wilmington, Charleston, Savannah — connecting the Confederate capital with the ports on the Atlantic.

2. Richmond, Lynchburg, Chattanooga, Memphis, New Orleans; and

3. Richmond, Greensboro, Columbia, Atlanta, Pensacola — connecting Richmond with the Mississippi and the Gulf.

4. Louisville, Nashville, Chattanooga, Atlanta, Mobile;

5. Cairo, Corinth, Mobile; and

6. Cairo, Memphis, New Orleans — connecting the Ohio with the Gulf of Mexico.

The railroads of the South were not only few in number, but they were also badly laid out for the strategic demands of the war. The lines were short, and were broken at frequent intervals because of the refusal of important cities to let them pass through. Between Richmond and Savannah, there were half a dozen changes: the most serious break was at Petersburg, where the line from Richmond stopped at the western edge, and the road to Wilmington began at the southern limit. Some of the gaps were filled during the war, but not in time to do much good. As it was impossible to manufacture new rails, those which gave out were replaced by rails taken from less important routes of traffic. It was the same with the rolling stock: in 1864, the Quarter Master General stated that a train could not run more than one hundred miles

---

[15] See Farrand, *Basis of American History*, Chap. I.
[16] See Frontispiece: " Means of Transit."

[11]

a day on the main line from Richmond to Georgia, and that a car could not go five hundred miles without breaking down.[17]

On the other hand, the North in 1861 was over-supplied with railroads, and many of them were on the verge of bankruptcy. The owners were glad to place them at the disposal of the Government, and the military engineers rebuilt them as fast as they came under Federal control. The soldiers acquired so much skill in making repairs that by 1864 it was an almost futile operation for the Confederates to break a railroad line. As a striking example of the efficiency with which the Northern lines were handled, we may mention the transfer in three weeks' time of Schofield's Army of the Ohio, thirty thousand strong, from Tennessee to the coast of North Carolina, after the battle of Nashville in December 1864.[18]

The wagon-roads in the Southern States were few and poor — there were no paved highways such as connect the principal places in Europe; but there were numerous navigable streams. Towns were few and far between; food and forage were not easily obtainable; the great rivers were bridged at rare intervals. Except over a comparatively small area, the Union armies met the same obstacles as did the soldiers of Cromwell and Turenne.[19]

The city of Atlanta, the heart of the Confederacy, was sixty days' march from the Potomac, the same distance as Vienna from the Channel, or Moscow from the Niemen. New Orleans was thirty-six days' march from the Ohio, the same distance as Berlin from the Moselle. " Had Napoleon in the campaign against Russia remained for the winter at Smolensk, and firmly established himself in Poland," writes Colonel Henderson, " Moscow might have been captured and held during the ensuing summer. But the occupation of Moscow would not have ended the war. Russia in many respects was not unlike the Confederacy. She had given no hostages to fortune in the

[17] See 22 *American Historical Review*, 794–810: " The Confederate Government and the Railroads."

[18] See Parsons, *Rail and River Army Transportation in the Civil War*.

[19] 1 Henderson, 131.

shape of rich commercial towns; she possessed no historic fortresses, and so offered but few objectives to the invader. If defeated or retreating, her armies could always find refuge in distant fastnesses. The climate was severe; the internal trade inconsiderable; to bring the burden of war home to the mass of the population was difficult, and to hold the country by force impracticable. Such were the difficulties which the genius of Napoleon was powerless to overcome, and Napoleon invaded Russia with half a million of seasoned soldiers." [20]

The conquest of the eleven seceding States which the Federal Government was about to undertake with an army of 75,000 volunteers, and without the least preparation, was in truth a gigantic undertaking. Without a trained staff and an efficient administration, an army is incapable of movement. It is no small task to keep a marching column supplied with food and forage; and the problem of transport taxes the ability of the most experienced commander. A march of a hundred miles into an enemy's country seems like an easy feat, but unless every detail has been carefully thought out, it may be more disastrous than a lost battle. During the first five weeks of the Russian campaign, between the Niemen and Vilna, a distance of only sixty miles, Napoleon lost one-third of his army from disease. " To handle an army in battle is much less difficult than to bring it on to the field in good condition." [21]

Richmond, the capital of the Confederacy, was situated less than a hundred miles south of Washington: this necessarily made Virginia the seat of the war in the East. The South undoubtedly made a mistake in placing her capital so near the frontier; Chattanooga or Atlanta would have been a better choice. But the Union capital was actually on the boundary line; batteries on Arlington Heights would render Washington untenable. The capture of either of the capitals might have momentous consequences, and prove decisive of the contest. These facts had a controlling influence on the general strategy of the Civil War. The objects aimed at by the opposing armies in Virginia were:

[20] 1 Henderson, 133.   [21] 1 Henderson, 130.

(1) the protection of their own capital; (2) the capture of the enemy's capital; and (3) the defeat of the opposing army.[22]

The approaches to the National capital were blocked only by the Potomac River; and the entrenched line on the south bank, opposite the city, could easily be turned by marching down the Shenandoah Valley. This avenue for the invasion of the North ran from about the centre of Virginia in a northeasterly direction to Harper's Ferry, where the Potomac was easily passable. Throughout all this distance, it was feasible, by guarding the mountain passes, or " gaps," as they were generally called, to prevent interference by the Federal forces. The Valley was fertile, and possessed good turnpikes. From Lexington, at its head, to the Potomac, the Valley was 140 miles long, by about 24 miles wide. Its chief town, and strategic centre, was Winchester, about twenty-six miles southwest of Harper's Ferry. From Winchester, two highways lead westward by Romney and Moorefield; four lead east and southeast, passing the Blue Ridge by Snicker's, Ashby's, Manassas, and Chester gaps. Through Manassas Gap ran the railroad connecting Front Royal in the Valley with Richmond via Manassas Junction. The Baltimore and Ohio Railroad, the main connection between Washington and the West, crossed the Potomac at Harper's Ferry, and followed the course of the river for a distance of 120 miles within the confines of Virginia.

On the other hand, the Shenandoah Valley offered no special advantages as a route for the Federal invader. It led away from Richmond, and the Union forces were liable to be taken in flank, or to have their line of communication cut, by way of the lower gaps. It would therefore be no easy matter to debouch from the Valley and occupy Gordonsville, the key to the railway system of central Virginia.[23]

The population of the twenty-two States which adhered to the Union was over twenty-two millions; that of the eleven seceding States was but little over nine millions, of whom about three millions and a half were slaves.

[22] 1 Ropes, 121.   [23] 1 Ropes, 124.

The slaves, however, instead of being a source of anxiety to the South, as many in the North predicted, proved entirely trustworthy and faithful. They raised the crops upon which the whole South subsisted during the war; and they were largely employed in building fortifications.[24]

Regarding the relative numbers of the combatants on the two sides, there are wide differences of opinion. While the Federal statistics are quite complete, official figures are lacking in the case of the Confederacy. Colonel Livermore, who is considered an authority on the question, concludes that there were over a million and a half on the Union side, as against a million among the Confederates. Colonel Wood, a Southern writer, puts the Confederate levies at no more than six hundred thousand. As there could not have been more than a million men of age for military service in the South, the latter estimate is probably nearer correct.[25] There is no doubt, however, that the Union armies were vastly superior, not only in numbers, but even more in resources and equipment. To offset these advantages, the North labored under many disadvantages: it was generally acting on the offensive, in a hostile country, where large detachments were necessary, as the armies advanced, to maintain communications, and hold the territory gained.

The self-sustaining power of the South was far greater than has usually been imagined. The area under cultivation was almost equal to that north of the Potomac and the Ohio. The amount of livestock — horses, mules, cattle, and sheep — was actually larger than in the North; and the shortage of the wheat crop was more than balanced by the great harvests of rice and corn.[26]

But in material prosperity, the North was far in advance of the South: in accumulated capital there was no comparison between the two sections. The North was full of manufactories of all kinds; the South had very few of

---

[24] 1 Ropes, 98.

[25] *Cf.* Livermore, *Numbers and Losses*, 40, 63; *Confederate Hand-Book*, 29; and 4 *B. & L.*, 767–768. For a full discussion of this subject, see final chapter.

[26] See U. S. Census, 1860.

any kind. In the North there was also a much larger measure of practical business capacity.

The command of the sea naturally fell at once into the hands of the North. All the navy-yards, except those at Norfolk and Pensacola, and the entire personnel of the Navy, with the exception of a few officers, remained under the control of the Government. Moreover, the mercantile marine of the United States, which, in 1861, was second only to that of Great Britain, was almost wholly owned in the North.[27]

The gravity of the coming struggle was realized by neither party. Men of high ability at the North prophesied that the South would be brought back to the Union within ninety days. Only General Scott declared that its conquest might be achieved " in two or three years, by a young able general — a Wolfe, a Desaix, a Hoche — with 300,000 disciplined men, kept up to that number." [28]

Notwithstanding the absolute lack of factories and foundries in the South, and the inability to manufacture cannon, powder, and ammunition, the orders first placed in Europe by the Confederate Government were on a trivial scale. Before the war, metals, machinery, rails, rolling-stock, salt, and even medicine, came mainly from the North. The principal staples of the South — cotton and tobacco — brought leather and cloth in exchange from England. There was but one way in which the South could have procured the means of buying abroad the material of every kind of which she stood so greatly in need. Had the Government promptly seized all the cotton in the country, paying for it the market price in Confederate money, sent it to England before the blockade was firmly established, and there stored it, to be sold as occasion required, available funds would have been secured to meet the largest requirements. But this wise course, though suggested, was not adopted.[29] The majority of the

[27] *Cf.* 1 Ropes, 99–101, and Channing (6, 488, note), who states that about one-fifth of the officers, of all grades, resigned.

[28] Letter to Seward, 3 March 1861. If this had been written after the secession of Virginia, North Carolina, and Tennessee, Scott probably would have raised his estimate to at least half a million men.

[29] 1 Ropes, 102. *Cf.* Johnston's *Narrative*, 421–424.

Southern politicians thought that England and France, a large portion of whose population depended for their livelihood on the harvests of the South, would not brook interference with their trade, and would never allow the North to enforce the blockade. In the War of Independence, the fleets of France and Spain had come to the assistance of the struggling Americans, and compelled England to let her colonies go; therefore, it was not likely that the North, confronted by the naval strength of England and France, would fail to yield. But, in forecasting the future, the history of the past is not always an infallible guide.[30]

Virginia, the most important State south of Mason and Dixon's line, was not a member of the Confederacy when the Government was established at Montgomery. Her people did not regard the election of a Republican President as a menace, and were not strongly in favor of the secession movement. Many of her leading citizens deprecated the hasty action of South Carolina, and during the earlier months of 1861 there were few signs of unrest. But the crisis was not long postponed. When President Lincoln called upon the State to furnish her quota of troops for the Federal army, Virginia promptly seceded, and, as already stated, her action was followed by Arkansas, Tennessee, and North Carolina.

As soon as the Richmond convention passed the ordinance of secession, on the 17 April 1861, nearly all the officers in the regular army from that State sent in their resignations, and offered their services to the Confederate Government. A few officers only, of whom the most distinguished were Lieutenant-General Scott and Major (afterwards Major-General) George H. Thomas, remained loyal to the Union.

Among the officers who then left the Union service were the two most famous soldiers of the Confederacy — Robert E. Lee and Thomas J. Jackson.

Lee was born in Westmoreland County, Virginia, 19 January 1807. He was the son of General Henry Lee,

[30] 1 Henderson, 138.

[17]

familiarly known as "Light-Horse Harry," of Revolutionary fame. His mother, Anne Carter, of Shirley, on the James River, was a direct descendant of Robert Carter, who, because of his vast landed possessions and high social position, was called " King Carter."

The Lees were of the oldest, wealthiest, and most patriotic families in Virginia. The original ancestor was Richard Lee, who settled in the Old Dominion as early as 1640. After the Revolution, General Harry Lee served in the Congress of the United States, and was three times governor of Virginia. In his funeral oration on the occasion of the death of Washington, he pronounced the immortal words, so familiar to every American: " First in war, first in peace, and first in the hearts of his countrymen."

Harry Lee died when his son Robert was only eleven years of age. The family, which seems to have had some financial reverses, had moved to Alexandria, where Robert was placed in school, and worshipped in the same church that Washington had attended. At the age of eighteen he entered West Point on an appointment secured for him by General Andrew Jackson. He graduated second in his class, and for the next five years served in the Engineer Corps.

In June 1831, Robert Lee married Mary Custis, a great-granddaughter of Martha Washington, and the heiress to the beautiful estate of Arlington   on the banks of the Potomac.

The Mexican War gave Lee his first opportunity to show his great military talents. General Scott made him chief-of-staff, and for distinguished services he received the brevet rank of colonel. After the war, General Scott declared that Robert E. Lee was the greatest living soldier in America. In 1852 he was appointed superintendent of the Military Academy, where he made a fine record during his three years of service.

In 1861, Lee was colonel of the 5th Cavalry, in Texas, and was generally considered the ablest officer in the Army. He was recalled to Washington, and on the 18

April was offered by President Lincoln the command of the Army of the United States, which he declined. He resigned his commission on the 20 April, and three days later took command at Richmond of the military forces of Virginia.

Though opposed to secession, and deprecating war, Lee felt that he could take no part in the coercion of the Southern States. When the issue was drawn, like so many other men of the South, he considered his allegiance to his native State paramount to his loyalty to the Nation.[32]

In personal appearance and in character, there was a marked contrast between Lee and his great lieutenant, Jackson. Lee was tall, handsome, of distinguished manners and courtly address; he was a patrician, born and bred.

Jackson also was tall, but his form was ungainly, his hands and feet enormous; he was a true son of the soil. He was born on the 21 January 1824 in the little town of Clarksburg, now the county seat of Harrison, but then no more than a village in the Virginia backwoods. His father was a lawyer, clever and popular, who had inherited a comfortable patrimony; generous and incautious, he found it easier to make money than to keep it, and when he died in 1827, every vestige of his property was swept away. The young widow married again, but lived only a year longer, and at the age of seven the boy Thomas found himself a penniless orphan. In 1842, when he was eighteen years of age, a vacancy occurred in the Military Academy at West Point which was to be filled by a youth from the Congressional District in which Clarksburg was included, and young Jackson sought and obtained the appointment.

Owing to his lack of previous training, Jackson's career at West Point was not distinguished, but by application and hard work he finally succeeded in graduating seventeenth in a class of seventy, and his rank gave him a commission in the artillery. During the four years of his stay at West Point, the young Virginian gained in health and

---

[32] For a discussion of the obligation of officers to observe their oath of fidelity to the United States, see Upton's *Military Policy of the United States*, 240; also 6 Channing, 303–304.

strength, and attained his full height of five feet ten. He acquired the erect bearing of the cadets, but never overcame his natural awkwardness, and was always a poor horseman.

There was much in the boyhood of Jackson, as there was much in his later career, that recalls Napoleon to mind. Both were devoted to their families; both were indefatigable students; both were provincial, neither was prepossessing. They both had the same love of method and of order. An inflexibility of purpose, an absolute disregard of popular opinion, and an unswerving belief in their own capacity, were predominant traits in both. Neither sought sympathy, and both felt that they were masters of their own fate.[33]

The soubriquet of " Stonewall," by which Jackson will always be known, was really a misnomer: undoubtedly he could be steadfast on occasions, but he was stronger in offence than in defence. Like the great Corsican, the quality which above all others marked him was mobility — a swiftness in action which puzzled and generally confounded his adversaries, and which usually secured for him success.

Jackson was fortunate from the beginning of his military career. Before the Mexican War, the total strength of the regular army was not more than 8500 men, and nearly all this force was scattered in small detachments along the frontier, to control the Indian tribes. This warfare was monotonous, and there was but little chance to attain military distinction. The 1st Artillery, to which Jackson was attached, was ordered to the Rio Grande, and later was included in Scott's army of invasion. Jackson distinguished himself in several engagements, and came out of the war a major by brevet. None of his West Point comrades had made so great a stride in rank, and his future in his profession was assured.

Many of the generals with whom Jackson was later to be intimately connected, either as friends or enemies, are mentioned in Scott's despatches. Magruder, Ambrose Hill, McDowell, and Hooker, belonged to his own regi-

[33] 1 Henderson, 6–28.

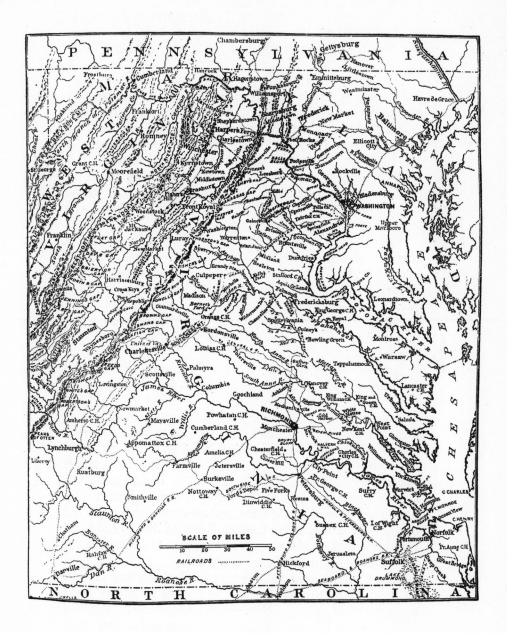

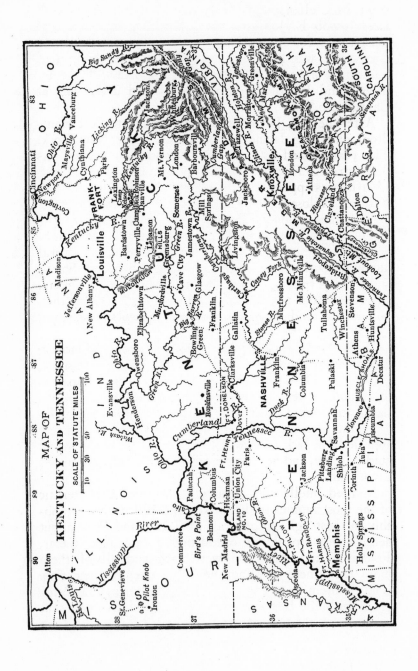

MAP OF
KENTUCKY AND TENNESSEE

SCALE OF STATUTE MILES

ment. McClellan and Beauregard served on the staff with Lee. Joseph E. Johnston, twice severely wounded, was conspicuous for his gallantry. Pope was a staff officer; Longstreet was bracketed with Pickett for conspicuous conduct; Porter and Reno did good service with the artillery, and Ewell had two horses killed under him at Churubusco.[34]

After the war, Jackson's battery was sent to Fort Hamilton, on Long Island, seven miles below New York. Two years passed without incident, and then Jackson was transferred to Florida, where his stay was brief. In March 1851 he was appointed Professor of Artillery Tactics and Natural Philosophy at the Virginia Military Institute. This college, founded twelve years previously, on the model of West Point, was located at Lexington, one hundred miles west of Richmond. It was attended by several hundred youths from Virginia and other Southern States, and was the training school of many Confederate officers. In all essential respects the Military Institute was then but little behind West Point: the discipline was as strict, the drill but little less precise.

In the well-stocked library of the Institute, Jackson found every opportunity to increase his professional knowledge. He was an untiring reader, and the campaigns of Napoleon were his constant study. He was an enthusiastic admirer of the genius of the Emperor; the swiftness, the daring, and the energy of his movements appealed to Jackson's every instinct. Ten years passed quickly away, and here we find him at the outbreak of the Civil War.

Marked intellectual capacity is the chief characteristic of the most famous soldiers. Ney and Blücher were probably the best fighting generals of France and Prussia, but neither was capable of conducting a campaign. Cæsar, Frederick, and Napoleon were each and all of them more than mere fighting men. No one of their time rivalled them in strength of intellect. It was this, combined with the best qualities of Ney and Blücher, that made them masters of strategy, and lifted them high

[34] 1 Henderson, 63.

above those who were tacticians and nothing more; and it was this that Jackson cultivated at Lexington.[35]

Finally, in estimating the relative power of the parties to this conflict, we must take into consideration their respective aptitudes for war. The South undoubtedly possessed a more military population than the North. Not only Virginia, but South Carolina, Louisiana, and other Southern States, possessed excellent military academies. A martial spirit was also cultivated by the conditions of life in the South: riding, hunting, fishing, — unusual physical exertions. The aristocratic régime of the slave-holding States was also conducive to a preference for military, rather than civil, pursuits, and the young men of the better classes eagerly embraced the profession of arms. They made excellent officers, while those below them in the social scale made admirable soldiers. In the North, on the other hand, there was very little of this enthusiasm for a military life. The people there were too busy with schemes for the development of the country, and for the acquisition of private fortunes.[36]

The organization of the Confederate army from the first was superior to that of the Federals. Although a few civilians were appointed to the rank of brigadier-general, all the chief commands were reserved for the graduates of West Point. The Confederate armies were commanded by officers of the full rank of general; the corps, by lieutenant-generals; the divisions, by major-generals, and the brigades, by brigadier-generals. Distinction of rank was uniformly based upon extent of command, as it ought always to be. In the Union army, on the other hand, armies, army-corps, or divisions, indifferently, were commanded by major-generals, to the general detriment of the service. Even General Scott was merely a lieutenant-general by brevet, and it was not until the autumn of 1863 that he was given the full rank of lieutenant-general. The grade of general was not created until 1866. Ignorance of military affairs, and an unworthy jealousy of distinctions of rank, which have always marked our public

[35] 1 Henderson, 94.   [36] 1 Ropes, 104–105.

men, were probably at the bottom of this unwise policy.[37]

The Confederacy was fortunate also, at the start, in having the services of some of the most efficient men in the " Old Army ": Adjutant General Cooper, Quarter Master General Joseph E. Johnston, and Commissary General Northrup; also Colonel Josiah Gorgas, who showed great genius in building up the ordnance service; as well as, in the field, those excellent organizers and disciplinarians, P. G. T. Beauregard and Braxton Bragg. So well did they all do their work that there were remarkably few changes in the personnel of the higher ranks of the Confederate army from the beginning until the close of the war. The only officer to come to the front at a later date was Robert E. Lee, who did not become prominent until the second year of the conflict. As General Cooper never served in the field, his name is not so familiar to the general public; but those who were in " a position to *know* what he did . . . will not fail to place him among those who contributed most to whatever was achieved." [38]

[37] 1 Ropes, 117.
[38] Letter of Mr. Davis to Fitzhugh Lee in 1877, quoted 7 Rowland's *Davis*, 553. Davis's acquaintance with Cooper dated back to the period before the Mexican War, when the two men worked together in the War Department — Davis as Secretary of War and Cooper as Adjutant General. (See 6 Channing, 400, note.)

CHAPTER TWO

APRIL–JULY 1861

MANASSAS

The News of Sumter — The President's Proclamation — Riot at
Baltimore — Washington Protected — The New Army — Gen-
eral Scott Retires — Political Officers — McDowell in Command
— The Military Situation — The Confederates at Manassas —
McDowell's Plan — The Army Organization — Johnston Joins
Beauregard — The Federal Advance — The Confederate Lines —
The First Skirmish — McDowell's Orders — The Turning Move-
ment — Opposed by Evans — Confederate Plans — The Morn-
ing Battle — Retreat of the Confederates — Henry House Hill
— Stonewall Jackson — The Federal Assault — Their Batteries
Destroyed — Defeat of the Union Army — No Pursuit At-
tempted — Losses on Both Sides — Confederate Organization —
Federal Strategy — Approved and Condemned — McDowell's
Plan Dangerous — His Poor Tactics — Opinions of the Critics
— The Lack of Cavalry — The Numbers Engaged — The Vic-
tory Due to Jackson — Elation of the South

WHEN the flag was fired on at Fort Sumter, the
Nation was powerless to resent the insult. The
military establishment was reduced to 13,000
men, scattered in distant garrisons. There was no reserve,
no transport, no organization for war. The navy consisted
of six screw-frigates, only one of which was in commission; of five steam sloops, some twenty sailing ships, and
a few gunboats. Although well armed, the majority of
the vessels were out of date; and 9000 officers and men
constituted the extent of the personnel.[1]

The news of the firing on Sumter reached Washington
on Saturday, the 13 April. The following morning, while
Anderson was preparing to evacuate the fort, the President called a special meeting of his Cabinet to discuss the
situation. With his own hand, Lincoln immediately
drafted a proclamation calling forth the militia of the

---

[1] 1 Henderson, 128. In all, there were thirty-four steam vessels on
the list, but some of these were very small. (6 Channing, 486).

[24]

several States to the number of 75,000 men " to cause the laws to be duly executed "; also convening both Houses of Congress in special session on the fourth day of July.[2]

This proclamation was published throughout the country on Monday morning, 15 April. Its effect in the North was instantaneous and universal. All uncertainty was at an end: the people were ready for war, and the response was simply magnificent. Only the " Old Bay State," however, was prepared. For several months, Governor Andrew had been giving special attention to the equipment and drill of the State militia, and five thousand men were ready, of whom three thousand were fully armed. Within twenty-four hours, the 6th Massachusetts mustered on Boston Common, and started for Washington. The regiment reached Baltimore on the 19 April, a date again to be made memorable by the shedding of the first blood in a great American war. In crossing the city between the two stations, which was necessary at that time, the regiment was attacked by a mob of Southern sympathizers, and several lives were lost on both sides. A few hours later, the regiment reached Washington, and took up its quarters in the Senate chamber at the Capitol. Until then the city had been guarded only by a small force of regulars and a few companies of local volunteers.

The 8th Massachusetts at once followed, under the command of Brigadier-General Benjamin F. Butler, well known in Boston as a lawyer and politician of rather unsavory reputation, who was now to become a national character. As the bridge across the Susquehanna at Havre de Grace had been burned, the regiment made its way by steamer to Annapolis, where it met the full and handsomely equipped 7th Regiment of New York. The arrival of these two regiments at Washington, for the moment, put an end to all apprehension.

Without waiting for the meeting of Congress, on the 3 May the President very wisely called for 42,034 volunteers for three years, for 22,714 men for the regular army, and for 18,000 men for the navy. These men, when enrolled, with the 75,000 previously called out, would

[2] Nicolay, *Campaigns*, 73.

raise the available army to 156,861 troops, and the navy to 25,600 men.[3] In his message to Congress, on the 4 July, the President recommended that this number be increased to 400,000 men. In these acts and recommendations Mr. Lincoln showed a comprehension of the magnitude of the task before him which was hardly to be expected from his lack of experience.

The work of organizing and directing these forces was at first entrusted to Lieutenant-General Winfield Scott, a veteran of two wars, but now past his three-score years and ten, and incapacitated by bodily infirmities. Though born in Virginia, he had remained loyal to the Union, and his sound military judgment was of great advantage to the Government at this time. The old general was loath to sheathe his sword, but his health soon forced him to resign from active service.

Out of the twelve hundred graduates of West Point, who, at the beginning of 1861, were still fit for service, a fourth were Southerners, and these, almost without exception, cast their lot with the Confederacy. The defection of Robert E. Lee, in particular, was a sad blow to General Scott, and a great loss to the Union cause.

It was necessary to relieve from active duty many other senior officers in the regular army, who were too old for service in the field, and their places should have been filled by promoting the most capable and promising of the younger officers. Unfortunately, however, the President, in making many of his appointments, was governed too much by political considerations. In the East, Butler and Banks, both men without any kind of military training or experience, were made major-generals of volunteers; while in the West, Fremont was appointed a major-general in the regular army, and succeeded in Missouri the brave and capable Lyon, to whose courage and skill the preservation of that State to the Union was largely due.[4]

---

[3] 1 Ropes, 111.

[4] Banks had been Governor of Massachusetts, and Speaker of the National House of Representatives. Fremont was the candidate of the Republican party for the Presidency against Buchanan in 1856. For the political reasons which influenced Mr. Lincoln, see Macartney, 29 *et seq.*, and 46 *et seq.*

On the 24 May, after the people of Virginia had ratified the ordinance of secession, the Federal troops crossed
the Potomac without opposition and occupied Arlington
Heights and Alexandria. A camp was established on the
south side of the river, and the line was entrenched from
the Chain Bridge to Alexandria. Brevet-Major McDowell, then on duty in the War Department, whose highest
rank of command had been lieutenant of artillery, was
made a brigadier-general, and placed in command of the
forces in Virginia.

Washington now being safe from attack, the Northern
newspapers and public began to cry out for a forward
movement before the expiration of the term of service of
the three-months men. General Scott wanted to wait until
the men of the second levy could be made ready for the
field. But, in the face of the newspaper clamor, the Government was finally forced to overrule the judgment of
the lieutenant-general, and he was ordered to make the
necessary arrangements for an advance.[5]

The military situation at this time was as follows: The
main army of the Confederacy, 20,000 volunteers under
General Beauregard, was stationed at Manassas Junction,
thirty miles southwest of Washington. Beauregard, a
classmate of McDowell at West Point, had been an officer
in the Engineers, and the capture of Fort Sumter had
added much renown to his already excellent reputation.
At Manassas Junction, on the Orange and Alexandria
Railroad, a branch line, coming from Front Royal in the
Shenandoah Valley, connected with the main line to
Richmond.

Near Winchester, in the lower Shenandoah Valley,
General Joseph E. Johnston, with about 11,000 men, confronted a Union force of some 18,000, under General
Patterson, a veteran of the Mexican War. Although
nearly seventy years old, he had recently been appointed
a major-general of volunteers from civil life, and given
this important command.

At Aquia Creek, thirty miles southeast of Manassas,
there was a Confederate force of 3000 men under General

---

[5] 1 Ropes, 127.

Holmes. At Fort Monroe, a small Federal force under General Butler was opposed by Generals Huger and Magruder.

All the Confederate detachments were under the direction of President Davis, at Richmond, who seems to have had General Lee as his military adviser; [6] while General Scott, under President Lincoln, commanded the Union forces at Washington.

There were two main roads running south from the National capital, one from Alexandria to Richmond via Fredericksburg, the other by way of Warrenton. The strategic importance of Manassas was due to the fact that it was located on the Warrenton Turnpike, and on the main line of railway from Washington to the Southern States. Beauregard's position there also guarded the junction of the branch line to the Shenandoah Valley, by which Johnston's army communicated with the Confederate base at Richmond. [7]

Manassas Junction lies on a high, open plateau. The Confederate position was protected by some slight fieldworks, armed with fifteen heavy guns. To the north and east of Manassas, at a distance of about three miles, flows Bull Run, with wooded heights in most places close to the banks. The stream is winding and sluggish, and fordable in many places, although, here and there, the banks are steep and rocky. The Confederate army guarded the various fords, extending on a line about eight miles long from the Stone Bridge on the Warrenton road to the railway. [8]

In reluctant response to the popular cry for a forward movement, Scott asked McDowell to submit a plan of operations, and he complied on the 24 June. His plan was " to turn the enemy's position and force him out of it by seizing or threatening his communications." He counted upon Patterson and Butler to contain the forces in their respective fronts. Estimating that Beauregard would still receive reënforcements enough to raise his army to about 35,000 men, McDowell thought that he should have a

---

[6] It is not entirely clear in what capacity General Lee acted at this time (see 1 Ropes, 133, note); but Maurice (65) says that his position was that of Chief of the General Staff.

[7] Steele, 132.　　　　　　　　　　[8] Nicolay, 176.

force of 30,000 of all arms, with a reserve of 10,000. At the same time he urged that he might be allowed to put his regiments into brigades: this fact, of itself, shows the very rudimentary state of the Union army.

McDowell's plan was fully discussed, and finally approved, at a council of war held on the 29 June at the Executive Mansion, in which took part the President, his Cabinet, and the principal military officers. McDowell stated emphatically that he could not hope to beat the two Confederate armies if united, and Scott gave him the positive assurance: " If Johnston joins Beauregard, he shall have Patterson at his heels."

It is perhaps unnecessary to state that the operation upon which the Federal authorities had decided was a complicated one, which should never have been undertaken with inexperienced generals and raw troops. It was tempting fortune to subject the issue of arms to the success of a coöperative movement. Instead of relying upon Patterson's ability to detain Johnston in the Shenandoah Valley, the bulk of his army should have been brought to Washington as soon as it was decided to make the forward movement. For this failure, General Scott was largely responsible.[9]

McDowell was ordered to begin his movement on the 8 July; but owing to various delays it was not until a week later that his force was raised to the stipulated strength.

On the 16 July, McDowell issued his orders to march that afternoon. His army was organized as follows.[10]

> *First Division:* TYLER
> Brigades: Keyes, Schenck, Sherman, Richardson... 9,936
> *Second Division:* HUNTER
> Brigades: Porter, Burnside.................... 2,648
> *Third Division:* HEINTZELMAN
> Brigades: Franklin, Willcox, Howard........... 9,777
> *Fourth Division:* RUNYON
> No brigade commanders..................... 5,752
> *Fifth Division:* MILES
> Brigades: Blenker, Davies................... 6,207
>
> Total 34,320

[9] 1 Ropes, 128.   [10] Nicolay, 174.

There were also seven troops of regular cavalry, and eight companies of infantry under Major Sykes. There were 49 guns, and seven of the batteries were also of the regular army. McDowell's force aggregated 35,000 men, but Runyon's division was held back to guard the line of communications, and took no part in the battle of Manassas. On the field, therefore, McDowell had only 30,000 men.

Through his spies in Washington, Beauregard was kept informed of the Federal plans, and on the 17 July he telegraphed to Richmond that the advance had begun. Davis immediately ordered Johnston and Holmes to Manassas. That same day, Patterson, after advancing within nine miles of Winchester, retired to Charlestown, and telegraphed General Scott that Johnston's force was 35,000 strong, although in fact it was not more than two-thirds the strength of his own.

This left Johnston free to depart, and on the 18th he marched his army by way of Ashby's Gap to Piedmont, where the infantry was placed in railway cars, while the cavalry and artillery proceeded by road. On the afternoon of the 20 July, he had joined Beauregard with the bulk of his forces.

It is hardly worth while to go into the details of the story of Patterson's failure to fulfill the expectations of his chief. As Mr. Ropes says, he " was really more to be pitied than blamed; . . . if Scott expected that Patterson would fight Johnston, as he says he did, . . . he should have given him orders to that effect, and he cannot be exonerated from blame for not having done so." [11]

McDowell began his advance from Alexandria on the afternoon of the 16 July, and on the morning of the 18th, the greater part of his force of 35,000 men was concentrated at Centreville, twenty-two miles from Washington, and five and a half miles northeast of Manassas. It should have been possible to have attacked the following morning, but the Federal commander was confronted by many obstacles. The maps were poor, and it was impossible to secure local guides. The army was much larger

[11] 1 Ropes, 130.

than any ever assembled on the American Continent; the general, his staff, and the troops were alike inexperienced. " To deploy 10,000 or 20,000 men for attack is a difficult operation, even with well-drilled troops and an experienced staff," says Colonel Henderson. " The troops had received no instruction in musketry, and many of the regiments went into action without having once fired their rifles. . . . Ignorance of war and contempt for the lessons of history were to cost the nation dear." [12]

In McDowell's report, he states that it was his intention to attack at once, but he could not get the troops into line earlier than he did. The men were not accustomed to marching, and the supply trains moved with difficulty and in disorder, so that there was a day's delay in getting the provisions forward. [13]

Beauregard's army, then called the Army of the Potomac, consisted of six and a half brigades. It was posted in a line about eight miles long, behind Bull Run, from the Stone Bridge on the Warrenton Pike to Union Mills Ford. The bridge was held by Evans's half-brigade, and the fords to the east by the brigades of Cocke, Bonham, Longstreet, Jones, and Ewell, with Early in the rear. Holmes, on his arrival, was placed in reserve, as were also the brigades of Jackson, Bee, and Bartow, of Johnston's Army of the Shenandoah, when they came on the field. From these arrangements it is evident that Beauregard expected the Federals to attempt to cross the creek by the fords to the east of the Stone Bridge. This was indeed McDowell's first intention, but he gave it up on account of the difficulty of an attack on that side.

Centreville is on an elevation from which the ground slopes in all directions. The Warrenton Pike runs almost due west, and good dirt roads lead to all the fords. The country toward Bull Run is cut up by small streams; and covered with farms, and thick woods which furnish good cover for troops.

On the morning of the 18th, McDowell ordered Tyler, whose division was in the lead, to make a reconnaissance, but strictly enjoined him not to bring on an engagement.

[12] 1 Henderson, 167.   [13] 2 Official Records, 324.

Tyler advanced along the road to Mitchell's Ford, and opened fire with artillery on the Confederate forces posted on the south side of the stream. He also sent forward two regiments of infantry and a squadron of cavalry into the thick woods along the creek. The troops of Bonham and Longstreet returned the Federal fire at short range, and the Union forces were driven back in disorder. This first affair, small as it was, had a very depressing effect upon McDowell's army, and greatly encouraged the Confederates.

This experience confirmed McDowell's impression that it was impossible with his raw troops to carry the line of Bull Run by a frontal attack. His stay of two days at Centreville, necessitated by the impossibility of concentrating sooner his loosely organized force,[14] had given time for his engineers to examine the position of the enemy, and on their report he decided to turn the Confederate left by making a détour to the northwest with his right wing. Unaware of the fact that Johnston was already on his way to join Beauregard, he also hoped to prevent their junction by destroying the railway to the Valley.

McDowell's orders, issued on Saturday, the 20 July, were as follows: Miles's division, with one brigade of Tyler's division and a strong force of artillery, was to remain in reserve at Centreville, and to threaten Blackburn's Ford. The rest of Tyler's division, with four batteries of regular artillery, was to advance along the turnpike and make a " secondary attack " at daybreak by way of the Stone Bridge. The divisions of Hunter and Heintzelman, about 13,000 men in all, were to make the turning movement. They were to march along the pike to a point two miles west of Centreville, there to take a road through the woods to the right, cross Bull Run at Sudley Springs, and move down upon the flank and rear of the enemy. Five batteries, twenty-four guns in all, were to accompany this column, the whole under the personal command of General McDowell. As soon as this movement had forced the left of Beauregard's army away from

[14] 1 Ropes, 137.

the Stone Bridge, Tyler was to cross and join in the main attack.[15] The division of Miles, 6200 strong, was to remain near Centreville to guard the communications of the army.

As anticipated, no resistance was encountered at Sudley Springs, but the turning column was delayed in starting, by Tyler's division getting in the way, and did not reach the ford until nine o'clock Sunday morning, instead of seven, as was calculated.

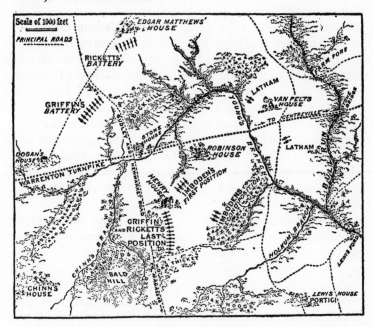

After fording the creek, and resting perhaps half an hour, the troops resumed their march in a southerly direction. They had proceeded about a mile when the enemy was encountered, posted on some heights near the Matthews house north of the Warrenton road. This was about ten-thirty.[16]

These troops were part of the demi-brigade of General Evans which held the extreme left of the Confederate line. Evans, who was an officer of the Old Army, and a good soldier, had soon divined that the Federal attack on

[15] Steele, 136.   [16] Porter's Report: 2 O. R., 383.

the Stone Bridge was only a feint; and, before long, he suspected that a movement to turn his left flank was in progress. His suspicions were confirmed by a courier from a picket at Sudley Springs, and by a " wig-wag " message from Beauregard's signal officer, Captain E. P. Alexander.[17] Leaving four companies and two guns to defend the bridge, and sending word to Cocke on his right, Evans marched the rest of his command, eleven companies and two guns, to the left, and took up a strong position on high ground about three-quarters of a mile north of the pike, with his left resting on the Sudley road.

On Johnston's arrival the day before, in virtue of his superior rank, he had taken command of the Confederate army, but he wisely left the actual direction of the troops to Beauregard. The latter had formed an ambitious plan of crossing by the lower fords, turning the left of the Federals, and cutting off their line of retreat. In fact, the two generals waited from half-past eight to half-past ten, Sunday morning, on a hill in the rear of Mitchell's Ford for this movement to begin. But the order to Ewell, who was to have been the first to cross, had miscarried, and now, as General Beauregard himself puts it, " the enemy was about to annihilate the left flank " of the Confederate army, " and had to be met and checked there, for otherwise . . . all would have been lost." [18]

After despatching orders for the two brigades of Holmes and Early to move up toward the Warrenton Pike, Johnston and Beauregard set off at a rapid gallop to join their troops engaged four miles away.[19] Ewell, Jones and Longstreet, at the same time, were ordered " to make a strong demonstration all along their front on the other side of the Run."

Upon finding Evans drawn up before him, Burnside promptly formed a regiment in line of battle and attacked. Other regiments came forward one after another and were repulsed: there was lack of concert and combined power. The Federal tactics were poor and timid.[20] Porter came to the support of Burnside, but Evans maintained

[17] 1 Ropes, 141; Alexander, 30.   [19] Johnston's *Narrative*, 48.
[18] Beauregard's *Manassas*, 117.   [20] Alexander, 33.

his position alone for more than an hour. Then he was re-enforced by the brigades of Bee and Bartow; and from the Henry House Hill, Imboden's battery lent its aid.

Meanwhile the leading regiments of Heintzelman's division had come up and prolonged the Federal line to the right. Part of both the hostile lines was in the woods and part in the open fields, and at some points the lines were only a hundred yards apart.

Soon after the arrival of Bee and Bartow, with their four regiments, the right of the Confederate position was taken in flank and rear by the brigades of Sherman and Keyes of Tyler's division. Under the mistaken impression that the Stone Bridge was mined, and defended by a heavy abattis, the Federal troops had found fords and crossed Bull Run about halfway between the bridge and Sudley.[21] Thus enveloped on their right, after having maintained their position for over two hours against superior numbers, the Confederates at last gave way and fled in confusion across Young's Branch.

In the angle south of the turnpike there is a commanding ridge called the Henry House Hill, generally level on top, and some two hundred yards across. The inner edge of the ridge afforded some cover both from view and from fire, and formed a good position for a defensive line of battle. Gentle slopes led down from the hill to the valley of Young's Branch; but they were cut up by little ravines, and partly covered with patches of young pines. Upon the northwest brow of the plateau stood the Henry house; and a third of a mile northeast of it, on a projecting spur, was the Robinson house, surrounded by dense trees and shrubbery. Both houses were small frame buildings, and neither had any defensive strength. At the rear of the plateau, along the eastern borders, was a thick fringe of young pines, which merged into a dense oak woods, of considerable extent, lying on both sides of the Sudley-Manassas road.[22]

Jackson, who had marched to the sound of the firing, had formed his brigade in the edge of the pines along the

[21] Alexander, 25, 33.
[22] Steele, 138; Beauregard, 1 B. & L., 207; Alexander, 35.

eastern brow of the plateau. He was just in time to support Imboden's battery, which, badly cut to pieces, was withdrawing from the fight. At this moment appeared General Bee: he was covered with dust and sweat, his horse foaming. " General," he said, " they are beating us back! " " Then, sir, we will give them the bayonet," replied Jackson, as his thin lips closed like a vise. Inspired with renewed confidence, Bee galloped back to the ravine where his officers were trying to reform their broken companies. Pointing with his sword to the line on the heights above, he cried: " Look! there is Jackson standing like a stone wall. Rally behind the Virginians! " [23] Bee died that day, but his words will live forever: from that hour, Thomas Jonathan Jackson was universally known as Stonewall Jackson.

Beauregard and Johnston were now on the ground: the former took personal command of the troops, while the latter rode back to the headquarters at the Lewis house to hurry up reënforcements.

It was now about two o'clock. General McDowell, who was present, in direct command of the Union forces, decided to complete the victory by carrying the Confederate position on the Henry House Hill. He had allowed Burnside to withdraw his brigade, which was exhausted from the morning's work, but he had in hand for the attack the brigades of Porter, Willcox, Sherman, and Franklin, a squadron of regular cavalry, and four batteries of artillery, about 10,000 men. Tyler, with Keyes's brigade of his division, after a feeble demonstration against the Confederate right, had recrossed Young's Branch, and took no further part in the battle. Schenck's brigade and Tyler's artillery were still on the other side of Bull Run. Howard's brigade had not yet come up. The Confederate force on the hill comprised about 6500 infantry, Stuart's squadron of cavalry, and thirteen pieces of artillery.[24]

After the withdrawal of the Confederates from their first position on the Matthews Hill, McDowell placed the two fine regular batteries of Ricketts and Griffin on a hill

[23] 1 Henderson, 177.   [24] 1 Ropes, 147.

near the Dogan house, in the angle between the turnpike and the Sudley road. From this position they swept the summit of the Henry Hill with a destructive fire. Knowing the moral support which artillery always gives to infantry, before assaulting the new Confederate position McDowell ordered Major Barry, his chief-of-artillery, to send forward these two batteries to a position beyond and to the south of the Henry house.[25] It was a strange procedure to expose these valuable batteries, without any infantry support, to a close musketry-fire, which of course they could not return. Ricketts and Griffin were amazed to receive such an order, but they promptly obeyed, and went into battery near the Henry house, within musket-shot of the woods south of it.[26]

Here the batteries were charged by Stuart's cavalry, stationed on the left of the Confederate line, and the Zouave regiment, which had been assigned as a support, at once gave way.

While Colonel Willcox was endeavoring to rally the Zouaves, the 33d Virginia suddenly appeared from the woods at the south and advanced toward the batteries. At this early date, the uniforms in the two armies were very much alike, and from the direction of the advance Major Barry thought that this was a Federal regiment sent to their support. He therefore ordered Griffin to withhold his fire. A moment later the doubtful regiment proved its identity by a deadly volley, delivered at a range of seventy yards. Every gunner was shot down, several officers fell killed or wounded, and the batteries were rendered useless for the rest of the day. Griffin managed to drag off three of his guns; but Ricketts was badly wounded and captured.[27]

Although somewhat discouraged by this reverse, McDowell had no idea of giving up the fight. The Federals crossed the valley of Young's Branch, mounted the northern slopes of the hill, and gained the plateau beyond the Henry house. Here the fighting became fierce.

[25] Imbodem terms this order "the fatal blunder of the day," 1 *B. & L.,* 234.

[26] Willcox's Report: 2 O. R., 408.

[27] Alexander, 39; 1 Henderson, 183; 1 Ropes, 148–151.

The batteries were taken and retaken. The hill at times was covered with the Federal regiments. The enemy more than once was driven back into the woods which bordered the plateau on the south and east, and into which the Federal troops could not venture to follow. For more than an hour, the battle raged backward and forward across the plateau, without any material change in the situation. About three o'clock, Howard came up, but too late to affect the result. Then the Confederates received reënforcements which turned the day in their favor. Early's brigade came up from the lower fords; Kirby Smith's brigade of Johnston's army reached Manassas by rail from the Valley, and marched at once to the field. These fresh troops were placed far out on the Confederate left, thus enveloping the right flank of the Federals. As Smith led in his troops, he was severely wounded and had to turn over the command to Elzey. Beauregard now ordered an advance all along the line, and the effect was decisive. The Union soldiers, without any show of panic, simply broke ranks, and started home, retiring, for the most part, over the roads by which they had come. The retreat was covered by Sykes's battalion of infantry and Palmer's squadron of cavalry, both of the regular army. " By six o'clock there was not a Union soldier, but the dead, the wounded, and the captives, on the south side of Bull Run." [28]

No effective pursuit was made by the Confederates. " Never did an enemy make a cleaner escape, out of such an exposed position, after such an utter rout," says General Alexander.[29]

Early in the afternoon, President Davis arrived at Manassas by rail from Richmond. Mounting a horse, he rode to the field. To the long procession of stragglers, retiring from the battle-field, he cried; " *I am President Davis. Follow me back to the field!* " Not far off, Stonewall Jackson was having a wound in his hand dressed by a surgeon. Hearing the words of Davis, he shouted: " We have whipped them! They ran like sheep! Give me five

[28] Steele, 140.
[29] Alexander, 50.

thousand fresh men, and I will be in Washington City to-morrow morning! " [30]

In fact, Jackson seems to have been the only man to grasp the situation and realize the great opportunity before them. The President and his two generals spent the rest of the afternoon in riding over the field. Although it was not sunset until after seven, and there was a nearly full moon, no serious pursuit was attempted. For this failure to follow up their success, the Confederate generals have presented many excuses. " Our army," says General Johnston, " was more disorganized by victory than that of the United States by defeat." [31]

McDowell intended to make a stand at Centreville, but the men could not be stopped there, and the Federal army retired within the defences of Washington.

The losses at Manassas, which the Federals call the battle of Bull Run, were as follows: [32]

	Federals	Confederates
Killed	460	387
Wounded	1,124	1,582
Missing	1,312	13
Totals	2,896	1,982

Estimated on the basis of the Confederate losses, probably 750 of the Union prisoners were wounded, which would make the total Federal loss in killed and wounded over 2300, or approximately 12 per cent. of the number actually engaged. The Confederate loss was not quite so large — about 11 per cent. These figures show hard fighting.

On the Federal side, Hunter and Heintzelman were wounded, Willcox, wounded and captured. On the Con-

[30] Alexander, 42.

[31] 1 B. & L., 252; Johnston, 60. See also letter of 4 August 1861, from Davis to Beauregard, in which he says: " It would have been extremely hazardous to have done more than was performed." (5 Rowland's Jefferson Davis, 120.)

[32] 1 B. & L., 194–195. Livermore (77) gives the Federal losses as 2708.

federate side, Bee and Bartow were killed, Jackson and Kirby Smith, wounded.

In the organization of its first army, the Confederacy displayed more ability than the Government at Washington. Mr. Davis was a graduate of West Point, and had served seven years in the regular army; he had commanded a volunteer regiment in the Mexican War, and had later been Secretary of War. He was acquainted, personally or officially, with most of the higher officers of the Old Army, and his selections for command were generally good. He had the professional soldier's horror of putting troops in charge of men who knew nothing of the business of war. No citizen soldier was given a high command until he had demonstrated his fitness. He did not make the mistake of Mr. Lincoln, with his lack of military experience, and appoint to important commands such men as Banks and Butler.

The Union army of 35,000 men was the largest ever assembled on this Continent, yet it was not organized into higher units than regiments until just before it left Washington.

McDowell's halt of two days at Centreville, necessitated by the " disorganized state " of his army, was fatal. It gave time for the transfer from the Valley of Johnston's Army of the Shenandoah, which decided the battle on Sunday afternoon.

The strategy of the Federal commander has been approved by many writers.[33] For example, General Sherman says: " It is now generally admitted that it was one of the best-planned battles of the war, but one of the worst-fought." Colonel Henderson also writes: " The turning movement by Sudley Springs was a skillful manœuvre, and completely surprised both Johnston and Beauregard. It was undoubtedly risky, but it was far less dangerous than a direct attack on the strong position along Bull Run."

These opinions seem to be based upon an erroneous impression of the formidable strength of the Confederate

[33] 1 Sherman, 181; Johnston, 57; 1 Comte de Paris, 228; Nicolay, 206; 1 Henderson, 196. On the contrary, Mr. Ropes thinks the strategy was poor: see 1 Ropes, 158.

position, and it is therefore somewhat difficult to agree entirely with these eminent authorities.

Colonel Henderson writes: " The Confederates were strongly posted. . . . Even with regular troops a direct attack on a single point of passage would have been difficult." [34]

Mr. Ropes says that Bull Run " presented a formidable obstacle for such raw troops as those which constituted the United States forces." [35]

On the other hand, Captain (afterwards General) Alexander, of the Confederate army, who was present at the battle, says: " Our army was weak and badly posted and could not have withstood a vigorous attack by the force in front of us. Both of our flanks were in the air, and Bull Run could be crossed by infantry in many places. Our centre was a large salient whose lines the enemy could enfilade. The ground on their side was commanding and afforded close approach under excellent cover. On our side it was low and gently rising to the rear, giving no cover whatever, except of the woods." [36]

In McDowell's report he states that he could not make the attack earlier than he did. " I wished to go to Centreville the second day," he writes, " but . . . I was told that it was impossible for the men to march further. They had only come from Vienna, about six miles, and it was not more than six and a half miles further to Centreville, in all a march of twelve and a half miles; but the men were foot-weary." [37]

Nevertheless, in the face of this experience, of only two days before, McDowell laid his plans for five of his eight brigades to make a night march of nine or ten miles by a circuitous route which would take them dangerously far from his other forces: in other words, he took the risk of having his army split in two by a formidable obstacle. The success of his project depended upon his rolling up the left flank of the enemy, and clearing the path for his own forces to unite by way of the Stone Bridge. It further

[34] 1 Henderson, 171.
[35] 1 Ropes, 135.
[36] Alexander, 22. *Cf.* Beauregard, 1 *B. & L.*, 196.
[37] 2 O. R., 324; McDowell's Report.

involved the hazard of forming his line of battle parallel to the Warrenton Pike, his line of retreat; or with his back to the stream; or with his face to the rear.[38]

In fact, McDowell deliberately took the risk of leaving his small rear guard to maintain his line of communications, and cut loose from his base, for the purpose of turning the enemy's left. His main body was further from Centreville than was the Confederate right, and he did not dare to call on his reserves for reënforcements. Unless he won a decisive victory, his position would be untenable, and he would be forced to withdraw across the stream.[39]

But General Sherman is quite right in saying that the battle was not well fought. From every tactical point of view, the attack was badly made. Instead of setting up his headquarters somewhere in the rear, and directing the operations as a whole, McDowell was at the very front, and scarcely exercised any influence on the action. As so often happened in the battles of the Civil War, regiments and brigades went into the battle without any sort of order or concert of action. The assaults were all straight to the front: there was no effort to make a flank attack.

Although the Stone Bridge was open, McDowell did not summon his reserves from Centreville, only four miles away; he did not call Schenck's brigade, and the batteries with it, across the Run; he did not order Burnside back into action; he allowed Keyes to lie idle under cover of Young's Branch throughout the afternoon.

General Johnston says: " If the tactics of the Federals had been equal to their strategy, we should have been beaten." [40] And General Alexander writes: " The Federal tactics were poor and timid: . . . there was lack of concert and combined power." [41]

Colonel Henderson, after paying a tribute to the accuracy of the fire, the fine discipline and staunch endurance of the Federal gunners, who were all old soldiers, says: " The infantry, on the other hand, was not well

[38] Steele, 145.
[39] See the remarks of General Beauregard, 1 B. & L., 218. Also Alexander, 28.
[40] Johnston, 57.
[41] Alexander, 33. Here again Mr. Ropes disagrees: see 1 Ropes, 159.

handled. The attack was purely frontal. No attempt was made to turn the Confederate flanks, although the Stone Bridge was now open and Johnston's line might easily have been taken in reverse. Nor does it appear that the cavalry was employed to ascertain where the flanks rested. Moreover, instead of massing the troops for a determined onslaught, driven home by sheer weight of numbers, the attack was made by successive brigades, those in rear waiting till those in front had been defeated; and in the same manner, the brigades attacked by successive regiments. Such tactics were inexcusable." [42]

Mr. Ropes states that the work of Colonel Henderson was not seen by him until his own book was in press, but he met this criticism in advance by the following explanation of McDowell's course: " He did not undertake to coordinate the movements of his divisions and brigades, as he doubtless would have liked to do, because he thought it very doubtful if he could succeed in such an undertaking with raw troops and inexperienced generals, and because moreover it would have taken precious time to make the attempt." [43] Later, Mr. Ropes states: " McDowell could not, with the number of troops at his immediate disposal, turn his adversary's position; he had not a sufficient superiority in force." [44]

As bearing on this point, it may be stated that, at the period of the battle on the Henry Hill, Henderson estimates that the Federals had 16,000 infantry available, while both Ropes and Alexander state that McDowell had under his immediate control not much more than 9000 men, allowing for casualties and stragglers, and taking into account the absence from the firing line of the four brigades of Howard, Burnside, Keyes, and Schenck. All the authorities agree that Beauregard was holding the hill with about 6500 men; but the chances were rather in his favor, as he was standing on the defensive, and the Federal troops, after marching and fighting for twelve hours, were nearly exhausted. [45]

[42] 1 Henderson, 181.
[43] 1 Ropes, 149.
[44] 1 Ropes, 152.
[45] *Cf.* Alexander, 38; 1 Henderson, 181; 1 Ropes, 145, 147.

The Federal army should have contained a brigade of cavalry, but it had only seven little troops, and they were mostly split up into small details. The Confederates had 1800 horsemen, but they were split up in the same manner. With the exception of Stuart's charge on the Zouaves, the cavalry played a very insignificant rôle in the battle.[46]

Beauregard's handling of his troops was equally bad, but fortunately for the Confederacy he had an able associate in Johnston, who hurried up reënforcements at the critical moment, in time to save the day.

Out of McDowell's army of 35,000 men, only 18,500 crossed the Run; and of these the brigades of Burnside and Keyes took little part in the action. Beauregard had about 32,000 men on the field, but he put only 18,000 into the battle. In very few actions of the Civil War were the numbers engaged so nearly equal, but the Confederates had the advantage of acting throughout on the defensive.

Only two officers handled their men well: Sherman on the Union side, and Jackson on the Confederate. It was the latter's wise choice of a position on the further edge of the open plateau, and McDowell's failure to take it in flank, which enabled the Confederates to hold out for four hours against superior numbers, and made their victory possible.[47]

In the opinion of Colonel Henderson, the position chosen by Jackson was the strongest that could be found — a position from which the view is limited, well in the rear of a crest line. The brow of the hill which looks down upon Young's Branch gave an extended view and a wide field of fire upon the advancing Federals, but both flanks would have been exposed. Later, at the battle of Chattanooga, we shall see the dangers of such a position, where the defenders could see the hosts of the enemy preparing for the assault.

The catastrophe of Manassas may be termed one of those unavoidable accidents that so frequently occur in war. But, for a few days, the North seemed dazed: stocks

[46] Steele, 148.　　　[47] Steele, 147.

went down, and money went up. Then stern resolve took
the place of despair. To the President's call for volunteers, there was a magnificent response: the men enlisted
with a spirit that has never been surpassed.

To the South, on the other hand, Manassas was a
Pyrrhic victory. It gave their people a very unwarranted
opinion of the superior fighting qualities of their troops.
To many, the war seemed to be over: volunteering
stopped, and even in South Carolina it proved to be impossible to raise sufficient troops to garrison the seacoast
defences. The Government indulged in vain hopes of
foreign intervention. Few were wise enough, like General
Johnston, to realize that the Southern victory was not
"due in any degree to lack of prowess in their assailants." [48]

Many of the officers engaged in this first great battle
of the war subsequently attained high rank in the
two services. On the Union side, Sherman, Burnside,
McDowell, Keyes, Heintzelman, Franklin, Porter, and
Howard became army or corps commanders; on the Confederate side, Johnston and Beauregard became full generals, and Jackson, Longstreet, Ewell, Early, and
Holmes, lieutenant-generals.

[48] Johnston, 50.

CHAPTER THREE

FEBRUARY 1862

HENRY AND DONELSON

McClellan Appointed Commander-in-Chief — His Plan of Campaign
— Kentucky and Missouri — Importance of Kentucky — Means
of Transit — Albert Sidney Johnston — His Position in Kentucky — General Polk — Forts Henry and Donelson — The
Union Commanders — General Halleck — Buell's Plan — Victory of Mill Springs — General Thomas — Halleck Orders an
Advance — General Grant — Capture of Fort Henry — Fort
Donelson Invested — The Confederate Works — The Commanding Officers — The Union Fleet Repulsed — Discouraging Outlook — The Confederate Sortie — Success Followed by Withdrawal — Grant Orders an Assault — Its Unexpected Success —
Donelson Surrendered — The Losses on Both Sides — Importance
of the Victory — Grant, a National Hero — Comments on the
Campaign

DECISIVE as was the victory of Manassas, it is not
probable that the Confederates could have captured Washington at that time. Three of the
Federal divisions had taken no part in the battle, and were
in good condition for the defence of the capital. President Davis discussed the situation fully with Johnston
and Beauregard, the night after the battle, and they all
agreed that the attempt would be hopeless.[1]

While the loss of the battle was a terrible shock to the
North, it caused no wavering in the determination to
prosecute the war. On the day after the battle, the House
of Representatives voted for the enlistment of 500,000
volunteers. The same day, President Lincoln summoned
Major-General McClellan to Washington, and assigned
him to the command, under General Scott, of all the
troops at the capital. In October, Scott insisted on being
allowed to retire from active service, and, on the first day

[1] *Cf.* 1 Davis, *R. & F.*, 360; Johnston, in 1 *B. & L.*, 252; Beauregard,
1 *B. & L.*, 219.

of November, McClellan was appointed commander-in-chief of all the armies of the United States.

Prior to this date, however, on the 4 August, at the request of Mr. Lincoln, McClellan had drawn up a memorandum on the object of the war and his general plan of operations. The main campaign, from which he expected the most decisive results, was to be in the East, but he made a number of judicious suggestions, such as that " a strong movement be made on the Mississippi, and that the rebels be driven out of Missouri." [2]

As the principal military operations of the following winter and spring took place in the West, we shall now turn to the Mississippi Valley.

It will be remembered that when the other Southern States seceded and organized the Confederacy, Kentucky wavered in its loyalty to the Union. The governor was for Secession, but the legislature was for the Union, so the State at first endeavored to compromise by declaring its neutrality (September 1861). Before we take up, however, the narrative of the military operations which this attitude of Kentucky forced upon the Government, it is necessary to trace very briefly the course of events in Missouri. In the summer of 1861, the Confederates made a determined effort to secure control of that State. In August a Confederate force of 10,000 men defeated Lyon, after a hard-fought action in which that promising officer lost his life. Later, a Union army under General Curtis drove the principal Confederate force under Van Dorn out of the State, and in March 1862 totally defeated it in an obstinate engagement at Pea Ridge in Arkansas. This decisive battle settled the fate of Missouri, although the large secessionist population in the State never ceased to give some cause for anxiety.

It was evident to all intelligent observers that the neutrality of Kentucky could not last: its position was too important. On the north the State was bounded by the Ohio River, which separated it from the Union States of Ohio, Indiana, and Illinois; on the south, by the Confederate State of Tennessee; on the east by Virginia, from

[2] 5 O. R., 7.

which it was separated by the Cumberland Mountains, which could be crossed only at certain passes, of which the most important was Cumberland Gap; on the west, by the Mississippi River. Through its borders ran the rivers Tennessee and Cumberland — two most important military thoroughfares.

In this territory there were seven principal lines of railway: [3]

1. Louisville and Nashville, running south through Bowling Green 170 miles to Nashville, where connection was made with —

2. Nashville and Chattanooga, joining these two cities, and —

3. Nashville and Decatur, leading into Alabama.

4. Memphis and Ohio, running from Bowling Green via Paris and Humboldt 250 miles to Memphis. From Humboldt, a branch line, 170 miles long, led to Columbus; and two lines, the Mississippi Central and the Mobile and Ohio, ran into Mississippi.

5. Memphis and Charleston, which passed through northern Mississippi and Alabama to Chattanooga, where it connected with —

6. Georgia Central, to Atlanta, and —

7. East Tennessee and Georgia, the main line of communication between Virginia and the Gulf States.

There were a few metaled pikes in Kentucky and Tennessee, but the highways were mainly the ordinary dirt roads — good in summer, but nearly impassable in winter and spring.

The neutrality of Kentucky was not long recognized either by the Union or the Confederacy. On the 3 September 1861, General Polk occupied Columbus, and two days later General Grant took possession of Paducah. President Davis then gave the chief command in the West to Albert Sidney Johnston, who was generally regarded as one of the ablest of American soldiers. He was a native of Kentucky, of New England descent. A graduate of West Point, he had served with distinction in the Mexican War. Like Lee, he had been opposed to secession, but

[3] See Frontispiece: "Means of Transit."

when his adopted State, Texas, seceded, he offered his sword to the Confederacy. He was then in his fifty-ninth year, handsome in person and winning in manner, of lofty character, heroic courage, and undoubted ability.[4]

Johnston made his headquarters at Bowling Green, the key to the railway system of Kentucky, where he formed an entrenched camp, with about 22,000 effectives. His line extended from Columbus, on the left, to Cumberland Gap, on the right. In January 1862, Columbus, which was fortified, was held by General Polk, with 18,000 men, and there was another fortified camp at Cumberland Gap.

General Leonidas Polk was one of the picturesque figures of that time. A nephew of President Polk, he had been educated at West Point, but had soon left the army to study theology. At the outbreak of the Civil War he had been for twenty years the Episcopal Bishop of Louisiana; he soon changed his surplice for the uniform of a major-general, and was at once placed in command of the Confederate forces in western Kentucky.

Below Columbus, the Mississippi was guarded by two or three garrisoned forts, and the Tennessee and Cumberland were protected by two forts erected just south of the Kentucky border, where the rivers were about twelve miles apart. Fort Henry stood on the east bank of the Tennessee, and Fort Donelson on the west bank of the Cumberland. Better positions could have been chosen, a few miles further down, at a point where the rivers are separated only by a space of three miles, but the sites were selected at the time that the neutrality of Kentucky was respected, so they were kept within the limits of Tennessee. These two forts were held by General Tilghman with 5000 or 6000 men.

Opposed to Johnston's Confederate forces, General Buell had an army of some 45,000 men, with headquarters at Louisville. General Halleck was in chief command in Missouri, with headquarters at St. Louis, and his territorial department included that part of Kentucky west of the Cumberland River. The commands of these two generals were absolutely independent. At Cairo there

[4] Fiske, 53.

was also a strong Union fleet of ironclad gunboats under Commodore Foote.

On becoming commander-in-chief, McClellan had given this important post in the West to Halleck, whose good fortune was soon to carry him to the supreme position in the army at Washington. Yet he was a worse than mediocre man. He possessed a thorough knowledge of the art of war as it exists in books, and could sit in his study and plan campaigns, but he had had no practical experience of operations in the field, and was later to be responsible for some of the most terrible disasters of the war.[5]

The situation of the Confederates in Kentucky, as Johnston well knew, was extremely precarious. The capture of Fort Henry and Fort Donelson, and the destruction of the railway bridges across the rivers, would break his lines of communication with the garrisons on the Mississippi; would necessitate his retreat from Bowling Green, and would also probably result in the evacuation of Columbus by Polk.

Johnston tried in vain to secure reënforcements: his forces were too small, and the men he had were badly armed. He knew also that the Federal fleet was far superior to anything that the Confederates could assemble in the three rivers.

The plan proposed by Buell for the opening campaign of 1862 in this theatre was for Halleck to ascend the Tennessee and the Cumberland with 20,000 men, supported by the ironclad fleet, while he himself advanced southward along the line of railway to Bowling Green. Halleck did not favor this plan, but wanted the bulk of Buell's forces joined to his own, so that he could move up the Cumberland with an army of 60,000 men, while Buell, with the rest of his command, acted as a containing force in front of Bowling Green. McClellan would not give his approval to either of these plans, but kept urging Buell to advance into East Tennessee, to secure possession of the railroad there, and to support the inhabitants of that region, who were intensely loyal in their sentiments.

[5] Fiske, 34.

In December and January, there were some minor
military operations in this territory, the most important
of which was the battle of Mill Springs. Here, on the
19 January 1862, General Thomas, with a division of
Buell's army, defeated a force of Confederates, and drove
it back into the mountains at Cumberland Gap.

George Henry Thomas, whom Professor Fiske terms
" one of the most attractive characters in American history
since George Washington," [6] was a native of Virginia. He
was educated at West Point, and served with distinction
in the Mexican War. Like Lee and both the Johnstons he
was confronted with the painful question of allegiance,
but, unlike them, his sense of loyalty prevailed over his
love for his native State.

It has always been a matter of much debate as to who
was entitled to the credit of the plan for the expedition to
Forts Henry and Donelson, which struck the first ef-
fectual blow at the Confederacy. Halleck claimed the
credit, and Sherman seems to accord it to him,[7] but Buell
and Grant have also been awarded the honor.

On the 29 January, Halleck received a telegram from
McClellan stating that a Confederate deserter had reported that Beauregard was under orders to leave Manassas for Kentucky with fifteen regiments. Three days later,
without awaiting further instructions from Washington,
or arranging for any coöperation from Buell, Halleck
ordered General Grant, with 17,000 men and Foote's
ironclads, to ascend the Tennessee and attack Fort Henry,
in order to anticipate the arrival of Beauregard's forces.[8]

Not until the age of thirty-nine did the call come for
Ulysses Simpson Grant, who now enters upon the scene
of History. Born in 1822, on the banks of the Ohio; educated at West Point, where he achieved no distinction;
present in every battle, except one, of the Mexican War,
where he gained little reputation, he had been engaged
since, without success, in several lines of business. At the
outbreak of hostilities in 1861, he was earning a scanty
subsistence in the leather trade at Galena, Illinois — a

---

[6] Fiske, 54. [7] 1 Sherman, 248.
[8] For a full discussion of this move, see 2 Ropes, 7–10.

broken, dissipated man, for whom no one would have dreamed of predicting a brilliant future.[9]

When the President's call for troops came in April, Grant raised and drilled a company of volunteers. Presently he passed to the charge of a district, then to the command of the great dépôt at Cairo. He was soon a brigadier, and in November, at the head of a little force of 3000 men, he fought the battle of Belmont. This was only a small affair, but it made him known to his superiors as a leader cool and adroit in the field, and secured for him the command of the Fort Henry expedition.

The expedition started the 2 February. As there were not enough boats to transport all the troops at once, McClernand's division went first, and landed about nine miles below Fort Henry. General Grant followed with the remainder of the troops, and on the 5th moved his army by boats up to a point four miles below the fort.

Fort Henry was a regular bastioned work, enclosing a space of about ten acres. It was in a bend of the river, so that twelve of its seventeen guns had a perfect sweep of the water, but they were nearly at the water level, which made their fire ineffective against the Union gunboats. The fort was badly located: it was not only surrounded by higher ground, but was perfectly commanded by heights on the opposite bank, where the Confederates had built another work, called Fort Heiman.

At this time, General Tilghman had about 2500 men in the two forts on the Tennessee, but on the morning of the 6th he sent all of his troops to Fort Donelson, except about seventy men, whom he kept at Fort Henry, under his own command, to hold the fort, and serve the guns, until the infantry was well on its way.

At eleven o'clock on the morning of the 6 February, General Grant moved on the forts, with his land forces, and Foote's fleet consisting of four ironclads and three wooden gunboats. At a distance of a mile, the fleet opened fire, and two hours later Tilghman lowered his colors and ran up a white flag. The Union troops were so much delayed by the high water in the creeks, and the muddy

[9] Fiske, 43; Buchan, 39.

roads, that the Confederates had time to make good their retreat to Fort Donelson.

Immediately after the fall of Fort Henry, two of the gunboats proceeded up the river and destroyed the bridge of the Memphis and Ohio Railroad. Then they continued on up the river as far as the Muscle Shoals, in Alabama, destroying large quantities of Confederate supplies, and spreading alarm through the whole region.[10]

As soon as General Johnston learned of the fall of Fort Henry, he sent about half of his force under General Floyd to Fort Donelson, and with the remainder of his army, some 14,000 men, retreated to Nashville, where he arrived on the 16 February.

There were two roads leading from Fort Henry across to Fort Donelson, about twelve miles east on the Cumberland. The intervening country was cut up by creeks and marshes, hills and ravines; and was heavily wooded. The water was high in all the creeks, and the roads were in very bad condition. Grant wanted to proceed at once to Fort Donelson, but it continued to rain, and his artillery and wagons could not move. He was also delayed by the time necessary for the fleet to run down the Tennessee and ascend the Cumberland, as he did not " feel justified " in attacking without the coöperation of the fleet. So it was not until the 12 February that his army moved. On that day he started with the divisions of McClernand and C. F. Smith. Another division which had just arrived, under Lew Wallace, and which included a brigade sent by General Buell, went around by water. Before night the neighborhood of the fort was reached by McClernand and Smith, and the troops took up a position surrounding the work. The next day Wallace arrived, the lines were rectified, and some fighting took place.[11]

Fort Donelson was a larger and more elaborate work than Fort Henry. The main fort was an irregular, bastioned parapet, enclosing a space of about 100 acres, nearly 500 yards long in its greatest dimension. It stood 100 feet above the river, at the eastern end of a ridge which narrowed down to a mere neck just west of the

[10] 2 Ropes, 17.　　　　　[11] 2 Ropes, 24.

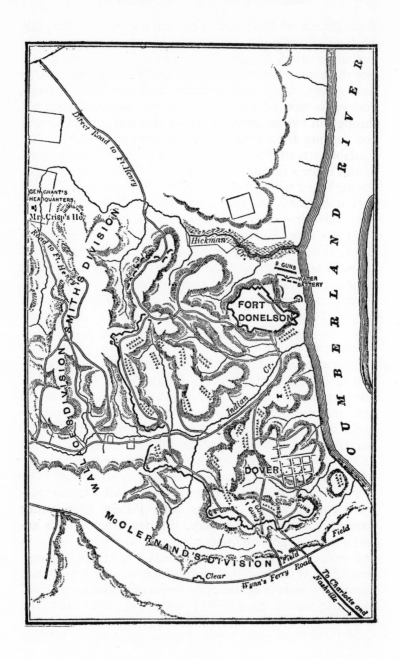

fort. Except at this point, the ground sloped from the work on all sides. On the north, Hickman Creek, which was unfordable, formed a perfect barrier. On the river side there were two water batteries fifty or sixty feet above water level, commanding the river to the north. About 700 yards west of the main work was another ridge, cut through in two or three places by forks of Indian Creek, and curving from Hickman Creek around to another unfordable stream south of Dover. On the irregular crest of this ridge a line of entrenchments had been constructed, strengthened with abattis. This line, which was two and a half miles long, was what came to be called, later in the war, rifle-pit — a trench with the earth thrown up on the outer side. Batteries were constructed at nine points in the line, and armed with the guns of eight field batteries. The entire line followed the face of ridges from fifty to eighty feet high, except toward the south where a break was made by the valley of Indian Creek, and faced on valleys or ravines filled with forest and underbrush. The position was a strong one, but possessed the common fault of the Confederate works — it was so large as to need several thousand men to defend it, and a small army in case of an obstinate and protracted siege. " Such conditions," says Mr. Ropes, " made too heavy a draft on the limited resources of the Confederate armies. Thousands of men were shut up in these works who should have been serving in the field with the active armies." [12]

This strong position was held by an army of 19,000 men, commanded by General Pillow, an officer of but little merit. Second in command was General Buckner, an excellent soldier, whose relations with Pillow were rather strained. On the 13 February, the day after Grant's arrival, a third general, senior in rank to Pillow, came in and took command. This was John B. Floyd, lately Secretary of War under President Buchanan. He was a man absolutely unfit for such an important command, and Johnston made a great mistake in sending him there. [13]

[12] 2 Ropes, 15. *Cf.* Johnston's *Johnston*, 85, 86; also Johnston's *Narrative*, 152.
[13] Fiske, 58.

Upon its arrival, the army of General Grant took up its position on another ridge about 600 or 700 yards from the Confederate line, and approximately parallel to it. McClernand's division was on the right, Smith's on the left, and Wallace's, after its arrival the next day, held the centre. Grant now had about 25,000 men on the field, the divisions were all closed up, and the line was extended around to the right so as to bar the road to Charlotte and Nashville, the only Confederate line of retreat.

General Grant considered the enemy's works too strong to be assaulted successfully by the raw troops at his disposal, and relied upon the fleet to reduce the fort. On the 14th the fleet arrived, and Commodore Foote at once took his ships into action. But the gunboats found no such easy task as the reduction of Fort Henry. The Confederate guns, placed 32 feet above the river, were served skillfully, and their fire was very effective. Two of the ironclads had their steering apparatus shot away and helplessly drifted down the river out of the action. The other two were so badly damaged as to be compelled to withdraw. The whole fleet was put *hors de combat*, and Foote himself was severely wounded. It would be necessary to send the disabled vessels back to Cairo for repairs, and further coöperation by the fleet seemed for the moment out of question.

After he had witnessed the repulse of the fleet, Grant felt that a speedy victory was not to be expected, and looked forward to a protracted siege. To make the situation even more discouraging, the weather had turned intensely cold, the temperature dropping to twenty degrees below the freezing-point. The men were without tents, and could not build fires, within full range of the enemy's guns. Many of them, in their inexperience, had thrown away their blankets, and were frost-bitten — some even frozen to death. The wagons had not all come up, and rations were scarce. " The sun went down on the night of the 14 February 1862, leaving the army confronting Fort Donelson anything but comforted over its prospects." [14]

[14] 1 Grant, 303.

The Confederates also were much discouraged, and Grant's problem was nearer a solution than he imagined. It was feared that the Federal troops would gain the bank of the river above the fort, establish batteries there to command the stream, and thus prevent supplies from reaching the defenders. At a council of war held that evening, the three generals decided to attack the Union right at daybreak, with the object of forcing it off the Charlotte road, and opening up an avenue of escape. The plan was an excellent one, and it was well executed; but it failed in the end because no orders were issued, or arrangements made, for an immediate retreat in case of success.

The next morning, the 15th, the Federal right wing under McClernand was vigorously attacked, and rolled up against Wallace. By one o'clock the Confederates had gained their object, and the road to Nashville was open. Then, in the very moment of victory, Pillow, who had directed the attack, made the fatal blunder of ordering the men back into their works.

At this hour, General Grant arrived on the scene. On account of his wound, Commodore Foote had asked Grant to come aboard his flagship for a conference; it thus happened that the Union commander was absent all the morning. When Grant reached the field, the fighting was all over, and the victorious Confederates were retiring to their works.

Grant sent a despatch to Foote, telling of the events of the morning, and adding, " I must make a charge to save appearances." He asked Foote to make a demonstration with the gunboats and fire a few shells at long range. He said, this " may secure a victory: otherwise all may be defeated."

" It is clear," comments Mr. Ropes, " that he did not expect any important result from the charge; it was, he saw, the proper thing to order, but he relied mainly on the reappearance of the fleet to restore confidence to his troops." [15]

After sending his message to Foote, Grant rode over

[15] 2 Ropes, 31.

to find Smith on his left, and gave the order for an immediate assault on the works in his front. The veteran Charles F. Smith, one of the finest officers in the Union service, led the attack in person, and inspired his raw troops with his own dauntless courage. Fortunately for the attacking party, the Confederate troops who had held this part of the line had not yet had time to regain their entrenchments after the morning sortie, and the works were easily carried, although the few troops left in this part of the fort defended themselves with great tenacity. The position thus carried by Smith was found to possess unusual importance: it was an angle inside the fort, which practically commanded the entire work.[16]

In the meantime, under orders from General Grant, Wallace and McClernand had advanced, and reoccupied the positions from which they had been driven in the morning. By nightfall the Union forces again blocked the Confederate line of retreat.

That evening another council of war was held within the fort, and it was decided to surrender the works on the best terms possible. Then ensued a remarkable scene. Floyd, who was at that moment under indictment at Washington for misuse of public funds, said that he would rather die than fall into the hands of the Federals. So he passed the command over to Pillow, who, in turn, transferred it to Buckner, and these two generals escaped up the river on a small steamboat. At the same time, Forrest, with the greater part of his cavalry, succeeded in getting by the Union right, and evading capture.

At daybreak Buckner sent a note to General Grant proposing the appointment of commissioners to agree upon terms of capitulation. Grant wrote back the since famous reply: " No terms except unconditional and immediate surrender " would be accepted, and added that he proposed " to move immediately " upon the enemy's works. Without further parley, Buckner thereupon surrendered his command.

" With plenty of food and ammunition," says Major

16 2 Ropes, 32.

[58]

Steele, "there does not appear to have been any adequate excuse for surrendering at that time." [17]

The Union losses at Fort Donelson were about 2600 killed and wounded, 224 missing. It is impossible to give any reliable statement of the Confederate casualties, but they probably did not exceed 2000 killed and wounded.[18]

There are also no reliable figures regarding the number of the garrison, or the number of prisoners captured. There were probably some 19,000 men in the fort, of whom about a quarter escaped. Badeau states that rations were issued at Cairo to 14,623 prisoners, which seems to be the most trustworthy statement of the number captured. Mr. Ropes says: "About 11,500 men with 40 guns were the fruits of this great victory." Mr. Fiske states: "The surrender delivered up to Grant nearly 15,000 prisoners, with 65 cannon and 17,000 muskets." [19]

The capture of Fort Donelson was the greatest military achievement that the American Continent had yet witnessed, but its moral and strategic results were out of all proportion to its physical dimensions. The two great rivers were laid open for hundreds of miles. There was a panic at Nashville. The State government fled, with the archives and the money in the treasury. Johnston evacuated the city, and fell back to Murfreesboro. Just a week after the surrender, a division of Buell's army occupied the capital of Tennessee. On the Mississippi, the results were equally decisive. Columbus was no longer tenable, and Polk soon retreated as far as Corinth, in Mississippi.

At one bound, General Grant became a national hero, and this he deserved to be. No criticism can be made of his conduct of the campaign. He had the good sense to rely upon the gunboats to reduce the fort, and, "with a discretion which on similar occasions afterwards he did not always show, he did not waste the strength of his troops by assaulting the unbroken and well-manned fortifications of his antagonists." [20] He well merited the praise

[17] Steele, 164.
[18] See Livermore, 78.
[19] Cf. 2 Campaigns, 60–64; 2 Ropes, 33; Fiske, 64; Grant, 314–315.
[20] 2 Ropes, 35.

which came to him from the public, and the promotion which the Government at once bestowed upon him.

The general strategy of the war in the West may be regarded as a flanking movement on a vast scale, by which, after four years, the left of the Confederacy was at last turned and its overthrow accomplished. At the opening of 1862, of course, no such plan was considered. The Federal objective was to break the Confederate line of defence at its most vulnerable point; and the Donelson campaign was an example of what the text-books call "strategic penetration." The two wings of the Confederate army were at Columbus and Bowling Green, 170 miles apart, or less than one day, in point of time, by rail. The capture of Henry and Donelson, the destruction of the railway bridge over the Tennessee, and the occupation of Clarksville by the Federal forces, broke the line of communication between the two wings of Johnston's army, and compelled their retirement.[21]

Although this brief campaign was most successful, it had not been free from a certain measure of risk. General Halleck had begun it without any authority from Washington, and without any understanding with Buell either for support or coöperation. Buell was perfectly willing to cause a diversion by advancing in force on Bowling Green, but he was still under orders to invade East Tennessee. He offered Halleck one of his brigades, which arrived in time to take part in the capture of Donelson; and he placed at his disposal eight new regiments then in Ohio and Indiana. He also wrote McClellan, on the 5 February, advocating the postponement of the East Tennessee movement, and finally obtained his approval of the advance on Bowling Green. From that moment, McClellan did all in his power to coördinate the operations of the forces under Halleck and Buell.

To reënforce Grant, Buell had to send troops around by the Ohio River, while Johnston had the short line of the railroad and the highways. This gave Johnston a chance which he failed to improve. He should have left

[21] Steele, 162.

a small force at Bowling Green, to hold back Buell, and himself led the remainder of his army against Grant. Instead of doing this, he sent an incompetent general, Floyd, with 12,000 men to Donelson, while he himself fell back with 14,000 to Nashville.

"In all of the operations of the Civil War," says Major Steele, "it would be hard to find another example of such crass incapacity as was displayed by the Confederate commanders at Fort Donelson. . . . Not one, but several opportunities offered, . . . which, if made use of by a bold and skillful general, might have resulted in a Confederate success." [22]

At the opening of the campaign, Johnston had the advantage of interior lines and could have concentrated his forces more quickly than Halleck and Buell, but after the capture of Henry and Donelson the case was exactly reversed. His line was penetrated; the railway was in the possession of the Federals, and they had on their side all the strategic advantages. Johnston was forced to abandon Bowling Green and fall back to Nashville. He should have left the defence of Donelson to its own little garrison, and kept his forces united; or if he wanted to defend that point, he should have gone there himself. He never would have made the mistake of shutting his army up within the fort to be besieged, and he did not expect Floyd to do so. "He wished Donelson defended if possible, but he did not wish the army to be sacrificed in the attempt." One of his last telegrams to Floyd said: "If you lose the fort bring your troops to Nashville if possible." [23] Any general of average ability would have found it "possible."

All the commanders had cavalry, but with the exception of Forrest's work at Donelson, their rôle in this campaign was insignificant. The generals had not yet learned how to employ this important arm of the service in the strategic duty of "security and information." Even Forrest, who later became one of the ablest cavalry commanders in the Confederate army, up to this time had

[22] Steele, 163. Floyd was subsequently placed in command of Virginia State troops, and Pillow became a pursuer of Confederate conscripts.
[23] W. Preston Johnston, in *B. & L.*

[61]

done no more than forage and fight. General Grant had cavalry at Donelson, but did not employ it to any extent. It should be stated, however, that his cavalry was made up of volunteers, lately enlisted, and neither officers nor men had had any experience.

This was the first instance in the Civil War in which a river was used as the line of operations, and it furnished nearly the only successful instance in any modern campaign. The ease with which transports can be harassed by the enemy on shore renders the use of rivers as lines of operation very exceptional.[24]

No other Union victory, except Gettysburg, had so disheartening an effect upon the people of the South, and none caused so much exultation in the North, as the capture of Forts Henry and Donelson. " The effect," says Mr. Ropes, " was electrical. It was the first great success won by the Union arms within the limits of the Confederacy." Professor Fiske also chronicles the hopeful feeling throughout the North: " In the gloomy record of the anxious and impatient year which had just passed, this great victory was the one bright spot. The victor became a popular hero."

Halleck, who was personally entitled to so little credit, asked the Government to enlarge his command so as to cover all of the armies west of the Alleghanies, and on the 11 March his request was granted. The territory was divided into three departments, Pope in Missouri commanding the right, Grant on the Tennessee the centre, and Buell at Nashville the left. Grant had already been made major-general of volunteers, and Buell, Pope, Smith, McClernand, and Wallace were raised to the same rank.

[24] Steele, 167.

CHAPTER FOUR

APRIL 1862

SHILOH

The Union Camp at Pittsburg Landing — Lack of Entrenchments —
The Divisions — Dangers of the Position — Responsibility of
Halleck and Grant — The Confederate Army — Its Command-
ers — Advance to Shiloh — Buell's March — Nelson's Arrival —
Blind Confidence of Grant and Sherman — The Confederate
Attack — Grant Absent — Sherman Driven Back — The Hor-
net's Nest — Johnston Killed — The Union Centre Broken —
Prentiss Surrenders — Grant Arrives — The Final Stand — The
Confederates Withdraw — Grant's " Incompetence " — Poor
Tactics of the Confederates — The Monday Battle — The Con-
federates Defeated — Heavy Losses — Comments — The Tactics
Bad on Both Sides — Failure to Pursue the Enemy — Results
of the Campaign

THE first of April 1862 General Grant's command,
now called the Army of the Tennessee, was encamped on the west bank of the Tennessee River at
Pittsburg Landing, a point about a hundred miles south
of Fort Henry, and twenty miles north of Corinth, where
Johnston was assembling his army. Grant's headquarters
were at Savannah, a small town about nine miles further
down on the other (east) bank of the river.

A few weeks prior to this date, Grant had been temporarily suspended, owing to a misunderstanding with Halleck,[1] and the site of the camp was selected by C. F. Smith,
who was at first in charge of the expedition. But that excellent officer met early in March with a serious accident,
from the effects of which he never recovered.

The ground upon which the camp stood, and upon
which the battle of Shiloh was fought, was an irregular
triangle, with sides three or four miles long, bounded on
the north and west by Snake Creek and its tributary Owl

---

[1] See 1 Grant, 326–327.

Creek; on the east by the Tennessee; on the south by Lick Creek and its branch, Locust Grove Creek, a small brook in quite a deep ravine. At that time all of these streams were more or less flooded.

The highest ground, about 200 feet above the river, was a ridge lying north of Locust Grove Creek, and from this point the land sloped gradually to the level of the camps, 100 feet below. The ground, uneven and thickly wooded, was mostly impassable for cavalry, although there were several clearings of from 20 to 80 acres. A number of small roads intersected the field, and on one of these, running out toward Corinth, near the west of the position, was a rude meeting-house built of logs and known as Shiloh Church, which gave the name to the battle.

The greater part of the army was arranged across the base, or open front, of the triangle between Owl and Lick creeks, which protected its two flanks. This open front was the only quarter in which the army was exposed to assault. At a later period of the war this line would have been entrenched, and the whole position made impregnable.

The right of the line, near the crossing of Owl Creek by the Purdy road, was held by Sherman, with Prentiss next to him on the left. On Sherman's left, and rear, was McClernand, while Stuart's brigade of Sherman's division held the extreme left, resting upon Lick Creek. From a mile to a mile and a half in the rear, stretching from a point just above the Landing nearly across to Snake Creek, were the divisions of Hurlbut and C. F. Smith — the latter now under the command of William Wallace, owing to Smith's injury. The division of Lew Wallace was five miles down the river at Crump's Landing, whence a road runs west to Purdy. Another road, parallel with the river, connected Wallace with the Union position by a bridge lately built over Snake Creek.

From Pittsburg Landing two roads led direct to Corinth, only twenty miles away, where it was known that Johnston was assembling an army, estimated at from 50,000 to 80,000 men; but, as above stated, no works of

[64]

any kind were thrown up on the exposed side of the Federal position; nor was there arranged any line of defence or plan of action in case of attack. Furthermore, there was no possibility of retreat from the position: no bridge could be thrown across the Tennessee, which, at the time, was very high, overflowing its banks. In the rear were deep and muddy creeks, which were practically impassible. The whole arrangement was manifestly faulty, and indicates great carelessness on the part of General Grant. His headquarters were nine miles away, and all the well-known maxims of war, applicable to such a situation, were unheeded by him. Probably there never was an army encamped in the heart of a hostile country with so little regard to the manifest risks which are inseparable from such a position.[2]

For this state of affairs, Halleck was largely responsible. It was by his permission and approval that Grant, with over 40,000 men, was encamped at Pittsburg Landing, in such an exposed position. But Grant, who was on the ground, cannot escape his share of the responsibility.

Halleck had, indeed, ordered Buell to direct his march on Savannah, but in his correspondence he never once intimated to Buell that Grant's army was in peril until it was joined by the troops coming from Nashville. In reality, that danger was imminent.

As we have seen, the army under the command of Johnston had retired from Nashville to Murfreesboro. Thence it marched south over very bad roads to Decatur, in Alabama. Here, about the middle of March, the Tennessee River was crossed, and the march resumed in a westerly direction, the head of the column reaching Corinth, in Mississippi, about the 18th. Johnston had with him some 20,000 men, and he was almost immediately joined by General Bragg, with about 10,000 troops from Pensacola and New Orleans. To this point also Beauregard, his able second in command, directed the forces of Polk, who, since the evacuation of Columbus, had been at Humboldt and Jackson.

On the 29 March, Johnston formally assumed the com-

[2] 2 Ropes, 56–58.

mand of these forces, to which he gave the name of the
" Army of the Mississippi." Bragg was made chief-of-
staff, and Beauregard was designated as second in command. The army was divided into three corps, under the
command of Polk, Bragg, and Hardee. There was also a
reserve division of infantry, under Breckinridge, lately
the Vice-President of the United States. The army numbered nearly 40,000 men, of whom 35,000 were infantry
and the rest cavalry and artillery.[3] There were about 100
guns.

The Confederate forces were ably commanded. Johnston was generally considered to be one of the finest
officers in the service. Bragg, who subsequently commanded the army, stood very high as an organizer and
disciplinarian, and was a good general, although not a successful strategist. Breckinridge, although a civilian, was a
gallant and efficient officer.[4]

Johnston, who was well-informed regarding the position of the Federals, was anxious to strike Grant before
Buell could arrive, but it was impossible to complete the
organization of his new army before the first of April.
Orders for the advance were finally issued on the 3rd.
Then, the roads were found so bad, and the weather was
so rainy, it was impossible to cover the short distance of
twenty miles under three days, so that the army did not
get within striking distance until Saturday afternoon, the
5 April. Beauregard felt certain that Buell's army must
have joined Grant by this time, and advised that the plan
be given up, but to this Johnston would not consent. Accordingly the orders were issued to attack the enemy at
daybreak on Sunday, the 6th.

The Federal forces under General Grant comprised six
divisions of infantry, and numbered on paper nearly
45,000 men, of whom about 3000 were cavalry. There
were over 20 batteries — more than 100 guns.[5] All of
the division-generals were men of unquestioned bravery,

[3] See 7 O. R., 259, 261; 11 O. R., 339, 340, 370; Johnston, 548.
[4] 2 Ropes, 61, 62.
[5] Grant (1 *Memoirs*, 366) places the number of his effective force
at only 38,000. Force (180) puts it at about 40,000.

and perfectly equal to their tasks. Sherman subsequently rose to the command of this army.[6]

In the meantime, the Army of the Ohio, under General Buell, was slowly marching across the country, from Nashville, on the Cumberland, to Savannah on the Tennessee. His force consisted of five divisions, under Thomas, McCook, Nelson, Crittenden, and Wood, and numbered about 37,000 men, with a full complement of artillery, and some cavalry.[7]

The army marched steadily, but without haste, covering about fifteen miles a day. At Duck River, it was found that the bridge had been burned by the enemy, and this caused a delay of nearly two weeks. The movement was not pressed, because Buell had no intimation, from either Halleck or Grant, that the army at Pittsburg Landing was in any danger of attack. In fact, to use Buell's own words, he understood that he was " not to succor General Grant's army, but to form a junction with it for an ulterior offensive campaign."

Nelson, who was in the lead, arrived at Savannah with his division on Saturday, 5 April, about noon, and with one of his brigade commanders, Ammen, saw Grant that same afternoon. Ammen suggested that the division should cross the river at once, and join the army encamped at Pittsburg Landing, but Grant declined the offer — remarking that there would be no battle there, and that they would have to go to Corinth.[8] The same day Grant wrote to Halleck that he had " scarcely the faintest idea " that an attack would be made upon him, but that he should be prepared if it took place.[9] Such blind confidence is hard to explain, when he thought that Johnston had at Corinth, on his own estimate, " not far from 80,000 men." [10]

Sherman, who appears to have been in command when Grant was not at the camp, shared in full the confidence of his chief. On the 5th he wrote Grant: " I do not apprehend anything like an attack on our position." Both

[6] 2 Ropes, 64.
[7] 1 Van Horne, 99.
[8] 10 O. R., 331.

[9] 10 O. R., 89.
[10] 11 O. R., 94.

Sherman and Prentiss, however, sent out small parties to reconnoitre. Several bodies of the enemy were encountered on Saturday, and on Sunday morning at three o'clock Prentiss despatched an entire brigade to ascertain the extent of the Confederate forces. About six o'clock these troops came in contact with the enemy's first line, under Hardee, and were driven back with loss.[11]

The original Confederate order was to attack at three o'clock on the morning of Saturday, the 5th, but the troops were not in position until late that afternoon. All day Friday they had advanced over muddy roads, hindered by a pelting rain. After midnight a violent storm broke upon them, as they stood under arms in the pitch darkness, with no shelter but the trees. This was followed by clearing weather, and the sun set on Saturday evening in a cloudless sky. Sunday morning broke upon a scene so fair that it left its memory on thousands of hearts. The sky was clear overhead, the air fresh; and when the sun rose in full splendor, the advancing host passed the word from lip to lip that it was the " sun of Austerlitz." [12]

The Confederates advanced to the attack in three parallel lines, under the command of Hardee, Bragg, and Polk. With the reserve of Breckinridge, they numbered 39,630 men, including 4300 cavalry. The first gun was fired at 5:14, as General Johnston was taking coffee with his staff. They at once mounted and galloped to the front.[13]

Two hours later the Confederate artillery opened fire, and Johnston's army advanced with a rush, confident of victory. The Union troops, suddenly alive to the fact that they were attacked in great force, hardly had time to seize their muskets and fall in before the first Confederate line was upon them. Not expecting any attack, and not being in order of battle, for the first few hours they were at the mercy of their antagonists.[14] The resistance they offered was therefore of a fragmentary and disconnected character — each body of troops making the best defence it could, often isolated from the other bodies of troops in

[11] 10 O. R., 277–278.
[12] Johnston, 1 B. & L., 556.
[13] Ibid, 557–558.
[14] 2 Ropes, 68.

its vicinity, and therefore exposed to having its flanks turned by the well-supported lines of the Confederate army.[15] To make matters worse, for several hours there was no commanding general on the field, and each division commander was thrown upon his own resources, with such assistance as he could get from his nearest neighbor.

The first shock fell upon the two divisions of Sherman and Prentiss, which were almost entirely composed of raw troops, and they soon gave way, but for the most part fell back to new positions. This gave time for the divisions of McClernand, Hurlbut, and Wallace, to get under arms and form in order of battle.

Sherman's division naturally retired on that of McClernand, and Hurlbut sent one brigade to their assistance. These troops fought gallantly and stubbornly during the whole day, without the slightest aid from the centre, from which they were separated by a wide gap. Falling back from one position to another, at the close of the day they covered the bridge over Snake Creek by which Lew Wallace was expected to arrive. In his report McClernand states that this was the eighth position he had occupied during the battle.[16]

Prentiss's division, also composed of raw troops, fell back upon the two remaining brigades of Hurlbut, and William Wallace brought up his division to their assistance. About ten o'clock these three bodies of troops, constituting the centre of the army, took up a very strong position, which the Confederates called the " Hornets' Nest." This was located near the centre of the Union line, about halfway between the church and the river. It was a wooded area with dense undergrowth, and was well suited for defence. Here they held out for five or six hours, against the repeated assaults of the enemy, whom they again and again beat back with severe loss. It was in directing one of these assaults, about two-thirty, that General Johnston was killed. He was struck by a rifle-ball which cut an artery in the leg. If a tourniquet had been applied, the wound need not have been fatal; but John-

---

[15] Force, *Campaigns*, 124.   [16] 10 O. R., 250, 119.

ston, absorbed in his work, paid no attention to it, and suddenly fell dead from loss of blood. His death was a greater misfortune to the South than the loss of the battle.[17]

Finally, after four o'clock, Bragg abandoned these costly frontal attacks, and advanced beyond the Federal position. Hurlbut, finding himself flanked, retired to the Landing. This exposed Prentiss's left, and forced him to change front. Soon afterwards, about five o'clock, the two divisions of Prentiss and Wallace were attacked by the Confederate corps of Polk and Hardee in front and on both flanks. In trying to withdraw his command, Wallace was killed, and between five and half-past five o'clock Prentiss was forced to surrender, with about 2200 men. This ended the resistance of the Federal centre.

The isolated brigade of Stuart, on the extreme left, maintained its position until after three o'clock, and then succeeded in retiring to the Landing, having lost about half its men.

Late in the afternoon there were from 5000 to 15,000 fugitives crowded under the high bluff near the Landing. Efforts were made from time to time to rally them, but they were thoroughly demoralized and would not budge from their shelter.[18]

General Grant was taking an early breakfast at Savannah when he heard the sound of heavy firing at the Landing. He ordered Nelson to march his division up the river to a point opposite the Landing, ready to be ferried over. Then he started up the river himself in a steamer, stopping at Crump's Landing to direct Lew Wallace to be ready to march on receipt of orders. Finding on his arrival that the attack was very serious, he sent a staff-officer to order Wallace to march at once. He then rode to the battle-field, saw Sherman about ten o'clock, and afterwards Prentiss at the Hornets' Nest, which he ordered him to maintain at all hazards. Realizing then how dangerous the situation was, at noon he despatched

[17] See 2 Davis, 69.
[18] 2 Ropes, 74. But see also Grant (344), who states that many returned to the field.

an urgent note to Buell, asking him to get his troops on the field at once.

The final Federal position of the day was on a line running from just above the Landing to the bridge across Snake Creek. The left of this position was covered by a ravine partly overflowed with backwater. Here a force of some 4000 men was collected; and a battery of twenty pieces was planted on the bluffs, by Colonel Webster of Grant's staff, just as three Confederate brigades were advancing to the attack. These guns opened upon them, while at the same time two of the Union gunboats enfiladed the Confederate lines. The Confederates, loath to abandon the contest, in which victory seemed almost within their grasp, rushed down into the ravine, and climbed the steep slope on the further side. Here they received the terrible fire of the battery, and the destructive volleys of the Union infantry. Again and again they attempted to reach the crest, but were as often forced to retire. The sun was fast disappearing and little time was left to finish the work of the day. Just as night set in, Beauregard, who was now in supreme command, ordered the troops to withdraw.[19] For this he has been severely criticised, but nothing was to be gained that afternoon by prolonging the action.[20]

In his review of the battle, General Buell, speaking of the final Confederate assault, says: " The attack was poorly organized, but it was not repulsed until Ammen [of Nelson's division] arrived. . . . Had the attack been made before Nelson could arrive, . . . it would have succeeded beyond all question." [21]

As a matter of fact, Ammen's brigade " was ferried across the river just in time to see the end; it had two men killed and one wounded." [22] The arrival of Nelson, therefore, did not affect the result in the smallest degree.

Buell's statement is also directly contradicted by Beaure-

[19] 10 O. R., 466, 472, 550, 551, 555.

[20] *Cf.* 2 Ropes, 82; Steele, 189. See also his own statement below.

[21] 1 *B. & L.*, 507: " Shiloh Reviewed."

[22] Steele, 179. See also Upton, 272: " The last desperate charge was repulsed just as the leading division of Buell's army succeeded in crossing the river."

gard's article on the battle. He writes: "After the capture of General Prentiss no serious effort was made to press the victory by the corps commanders. In fact the troops had got out of the hands of the corps, divisional, and brigade commanders; and for the most part, moreover, at the front, were out of ammunition. Several most gallant, uncombined efforts . . . were made to reach and carry the Federal battery, *but in every instance the effort failed*." He adds that, " really the attack had ceased at every point," before he issued orders at six o'clock to suspend hostilities and withdraw the troops from under fire.[23]

Professor Fiske considers General Buell's article as " one of the most masterly pieces of military criticism . . . in any language." But Buell was so biased by his jealousy and hatred of General Grant that his statements cannot be accepted without many qualifications.

Mr. Ropes, also, shows his animosity to General Grant in his declaration that the final attack would probably have succeeded but for the arrival of Buell's fresh and well-disciplined troops. He says that, if the Landing had been seized and occupied by the Confederates, they could easily have prevented Nelson's division from crossing, and what was left of Grant's army might have been forced to surrender.[24] " *But*," says General Beauregard, " *in every instance the effort failed*."

Nelson's division was delayed in reaching the field through the neglect of Grant to provide steamers to transport the troops from Savannah. They were forced to march up the east side of the river, through a swamp in which the artillery had to be abandoned. The division of Lew Wallace, of Grant's army, took the wrong road in the morning, and did not arrive until after dark. Probably not more than 12,000 men of the Army of the Tennessee were with the colors that night.[25]

" It is evident from all the accounts — Grant's included — that the battle of Sunday was fought by the Union army without any directing head," says Mr. Ropes.

[23] 1 *B. & L.*, 590. The italics are General Beauregard's.
[24] 2 Ropes, 80.   [25] 2 Ropes, 81.

"Fortunate was it for the Union cause that five such gallant and capable division-commanders were on the field. They did all that could be done in the circumstances in which they were placed. But it cannot be supposed that their efforts would not have been better employed and therefore more successful had they found in Grant a general who was capable of assuming the entire control and direction of a great battle. Grant, however, was not a general of this sort. He had neither the ability nor the experience for such a task." [26]

The battle of Sunday was fought by the Confederates with the greatest energy and courage, but it failed of final success because of tactical errors. Their plan was to turn the Union left, so as to cut the Federals off from the Landing, and surround them in the angle of Owl Creek, in which event they hoped to insure a surrender. But in the heat of the conflict this excellent plan was lost sight of, and their strength was wasted for hours in a vain effort to take the Hornets' Nest by a frontal attack. With all his great abilities, it must be admitted that Johnston did not attempt on this day to fill the rôle of an army-commander. He left the general control of the action to Beauregard, and confined himself to directing the assault on the Union centre, where he lost his life.

During the night the remainder of Nelson's division arrived, also that of Crittenden, and early in the morning McCook came up. These three divisions of Buell's army, numbering about 20,000 men, were placed on the left of the Union line. The right was held by the divisions of Hurlbut and McClernand, which still preserved their organization, and the 5000 fresh troops of Lew Wallace. The divisions of Sherman and William Wallace were broken up, but many of the men were in line for the second day's battle.

Grant and Buell determined to assume the offensive as early as possible. Buell took the personal direction of his own troops, and handled them in masterly fashion. [27]

[26] 2 Ropes, 83–84. Here again Mr. Ropes shows his antipathy for General Grant.
[27] 2 Ropes, 88.

The defeat of the Confederates in the battle of the second day was inevitable. They could put only 20,000 men in line, while the Federals had 25,000 fresh troops, besides at least 10,000 who had taken part in the action of Sunday. As Professor Fiske remarks, the Civil War proved that in fighting quality there was little to choose between the soldiers of the North and the South, so that, under similar conditions, victory always took the side of the heaviest battalions.[28]

The Confederates held practically the same line, to the north of Shiloh Church, which had been occupied the previous day by the Union camp. Bragg was on the extreme left, with Polk and Breckinridge next, and finally Hardee, on the extreme right, next to the river. Beauregard handled his troops bravely and skillfully, and was ably seconded by his corps-commanders. No final or critical stand was made anywhere, and by four o'clock the Confederate army had fallen back beyond Shiloh Church. Here General Grant stopped the Federal advance.

Considering the numbers engaged, the losses on both sides had been very heavy:[29]

	Federals	*Confederates*
Killed	1,754	1,728
Wounded	8,408	8,012
Missing	2,885	959
Totals	13,047	10,699

The Federal casualties amounted to over 24 per cent., and the Confederate to more than 26 per cent. — a larger percentage than in any battle of the Civil War except Chickamauga. In his *Memoirs*, Grant says: " Shiloh was the severest battle fought at the West during the war. . . . I saw an open field . . . so covered with dead that it would have been possible to walk across the clearing, in any direction, stepping on dead bodies, without a foot touching the ground." [30]

[28] Fiske, 95.
[29] Livermore, 79–80.
[30] 1 Grant, 356.

SHILOH

For many years the battle of Shiloh was a subject of bitter controversy in the North. " Probably no single battle of the war," says General Sherman, " gave rise to such wild and damaging reports. It was publicly asserted at the North that our army was taken completely by surprise; that the rebels caught us in our tents; bayoneted the men in their beds; that General Grant was drunk; that Buell's opportune arrival saved the Army of the Tennessee from utter annihilation, etc." [31]

These reports were quite generally believed, and were in a measure sustained by the published articles of Buell, Nelson, and others; even Mr. Ropes, who is generally very fair in his criticisms, has many severe comments to make on the subject of General Grant. But after the lapse of sixty years it may now be possible to take a less prejudiced view of the events and incidents of the battle. The falsity of some of the charges, mentioned by General Sherman, will be apparent from the above narrative, but others may be considered here in somewhat greater detail.

General Sherman says: " We did not fortify our camps against an attack, because we had no orders to do so, and because such a course would have made our raw men timid. . . . At a later period of the war, we could have rendered this position impregnable in one night, but at this time we did not do it." [32]

General Grant writes: " The criticism has often been made that the Union troops should have been entrenched at Shiloh. Up to that time the pick and spade had been but little resorted to at the West. I had, however, taken this subject under consideration soon after reassuming command in the field, and, as already stated, my only military engineer reported unfavorably. Besides this, the troops with me, officers and men, needed discipline and drill more than they did experience with the pick, shovel, and axe. . . . Under all these circumstances I concluded that drill and discipline were worth more to our men than fortifications." [33]

On this point it may be remarked that even so good a

[31] 1 Sherman, 244.
[32] 1 Sherman, 229.
[33] 1 Grant, 357.

[75]

soldier as Robert E. Lee did not employ field entrenchments at Antietam six months later, in the autumn of this
same year. It is therefore hardly fair to condemn Grant
and his able division-commanders for not having taken
such a precaution at this early period of the Civil War.

Grant has also been criticised for maintaining his headquarters at Savannah, nine miles from the camp. He states
that it was his intention to move to Pittsburg, but Buell
was expected daily, and would come in at Savannah; he
therefore remained at that point a few days longer than
he otherwise would have done in order to meet Buell on
his arrival.[34] The relations between Grant and Buell had
never been very cordial, and for this reason Grant wished
to show his rival every consideration. Buell, however, was
less courteous: although he reached Savannah on Saturday night, he did not make his presence known to Grant;
and they did not meet until one o'clock the following
day.[35]

On Friday night, the 4 April, when returning from the
front, where firing had been heard, Grant was badly injured by a fall of his horse. In the darkness, with the
rain pouring down in torrents, on the way back to the boat,
the horse fell with Grant's leg under its body. Only the
softness of the ground saved the general from a very
severe injury. As it was, his boot had to be cut off, and
for several days he was unable to walk except with
crutches.[36]

It is well known that Grant, on account of his habits,
had been somewhat under a cloud when he left the regular army. On the first day of the battle he was under a
terrible physical and mental strain, and it would not be
strange if he resorted to stimulants, but there is nothing
in any of the reports of the battle to show that he was
not in the full possession of his faculties.[37]

In his memoirs General Grant denies emphatically the
statement so often made, that his troops were badly beaten
on the first day of Shiloh. He says: " There was in fact

[34] 1 Grant, 334.
[35] See 1 Grant, 336.
[36] 1 Grant, 334.
[37] *Cf.* Fiske, 68.

no hour during the day when I doubted the eventual defeat of the enemy." [38]

This statement is borne out by the account of Whitelaw Reid, who has pictured Grant at the moment of the last Confederate attack. He sat his horse, quiet, thoughtful, almost stolid. "Does not the prospect begin to look gloomy?" some one asked. "Not at all," was the quiet reply. "They cannot force our lines around these batteries to-night. To-morrow we shall attack them with fresh troops and drive them of course." [39]

It is a principle often illustrated in war that when two armies have fought until their strength is well-nigh spent, the one that can soonest summon its jaded energies to a final assault is almost sure to win. Grant was a very brave, resolute, obstinate man, and a hard fighter. Whatever might be the chances, he was determined to hold out to the last. There is little doubt, therefore, that, even without the arrival of Buell, he would have resumed the battle the next morning with the fresh troops of Lew Wallace, and what was left of his other divisions. He would have had about 17,000 men in line; and the Confederate army was reduced to not more than 20,000 troops, all of whom were in organizations which had been greatly shattered by the casualties of the battle of Sunday, as well as weakened by the loss of many valuable officers.[40] There was at least an even chance of winning. As Grant tersely remarks: "The victory was not to either party until the battle was over." [41]

Grant admits that an immediate pursuit of the enemy after the battle "must have resulted in the capture of a considerable number of prisoners and probably some guns." "I wanted to pursue," he says, "but had not the heart to order the men who had fought desperately for two days, lying in the mud and rain whenever not fighting; and I did not feel disposed positively to order Buell, or any part of his command, to pursue. Although the senior in rank at the time, I had been so only a few

[38] 1 Grant, 363.
[39] 1 Reid, *Ohio in the War*, 375.
[40] See 2 Ropes, 88.
[41] 1 Grant, 364.

weeks. . . . I did not meet Buell in person until too late to get troops ready and pursue with effect." [42]

Grant was a very shy, modest, unassuming man, and, in view of the somewhat strained relations between Buell and himself, it is easy to understand his attitude. But General Buell, as Grant himself states, was a brave, intelligent officer, with much professional pride and ambition,[43] and Buell himself should, not only have proposed, but even insisted upon, taking up the pursuit with his fresh troops, who had not been engaged in the battle. That he did not do so, was doubtless due to the jealousy of Grant which he showed on this, and on many later occasions. He was far more to blame than Grant for not securing the full fruits of the victory.

On this same subject General Buell writes: " I make no attempt to excuse myself or blame others when I say that General Grant's troops, the lowest individual among them not more than the commander himself, appear to have thought that the object of the battle was sufficiently accomplished when they were reinstated in their camps; and that in some way that idea obstructed the reorganization of my line until a further advance that day became impracticable." [44]

And Professor Fiske says: " I suspect that the true explanation, after all, may be that our peace-loving people had not yet come to realize what a terrible affair war is, when truly effective, and especially when waged against our own kin. . . . We were satisfied with thwarting the hostile army, and did not appreciate the need for terminating its existence." [45]

More than any battle of modern times Shiloh resembled the conflicts of the Middle Ages, in which knight fought against knight in the general mêlée. An attempt to recount in detail all the incidents of the day would be both tedious and unprofitable: it was like a gigantic kaleidoscope, in which objects were constantly shifting —

[42] 1 Grant, 354.
[43] 1 Grant, 358.
[44] 1 B. & L., 534.
[45] Fiske, 98.

but never repeated in symmetrical patterns. For this confusion, there were two reasons, principally:

First, the Confederate attack was made in very unusual tactical formation. Instead of the three corps-commanders — Hardee, Polk, and Bragg — taking charge respectively of the left, centre, and right, as was arranged later in the day, Beauregard ordered that the three corps should advance in line, one behind the other. Hardee's corps, with a brigade from Bragg's, was to constitute the first line, the remainder of Bragg's corps the second line, and Polk's corps, with Breckinridge's division, the third.[46]

Second, the camps in which the Federals were taken by surprise were established to suit the convenience of the several commanders, and without any pretence of system. The army was not in the least prepared to receive an attack — it was not even in order of battle.[47] The resistance, therefore, which it offered to the Confederate attack was necessarily of a fragmentary and disconnected character — each body of troops making the best defence it could, often isolated from the other bodies of troops in its vicinity.[48] The course which the battle took was therefore what might have been expected under such conditions.

Of all the battles of the Civil War, that of Shiloh, says Major Steele, is the hardest problem for the military student — the most difficult in which to apportion the credit and the blame.

" It is not an easy task," writes Mr. Ropes, " to follow the movements of General Halleck's mind during the ten days which succeeded the fall of Fort Donelson." [49] It is certain, however, that he did not do what McClellan expected of him, and that was to occupy Nashville at once. He did little except to bombard the Government with applications to be given the chief command in the West. " Give it to me," he wrote on the 19 February, " and I will split secession in twain in one month." Finally, on the 11 March 1862, in anticipation of the forward movement in the East, McClellan was relieved of the general

[46] 10 O. R., 386.
[47] 2 Ropes, 69.
[48] Force, 124.
[49] 2 Ropes, 49.

command of the armies, and Halleck's wish was granted. His department comprised all of Kentucky and Tennessee, and the army of General Buell was placed under him. Although it was a great advantage to the Union cause to have all the forces in this territory under one general, the appointment of Halleck was a mistake. He had been educated at West Point, but most of his life had been passed out of the army, and he had little natural aptitude for military affairs. He was, moreover, careless, indolent, and inexact to a high degree.[50]

Before being placed in command, Halleck did nothing until about the first of March, when he sent C. F. Smith on a sort of " steamboat raid " up the Tennessee. This led to the selection of Pittsburg Landing as a site for the camp of Grant's army. As soon as Halleck was appointed to the supreme command, he ordered Buell to march on Savannah. This was practically the only act of Halleck's in the campaign which was of value: it brought Buell's army to Shiloh in time to turn a Union reverse into a victory; possibly in time to save Grant's army from capture.[51]

It is impossible to say anything in commendation of the tactics employed at Shiloh on either side. Neither of the hostile armies on that day was really *commanded*. The two armies in fact fought without any control, and to this fact nearly all the mistakes can be charged. Neither Grant nor Johnston established headquarters from which to direct his forces. Grant " visited " his several division-commanders, and issued a few verbal orders, but that was about all. Johnston " was killed doing the work of a brigadier." [52] As army commanders, neither Grant nor Johnston exerted any influence upon the tactics of this great battle.

The Confederate plan to turn the Union left, and hem Grant's army into the pocket of Snake and Owl creeks was never carried out. An attempt was made to turn both

[50] 2 Ropes, 58.
[51] Steele, 185.
[52] Lecture by Major Swift, quoted by Steele, 187.

flanks, and break the centre, all at once — an effort entirely beyond the strength of Johnston's army.

The Confederate attack, in long lines, instead of deep formation, was also an error. Corps, divisions, and brigades, were soon mixed in hopeless confusion: the action degenerated into a series of isolated combats, which, without any general plan, were ineffective. By eleven o'clock there was not a reserve on the field.[53]

On the Federal side, the tactics were fully as bad. With no prearranged plan, no line or order of battle, it was impossible to have any concert of action. A regiment was rarely overcome in front, but fell back because the regiment on its right or left had done so, and exposed its flank. It continued its backward movement until it was well under shelter, thus exposing the flank of its neighbor, who then was also compelled to withdraw. Once in operation the process repeated itself indefinitely.[54]

In his own story of the battle,[55] Beauregard admits that he knew on Sunday night that at least three of Buell's divisions had arrived. If so, he made a great mistake in staying on the field, instead of retreating at once. The battle of the second day was a useless sacrifice of life. Nothing was to be gained by continuing the struggle against such overwhelming odds.[56]

In later years, both Grant and Sherman were very sensitive to the criticisms of their failure to pursue the enemy, and secure the full fruits of the victory. The explanations given in their memoirs are not at all convincing. Bragg reported the next morning that his troops " were utterly disorganized and demoralized." Breckinridge declared, " My troops are worn out, and I don't think can be relied on after the first volley." Grant and Buell had at least 20,000 fresh men to take up the pursuit, which should have resulted in the capture or the complete dispersal of the Confederate army. In answer to an inquiry from Professor Fiske, regarding the failure to pursue the enemy, Sherman, after the war, made the humorous reply: " I assure you, my dear fellow, we had

[53] Steele, 188.
[54] 1 B. & L., 504.
[55] 1 B. & L., 593.
[56] Steele, 189.

had quite enough of their society for two whole days, and were only too glad to be rid of them on any terms! " [57]

Grant states that the nature of this battle was such that cavalry could not be used in front; he therefore formed his into line in rear, to stop the numerous stragglers.[58] On the Confederate side, Forrest's men charged a battery, capturing some of the guns, and were of service in compelling the surrender of Prentiss. On Monday, they covered the retreat, forming the last line of the rearguard.

Although much more should have been accomplished, the results of the campaign were on the whole satisfactory to the National Government. Kentucky, and all of Tennessee, except the eastern part, were again under Union control; besides this, the Mississippi was free as far as Vicksburg. To offset these advantages, the Confederate army, which should have been destroyed, was still intact.

[57] Fiske, 99. *Cf.* 2 Ropes, 90; also Upton 310, who writes: " The military commanders on the spot know after a battle the condition of their own army, while, unlike the critics, they do not know that of the enemy."

[58] 1 Grant, 343.

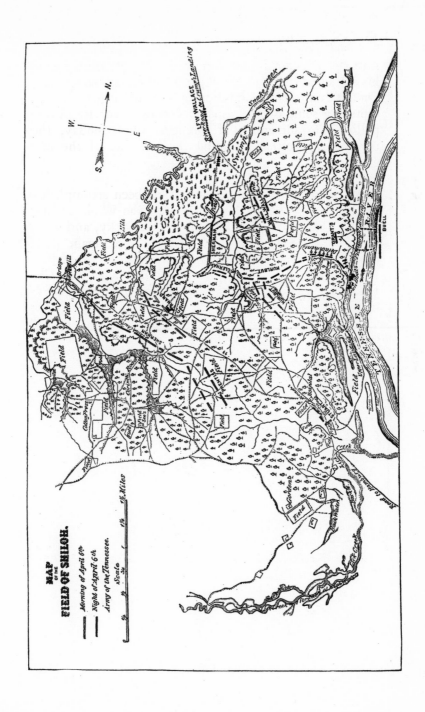

MAP OF THE FIELD OF SHILOH.

Morning of April 6th
Night of April 6th
Army of the Tennessee.

Scale

1/4 1/2 1 1 1/2 1 1/2 Miles

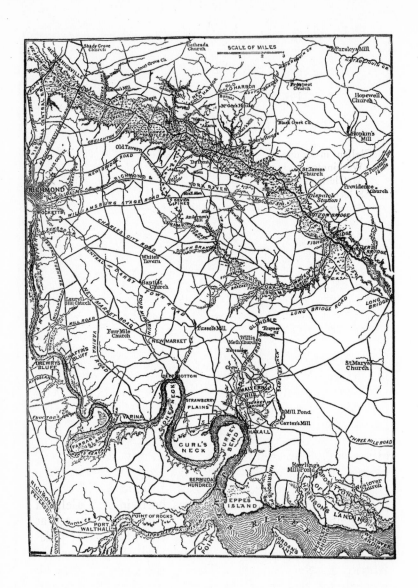

CHAPTER FIVE

JULY 1861 — JUNE 1862

THE PENINSULA

O N the 21 July 1861 the streets of Washington were crowded with stragglers from the disastrous field of Manassas, better known as Bull Run. The following day, General George B. McClellan was relieved from command of the Army of the West, and on the 27th, by order of President Lincoln, assumed control of the lately defeated troops in the vicinity of the capital. No appointment at that time could have been more acceptable to the people, the press, and the army.

George Brinton McClellan was born in Philadelphia 3 December 1826. Twenty years later he was graduated at West Point, the second in a class in which Stonewall Jackson was seventeenth. As an engineer with Scott's army in Mexico he won distinction. During the Crimean War he was selected as one of the Government's observers, and his report on the campaign was published by special act of Congress. After serving two years as captain of the 1st Cavalry, he resigned, to accept the appointment of chief engineer of the Illinois Central Railroad, of which he soon became vice-president. At the outbreak of the war he was president of the Ohio and Mississippi, with headquarters at Cincinnati. In all the various positions he had held, he had shown great zeal and capacity.[1]

When the President called for troops after the fall of Sumter, Governor Dennison, of Ohio, appointed McClellan major-general of the " Militia Volunteers " of that State, and he organized, equipped, and put in the field the Army of the Ohio. His operations in West Virginia were " brief and brilliant," and he was the only Union general who had yet scored a complete success. At the time he was called to Washington, McClellan was a man of fine soldierly appearance and engaging manners, thirty-five years of age.[2]

No better picture of the situation at the capital could be presented than is to be found in the general's own statement:

" All was chaos and despondency; the city was filled with intoxicated stragglers, and an attack was expected. The troops numbered less than fifty thousand, many of whom were so demoralized and undisciplined that they could not be relied upon even for defensive purposes. Moreover, the term of service of a large part had already expired, or was on the point of doing so. On the Maryland side of the Potomac no troops were posted on the roads leading into the city, nor were there any entrenchments. On the Virginia side the condition of affairs was better in these respects, but far from satisfactory. Sufficient and fit material of war did not exist. The situation was difficult, and fraught with danger.[3]

General McClellan immediately appointed his general staff, and the work of organizing and equipping a large army was forthwith undertaken. Ninety days later, on the 27 October, the general officially reported to the Secretary of War that he had an aggregate strength of 168,318, with 147,695 present *for duty*. Of this number, some 13,000 were only partially armed, leaving an effective force of about 134,000.

---

[1] Webb, *Campaigns*, 2–3.   [3] 2 *B. & L.*, 160.
[2] Steele, 191.

THE PENINSULA

As the new levies of infantry arrived at Washington, they were formed into provisional brigades, and stationed in the suburbs of the city, to be perfected by instruction and discipline. By the opening of the spring of 1862 McClellan had created " as noble a body of men as could have been raised, under similar circumstances, the world over." [4] Exclusive of the detachments necessary to guard the defences of Washington, the Potomac, and the lower Shenandoah Valley, which required about 55,000 men, there was a field army 158,000 strong.

On the first of November 1861, General Scott retired, and McClellan was appointed to succeed him as commander-in-chief. But, even before this date, McClellan had prepared, at the request of the President, a memorandum setting forth his views as to the proper method of suppressing the rebellion. War all along the line was his purpose. He proposed to strike at the two centres — Richmond in the East and Nashville in the West — while at the same time expeditionary forces were to assail the principal points on the coast and on the Mississippi. Upon these plans, the subsequent successful campaigns were practically based.

Meantime the Confederate army under Joseph E. Johnston remained in its position at Manassas, and no steps were taken by McClellan to destroy or dislodge it. The Confederates were also allowed to set up batteries on the lower Potomac, which closed the navigation of the river, and the general refused to take any action to capture them. Finally, the last of October, occurred the unfortunate affair of Ball's Bluff, in which Colonel Baker, who had lately resigned his seat in the Senate, was slain, and nearly all his men were killed or captured. The people of the North could not understand this prolonged inaction, and became impatient.

The autumn of 1861 passed, and no move was made. The winter was now at hand, and the roads in Virginia had become almost impassable. To make matters worse, McClellan took typhoid fever and was ill for several weeks, in December and January. The Government debt

[4] Webb, 8.

[85]

was piling up, and had reached over half a billion dollars. Dissatisfaction was general, especially at Washington, in Government circles, and in Congress.

Finally, President Lincoln issued the first of his famous " War Orders," in which he directed that the army should advance against Manassas on or before the 22 February — a date chosen doubtless for sentimental reasons. This order was not carried into effect, and two other orders were issued by the President — all for the purpose of allaying the popular impatience.

At length McClellan was forced to divulge his plans, and on the 8 March a forward movement on Richmond by way of Urbana was finally decided upon. The very next day, Johnston withdrew his forces from Centreville and the Potomac, and took up a position south of the Rappahannock, with his right at Fredericksburg and his left at Culpeper Court House. The movement placed the Confederate army as near Richmond as the Union forces would be at Urbana, and compelled the abandonment of that route. It was therefore decided to transfer McClellan's army by water to Fort Monroe, which was held by a Federal garrison, and make that fortress the base for an advance on Richmond by way of the peninsula between the York and James rivers.

On the same day that the Urbana plan was approved, an order was issued forming army corps and assigning the senior general officers to their command. This action was taken without the knowledge of McClellan, and against his judgment that the appointments should have been postponed until the generals had been tried in the field. The organization was as follows:

First Corps: McDowell — Divisions: Franklin, McCall, King

Second Corps: Sumner — Divisions: Richardson, Blenker, Sedgwick

Third Corps: Heintzelman — Divisions: Porter, Hooker, Kearny

Fourth Corps: Keyes — Divisions: Couch, Smith, Casey

Before leaving for the Peninsula, McClellan decided to march his army out to the abandoned Confederate camps at Centreville, in order " to give the troops a little experience on the march and in bivouac, get rid of extra baggage, and test the working of the staff-departments." During this absence, an order was published, without any previous intimation to McClellan, relieving him from the general command of all the armies, and confining his authority to the Department of the Potomac.[5]

Fort Monroe, which McClellan had selected as his base, was a large and very strong work, situated at the southeastern extremity of the Peninsula, about seventy miles from Richmond. His original plan of operations was based entirely upon the coöperation of the navy, which he expected not only to carry his supplies, but also to transport his troops up the York or the James, so as to turn and compel the evacuation of each and every line of defence which the enemy might take up. When his army had thus manœuvred the Confederates back to the immediate vicinity of Richmond, he expected to fight his great battle, destroy the enemy's main army, and capture the capital of the Confederate States.

But his expectations regarding the coöperation of the navy, at least for a time, were disappointed. On the 8 March the *Merrimac* had steamed out of Norfolk, and sunk two Federal frigates in Hampton Roads. The next day the ram had engaged the *Monitor*, and been forced to return to port in a damaged condition. The vessel was not destroyed, however, and the Federal Navy advised against any attempt to use the James River. At the same time it was discovered that the Confederates had batteries at Yorktown and Gloucester Point on the York which the navy could venture neither to attack nor to pass.

The Peninsula, less than six miles wide at its narrowest point, is a low, level, and marshy region. The highways at that time were all dirt roads. The York River, formed by the junction of the Mattapony and the Pamunkey, was navigable up to the junction joint, where stood West Point, the eastern terminus of the Richmond and York River Railway. Richmond was at the head of navigation, on the north bank of the James.

[5] 2 *B. & L.*, 168.

The only formidable natural obstacle to an advance up the Peninsula was the Chickahominy River and adjacent swamps. This river rises some fifteen miles northwest of Richmond and enters the James about forty miles below that city. Between Meadow Bridge, north of Richmond, and Bottom's Bridge, directly to the east, the river at its ordinary stage is some forty feet wide, fringed with a dense growth of heavy forest trees, and bordered by low marshy lands, varying from half a mile to a mile in width. Within these limits, the firm ground, above highwater mark, seldom approaches the river on either bank, and in no place on both banks. The river was subject to frequent, sudden, and violent floods, and a single severe storm, even of brief duration, would cause an overflow of the bottom-lands, rendering the river impassable for many days, without long and strong bridges.[6]

Of nearly all these facts, General McClellan was fully aware before he went to the Peninsula;[7] but with his "characteristic persistence" he adhered to his original plan even when circumstances had so changed as to make it no longer equally attractive. Accordingly, during the month of March, the Second, Third, and Fourth corps were transported to Fort Monroe.

McClellan already knew that the works at Yorktown, some twenty-five miles up the Peninsula, were held by Magruder with some 15,000 Confederates; also that Johnston's main army would be able to march promptly to this quarter. He therefore "determined to move at once with the force in hand, and endeavor to seize a point — near the Halfway House — between Yorktown and Williamsburg, where the Peninsula is reduced to a narrow neck, and thus cut off the retreat of the Yorktown garrison and prevent the arrival of reënforcements."[8] In reaching this decision he was misled by the erroneous "Cram" map[9] which depicts the Warwick River as coming down to Lee's Mills from the north, instead of

---

[6] 2 B. & L., 174–175.
[7] 1 Ropes, 245, 267–269.
[8] 2 B. & L., 169–170.
[9] See Webb, 55.

stretching across the Peninsula from Yorktown to the James, as proved to be the case.[10]

The forward movement began on the 4 April in two columns, Heintzelman on the road to the right, and Keyes on that to the left. On the following afternoon both columns had been stopped, the right by the works in front of Yorktown, the left at Lee's Mills, where the Warwick was found to be unfordable and strongly entrenched. By means of several dams Magruder had made the river too deep to ford at almost every point; and he had also constructed a strong line of field-works, thirteen miles long, entirely across the Peninsula. "Thus," says General McClellan, "all things were brought to a stand-still, and the intended movement on the Halfway House could not be carried out." [11] In his report McClellan expresses great surprise at this "unexpected" halt, but General Webb says: "Just such a halt *ought to have been expected*. Nothing less than a continuous front of opposition from the York to the James should have been looked for." [12]

McClellan concluded that the line was too strong to be carried by assault, so he brought up Sumner's corps, and prepared for a regular siege. At this moment he was also on the point of ordering McDowell's corps to move against Gloucester, when he learned that it had been withdrawn from his command and detained near Washington.[13] This reduced the force of 155,000, upon which he had counted at the beginning of the campaign, to about 92,000 men, or some 85,000 present for duty.

To make matters even worse, at this same time the region from the Alleghanies to the sea was parceled out among four independent commanders, and an order was issued from the War Department discontinuing all recruit-

---

[10] 2 *B. & L.*, 169. It seems strange that the topography of the Peninsula was not better known to McClellan, for the whole region was carefully surveyed by the French engineers during the Revolution, and the maps printed in Marshall's *Washington*, and several other early historical works, show the correct course of the river. (See 6 Channing, 466, note.)

[11] 2 *B. & L.*, 170.

[12] Webb, 54. The italics are General Webb's.

[13] The Government, however, sent him by water, on the 22 April, Franklin's division of this corps.

ing for volunteers and closing the recruiting stations.[14] The pernicious policy was also adopted of raising new regiments, instead of maintaining the existing organizations in the field at their full strength. A course more in accordance with well-established military principles would have saved the country millions of treasure and thousands of valuable lives.[15]

Meanwhile the siege operations had been pushed, and the batteries would have been ready to open fire not later than the morning of the 6 May, but during the night of the 3rd the enemy evacuated his positions and retreated up the Peninsula. About the first of May, Magruder had been joined by Johnston's army; and the latter took command of the combined Confederate forces.

The pursuit of the Confederates was at once taken up by all the available Federal cavalry, supported by two divisions of the Third and Fourth corps. About two miles in front of Williamsburg, Magruder had constructed a strong line of defence. Here on the 5 May the Confederates fought a rear-guard action to hold back the Federals until the trains could get well on their way. The battle lasted nearly all day, and that night the Confederates withdrew.

The Union advance was delayed by " dreadful weather and terrible roads," but by the 16 May all the corps were within supporting distance, and a new dépôt was established at White House. On the 18th, the Fifth and Sixth corps were formed, so that the organization of the Army of the Potomac was then as follows:

Second Corps: SUMNER — Divisions: Sedgwick and Richardson

Third Corps: HEINTZELMAN — Divisions: Kearny and Hooker

Fourth Corps: KEYES — Divisions: Couch and Casey

Fifth Corps: PORTER — Divisions: Morrell and Sykes

Sixth Corps: FRANKLIN — Divisions: Smith and Slocum

The destruction of the *Merrimac* on the 11 May had opened the James River, and McClellan wished to use that line for his future operations, but his plan was

[14] 2 *B. & L.,* 170. [15] 2 *B. & L.,* 171.

changed by orders from Washington. On the 18th, a telegram from the Secretary of War informed him that McDowell would advance from Fredericksburg, and directed him to extend the right of the Army of the Potomac to the north of Richmond so as to establish communications with McDowell's corps. The same order directed McClellan to maintain his base at White House. To these orders, McClellan attributes the failure of his campaign,[16] and there is certainly great weight in his contention. Mr. Ropes says: " Petersburg was absolutely undefended, and could be occupied without opposition. . . . This last line of operations was in truth the one which promised the best results. If Petersburg should be occupied in force by the Federals, it is hard to see how the Confederates could expect long to retain their hold on Richmond." [17]

The Confederate authorities were well aware that McClellan's army, apart from McDowell's corps, outnumbered that of Johnston nearly three to two, the latter being only about 50,000 strong; [18] and the situation seemed so desperate that preparations were made for the removal of the military papers from Richmond. The greatest danger was apprehended from the advance of McDowell's corps, from Fredericksburg, upon the flank of Johnston's army, and it was determined to do everything possible to prevent this movement. General Lee, who was in general charge of the military operations of the Confederacy, accordingly sent Ewell's division to reenforce Jackson in the Shenandoah Valley.

To avoid interrupting the narrative of events in the Peninsula, the story of Jackson's operations in the Shenandoah has not yet been told.[19] Soon after the battle of Bull Run, Jackson was promoted to the rank of major-general; and on the 28 October 1861 he was ordered to Winchester to assume command of the Valley District.

[16] 2 B. & L., 173.
[17] 2 Ropes, 113.
[18] 2 Ropes, 114.
[19] These two operations " were so closely related that, to comprehend the strategy of either, it is necessary to study them together." (Steele, 191.)

The Shenandoah Valley has already been described in some detail.[20] On its eastern or exposed flank it was covered by the Blue Ridge Mountains, which could only be crossed at certain gaps, through most of which there were good roads. The Valley was connected with Richmond by two lines of railway: the Manassas Gap, mentioned in connection with the Manassas campaign, and the Virginia Central, running from Staunton by way of Rockfish Gap, Charlottesville, and Gordonsville. A good system of roads connected all of the towns and villages. The main thoroughfare was the Valley Turnpike, stretching from Staunton, near the head of the Valley, to Martinsburg at its lower end, a distance of 120 miles. The main valley, averaging about twenty miles in width, is closed on the western side by the Alleghanies.

The two forks of the Shenandoah River, in the upper part of the Valley, flow parallel to each other, about eight miles apart, for a distance of forty or fifty miles, but separated by an isolated ridge called Massanutten Mountain, as high as the Blue Ridge. At Strasburg this ridge drops suddenly to the level of the Valley, and the North Fork of the Shenandoah sweeps around its base and joins the South Fork at Front Royal. The Shenandoah, thus formed, flows along the very base of the Blue Ridge to Harper's Ferry, where it enters the Potomac. The valley between the Blue Ridge and the South Fork, at the foot of Massanutten Mountain, is known as Luray Valley.

Jackson's command at first consisted only of a weak body of militia; but he was soon reënforced with his old brigade, and later with 6000 poorly disciplined troops under Loring. These, with Ashby's cavalry, raised his forces to about 10,000 men.

The Union troops in this district, about 18,000 strong, were commanded by General Banks, whose headquarters were at Frederick City, in Maryland. General Kelly, with a detachment of 5000 men, garrisoned Romney, a town about thirty-five miles northwest of Winchester by a good road. In January, Jackson marched against this point, hoping to capture the Federal force, but it escaped. This

[8] See *ante*, page 14.

operation, which was attended by great hardships, amounted to nothing in the end.

During the winter, from various causes, Jackson's little army was greatly reduced, so that at the beginning of March he did not have over 5000 men available. Having retired up the Valley, he learned that the enemy had begun to withdraw troops and send them to McClellan. He resolved to check this by a demonstration against Winchester, then occupied by General Shields with a Union force of some 10,000 men. On the 23 March Jackson occupied a ridge at the hamlet of Kernstown, four miles south of Winchester. Here he was attacked by Shields, and finally forced to retreat, after a severe engagement of several hours. The pursuit was not vigorous, and Jackson retired in good order to the vicinity of Swift Run Gap.[21]

Although defeated, Jackson had succeeded in his object of stopping the withdrawal of Federal troops from the Valley, and General Lee was so pleased that he decided to reënforce the Valley army by sending Ewell's division to Jackson, thus giving him an aggregate force of some 15,000 men.

On the first of May, the situation was as follows: Milroy was at McDowell, about forty miles from Staunton, with a Union force of 4000 men, and Schenck's brigade of 2500 was near Franklin, where 20,000 troops of Fremont's army were concentrating. Banks had fortified Strasburg, seventy miles northeast of Staunton on the turnpike, and had pushed forward a force of 20,000 men to Harrisonburg. The total Union forces in the Valley under various commanders aggregated not less than 65,000 men.[22]

Jackson decided first to strike Milroy's detachment, and then to turn against Banks. To mask his movement, he marched over the mountains to a small station a few miles west of Charlottesville, leaving friends and foes to think that he was en route for Richmond. Cars were waiting for his troops, but instead of going east, the trains

[21] 2 B. & L., 283–284.
[22] 2 B. & L., 285. The number given is probably too large by about 20,000 men.

went west to Staunton. Jackson immediately started his troops on the road from Staunton to McDowell, where on the 8 May he fought a severe and bloody engagement with Milroy and Schenck. The Federals were defeated, and fled toward Franklin to unite with Fremont. Jackson then returned to the Valley, leaving his cavalry under Ashby in front of Fremont to screen the movement.

In the meantime, Banks had fallen back to Strasburg. Shield's division had been sent to General McDowell, and he had only 8000 men, of whom he had placed 1000 under Colonel Kenly at Front Royal, while he himself was entrenched at Strasburg with the remainder.

On the 21 May Jackson started northward with his little army, along the turnpike, but suddenly turned to the right and crossed the Massanutten to Luray. On the morning of the 22d he took the road down the valley, and the next day fell upon Kenly's detachment at Front Royal. The Federal force was almost entirely wiped out, 154 being killed or wounded, and 600 captured. The Confederate losses were only eleven killed and fifteen wounded.

Banks retreated to Winchester, where he made a use-less stand, " to test the strength of the enemy," and then withdrew across the Potomac. After a rest of two days, Jackson advanced to within three miles of Harper's Ferry, to increase the fear at the North, and to give his wagons, with the spoils of Winchester, time to get away on the road to Staunton.

Returning by train to Winchester, ahead of his army, Jackson learned on the 30 May that Shields, command-ing McDowell's vanguard, had captured Front Royal; also that Fremont was twenty-five miles west of the Valley Turnpike on the road from Moorefield to Stras-burg. Winchester is only eighteen miles from Strasburg, but Jackson's troops were from seven to twenty miles further back on the pike. Banks, in his rear, had 15,000 men; Fremont, also 15,000; and Shields, 10,000, with 10,000 more a few miles behind. Jackson had only 15,000 troops to meet these 50,000 Federals, and he was en-cumbered with 2000 prisoners, besides a double train of wagons seven miles long. He was in a trap, and nothing but the incompetency of the Union commanders saved him. None of them knew the exact location of the other Federal detachments, and they all stood in awe of Jackson. Fremont was checked by Ashby's cavalry six miles west of Strasburg, and Shields was kept back on the east by a small brigade.

Jackson concentrated his troops at once, and on the 31 May his main body bivouacked at Strasburg. The next morning Ewell's division relieved the cavalry in front of Fremont, and kept him back until the trains and the Stonewall brigade had passed. That night the whole command was at Woodstock, with Ashby's cavalry protecting the rear. The forces of McDowell and Fremont did not get into communication with each other until the 2 June, when both columns took up the pursuit, Shields by the Luray Valley, and Fremont by the turnpike, on opposite sides of the Massanuttens. In anticipation of these movements, Jackson had destroyed the three bridges on the South Fork, to the north of Port Republic, and sent a detachment to hold the bridge at that place for the retreat of his own army. On the 4 June, the Confederates crossed the North Fork, and burnt the bridge. Heavy rains in the Valley, which raised the river, made it difficult for the Federals to throw over a pontoon-bridge, and this gave Jackson a lead of twenty-four hours. In a desperate skirmish on the 6th, Ashby was shot through the heart. The death of no other man, save Jackson, could have caused so great a loss to the army. He was the first cavalry leader in this war, or in any war since the time of Napoleon, to use his squadrons right.[23]

The night of the 7 June the hostile forces were thus situated: Shield's command was stretched out over twenty-five miles of road in Luray Valley; Fremont was at Harrisonburg; Ewell's Confederate division was near Cross Keys, and Jackson's main body was near Port Republic.[24] Jackson might now have easily made good his escape, but he had other plans in view. He proposed to hold Fremont back at Cross Keys with Ewell's division, while he

[23] Steele, 230. [24] 1 Henderson, 449.

crushed Shields with his main body, then to fall upon Fremont with his entire force.

On the 8 June, Fremont attacked Ewell at Cross Keys. Not knowing where Shields was, and supposing that Jackson's entire army was in front of him, the Federal commander made his attack in a timid, half-hearted fashion, only employing five of his twenty-four regiments present on the field. The Federals were repulsed, and the action was not renewed.

At an early hour the following day Jackson set out to attack Shields. About two miles down the river from Port Republic he encountered two Federal brigades under Tyler in a strong position. Here the battle of Port Republic took place. After a fierce action, which lasted for four or five hours, Tyler was driven off the field. In his retreat he met Shields, hurrying with the remainder of his division to the sound of the battle. Shields formed line and stopped the pursuit.

Before midnight Jackson's entire army was in bivouac at Brown's Gap, where it remained until it set out on the 17th upon its swift and secret journey to Richmond. The Valley Campaign was at an end.

During the period of fourteen days, from the morning of the 19 May to the night of the first of June, Jackson's army marched 170 miles, routed forces aggregating 12,500 men, threatened the North with invasion, drew off McDowell from Fredericksburg, and finally, though surrounded on three sides by 50,000 Federals, brought off a huge convoy without losing a single wagon.[25]

Lee had been the first to recognize the weak joint in the enemy's armor: the National anxiety for Washington. Kernstown induced Lincoln to form four independent armies, each acting on a different line. Two months later, when McClellan was in front of Richmond, and it was most important that these armies be combined, Jackson drove Banks across the Potomac, and again the Federal concentration was prevented. Finally, the battles of Cross Keys and Port Republic led Mr. Lincoln to make his worst mistake, and McClellan was left isolated when he

[25] 1 Henderson, 434.

most needed help. The brains of two great leaders —
Lee and Jackson — had done more for the Confederacy
than 200,000 soldiers had done for the Union. From
this instance it may be deduced that Providence is sometimes more inclined to side with the big brains than with
the big battalions.[26]

A week after Cross Keys and Port Republic, Jackson
had vanished from the Valley, and when he appeared on
the Chickahominy, Banks, Fremont, and McDowell were
still guarding the roads to Washington, and McClellan
was waiting for McDowell — 175,000 men absolutely
paralyzed by 16,000! Only Napoleon's campaign of 1814
affords a parallel to this extraordinary spectacle.[27]
" These brilliant successes," writes Lord Wolseley, " appear to me models of their kind, both in conception and
execution. They should be closely studied by all officers
who wish to learn the art and science of war." [28]

The use Jackson made of his cavalry was perhaps the
most brilliant tactical feature of the Valley Campaign.
Such tactics had not been seen since the days of Napoleon.
The great cloud of horsemen which veiled the march of
the Grand Army had been forgotten. The vast importance ascribed by the Emperor to procuring early information of his enemy and hiding his own movements had been
overlooked; and it was left to an American soldier to re-
vive his methods.[29]

To return now to the Peninsula.

On the 17 May, McClellan resumed his advance on
Richmond, and encountered but little resistance, as Johnston had withdrawn to the further side of the Chickahominy. The army moved very leisurely, taking three
days to cover the twelve miles from White House to the
river. By the 25th the corps of Heintzelman and Keyes
had crossed at Bottom's Bridge, and taken position on the
south side of the stream. The three other corps remained

[26] 1 Henderson, 502–503. *Cf.* Maurice, 98.
[27] 1 Henderson, 508.
[28] *North American Review*, vol. 149, p. 166. On the other hand, see
the inconsequential remarks of Professor Channing (6 Channing, **469**,
note).
[29] 1 Henderson, 520.

on the north side, extending from the railway to the Mechanicsville Road. This dangerous position, astride the Chickahominy, was taken by McClellan when he was expecting to be rejoined by McDowell, but was not changed even after he was advised that McDowell would not join him. Bridges were built, to facilitate communication between the two wings of the army, but they were liable at any time to be carried away by high water.

In order to secure his line of communications by the York River railway, and to clear his right flank and rear of the enemy, on the 27 May McClellan despatched Porter against Branch's brigade of Confederates which was at Hanover Court House, fourteen miles north of Richmond. The objects of the expedition were accomplished; and, after destroying the bridges and railroad as far as Ashland, Porter returned to his old camps. This affair has been termed a " useless battle," but General Webb " considers the moral effects of that success to have been of the greatest importance in the subsequent battle of Gaines's Mill." [30]

Johnston's army was now within the entrenchments before Richmond. Having received some reënforcements, it was about 63,000 strong. The army, which had not yet been divided into corps, was organized in four strong divisions, under Longstreet, D. H. Hill, Magruder, and Smith; two small divisions, under A. P. Hill, and Huger; and Stuart's cavalry.

Johnston's first plan was to attack that part of McClellan's army which lay north of the Chickahominy, but when he learned that McDowell had been sent to the Valley, he decided to destroy the two Federal corps which had crossed the river and were encamped within a few miles of Richmond. He accordingly issued orders for his troops to be in position to attack at daybreak on the 31 May.

On this day the Federal position was as follows: Casey's division of the Fourth Corps (Keyes) occupied some rifle-pits and a redoubt about three quarters of a mile west of Seven Pines, a tavern on the Williamsburg stage road.

[30] Webb, 93–96, and 186.

The other division, under Couch, was a little to the right and rear. Heintzelman's Third Corps had not advanced much beyond the Chickahominy: the division of Kearny was at Bottom's Bridge, five miles from Casey's advanced line, and Hooker's division was seven miles to the south, guarding White Oak Bridge. Each of these four divisions numbered about 8500 men. It is apparent that General Heintzelman, who was in command of both corps, had not sufficiently concentrated his forces.[31]

To the south of the stage road the ground was swampy, and this gave some protection to the Union left; but to the north, as far as Fair Oaks station on the York River railroad, the country was favorable. It was, of course, to be expected that McClellan would throw his Second Corps, under Sumner, across the river, but the Confederate plans were favored by a violent storm on the afternoon and night of the 30th, which rendered the river unfordable and made the bridges unsafe for the passage of men and guns.

Johnston's plan was simple, and should have been effective. Longstreet was to command the main attack, which was to fall upon the troops at Fair Oaks and Seven Pines. He was to move by the Nine-mile Road, D. H. Hill by the Williamsburg Road, and Huger by the Charles City Road. Smith's division was to remain at the road-fork near Old Tavern, to protect the Confederate left against any movement from the north side of the river. Magruder and A. P. Hill were to remain in position north of the Chickahominy.

The whole plan miscarried through Longstreet's misunderstanding of his orders, which were given him verbally. He got part of his division on the Charles City Road in front of Huger, and part on the stage road in rear of D. H. Hill. Instead of attacking at daybreak, it was one o'clock before the action began, and then D. H. Hill attacked alone. At first the Confederates gained some advantage, but after several hours Kearny came up with his division, and the Union line of battle was reëstablished. Later, Hill was reënforced by one of Longstreet's bri-

[31] 2 Ropes, 138.

gades, and the Federals were driven back to a point a mile and a half east of Seven Pines, where the battle at this part of the line ceased, at about six-thirty.

Huger's division and six of Longstreet's brigades had scarcely fired a shot; but there was a sharp engagement about five o'clock, near Fair Oaks, between Smith's division and part of Sumner's corps, which had marched to Keyes's assistance by way of Grapevine Bridge. The Confederates were repulsed with heavy loss, and the troops of Sumner remained masters of the field.

Before sundown Johnston recognized that his attack was a failure, and he was about to suspend the action, when he received two severe wounds. He was carried from the field, and was incapacitated for service until the middle of November.[32]

G. W. Smith, the next in rank, assumed command of the Confederate army, and he ordered Longstreet to renew the attack " as soon after daybreak as practicable." Longstreet's attack was feebly made, and was repulsed with heavy loss. This ended the battle. General McClellan arrived on the field early in the afternoon, but gave no orders for an attack.

About two o'clock, General Lee appeared at Smith's headquarters, and, by orders from President Davis, assumed command of the Confederate army. That night he withdrew the troops within the defences of Richmond. General Smith, on account of illness, retired temporarily from active duty, and Whiting took command permanently of his division.

In the battle of Seven Pines, or Fair Oaks, as it is variously called, the Confederates lost about 6000 men, and the Federals, 5000.[33] The attack was a complete failure,[34] and left the Confederates in a very disheartened condition. Lee set his men to work strengthening the lines in front of Richmond, and their spirits soon revived, with the sense of security that this gave them.

At the time of his appointment to the command of the Army of Northern Virginia, General Lee was fifty-five

[32] Alexander, 87; Johnston, 138.
[33] Livermore, 81.
[34] Johnston (143) claims that it was a success.

years of age, in perfect health, vigorous and robust.[35] As military adviser to the President, a position similar to that of Chief of the General Staff, he had won the full confidence of his chief, but it is a mistake to say that at this time he possessed " the unquestioning and enthusiastic devotion of the army." [36] His only active service had been in West Virginia in the autumn of 1861, and this campaign had generally been considered a failure. His appointment, therefore, " did not at once inspire popular enthusiasm." [37] As he had fought no battles in West Virginia, there was quite a general impression that he would not be an aggressive commander, and this was strengthened when he set his men to work on the fortifications of Richmond. This action, to some of his amateur critics in the public press, seemed a confession of cowardice. Only a few people, who knew him well, then believed that he had the audacity to assume the offensive — to run greater risks and take more desperate chances, than any other general, North or South.[38] These doubts, however, were soon removed, and long before the end of the war, Lee's position was unique — no other commander, on either side, was so universally believed in, so absolutely trusted. " Nor was there ever a commander," says Mr. Ropes, " who better deserved the support of his government, and the affection and confidence of his soldiers." [39]

During the first three weeks of June neither army made any aggressive movement. Lee was engaged in strengthening the defences of Richmond, and McClellan employed his troops in building bridges to connect the wings of his army. These bridges had to be long enough to cross not only the Chickahominy itself, but the marshes on either side, and the task involved no little labor and difficulty. It was, moreover, aggravated by the bad weather which prevailed during the first half of June.[40] McClellan also constructed elaborate field-works on the south side of the river, which completely covered the front from Golding's farm to White Oak Swamp, and rendered this part of the Federal line practically impregnable. Works were also

[35] 2 Ropes, 157.
[36] 2 Ropes, 158.
[37] Alexander, 109. Cf. Maurice, 108.
[38] Alexander, 109–110.
[39] 2 Ropes, 158.
[40] 2 Ropes, 158.

thrown up on the north side, behind Beaver Dam Creek. The two corps of Sumner and Franklin were permanently established on the south side of the river, and only the Fifth Corps, of Fitz John Porter, remained on the north side.[41]

On the 20 June the bridges had been completed, and the weather was fine. This was obviously McClellan's time to attack, if he ever intended to do so. He had received reënforcements which had brought his army up to an aggregate of 105,000 men, and there was no immediate prospect of a further increase in numbers. It was plain that the chances of success were better now than they would be after General Lee was strengthened by the arrival of Jackson's command from the Shenandoah. At this time Lee had only 68,000 men within the lines of Richmond, and McClellan outnumbered him by more than three to two.[42] These odds, according to Napoleon, are sufficient, and if a general cannot discover from the attitude of his enemy what the odds are, he is unfitted for supreme command. McClellan was a man of undoubted ability, but his good qualities were accompanied by marked defects. Bold in conception, he was terribly slow in execution: his will was less powerful than his imagination.[43]

Lee had served on the same staff with McClellan in the Mexican War, and had personal knowledge of his capacity and character: " he read him like an open book." [44] McClellan, on the other hand, failed to draw a single correct inference. It is true that he was misled by his famous detective staff, and believed the garrison of Richmond to number at least 200,000 men. But he made no effort whatever to supplement or check up this information. It must be admitted that his cavalry, which numbered only 5000 sabres, was weak in proportion to his other arms, and also of inferior quality, but he scarcely employed it at all.

Lee, on the other hand, had found means to acquire ample information of the dispostion of his adversary's forces on the north bank of the Chickahominy, the point

[41] 13 O. R., 490.
[42] See 2 Henderson, 11.
[43] 2 Henderson, 4.
[44] Cf. Maurice, 35.

he had decided to attack. His cavalry, also, was below the usual proportion of one trooper to every six men of the other arms, numbering not more than 3000; but it was of superior quality, familiar with the country, and united under the command of J. E. B. Stuart, one of the ablest cavalry leaders developed during the Civil War.

"Early on the 12 June, with 1200 horsemen, and a section of artillery, Stuart rode out on an enterprise of a kind which at that time was absolutely unique, and which will keep his memory green so long as cavalry is used in war." [45] He encountered and defeated a small Federal force near Old Church, and reached Tunstall's Station on the York River railroad without further opposition. He had then accomplished the object of the expedition, which was to ascertain the nature of the region lying north of the Chickahominy, and the arrangements of McClellan to protect his line of supplies. Stuart now realized that it would be dangerous, if not impossible, to return to Richmond by the route by which he had come, so he determined to make a complete circuit of the Union army. This feat he successfully accomplished, crossing the Chickahominy fifteen miles below Bottom's Bridge, and reaching Richmond by way of the James River Road on the 15th. He had marched nearly 150 miles, in four days; captured many prisoners, and lost but one man. [46]

On the whole, however, this brilliant raid cost the Confederates more than its results were worth. It seriously alarmed McClellan for his line of supplies, and he immediately gave orders to begin loading the transports, preparatory to a change of base to Harrison's Landing on the James River. If these preliminary arrangements had not been made, the results of the campaign would have been much more favorable to the Confederates. [47]

At the same time, McClellan caused a survey to be made by his engineers of the region between the railroad and White Oak Swamp. From the data furnished by these officers, maps were prepared for use in case the movement to the James should be found advisable. [48]

[45] 2 Henderson, 7.
[46] 2 B. & L., 271–275.
[47] Alexander, 114. Cf. Maurice, 115.
[48] Webb, 128.

General Lee had also been largely reënforced during the month of June, and when joined by Jackson would dispose of 86,500 men.[49]

He now decided to take the offensive, and made arrangements for the coöperation of Jackson, which was essential to the success of such a movement. At this time, the Federal troops in the Shenandoah had fallen back, and no further trouble from them was anticipated for the time being. Jackson was therefore ordered to leave a small force to guard the passes, and to join the main army as soon as possible, moving east to Ashland, on the Richmond and Fredericksburg Railroad.

Before issuing on the 24 June the orders for the battle of Gaines's Mill (General Orders No. 75), General Lee called a conference at his headquarters, of Jackson, Longstreet, A. P. Hill, and D. H. Hill, to arrange all details. When summoned to this meeting on Saturday, 21 June, Jackson was near Gordonsville. He started on a freight train bound to Richmond, but left the train before midnight that night at a station [50] where he spent Sunday, attending church twice. At midnight he set out on horseback for the conference at Richmond some fifty miles away, arriving about three o'clock Monday afternoon.[51] If he had kept on the train he would have reached Richmond early Sunday morning. His infantry followed by train, but the artillery and cavalry marched all the way. His brigades, on the march, also kept Sunday in camp, as usual.

At the conference, Longstreet asked Jackson to fix the date for the attack, and he named the 25 June, but on Longstreet's suggestion that he allow more time, the 26th was selected.

[49] Mr. Ropes (Part II, 164) says: "These and other troops added some 25,000 men, at least, to the Confederate force in Virginia, raising it to about 90,000 men." In this estimate, he evidently includes Jackson's command, of some 18,500, in the Valley.

[50] Henderson says it was Frederick Hall, other reports say Louisa C. H.

[51] Mr. Ropes states that this long ride was due to "excessive caution" — "for fear of being recognized as a passenger on the train." (2 Ropes, 165.)

CHAPTER SIX

JUNE — JULY 1862

THE SEVEN DAYS

McClellan's Plans — The Federal Position — Lee Prepares to Attack
Porter — His Objects — His Opinion of McClellan — Jackson's
Movements — Battle of Beaver Dam Creek — The Confederates
Repulsed — Jackson Fails to Coöperate — Porter Falls Back to
Gaines's Mill — His Position and Forces — Battle of Gaines's
Mill — The Federals Defeated — McClellan Responsible —
Porter's Fine Tactics — McClellan Decides on a Change of
Base — Lee's Orders for the Pursuit — Battles of Savage Station
and Glendale — The Confederates Repulsed — Jackson's In-
activity on Both Days — Confederate Tactics Poor — Jackson's
Excuses — White Oak Swamp — Strong Federal Position at
Malvern Hill — The Confederate Attack Fails — The Federals
Withdraw to Harrison's Landing — Losses During the Seven
Days — Comments — Criticisms of Jackson and McClellan —
The Army Withdrawn

THE morning of Thursday, the 26 June, dawned
clear and bright, giving promise that the day would
be a brilliant one. For twenty-four hours, General
Porter, in command of the Fifth Corps, on the north bank
of the Chickahominy, had been expecting an attack from
the enemy. At midnight on the 24th, General McClellan
had telegraphed him that a deserter had given information that Jackson was in the immediate vicinity, ready to
unite with Lee in an attack upon his command. In the
far distant northern and western horizon, vast clouds of
dust indicated the approach of Jackson's army.

A despatch on the 23 June, from McClellan's chief-
of-staff, had stated to Porter: " If you are attacked . . .
the troops on this side will be held ready either to support you directly or to attack the enemy in their front.
If the force attacking you is large, the general would
prefer the latter course, counting upon your skill and the
admirable troops under your command to hold their own
against superior numbers long enough for him to make

the decisive movement which will determine the fate of Richmond." This was an admirable plan, if only McClellan had had the energy to carry it out!

The Federal position on Beaver Dam Creek was naturally very strong. The banks of the valley were steep, and forces advancing to the attack, on the adjacent plains, would present their flanks, as well as their front, to fire of both infantry and artillery, safely posted behind entrenchments. The stream was over waist-deep and bordered by swamps. Its passage was difficult for infantry at all points, and impracticable for artillery except at the bridge-crossing near Mechanicsville, and the one below, at Ellerson's Mill.[1]

General Lee's plans for the initial operations were of a somewhat complicated nature. Magruder, who had so successfully imposed on McClellan at Yorktown, with 28,000 men was relied upon to hold Richmond until Porter was crushed. With the remainder of his army, 35,000 men all told, Lee would cross the Chickahominy and attack the front of the Federals, while the 18,500 troops under Jackson descended on their flank and rear.

Four bridges crossed the river on Lee's left, but only two of these could be used for the attack — Mechanicsville Bridge, and Meadow Bridge, about a mile and a half up stream. Five and a half miles above Mechanicsville, at the Half Sink, there is Winston's Bridge, where Branch, of A. P. Hill's division, was to cross; and three and a half miles below is New Bridge. With the exception of the passage at the Half Sink, the northern approaches to all these bridges were in possession of the Federals, so it was a difficult operation to transfer the Richmond troops from one bank of the Chickahominy to the other.[2]

Lee's first object was to secure the two centre bridges, which he expected to achieve by the advance of the Valley army. Then, as soon as the Federals fell back, Longstreet and the two Hills would cross the river and strike Porter in front, while Jackson attacked his right. A victory would ensure the possession of New Bridge, and put the troops north of the river in close communication with Magruder.

[1] 2 B. & L., 326–328. [2] 2 Henderson, 14–15.

We can now see how, in the hands of a skillful general, entrenchments may form a " pivot of operations," — the means whereby he covers his most vulnerable point, holds the enemy in front, and sets his main body free for offensive action. This is clearly exposed in Lee's report, and shows that he contemplated this action from the first. Yet it is very doubtful whether he would have taken such a desperate chance if he had not known McClellan as he did. " From Hannibal to Moltke," says Colonel Henderson, " there has been no great captain who has neglected to study the character of his opponent, and who did not trade on the knowledge thus acquired; and it was this knowledge which justified Lee's audacity." [3]

Lee's plans all hinged upon the movements of the Valley army. On the morning of the 24 June, Jackson, with his infantry, was at Beaver Dam Station, on the Virginia Central road, about 18 miles from Ashland, and was expected to reach Ashland that night. The following night, the 25th, he was to halt near Merry Oaks Church, just west of the Virginia Central Railroad. At three o'clock on Thursday morning, the 26th, he was to advance on the road leading to Pole Green Church, and, bearing well to the left, turning Beaver Dam Creek, to proceed toward Cold Harbor. [4]

At three o'clock on the morning of the 26th, however, Jackson was still at Ashland, and it was not until nine that he crossed the railroad. Branch, on hearing that the Valley army was at last advancing, crossed at Winston's Bridge and moved on Mechanicsville. Meanwhile, A. P. Hill was waiting near Meadow Bridge until the advance of Branch and Jackson should clear the way for his passage. At two o'clock, hearing nothing from his associates, and fearing that further delay might result in the failure of the whole plan, he gave orders to seize the bridge. The Federal pickets fell back, followed by Hill, who, after a short march of three miles, found himself under fire of Porter's artillery. [5]

About two o'clock on the afternoon of the 26th, the

[3] 2 Henderson, 13.   [5] 2 Henderson, 19.
[4] General Orders No. 75.

boom of a single cannon, the signal agreed upon, announced to Porter that the enemy was crossing the Chickahominy. His divisions were promptly formed, and took the positions to which they had previously been assigned. An hour later, the Confederates, under Longstreet and the two Hills, crossed the two centre bridges in force, and pushed down the roads leading to Beaver Dam Creek, the Union outposts falling back across the creek, and destroying the bridges behind them.

A part of the Confederate forces took the road to the right to Ellerson's Mill, but the main body advanced directly into the valley of Beaver Dam Creek. Suddenly, when halfway down the valley, the Federals opened up with rapid volleys of artillery and infantry, which drove the attacking force back in hasty flight. Later in the afternoon they returned again to the attack, but were once more repulsed with terrible slaughter. The forces directed against Ellerson's Mill suffered an even more disastrous defeat. When night came on, they all fell back beyond gun-shot, and the contest was over. The Union loss was only 361, while the Confederates lost nearly 1500 out of some 10,000 attacking.[6]

General McClellan came on the field at an early hour in the afternoon, and remained with Porter until about one o'clock the next morning. After his return to his headquarters, south of the river, he sent orders, about three o'clock, for Porter to withdraw to a well-selected and very strong position east of Gaines's Mill. These orders were immediately executed.

About 4:30 P.M., Jackson had reached Hundley's Corner, three miles north of the Federal position, but separated from it by a dense forest and the windings of the creek. Here, after establishing his outposts, he ordered his troops to bivouac. Although the cannonade was distinctly heard, he made no attempt to assist his comrades, who, not three miles away, were assaulting the Federal lines. The victor of the Valley campaign, on his first appearance in combination with the main army, had proved

---

[6] Livermore, 82. In 2 *B. & L.*, 350–351, the Confederate losses are given as nearly 2000.

a failure, and wrecked General Lee's plans. His biographer, Colonel Henderson, offers many excuses for his lack of energy, but none is convincing. " To fix an hour so long in advance," he says, " was worse than useless, and Jackson cannot be blamed if he failed to comply with the exact letter of a foolish order." [7] But Jackson himself had proposed a time twenty-four hours earlier! [8]

The position selected for the final Federal stand was east of Powhite Creek, about six miles from Beaver Dam Creek. The line of battle was semicircular, the ends being in the valley of the Chickahominy, while the central part occupied the high grounds along the bank of a creek, and curved around past McGehee's to Elder Swamp. Part of the front was covered by the ravine of the creek, and, toward the east, by a series of boggy swamps, covered with dense brush. Near McGehee's, and beyond, the ground, elevated and drier, was broken by ravines swept by the Union fire. The high land at the centre was cleared, and the numerous fences and ditches afforded cover to both infantry and artillery.[9]

The new line of battle was strong, but it was too extended to be held by Porter's forces, and he certainly had a right to expect that enough troops would be sent by McClellan to enable him to maintain his position during the day. But this obvious duty McClellan did not perform.[10]

Porter's force consisted of three divisions of infantry, six regiments of cavalry, and twenty batteries of artillery, — in all about 30,000 men. The men were well disciplined, and they were well commanded. Porter himself was a graduate of West Point, an officer of the Old Army, who had seen service in Mexico under Scott, and he was known to be a brave and skillful general.[11]

The battle, which took its name from Gaines's Mill on the creek, began about two o'clock with a furious assault

[7] 2 Henderson, 20–21.
[8] See *ante*, page 104.
[9] 2 B. & L., 331. Porter's " hasty entrenchments " were the germ of the works so universally used on all the battle-fields in the later stages of the war. (2 Ropes, 380.)
[10] 2 Ropes, 175.
[11] 2 Ropes, 176.

by A. P. Hill, who was finally repulsed with great loss. For several hours the efforts of the Confederates were absolutely fruitless, and General Lee began to imagine that he was confronted by the principal part of the Federal army. He continued, however, to press the attack, with Jackson and D. H. Hill on the north front, A. P. Hill and Longstreet on the west. When Slocum's division, from Franklin's corps, arrived to reënforce Porter, about four o'clock, the Union reserves were entirely exhausted. With these fresh troops, Porter held out for about two hours more, but toward evening the Confederates succeeded in breaking the centre of his line, and the Federals were forced to retreat. Their withdrawal was aided by the appearance on the field of two brigades of Sumner's corps. During the night all the Federal troops crossed to the south bank of the Chickahominy, destroying the bridges behind them. The Confederate loss in killed and wounded was about 9000.[12] The Federal loss is reported as 6837 men, killed, wounded, and missing, including some 2800 prisoners, of whom about 1200 were wounded, left in the hands of the victorious Confederates. There were also 22 guns abandoned on the field.

" No one can read the accounts of this action," says Mr. Ropes, " without coming to the conclusion that 10,000 or 15,000 more men sent to Porter would have enabled him to hold his own till nightfall, and then to have effected the withdrawal of his command with entire safety." [13] General Alexander expresses the same opinion in even stronger terms. He writes: " Porter himself was perhaps the hardest opponent to fight in the Federal army. . . . Indeed, had McClellan reënforced Porter, as he should have done, with a whole corps, he might have won a great victory." [14]

McClellan might also have relieved the pressure on Porter by an attack on Magruder, who himself believed that his lines might have been carried. But that prince of " bluff " maintained such a brisk demonstration against McClellan's front, that the Union commander, with his

[12] Livermore (83) estimates their losses at 8751.
[13] 2 Ropes, 179.
[14] Alexander, 123.

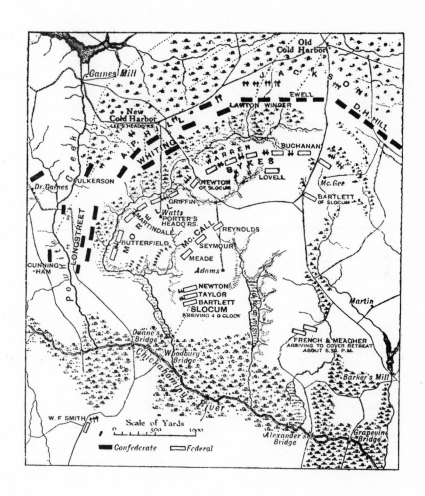

Scale of Yards
0   500   1000

■ Confederate   □ Federal

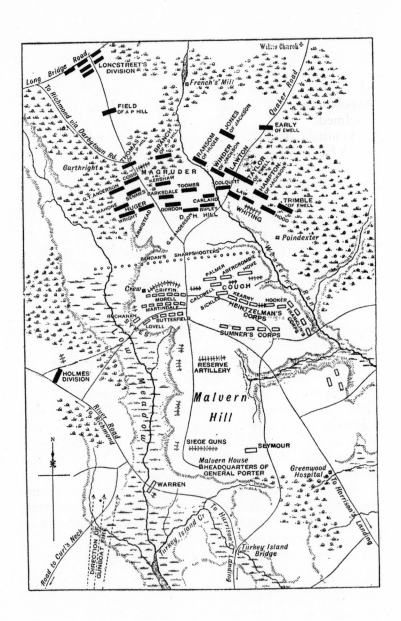

exaggerated estimate of the numbers opposed to him, postponed moving his reserves until it was too late. With 66,000 men on the south bank of the Chickahominy, McClellan was held in his entrenchments throughout the day by 28,000 Confederates. " Intent on saving his trains, on securing his retreat to the river James, and utterly regardless of the chances which fortune offered, the ' Young Napoleon ' had allowed his rear-guard to be overwhelmed." [15]

As usual, McClellan was not seen on the field of battle, which his devoted troops so well defended, but Porter was more than a sufficient substitute for the commander-in-chief. Porter's tactics were admirable; and, when his front was broken, he conducted the withdrawal in a masterly manner. The Federal retreat was favored by the absence of Stuart, who, in common with Lee and Jackson, thought that the enemy would endeavor to reach the White House, and dashed in that direction with his 2000 horsemen. When he learned his error, darkness had already fallen, and it was too late to accomplish anything.

The Confederate tactics in the battle were poor, and nearly lost them the victory. The attack was made too late in the day, and then their energies were not concentrated, or their assaults properly coördinated. This made the victory much more bloody than it need have been. [16]

It is a curious fact that all the severe battles in this campaign began after noon, which, even in the long June days, caused the Confederates on many occasions to lose the precious hours of daylight necessary to gather the fruits of victory.

At Gaines's Mill, the French princes, who were volunteer aides on General McClellan's staff, served with General Porter, and displayed the greatest gallantry — exposing themselves to every danger. [17]

On the night of the 28 June, the day after the battle

[15] 2 Henderson, 48.

[16] Alexander, 123–124.

[17] These were the Prince de Joinville, the son of King Louis-Philippe, and his two nephews, Comte de Paris and Duc de Chartres. The Comte de Paris afterwards began, but never finished, a history of the Civil War.

of Gaines's Mill, the corps commanders were assembled at the Trent house, the headquarters of General McClellan. He then announced his intention to change his base to the James River, and handed each of the officers a map showing the route across the White Oak Swamp. It was a perilous undertaking, for he had only one narrow road to move by, a great swamp and a creek to cross, with his army encumbered by a train of 5000 wagons, and 2500 cattle. The bulk of the stores at White House was moved by water.

Porter, with the Fifth Corps, was sent ahead to occupy the strong position at Malvern Hill. He was followed by the Fourth Corps, under Keyes, who was ordered to take up a position south of the swamp, to cover the flank of the column on the side toward Richmond. The three other corps, of Sumner, Heintzelman, and Franklin, remained north of the swamp to cover the retreat.

Lee practically did nothing on the 28th, as he was still in the dark as to the intentions of the enemy. But by the morning of the 29th, he became convinced that McClellan was moving toward the James. He then ordered Magruder and Huger to push forward on the Williamsburg and Charles City roads; Longstreet and A. P. Hill, to cross by New Bridge and march to strike the Federal flank south of the swamp; Jackson and D. H. Hill, nearly 25,000 strong, to follow the shortest and most direct route, by the Grapevine Bridge, over which Porter had retreated across the Chickahominy.

Lee's orders were simple and obvious, but he would have done better to leave the pursuit of the Federal rearguard to Huger and Magruder, while he himself, with Jackson, Longstreet, and A. P. Hill, moved swiftly to the right by good roads, and placed the bulk of his army across McClellan's path near Malvern Hill.[18]

Magruder came upon Sumner, with his own and part of Franklin's corps, at Savage Station on the afternoon of the 29th, and immediately engaged the Federals. He was in momentary expectation of seeing Jackson fall upon the flank of the enemy from the direction of Grapevine

[18] Alexander, 134.

Bridge, but he was left without aid; his attacks were repulsed, and at nightfall the Federals resumed their march.

The excuse of Jackson, which Lee accepted, was that he found the bridge destroyed, and spent the day in repairing it; although he might have crossed by the ford close at hand. The real explanation is given by General Alexander: " But this was Sunday, and Jackson gave it strict observance. The greater part of his troops remained in camp all day and until after midnight Sunday night. Then they made a start at, or before, 2:30 A.M." [19]

The morning of the 30 June found the Army of the Potomac, with all of its artillery and trains, south of White Oak Swamp, and the bridge destroyed. Franklin remained to guard the crossing of the creek against the pursuit of the enemy. Five divisions took up a position near Glendale, where the Charles City, Darbytown, and New Market roads come together. The two corps of Keyes and Porter covered Malvern Hill.

The battle of Glendale or Frayser's Farm, on the 30 June, was the crisis of the " Seven Days." During the night, the entire Federal army had crossed the White Oak Swamp, and McClellan had accomplished one-half his retreat safely. He had only eight miles more to traverse; his trains were well on the way; and his army was concentrated to protect his flank. Whatever may have been McClellan's shortcomings on the field of battle, he had shown himself admirable in retreat, and the change of base had been handled most skillfully. With one day more, his flank would no longer be exposed, and his whole army would be united in the strong position of Malvern Hill, with the trains in safety.

On the 26th at Beaver Dam, on the 27th at Gaines's Mill, and on the 29th at Savage Station, the Federal army had been in danger of destruction, but had escaped through the poor tactics of the Confederates. At Glendale one more opportunity was offered, and every condition seemed favorable. Lee had in hand the forces of Holmes, Longstreet, A. P. Hill, Magruder, and Huger, a total

[19] Alexander, 136. Henderson (II, 58) accepts this flimsy excuse; also Ropes (II, 191).

of 24 brigades, or about 44,000 men, all ready for the attack.

At the same hour, Jackson, with his 14 brigades, 25,000 strong, was only four miles away in an air-line; he was expected to assault the enemy's rear-guard with the vigor he had displayed in the Valley, and make up for his lack of energy on the previous days. At last Fortune seemed about to smile on the Confederate cause.[20]

In a field of broom-grass and small pines, Lee, with Longstreet and Hill, waited impatiently for the signal. He was so close to the rear of his line of battle that officers on his staff were wounded by random shots. Hour after hour passed, and nothing happened. Four o'clock came, and the day was drawing to a close, but not a shot had been fired. Lee had waited for either Huger or Jackson, or both, to begin, and neither had done anything.

Briefly, this is what had happened: Holmes, in command of the extreme right of the Confederate columns was marching along the river road, from New Market to Harrison's Landing, which passes under and around the south side of Malvern Heights, between them and the James River. The ground is low and flat, and when the advance reached a point about 1000 yards from Malvern, the Federal trains, passing over the heights, were in plain view. Holmes could not resist the temptation to order his guns to fire upon these wagons. But no sooner did his six guns open than they were answered by thirty of the heaviest rifles of the Federal Artillery Reserve, aided by the fire of the heavy guns on the gunboats in the river at Turkey Bend. The Confederate guns were quickly wrecked, and Holmes's whole division was thrown into confusion. There was nothing to do but to withdraw. Lee directed Magruder's six brigades, on the adjoining Central Road, to march to the support of Holmes, but there was nothing for them to attack or defend. Thus 18,000 men, who were to have supported Longstreet's right, were diverted from the real work of the day.[21]

To turn next to Huger's division: This command, marching by the Charles City Road, which had been ob-

[20] Alexander, 139.   [21] Alexander, 140–141.

structed by the Federals, made very slow progress, and did not get through in time to take part in the battle. " It seems incredible," remarks General Alexander, " that this division, within four miles of Lee, could have been allowed to spend the whole day in a mere contest of axemen, wherein the Federals, with the most axes, had only to cut *down*, and the Confederates, with the fewest, to cut *up* and remove." [22]

It only remains to tell the story of Jackson's movements. He had always before acted alone and independently; so Lee had shown his supreme confidence by giving him only very brief and general orders, and then going to the furthest flank, " as if generously to leave to Jackson the opportunity of the most brilliant victory of the war." [23] But Jackson " did not try and fail, he simply made no effort." After spending the 29th (Sunday) in camp, in absolute disregard of Lee's instructions, he passed the 30th in equal idleness in White Oak Swamp. His 25,000 infantry practically did not fire a shot in the two days.[24] For some unaccountable reason, he contented himself with simply shelling Franklin's position. He made little effort to cross at the bridge, and none whatever to use the five fords in the neighborhood. He held his own and D. H. Hill's troops all day north of the creek.

Longstreet and A. P. Hill, under Lee's immediate command, therefore fought the battle without assistance; and instead of making a simultaneous attack with their whole force, they let their brigades go into the battle piecemeal. The fight was desperate, and lasted until long after dark. The Federal line was broken once, but was soon reestablished by reënforcements. The Confederates gained no strategical advantage, nor did they inflict a greater loss of men than they suffered.[25]

[22] Alexander, 143. General Lee never made any charges against his officers, or ordered them before courts of inquiry, but he had his own method of dealing with delinquents. After the Seven Days, Holmes and Magruder were sent to the trans-Mississippi area, where they remained in obscurity until the end of the war; while Huger was transferred to the Ordnance Department, and saw no more active service.

[23] Alexander, 144.
[24] Alexander, 144.
[25] 2 Ropes, 197.

It must be admitted that in this action, Lee was badly served by two of his lieutenants — Huger and Jackson. The inactivity of the latter has been severely criticised by both friends and foes.[26]

In Jackson's own account of the day he writes that he was "anxious to press forward, but the marshy character of the soil, the destruction of the bridge over the marsh and creek, and the strong position of the enemy for defending the passage, prevented my advancing until the following morning." Regarding this statement, General Alexander makes the caustic comment: "Considered as an excuse for Jackson's inaction during the whole day this report is simply farcical."[27]

This formidable obstacle, which held up Jackson for a whole day, was a small creek, averaging 10 to 15 feet wide and *six inches deep,* with a sandy bottom. The White Oak Swamp was merely a flat area densely grown up in trees and bushes, more or less wet in places, but generally with firm footing. Small farms and settlements were scattered along its edges, and residents and cattle had many paths in and through it. The swamp was widest, and the country flatter, near its source, about five miles from Richmond, between the Williamsburg and the Charles City roads. Near the bridge the country was rolling, and the swamp narrower. Above the bridge, there were four good crossings known to the natives, and one below; but besides there were many less-known paths.[28]

The battle of Glendale, says Mr. Ropes, closed the second act in the drama of the "Seven Days." For the second time, General Lee had failed in the attempt to strike his adversary a crushing blow during the change of base, and the critical period of the movement was over.[29]

During the night of the 30 June, the Federal troops fell back from Glendale to Malvern Hill, where the

[26] 2 Dabney, 206–208; Longstreet in 2 *B. & L.,* 402–403; D. H. Hill, *Ib.,* 389; Franklin, *Ib.,* 381; Alexander, 144–147. See also 2 Henderson, 60–72.
[27] Alexander, 147.
[28] See Alexander, 146.
[29] 2 Ropes, 200.

Army of the Potomac was once more united on the morning of the first of July.

The position of Malvern Hill was one of great natural strength. The open plateau at the top, at a height of 150 feet above the surrounding country, was a mile and a half in length by half a mile in width. On the northerly side, the slopes, covered with wheat, standing or in shock, fell gradually to the edge of the woods, 800 to 1600 yards from the commanding crest. The base of the hill, except on the easterly side, was covered with dense forest; and within the woods, at the foot of the declivity, ran a winding and marshy stream. The right flank was partially protected by a long mill-dam. On the left, which was more open, there was an excellent artillery position, commanding a broad expanse of meadow-land, drained by a narrow stream and deep ditches, and flanked by the fire of the Federal gunboats. Only three approaches, the Quaker and the river roads and a track from the northwest, gave access to the heights.[30]

The ground had been thoroughly examined by Fitz John Porter, who had been there for twenty-four hours; and General Hunt had had ample time to post the reserve artillery, which he had done with his usual skill. All the forenoon was spent in arranging the troops and guns, and resting.

In his report, General D. H. Hill speaks of the formidable strength of the Federal position, on a commanding hill, guarded by swarms of infantry, securely sheltered by fences, ditches, and ravines, with all the approaches swept by artillery. Tier after tier of batteries were grimly visible on the heights, rising in the form of an amphitheatre. The Confederates could only reach the first line of batteries by crossing an open space of from 300 to 400 yards, exposed to a deadly fire of grape and canister from the artillery, and musketry from the infantry. If that first line were carried, another and another, still more difficult, remained in the rear.[31]

General Lee appears to have hesitated as to ordering an assault upon the Federals, in this strong position, but late

[30] 2 Henderson, 74.   [31] 13 O. R., 627.

in the afternoon he decided to make the attack. He probably thought the Federal army was entirely demoralized, or he would not have taken such a desperate chance.[32]

The battle was opened at four o'clock by an assault on the centre of the Union line by D. H. Hill, whose division was repulsed with heavy loss. Later, an attack on the Federal left was made by Huger, supported by Magruder, which also was a failure. There were also other isolated, useless, and unsuccessful attempts, each resulting in a bloody repulse. The failure was complete: absolutely no impression was made on the Federal lines.[33]

The action lasted only three hours, but the Confederates lost over 5000 men, killed and wounded, while the Union casualties were not more than one-third of that number. General Hill states that more than half the Confederate casualties were from artillery fire — an unprecedented thing in warfare.[34]

The following day, the 2 July, the Army of the Potomac fell back to Harrison's Landing on the James, where it fortified itself. A reconnaissance of the position convinced Lee of the uselessness of making another attack, and he withdrew his troops within the defences of Richmond.

At the beginning of the "Seven Days' Battles," McClellan had 105,000 men, and Lee, 86,500. The losses were as follows:[35]

	Federals	Confederates
Killed	1,734	3,286
Wounded	8,062	15,909
Missing	6,053	940
Totals	15,849	20,135
	15%	23%

[32] Cf. 2 B. & L., 391; Allan, 136.
[33] Webb, 167.
[34] D. H. Hill, in 2 B. & L., 394.
[35] 2 B. & L., 187. Livermore (86) estimates McClellan's "effectives" at 91,169, and Lee's at 95,481, which he reduces to 90,000, in a note. Johnston (145) states that Lee had received some 50,000 reënforcements, including Jackson's command.

The Peninsula Campaign and the Seven Days have always been the subject of much controversy, both North and South.

The plans of General Lee were bold and excellent, but they fell short of success owing to the faults of his lieutenants — particularly Jackson.

It is difficult to explain the failure of Jackson during the Seven Days. As General Alexander says: "He nowhere, even distantly, approached his record as a soldier won in his every other battle, either before or afterward. . . . Nothing that he had to do was done with the vigor which marked all the rest of his career." [36]

His brother-in-law, General D. H. Hill, writes: "Jackson's genius never shone when he was under the command of another. It seemed then to be shrouded or paralyzed. . . . This was the keynote to his whole character. The hooded falcon cannot strike the quarry." [37]

But it is impossible to accept this explanation. Jackson was certainly under the command of Lee at Second Manassas and Chancellorsville, where he displayed all of his former activity and energy. During the Seven Days he was apparently suffering from the "mysterious malady" which attacked Napoleon on two or three occasions during his career, notably at Borodino and Dresden, and which was nothing less than absolute physical and mental prostration.[38]

The criticisms of McClellan have been equally severe, and in most cases these were fully justified, although in some instances they were due to misapprehensions.

The Federal position athwart the Chickahominy was not "chosen" by McClellan, but was forced upon him by orders from Washington at the time McDowell was expected to advance from Fredericksburg.

The change of base to the James had always been in his mind, but was precipitated by Lee's determination to break his communications with White House. Then his

[36] Alexander, 116.
[37] 2 B. & L., 389.
[38] See Lord Wolseley's *Decline and Fall of Napoleon*, 28, and 64. Also Maurice, 119.

only mistake was the delay of twenty-four hours in giving the order to march, which necessitated the actions at Savage Station, Glendale, and Malvern Hill.

The movement was dictated by the absolute necessity of establishing a new base of supplies, and was not the result of the Confederate attacks. The marching away of the Federal army after each engagement was not because it had been beaten: it was simply continuing the movement to the James. To speak of " the pursuit " and " the escape " of the Union army is therefore scarcely correct.[39] Yet, these views were generally held, both at the time, and for many years afterwards.

Two years later, General Grant, after losing 55,000 men, found himself literally *driven* into the position which McClellan reached *voluntarily*, with one quarter that loss. It was a position of rare strategic advantage, the key to Richmond, when properly utilized; and it seems strange that this was not realized in 1862. After his change of base, McClellan had nearly stumbled into this key-position, and he seems to have comprehended this fact, for his army was recalled to Washington against his violent protests and appeals.[40] " Here is the true defence of Washington," he wrote; " it is here on the banks of the James that the fate of the Union should be decided." These words were prophetic!

Considering the many difficulties of the operation, the change of base was made in a masterly manner. The critic will have a hard task to find a flaw in either the strategy or the tactics of the movement.

Nevertheless, as Mr. Ropes points out, the moral and political effect of the campaign was entirely to the advantage of the Confederates. Two years later, the Administration and the public had had more experience, and Grant was supported, where McClellan had been condemned.

But, for this attitude of the public mind, McClellan

[39] See Alexander, 133, 156.

[40] The order withdrawing McClellan did " greater injury to the Union cause " than any other order issued during the war " with the possible exception of that appointing Halleck general-in-chief." — 6 *Papers Mil. Hist. Soc. Mass.*, 14.

himself was largely responsible. He was an accomplished soldier and a very able engineer; he had a very rare genius for organization and administration; but he was hardly equal at this time to the position of commander of a field army. He lacked vigor and activity and aggressiveness. He was too methodical and too cautious.

While it would be unjust to state that McClellan was lacking in physical courage, he was not a *fighting* general. " He had," says Mr. Ropes, " a constitutional aversion to the risks inseparable from all military operations. He shrank from the test of battle." [41] In fact, on few occasions during the campaign did he order an attack made. He acted almost entirely on the defensive. Furthermore, he was usually absent from the field of battle, doing work which should have been delegated to a member of his staff. At Williamsburg he did not arrive on the field " until the action was practically over," having stayed at Yorktown to give his personal attention to the embarkation of some troops going up the York River.[42] At Fair Oaks and Seven Pines, he did not appear on the ground until about two o'clock on the afternoon of the second day, and then he " gave no orders looking to an attack." [43] At that time the Confederates were much demoralized from their severe losses, and the change of leaders, and many authorities are of the opinion that McClellan could have won an easy victory.[44]

During the " Seven Days' Battles," McClellan was never at the front. The two principal actions, Gaines's Mill and Malvern Hill, were fought by Fitz John Porter, the ablest of his corps commanders, without any personal direction from the commander-in-chief. At Savage Station, " General McClellan was not on the ground, and the senior corps-commander, Sumner, who ought promptly to have assumed command in his absence, evidently did not do so." [45] At the battle of Frayser's Farm, or Glen-

[41] 2 Ropes, 105.
[42] 2 Ropes, 110.
[43] 2 Ropes, 150.
[44] *Cf.* Webb, *Campaigns*, 116, 117, 186; 2 Comte de Paris, 71. **Ropes,** however, doubts this. See 2 Ropes, 155.
[45] 2 Ropes, 191.

dale, General Lee commanded in person, stationing himself where the fighting was going on, and where he could superintend the operations of Longstreet and A. P. Hill. "General McClellan, on the other hand, after giving in the morning certain directions to his corps-commanders, but apparently without handing over the command to any one of them, rode down to Malvern Hill, and even as far as Haxall's Landing, and conferred with Captain Rodgers of the navy in regard to the place where the army had better finally be stationed. . . . It is almost incredible that any intelligent man should have acted as General McClellan acted on this critical day." [46]

In speaking of the actions of the 29 and 30 June, and 1 July, General Alexander also says: "Unknown to us, another circumstance was rarely in our favor. . . . McClellan, on each day, left his army without placing any one in command during his absence, while he did engineer's duty, examining the localities toward which he was marching. Had the Confederates accomplished their reasonable expectations, the criticism of McClellan would have been very severe." [47]

One of the four conditions of the plan for the transfer of the Army of the Potomac to the Peninsula was: —

"That the force to be left to cover Washington be such as to give an entire feeling of security for its safety from menace."

As to whether General McClellan had a just grievance against the Government because President Lincoln detained McDowell's corps in the vicinity of Washington, authorities have always differed. General Webb thinks that this action was not warranted, and "in fact did everything to insure disaster to the Peninsula Campaign." On the other hand, Mr. Ropes maintains that "the Government was perfectly right." [48]

On the eve of the battle of Gaines's Mill, McClellan sent Stanton one of his characteristic communications. He

[46] 2 Ropes, 198. And Mr. Ropes adds (199): "If his army had been beaten on that day, McClellan would have been cashiered, and justly."

[47] Alexander, 139.

[48] Cf. Webb, 179–180; 2 Ropes, 213–216. See also, for a very able review of the subject, 2 B. & L., 435–438.

telegraphed the Secretary [49] that he thought Jackson was going to attack his right and rear; that the enemy's force was stated at 200,000 men; that he regretted his inferiority in numbers, but felt himself in no way to blame for it; and that, if a disaster should result, the responsibility could not be thrown on his shoulders, but "must rest where it belongs," that is to say — on the President and Secretary. To this insolent communication Mr. Stanton made no direct reply, but sent McClellan his best wishes.

After the battle, at 12:30 A.M. on the 28 June, McClellan sent a long telegram, in which he stated that his men were overwhelmed by vastly superior numbers *even after he had brought his last reserves into action*; that he had lost the battle because his force was too small; that the Government could not hold him responsible for the result; that the Government had not sustained his army; "if I save this army now, I tell you plainly that I owe no thanks to you *or to any other person in Washington. You have done your best to sacrifice this army.*" [50]

On reaching the James River, McClellan reported that he had saved the army, but would require reënforcement to the extent of 50,000 men — a number which he raised the next day to 100,000. In reply the President promised 31,000 men at once, and 10,000 more if possible. In a very kind letter, under date of the 2 July, Mr. Lincoln wrote: "If you think you are not strong enough to take Richmond just now, I do not ask you to try." On the 5th, Mr. Stanton also wrote: "Be assured that you shall have the support of this Department and the Government as cordially and as faithfully as ever was rendered by man to man." The next day Mr. Stanton followed this by a personal letter, couched in still warmer terms. General McClellan's reply was cold and formal.

The President visited Harrison's Landing to inform himself personally regarding the situation. Then McClellan handed Mr. Lincoln his well-known letter "upon a civil and military policy."

[49] 12 O. R., 51.
[50] Quoted 2 *B. & L.*, 438. The words italicized at the end are omitted in the despatch as printed in the report of the Committee on the Conduct of the War.

This was the last straw. On the 11 July the President appointed General Halleck commander-in-chief of the army, and Halleck, after a visit to McClellan's camp, recommended the withdrawal of the army from the Peninsula, and its union with the forces of General Pope. The orders for the removal followed. " There was, to my mind," General Halleck says, " no alternative." [51]

As we see it now, this was a great mistake, but under all the circumstances it is difficult to blame the Administration for its action.

" On the whole," says Major Steele, " the Peninsula Campaign was, on the part of the Confederates, a campaign of good plans and bad execution. . . . On the part of the Federals, it was a campaign of neglected opportunities." [52]

[51] See 2 *B. & L.*, 438.   [52] Steele, 215.

CHAPTER SEVEN

JUNE — SEPTEMBER 1862

SECOND MANASSAS

The Army of Virginia — Pope in Command — His Career — His Bombastic Proclamation — His Task — Theatre of the Compaign — The Military Situation — Lee's Plans — Battle of Cedar Mountain — Lee at Clark's Mountain — His Plans Disclosed — Jackson's Famous March — He Destroys the Union Base — Pope Retreats to Manassas — Jackson's Escape — Action at Groveton — Longstreet at Thoroughfare Gap — Battle of 29 August — Jackson's Strong Position — All the Union Attacks Fail — Story of the " Joint Order " — Longstreet Arrives — Federals Finally Repulsed — Pope's Fatal Error — Battle of 30 August — The Two Armies — Their Positions — Pope Badly Defeated — Retreats to Centreville — Thence to Fairfax — Stevens and Kearny Killed — Losses During the Campaign — Comments

ON the 26 June 1862 an order was issued by Mr. Lincoln consolidating the forces under Fremont, Banks, and McDowell, and the troops in Washington, into one army, to be called the Army of Virginia, and placing at its head Major-General John Pope. The victories of Stonewall Jackson over these separate commands in the Valley had convinced the President and Mr. Stanton that they made a mistake in the spring when they divided the territory east of the Alleghanies into four departments. All three of the superseded generals were seniors to Pope, and Fremont refused to serve under him. His corps, now called the First Corps of the Army of Virginia, was accordingly assigned to Sigel; Banks commanded the Second, and McDowell the Third, Corps.[1]

Pope was graduated from West Point in 1842, in the same class with Rosecrans, Sykes, and Doubleday, on the Union side, and Longstreet, D. H. Hill, and G. H. Smith, of the Confederate army. He was a handsome, dashing

[1] 18 O. R., 435, 437, 444.

officer, and a splendid horseman. He saw but little service until the Civil War, when he gained some reputation by the capture of New Madrid and Island No. 10, on the Mississippi. When he assumed command in the East, he was in the prime of life, less than forty years old, and had lost little, if any, of the dash and grace of his youth.[2]

The consolidation of the three armies was a wise measure, but the selection of Pope for the new command was a grave mistake; McDowell would have been a much better choice. For a brief period, Pope acted as military adviser to the President at Washington, but on the 11 July, General Halleck was appointed commander-in-chief of all the armies of the United States, and summoned to the capital. No selection for the supreme command could possibly have been more unfortunate, as Mr. Lincoln and the public were soon to find out.[3]

General Pope's first official act, on taking command the 14 July, was to issue a bombastic address to his troops, in which he displayed an absolute lack of tact. Not content with extolling the prowess of the Western troops, he was bitterly sarcastic in his references to McClellan and his army. " I have come to you," he said, " from the West, where we have always seen the backs of our enemies — from an army . . . whose policy has been attack and not defence. . . . I hear constantly of taking strong positions and holding them — of lines of retreat and of bases of supplies. Let us discard such ideas. . . . Let us look before and not behind."

At the time that Pope assumed command, the forces of Banks and Fremont were still in the Shenandoah Valley, and the two divisions of McDowell were at Manassas and Falmouth, respectively. The task laid out for him in the order constituting the new army was threefold: (1) To cover the city of Washington from attack; (2) to as-

[2] 2 B. & L., 524.

[3] The latter part of June, Mr. Lincoln made a secret journey to West Point to see General Scott. The only record of this mysterious meeting is a memorandum in the hand of Scott urging that McDowell's corps should be sent at once to McClellan. But it is generally supposed that at this time Scott advised the appointment of Halleck, and the union under Pope of the armies of Banks, Fremont, and McDowell. (See Macartney, 27–28.)

sure the safety of the Shenandoah Valley; and (3), so to operate on the Confederate lines of communications in the direction of Gordonsville and Charlottesville as to draw off, if possible, a considerable force of the enemy from Richmond, and thus relieve the operations against that city of the Army of the Potomac.[4]

General Pope thought that the first two of these objects could be accomplished best by withdrawing the corps of Sigel and Banks to the east side of the Blue Ridge. Accordingly these two commanders were ordered to cross the mountains and take position near Sperryville,[5] about twenty-five miles west of Warrenton. At the same time McDowell was directed to send the division of Ricketts to Warrenton, but to leave King's division at Falmouth "to protect the crossing of the Rappahannock at that point, . . . the railroad thence to Aquia Creek, and the public buildings which had been erected at the latter place."[6] This was contrary to General Pope's judgment, and he was undoubtedly correct in his position.

At this time the army of General Lee was still concentrated in the vicinity of Richmond, and his communications with the Valley by the Virginia Central Railroad remained unbroken. The important junction of this line with the Orange and Alexandria at Gordonsville was defended, as was also Charlottesville, whence one line ran to Staunton in the upper Valley, and another to Lynchburg, where it met the East Tennessee and Georgia, the main line to Chattanooga. The Manassas Gap, and the Orange and Alexandria, which came together at Manassas Junction, served to connect the Union forces with the lower Valley, and with their base at Washington. The junctions at Manassas, Gordonsville, and Charlottesville, were therefore points of great strategic importance. The former place was in the hands of the Federals, and the second was exposed to capture, as the Union forces could advance upon it easily, and be supplied directly from Alexandria: its protection was therefore of special concern to Lee.

[4] 16 O. R., 21.
[5] 18 O. R., 439, 440, 453, 468, 471.
[6] 18 O. R., 450; 16 O. R., 21.

Between the regions occupied by the Army of Virginia and the Confederate forces, flowed in an easterly direction the Rappahannock River and its branch, the Rapidan. Both were crossed by several bridges, and in the dry season were fordable at many points, but none the less they were quite formidable military obstacles. North and west of Gordonsville, the country was mountainous, and the entire theatre was more or less thickly covered with forest. The Bull Run Mountains could be passed only at a few gaps. The highways were mainly dirt roads, fairly good in dry weather, but difficult after a storm. There were a few macadam roads, like the Warrenton Turnpike, and the Little River Turnpike through Aldie Gap.

The military position in the early days of July was as follows: At Harrison's Landing on the James River, McClellan with some 80,000 men was still threatening Richmond. Pope, with about 47,000 troops in all, was near Sperryville with the two corps of Sigel and Banks, while one division (King's) of McDowell's corps was at Fredericksburg, and the other (Ricketts's) at Warrenton.

As Lee's army at Richmond was between the two Federal forces, it was obviously out of the question for Pope to march to the aid of McClellan, or to be sent to him by water without leaving the Capital and the Valley exposed. His efforts were therefore necessarily confined to threatening Gordonsville and Charlottesville. Accordingly, on the 7 July, and again on the 12th, and 14th, Banks was ordered to despatch his cavalry under Hatch to seize Gordonsville and Charlottesville. Much to the annoyance of Pope, this movement failed because Hatch did not march with sufficient celerity. At that time Gordonsville was held by only 200 infantry and a few cavalry, and could easily have been captured.[7]

To turn now to Lee: his first solicitude was to have McClellan's army recalled, and not reënforced, so that it could operate against Richmond from its new base. Knowing the inactivity of McClellan, he decided, with his usual audacity, to leave a small force within the defences of Richmond, and crush Pope before his army

[7] Alexander, 179.

could be joined by that of McClellan. He had received prompt reports of the advance of Pope, and on the 13 July he ordered Jackson to Gordonsville, with the divisions of Winder and Ewell. The Confederate army was not organized into corps until the following autumn, and Jackson and Longstreet were still only major-generals commanding divisions; but each now usually commanded other divisions besides his own, called a wing. Thus, Jackson's old division became Winder's (afterwards Taliaferro's), and Longstreet's became Pickett's.[8]

On his arrival at Gordonsville, Jackson was anxious to undertake some aggressive movement against Pope, but considered his force of 12,000 men too small; so he appealed to Lee for reënforcements. After some hesitation, on the 27 July Lee ordered A. P. Hill's division, about 12,000 strong, to Gordonsville.

On the 6 August, pursuant to orders from Halleck, Pope began an advance with his infantry, with the purpose of concentrating near Culpeper. The following day Jackson put his whole force in motion to fall upon Pope's army before it could be united. But the weather was very hot, and there were some blunders in the orders, so that it was three o'clock on the afternoon of the 9th before two of his divisions formed line in front of Banks's corps, which had been encountered at Cedar Mountain, some seven miles south of Culpeper. While awaiting the arrival of his other forces, Jackson brought up 26 rifled guns and opened fire on the enemy's lines. Banks at once attacked furiously, and routed the left of Jackson's line; but A. P. Hill arrived on the field with his division in time to save the day. Banks had begun the action without asking for reënforcements, and his unaided corps was " utterly overwhelmed and driven back with great loss." [9] It was now dark, but Jackson pursued by moonlight until he came upon Ricketts's division of McDowell's corps in line of battle beyond Cedar Creek, and was checked.

Such, in brief, was the battle of Cedar Mountain. Banks had about 8000 men on the ground, and Jackson some 20,000 at the end. The Federal loss was nearly 2400,

[8] Alexander, 175. [9] 2 Ropes, 250.

killed, wounded, and missing; the Confederate casualties were about 1300.

Both armies remained for two days in face of each other, and then Jackson wisely retired across the Rapidan toward Gordonsville. Pope followed as far as the river, but did not venture to cross, as he thought his " whole effective force was barely equal to that of the enemy." [10] In this he was entirely mistaken, for he had in hand nearly 40,000 men, while Jackson had hardly 23,000. On the 15 August, Pope was reënforced by 8000 men under Reno, from Burnside's command. He had then not less than 45,000 men, exclusive of cavalry. But his force was not an army: it was an amalgamation of corps and divisions which had never fought together, and which had no confidence in each other or in their commander. This heterogeneous body was now to be attacked by a real army, under the command of the most accomplished soldier of the day, General Robert E. Lee. [11]

McClellan's army abandoned its camp at Harrison's Landing on the 13 August, and the same day Longstreet was ordered to proceed to Gordonsville, where Lee himself took command on the 15th. Stuart's cavalry, and the remainder of the army quickly followed, with the exception of two brigades of infantry left to guard the capital against cavalry raids.

Lee now had about 55,000 seasoned troops; he occupied interior lines between Pope and McClellan, and he laid his plans to overwhelm the Army of Virginia before it could be joined by the Army of the Potomac. Pope's army, of about 45,000 men, had its centre at Cedar Mountain, with its right flank resting upon Robertson River to the west of the railway, and its left on the Rapidan to the east, the line being eight or ten miles long. Nearly opposite Pope's left flank, on the south side of the Rapidan, was a high wooded hill called Clark's Mountain, with spurs stretching down to the river at Sommerville Ford, about two miles above Raccoon Ford where the Union line rested on the Rapidan.

On Clark's Mountain Jackson had established a signal

[10] 16 O. R., 27.   [11] 2 Ropes, 253.

station from which there was an extensive view, covering a peaceful and pastoral district, which had not yet known the ravages of war, but whose rivers and villages were soon to become household words. Northward, beyond the green crest of Cedar Mountain, and the woods which hide the Rapidan, lie the wide and fertile plains of Culpeper. Just visible in the middle distance are the dim levels of Brandy Station, the scene of the great cavalry battle of the following June. On the horizon can be faintly traced the Bull Run Mountains, which mark the source of the creek, and the plateau of Manassas, the scene of the first battle of the war, and soon to be the field of an even more sanguinary conflict. To the east, as far as the eye can reach, is the great forest of Spottsylvania, where the armies of Grant and Lee were to meet in deadly combat; within whose gloomy depths the gallant Jackson was to receive his mortal wound on the field of Chancellorsville; and on the further edge of which Burnside was to wreck his brave army against the fieldworks of Fredericksburg.

On the 17 August, Lee had his army massed behind this mountain. His position gave him an excellent opportunity to cross at Sommerville Ford, fall upon Pope's left flank, and cut off his line of retreat. Probably at no time during the war was a finer chance put within his grasp.[12]

Lee's orders were to have Stuart's cavalry cross at a ford further to the east, dash for Rappahannock Station, and destroy the bridge behind Pope's position. Failure on the part of Fitz Lee to understand, or to execute promptly, an order of Stuart, caused a delay of two days, and also led to the capture of a staff officer carrying a copy of Lee's order, which disclosed his plan. Pope immediately took alarm, and withdrew his army behind the Rappahannock. No such unfortunate *contretemps* had occurred in war since the capture of Napoleon's orders to Bernadotte saved the Russian army from destruction during the Campaign of Poland in 1807.

Lee now advanced to the Rappahannock, which he found low and easily fordable. He then spent five days in making feints to find a favorable opening to cross, and

[12] Alexander, 186.

turn Pope's right. Meanwhile Stuart made a bold raid in rear of the Union army, and turned the tables by capturing Pope's headquarters, with his despatch-book containing much valuable information. Lee thus learned that the corps of Heintzelman and Porter, and Reynolds's division of Pennsylvania Reserves, 20,000 men in all, were within two days' march of Pope, and that the remainder of the Army of the Potomac was not more than a week behind. In this situation, Lee's only hope was in acting quickly, and he decided upon one of the most daring operations recorded in the annals of war. While he himself remained on the Rappahannock, with Longstreet's force of some 30,000 men, to occupy Pope's attention, he started Jackson, and Stuart's cavalry, about 24,000 men in all, to make a wide turning movement to the left, and strike at the Union line of communications.

Starting on the morning of the 25 August, Jackson marched that day to Salem, by way of Amissville and Orleans. The following day, without meeting any resistance, he pushed on through Thoroughfare Gap and Gainesville to Bristoe Station, on the Orange and Alexandria Railroad, where he arrived about sunset. That same night, Stuart's cavalry and two regiments of infantry captured Manassas Junction, a few miles to the north. The supplies of the Union army stored at Manassas " presented a sight to the ragged and half-starved Confederates, such as they had never before imagined." [13] There were acres of warehouses filled to overflowing; two miles of side-tracks covered with loaded cars; and immense quantities of goods of every kind stacked in the open fields under tarpaulin covers. After his men had feasted, and supplied themselves with everything they could wear, or store in their haversacks, Jackson gave orders to apply the torch. When Pope looked upon the ashes the next day, he must have regretted his words: " Let us study the probable lines of retreat of our opponents, and leave our own to take care of themselves."

The movement of Jackson's column on the morning of the 25th was observed by the Federals, but they thought

[13] Alexander, 194.

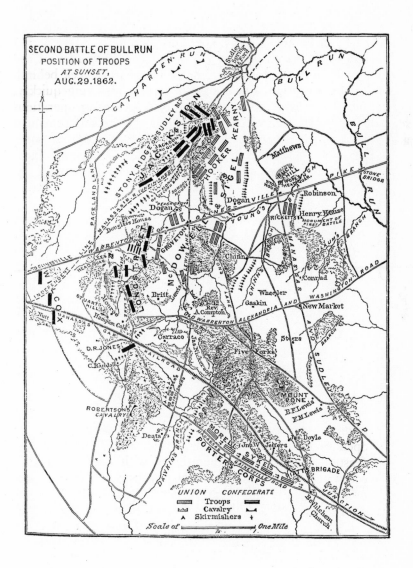

SECOND BATTLE OF BULL RUN
POSITION OF TROOPS
AT SUNSET,
AUG. 29. 1862.

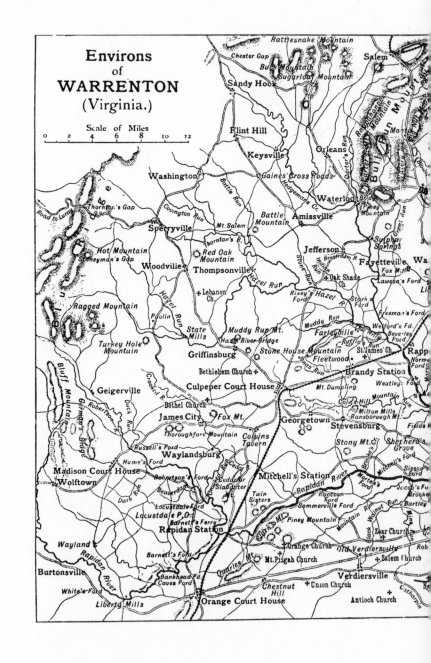

Environs
of
WARRENTON
(Virginia.)

Scale of Miles
0   2   4   6   8   10   12

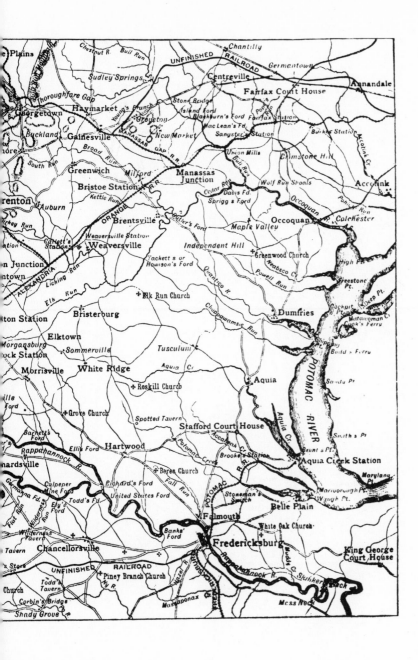

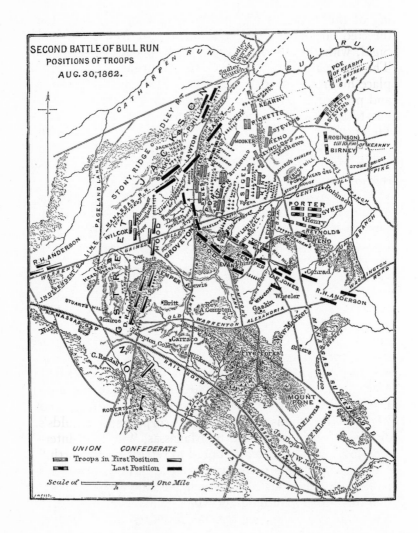

SECOND BATTLE OF BULL RUN
POSITIONS OF TROOPS
AUG. 30, 1862.

UNION   CONFEDERATE
Troops in First Position
Last Position

Scale of   One Mile

that it was going to the Valley, and no troops were sent to observe its march. Pope's army also made no move on the 26th, and that day Lee followed Jackson, with Longstreet's wing, which bivouacked at Orleans.

When Pope finally realized the situation, on the morning of the 27th, his first orders were very judicious. He directed on Gainesville the two corps of McDowell and Sigel, with the division of Reynolds, about 40,000 men. The occupation of this point with a strong force would place his troops directly between Jackson and Longstreet and prevent their junction: Gainesville was therefore the key to the whole position. In support of this movement, Heintzelman and Reno were sent to Greenwich, with three divisions; and Hooker was ordered to Bristoe, to attack Ewell, with Porter marching to support him. Banks remained in the rear to protect the trains.

McDowell and Heintzelman reached their destinations without opposition. At about two o'clock Hooker came in contact with Ewell at Bristoe, and attacked vigorously. Ewell was superior in numbers, but he had orders not to bring on a general engagement; so after an hour of resistance he retreated to Manassas.[14]

Pope now made the first of his many blunders in this campaign. As yet he had no conception that Lee was marching " to throw himself into the lion's den by the side of Jackson." Instead of manœuvring, therefore, in such a manner as to prevent their junction, his only idea was to " bag Jackson." [15] Accordingly, at 1 A.M. on the 28th he ordered Porter and Heintzelman to march to Bristoe; Reno from Greenwich to Manassas; and McDowell, with his own and Sigel's corps, and Reynolds's division, from Gainesville to Manassas, " so as to intercept Jackson in case he attempted to retreat to the north." He thus deliberately threw away the advantages of his position at Gainesville, and made possible the easy junction of the two Confederate wings. Only McDowell had sense enough, on his own responsibility, to order Ricketts's division of his corps to take position in front of Thoroughfare Gap. It was this order for all of his troops to march

14 Alexander, 194.   15 Alexander, 195.

on Manassas " at the very earliest blush of dawn," as
Pope poetically expressed it, which lost him the campaign.[16]

But Jackson did not wait at Manassas to be caught in a
trap. On the night of the 27th he sent the Stonewall
division [17] northward by the Sudley Springs road to cross
the turnpike and take position beyond Groveton. Early
the following morning Ewell's division marched to the
same place, crossing Bull Run at Blackburn's Ford, trav-
ersing the fields north of the stream, and recrossing to
the right bank at the Stone Bridge. Later in the day,
the division of A. P. Hill followed, marching north to
Centreville, and thence westward on the Warrenton
Pike. The divisions had been sent by these roundabout
routes for the purpose of mystifying Pope.

When Pope himself reached Manassas about noon on
the 28th he found Jackson gone, and could learn nothing
definite as to his destination. Later, he heard that Hill's
division had been seen at Centreville, and accordingly
issued orders at 4:15 for all his troops to march to that
place. Heintzelman and Reno went directly to Centreville; Sigel and Reynolds countermarched to the turnpike,
but did not cross Bull Run. King's division of McDowell's
corps turned eastward on the pike toward Centreville, and
about 5:30 was suddenly fired upon by Jackson's artillery.
Immediately afterwards it was attacked by the divisions
of Taliaferro and Ewell, and a fierce engagement ensued,
which lasted until seven o'clock, with heavy losses on both
sides. No advantage was gained by either party. Owing to
the length of the Federal column, or the late hour of the
day, only two of King's four brigades took any part in
the action. Both Ewell and Taliaferro were severely
wounded.[18]

Jackson, about a mile from the road, might have remained hidden and allowed King to pass, but he feared
that Pope would concentrate his entire army in an impregnable position behind Bull Run, and the main object

---

[16] Alexander, 196.
[17] Known as Taliaferro's since the death of Winder at Cedar Mountain.
[18] 2 Ropes, 272.

of the campaign be lost. He therefore attacked, even at the risk of drawing upon himself Pope's whole force.[19]

News of this action soon reached Pope, at his head-quarters near Manassas, and he jumped to the conclusion that Jackson was in full retreat from Centreville for Thoroughfare Gap. He therefore at once issued orders for the assembling of his troops on the Warrenton Pike. In his orders he wrote: "General McDowell has intercepted the retreat of the enemy, and is now in his front. . . . Unless he can escape by by-paths leading to the north to-night, he must be captured." Pope was entirely mistaken in his conjecture; and, in fact, he failed to draw a single correct inference during the course of this campaign. Not only was he in the dark regarding the intentions of his adversary, but he was also ignorant of the positions of his own corps. Therefore, instead of directing Hooker, who bivouacked south of Bull Run, to join Sigel by marching up the Sudley Springs road, he sent him by way of Centreville; and Porter, who was at Bristoe Station, was also ordered to make this wholly unnecessary détour.[20]

In the meantime the head of Longstreet's column had reached Thoroughfare Gap, about three o'clock on this same day, the 28 August. This gap is the outlet by which the Manassas Gap Railroad, passing from the Shenandoah, penetrates the last mountainous obstruction on its way to tide-water. It is a rough pass in the Bull Run Mountains, at some points not more than a hundred yards wide. A turbid stream rushes over its rugged bottom, on both sides of which the mountain rises several hundred feet. On the north the face of the gap is almost perpendicular. The south face is less precipitous, but is covered with tangled mountain ivy and projecting bowlders, forming an impregnable position when occupied by even a small force of infantry and artillery.[21]

At the eastern end of this gap, the Confederates encountered resistance from Ricketts's division, which, it will be remembered, McDowell had wisely ordered there, to

[19] Alexander, 199.   [21] 2 B. & L., 517.
[20] See 2 Ropes, 273, note.

postpone as long as possible the union of the two wings of Lee's army. Finding the position too strong to assail, Longstreet turned it by sending a force through Hopewell Gap, a few miles to the north. At nightfall, therefore, Ricketts retired to Gainesville, whence a short march would have united his division to that of King. Connecting with King on the right was the division of Reynolds; and on his right was the corps of Sigel. These forces were strong enough to hold their own until Pope could reenforce them in the morning. Nevertheless, King decided at 1 A.M. on the 29th to retire to Manassas; and this naturally induced Ricketts to fall back from Gainesville to Bristoe. Unfortunately McDowell was absent the whole evening, trying to find Pope, and was unable to rejoin his command until the next day.[22]

The morning of the 29 August, therefore, found the Union army badly scattered. The only troops in front of Jackson at Groveton were the corps of Sigel and Reynolds's division. Banks, Porter, and Ricketts's division of McDowell's corps, were at Bristoe; King's division of McDowell's corps, and Hooker's division of Heintzelman's corps, were at Manassas; the other division of Heintzelman (Kearny's) and Reno's two divisions were near Centreville.

It was hardly possible to unite all these forces for battle on that day; and there was nothing to prevent Longstreet from joining Jackson. The Union troops were much exhausted from their long and useless marches; rations were also scarce on account of the destruction of the dépôt at Manassas, and the fact that the trains under General Banks were so far in the rear. Under the circumstances, it would have been wiser for General Pope to withdraw his entire army behind Bull Run, for rest and refreshment, in a practically impregnable position, where he would be reënforced in a day or two by the corps of Sumner and Franklin from the Army of the Potomac.

"At the same time," writes Mr. Ropes, "notwithstanding all these facts, it was probably possible to inflict

[22] 2 Ropes, 274–275. For thus leaving his corps, McDowell was censured by a Court of Inquiry: 15 O. R., 330–331.

a severe blow on the corps of Jackson before it could be joined by that of Longstreet; but to effect this, it was necessary that General Pope should have a clear idea in his mind of what he proposed to do, and that no time should be lost by mistakes or delays, or by changes of purpose on his part." [23]

Longstreet had indeed cleared the gap, and the Federals who defended it had retired; but the main body of the Confederate army was still twelve miles away, and Jackson was confronted by vastly superior numbers. His forces had been reduced to about 23,000 effectives by the affair at Groveton. Less than two miles away, on the plateau of Manassas, were encamped 20,000 Federals, with the same number at the Junction; seven miles to the east, at Centreville, there were 18,000; and, at Bristoe Station, about the same distance, 11,000 — an aggregate of 69,000 men.

" Although it would have been sounder strategy, on the part of the Federal commander," writes Colonel Henderson, " to have concentrated toward Centreville, and have there awaited reënforcements," Pope decided to hurl his superior forces against Jackson before Lee could come up. Many motives may have influenced him to take this course; — ambition, anxiety to retrieve his blemished reputation, fear that he might be superseded by McClellan — all urged him forward.[24]

On the morning of the 29 August, the Confederate outlook was far from bright. Jackson did not yet know whether Longstreet had broken through, or even whether he *could* break through. In any event, his three divisions, worn with long marching and the fierce combat of the previous evening, would have to hold their own for several hours unaided.

The position chosen by Jackson was a very strong one. The long, flat-topped ridge, north of the Warrenton Turnpike, commands the approaches from the east and south. Some five hundred yards below the crest ran the line of an unfinished railroad, and behind the deep cuttings and high embankments the Confederate fighting-

[23] 2 Ropes, 276.   [24] 2 Henderson, 188.

line was strongly placed. The left, slightly thrown back, rested on a rocky spur, near Bull Run, commanding Sudley Springs Ford, and the road to Aldie Gap, his line of retreat. The front extended southwest for a mile and three-quarters. Early, with two brigades and a battery, occupied a wooded knoll, where the unfinished railroad crossed the pike, protecting the right rear, and stretching a hand to Longstreet.[25]

Before the right and right centre the open green pastures sloped gradually for a distance of 1300 yards to Young's Branch. The left centre and left were shut in by a belt of timber which obstructed the field of fire, but also screened the defenders from the enemy's artillery. Within the position there was ample cover for the reserves. Jackson's numbers were sufficient for the defence of the position, which was not only strong by nature, but strongly held. To every yard of the line, 3000 yards in length, there were more than five muskets, so that half the force could be retained in reserve.[26]

As Jackson was forming his lines at sunrise, the columns of Sigel and Reynolds were visible, nearly two miles away, deploying for the assault. They numbered only 19,000 men, so the attack was no stronger than the defence; and as the fire of the Federal artillery was restricted by the woods there could be little doubt of the result. The assault failed, and the Federals retreated across the fields.

But now Reno and Kearny, from Centreville, were coming on the field; and Sigel, calling on Reno for reenforcements, again made a desperate attack, which nearly broke the enemy's line. Jackson called up Branch's brigade from Hill's reserves; the wood was again cleared, and Sigel's division was put *hors de combat*. At this hour, about noon, Pope arrived on the field from Centreville. He immediately organized a fresh attack with the three divisions of Kearny, Hooker, and Reno. This assault was made about one o'clock, and portions of the attacking columns actually crossed the railroad, where a fierce hand-to-hand combat ensued. Jackson called up Pender's brigade from his reserves, and the Federals were at last

[25] 2 Henderson, 189.   [26] 2 Henderson, 190.

driven back. Pender incautiously followed, and was forced to retire under the hot fire of the Federal artillery. Seeing his retreat, Grover's brigade of Hooker's division, which was in reserve, was sent forward for a counterstroke. Grover broke through the Confederate line, and, if promptly and fully supported, had victory within his grasp.[27]

By this time, Longstreet's troops had begun to form on Jackson's right, relieving the brigades of Early and Forno, which were placed in reserve in the rear of the centre. These fresh troops, and other reserves, were sent in against Grover, who was driven back across the pike, with a loss of one-fourth his command.

The battle had now been going on for nine hours; four determined assaults had been made; and at least 4000 Federals had fallen. None of the attacks had had any chance of success, because made with too few men, and without proper support. Ignorant of Longstreet's arrival, and with fresh troops at hand, Pope was not yet willing to give up the effort, while the sun was still high above the horizon. The three brigades of Kearny, and the two of Reno were in good condition; and the corps of Porter and McDowell had not yet been in action.

In connection with Porter, there is much interesting history, which can only be briefly summarized here.

Pursuant to the 3 A.M. orders of Pope, on the morning of the 29th Porter was marching his corps from Bristoe to Groveton by way of Centreville (an unnecessary détour of ten miles), and had passed Manassas Junction, when he was met by a staff-officer of General Pope's, who gave him the purport of a written order (which was afterwards confirmed), to the effect that he (Porter) was to take King's division (of McDowell's corps) and move to Gainesville. His column at once faced about, and proceeded toward Gainesville through the Junction, where, about 11 A.M., he was joined by McDowell. An hour later he received a third order, addressed to McDowell as well as himself, known subsequently as the " Joint Order."

From this order two things are plain: (1) That Pope

[27] Alexander, 205–206.

believed that Jackson had retreated, and that they must not follow him even so far as Gainesville, because the army must be brought back at night to Centreville for needed supplies; (2) that if, contrary to his expectation, Jackson had not retreated, he would have to deal only with Jackson, and not with the whole of Lee's army united.

The two generals soon discovered that the situation was very different from that indicated in the Joint Order: Jackson had *not* retreated, and they had to deal with *the whole* of Lee's army. About 11:30, at a little stream called Dawkin's Branch, three and a half miles from Gainesville, they encountered the van of Longstreet's army, which had left Thoroughfare Gap that morning. At the same time it was evident from the clouds of dust in the direction of Gainesville that large bodies of troops were following.

The order in question contained a clause reading: " If any considerable advantages are to be gained by departing from this order, it will not be strictly carried out." After consultation, the two generals decided to avail themselves of this latitude. McDowell accordingly departed with King's division, leaving Porter where he was.

Porter, with only 9000 or 10,000 men, was thus left isolated. His plain task was simply to observe, or contain, the troops in his front, and this task he fully performed. Pope did not know that Longstreet had arrived, and when, at the close of the afternoon, he gave Porter a positive written order to attack Jackson's right flank, which he supposed to be " in the air," he could not understand Porter's failure to act. As ascertained later, the facts were, that when Porter arrived on the crest of the hills which descend to Dawkin's Branch, he encountered the advance of Longstreet's four divisions of 25,000 men; that Lee himself was on the field two or three hours before Pope in person arrived; and that " Porter with his two divisions saved the Army of Virginia that day from disaster due to the enemy's earlier preparation for battle." Furthermore, Porter's right was not in connection or communication with Reynolds, who held the left of the main line; and he was separated by Longstreet's entire corps from Jackson's right flank which he was ordered by Pope to attack.[28]

Late in the afternoon, about five o'clock, Pope again assaulted the Confederate left, with the two divisions of Kearny and Reno. In a very gallant and persistent attack, Hill's troops were forced back fully 300 yards, but at the critical moment Jackson once more called on his reserves, and the Federals were finally compelled to retire in disorder.

We must now return to Longstreet's corps, to explain the sixth and last combat of the day. On his arrival, Longstreet had formed his line, not in prolongation of Jackson's, but inclining forward, in a large obtuse angle. Lee's intention was to engage at once, but he finally yielded to Longstreet's request that he first be allowed to make a personal reconnaissance. This took an hour, and then the day was so nearly gone, it was decided to make only a reconnaissance in force, reserving the attack until early the next morning. Meanwhile McDowell had brought King's division on the field, and Pope had given orders for it to advance down the pike and fall upon Jackson's right, where, too, he was looking for Porter's attack. It thus happened that when King's division went forward to the attack, instead of finding Jackson in retreat, it met Longstreet advancing. King's weary troops were defeated in a fierce combat, which lasted until after nine o'clock.[29]

After the repulse and pursuit of King, Longstreet withdrew his men to the line from which they had advanced, and Jackson ordered his men back from the railroad cut, their line during the day, to the crest a few hundred yards in the rear. It thus happened that the Federals were left with a deserted battle-field in their front. Had this been a deliberate ruse, says General Alexander, it would have been a masterpiece. To Pope, it proved to be a fatal delusion and a snare. At daybreak he telegraphed Halleck

[28] The unjust sentence of the Court Martial, which ordered Porter to be cashiered, was reversed at a new hearing in 1878, when all of the facts were available, and he was restored to the army. See 2 B. & L., 695–697; Alexander, 207–208; 2 Ropes, 277–282; Upton, 341 et seq. Also the unwarranted comments of Steele (252).

[29] Alexander, 209–210.

that, after a terrible battle, with combined forces of the enemy, lasting from daylight until dark, the enemy was driven from the field which he then occupied. He concluded: " The news has just reached me from the front that the enemy is retreating toward the mountains."

This was Pope's last and greatest blunder, which made him the aggressor on the second day, and cost him the battle.

On the morning of the 30 August, Pope had united his entire army except the corps of Banks, which, not yet recovered from the affair of Cedar Mountain, was in charge of the trains near Bristoe. Before daybreak Porter had been withdrawn from his isolated position on the left, and brought around to the centre. Pope now had on the field 65,000 men and 28 batteries. Besides, the corps of Sumner and Franklin, and the divisions of Cox and Sturgis, about 42,000 troops in all, had landed at Alexandria, and were only twenty-five miles away.

Lee had in hand the force of Jackson, reduced to about 17,000, the troops of Longstreet, 30,000, and some 2500 cavalry, an aggregate of nearly 50,000 men. He also had about 20,000 reënforcements coming up, and already at the Rappahannock River.[30]

Pope spent several hours in forming his troops, and setting his army in battle array, with a view of avoiding the isolated attacks of the previous day, and pressing the " retreating " Confederates along the whole line.

The Union line was short and strong. From its right on Bull Run, in front of Jackson's left, to its left across the turnpike near Groveton, was less than three miles. About 20,000 infantry were deployed in the front line, with 40,000 more massed behind. Lee's line covered at least four miles. Jackson still held the left, in the strong position behind the railroad cut. Except for a battery of 18 guns, under Colonel S. D. Lee, which was placed on his right flank, he had received no reënforcements. Longstreet's line, as already stated, was not prolongation of Jackson's, but bent forward at an obtuse angle; and it considerably overlapped the Union left.

[30] Alexander, 211.

Pope, from his headquarters on Buck Hill near his centre, could see only a few Confederate batteries, supported by a strong line of skirmishers, and he could not be convinced by his officers that the enemy was not in full retreat. About noon the Federals attacked in force, and met a reception for which Pope was not prepared. The battle which followed was scarcely surpassed for desperation on either side during the war.[31]

The whole weight of the assault fell upon Jackson, who called for assistance. The Federals, in their attack, had advanced into the angle between Jackson and Longstreet, so that their line could be enfiladed. Longstreet sent several batteries into position, and opened upon the Union flank with a fire which nothing could withstand. In vain Pope sent in his reserves to stem the tide of retreat. Jackson ordered forward two brigades, in a counter-stroke, and Pope's battle was lost.

Seeing the effect of Longstreet's fire, about four o'clock Lee ordered a general advance. The objective point aimed at by Longstreet was the Henry House plateau, where Jackson's brigade, " standing like a stone wall," had made his name immortal thirteen months before. The capture of this position would have cut off the Federal retreat across Bull Run by the Stone Bridge, and here Pope made a desperate stand. Fortunately for the Federals the hour was too late for Lee to gather the full fruits of his victory; the daylight was also shortened by heavy clouds, and a rain set in about dusk which continued during the night and much of the next day.[32]

The Federal troops, in great disorder, poured across the bridge and through the fords toward Centreville. Here the whole army was concentrated on the corps of Franklin, which had arrived about six o'clock, only a few hours too late to reach the field and save the day.

As the Federal position at Centreville was very strong, Lee decided to turn it. On the morning of the 31st, Jackson's corps, preceded by Stuart's cavalry, was ordered to cross Bull Run at Sudley, and march by the Little River Turnpike on Fairfax Court House. Longstreet was to

[31] Alexander, 213.   [32] Alexander, 215.

collect the spoils on the battle-field, and then to follow Jackson. Progress was slow on account of the rain and mud.

Pope, although still claiming a victory, ordered Banks to destroy the trains at Bristoe, and join him by a night march. With Franklin, Banks, and Sumner, who arrived on the 31st, he now had 30,000 fresh troops, but he remained at Centreville only a single day. The whole army was withdrawn to Fairfax, where it was too close to its fortified lines to be flanked again out of position.

On the first day of September there was a small affair at Chantilly, in which Stevens, who commanded a division of Reno's corps, was shot through the head; and Kearny, who had ridden into the Confederate lines in the dusk, was killed in trying to escape. They both were prominent and distinguished officers. Stevens had graduated at the head of Halleck's class at West Point in 1839; and at the time of his death the Government was considering his appointment to the command of the now united armies of Pope and McClellan.[33]

The losses of the two armies for the entire campaign are summarized as follows: [34]

	Federals	Confederates
Killed	1,747	1,468
Wounded	8,452	7,563
Missing	4,263	81
Totals	14,462	9,112

The Confederates collected 30 guns and over 20,000 small-arms from the field of battle.

The results of the campaign are very ably summed up by General Alexander in two brief paragraphs: [35]

" While Lee had fallen short of destroying his greatly superior adversaries, he could yet look back with pride upon the record he had made within the ninety days since

[33] Alexander, 218.

[34] Alexander, 219. In 2 B. & L., 500, the Confederate losses are given as 9,474. Livermore (88) puts the Union losses at 16,054 and the Confederate at 9197.

[35] Alexander, 218.

taking command on the first of June. He had had the use of about 85,000 men, and the enemy had had the use, in all, of fully 200,000.

"At the beginning, the enemy had been within six miles of Richmond. He was now driven within the fortifications of Washington, with a loss in the two campaigns of about 33,000 men, 82 guns, and 58,000 small-arms. Lee's own losses had been about 31,000 men and two guns."

In his comments on the campaign, Mr. Ropes writes: "General Lee's operations had indeed been successful, but we must point out that his successes were due much more to the ability with which he improved the mistakes of his antagonist, than to any advantages which he procured for himself by the hazardous strategy which he employed. . . . Of these mistakes Lee took prompt advantage, and thus won his victory." [36]

These remarks, from a critic of the standing of Mr. Ropes, are surprising.

It is true that Napoleon, in his *Maxims*, warns against the division of an army into two columns unable to communicate; and especially against the strategy which places the point of junction in the very presence of a concentrated enemy. Both of these maxims Lee violated: *the first because he knew Jackson, the last because he knew Pope.* It is rare indeed that such strategy succeeds, and it has been remarked that, after Jackson's death, Lee never again attempted those great turning movements which had achieved his most brilliant victories.

"History," says Colonel Henderson, "often unconsciously injures the reputation of great soldiers. The more detailed the narrative, the less brilliant seems success, the less excusable defeat." [37]

"If," said Frederick the Great, "we had exact information of our enemy's dispositions, we should beat him every time."

"It is too often overlooked, by those who study the history of campaigns," says Colonel Henderson again, "that war is the province of uncertainty. The reader has the

[36] 2 Ropes, 311.   [37] 1 Henderson, 509.

[145]

whole theatre of war displayed before him. He notes the exact disposition of the opposing forces at each hour of the campaign, and with this in his mind's eye he condemns or approves the action of the commanders. In the action of the defeated general he often sees much to blame; in the action of the successful general but little to admire. But his judgment is not based on a true foundation. He has ignored the fact that the information at his disposal was not at the disposal of those he criticises; and until he realizes that both generals, to a greater or less degree, must have been groping in the dark, he will neither make just allowance for the errors of the one, nor appreciate the genius of the other." [38]

As a tactician, Pope was incapable. As a strategist, he lacked imagination, except in his despatches. Lee, with his extraordinary insight into character, played on Pope as he had played on McClellan, and his strategy was justified by success. If, as Moltke states, the junction of two armies on the field of battle is the highest achievement of military genius, the campaign against Pope has seldom been surpassed. Lee's strategy was certainly hazardous, but against an antagonist of different calibre he would never have attempted such manœuvres. To condemn them is therefore short-sighted criticism.[39]

"How often," says Napier, " have we not heard the genius of Bonaparte slighted, and his victories talked of as destitute of merit, because, at the point of attack, he was superior in numbers to his enemies. This very fact . . . constitutes his greatest and truest praise." It is often forgotten that Napoleon, in nearly all of his campaigns, was outnumbered in the whole theatre of war — not only in Italy, but in the campaigns of Ulm, Austerlitz, Eckmuhl, Dresden, Leipzig, France (1814), and Waterloo. He never waited for his adversary to become fully prepared, but struck him the first blow. The first principle of war is to concentrate superior force at the decisive point, that is, upon the field of battle. But this principle can never be observed by standing still and permitting the enemy to concentrate. True generalship is,

[38] 2 Henderson, 239–240.   [39] 2 Henderson, 230–232.

therefore, " to make up in activity for lack of strength ";
to strike the enemy in detail, and overthrow his columns
in succession. To claim therefore that Lee's victory was
due, less to his strategy, than to his ability to improve the
mistakes of his antagonist, is absurd.

Another of Napoleon's maxims says: " The first
qualification in a general-in-chief is a cool head — that is,
a head which receives just impressions, and estimates
things and objects at their real value." This, General
Pope certainly did not have. He never made a correct inference during the whole campaign, and consequently
committed one blunder after another. With each new report he changed his mind regarding the situation and
issued new orders. He wore his men out with marching
and countermarching, and destroyed what little confidence
they already had in him by his vacillating and contradictory orders.

After he knew of the arrival of Lee's army, he should
not have renewed his attack on the 30th, but have remained on the defensive, or withdrawn his army across
Bull Run, to await the arrival of the other corps of the
Army of the Potomac. But again he drew a false conclusion: he thought that Lee had begun to retreat, and accordingly gave orders to pursue.

It is difficult, moreover, to agree with the statement of
Mr. Ropes, adopted by Major Steele,[40] that the Union
army, though " beaten and badly beaten; still . . . was
not forced from the field "; and that it was only Pope's
retreat on the night of the 30th which " stamped the
whole campaign as a failure."

Pope, indeed, " with an audacity which disaster was
powerless to tame," reported to Halleck that the enemy
was " badly whipped." But these statements do not agree
with the descriptions of the utter confusion and disorder
of the Federal retreat as recorded by other writers.[41]

At the beginning of the campaign Pope handled his
cavalry very well. They " were employed with a boldness
which had not hitherto been seen." Led by two able young

[40] *Cf.* 2 Ropes, 302; Steele, 257.
[41] See Alexander, 215; also Powell in 2 *B. & L.*, 469; McClellan,
Ib., 549; Longstreet, *Ib.*, 521; and Upton, 373.

generals, Buford and Bayard, they did far better service than McClellan's detectives. There were frequent reconnaissances, and outposts were maintained twenty miles in advance of the army.[42] But at the end they were utterly broken down, — " worn out by courier and escort service "; so that at Centreville Pope had to send out a brigade of infantry on reconnaissance, because " there was absolutely no cavalry fit for service."

The work of the Confederate cavalry, as usual, was excellent. While the armies were facing each other on the Rappahannock, Stuart rode around Pope's flank, and captured his headquarters, with much valuable information. During Jackson's famous march, Stuart's cavalry was in the van, and covering the flanks. On the morning of the 31 August, Stuart reported to Lee before eight o'clock that the Federal army was at Centreville. Again, when Jackson moved out on the Little River Turnpike, Stuart led the way. If Pope had used his cavalry as well as Lee, there might have been a very different outcome to the campaign.[43]

[42] 2 Henderson, 104.   [43] Steele, 259.

CHAPTER EIGHT

SEPTEMBER 1862

ANTIETAM

Lee Invades Maryland — His Motives — His Army — His Line of
Communications — Jackson Sent to Harper's Ferry — McClellan
Reinstated — The Union Army Reorganized — The Advance to
South Mountain — The Famous "Lost Order" — Capture of
Harper's Ferry — McClellan Forces the Gaps — Lee Decides to
Stand at Sharpsburg — Comments — The Field of Battle —
Lee's Position — The Two Armies — McClellan's Delay — His
Plan of Battle — The Attacks of Hooker and Mansfield Fail —
Sumner Repulsed — The "Bloody Lane" — Cox Carries the
Burnside Bridge — End of the Battle — Numbers and Losses —
Final Comments

O N the morning of the 2 September, as soon as he
knew that Pope had found shelter within the defences of Washington, Lee ordered Jackson to
cross the Potomac, and form the vanguard of an invasion
of the North. Hitherto, the Confederates had been content to play the rôle of defenders, and they had played it
to perfection. Although they had awaited the attack within
their own frontiers, their tactics had been essentially offensive: it was by strategical and tactical counter-strokes
that the recent victories had been won. Like Napoleon,
Lee and Jackson believed that the best defence lies not in
strong positions, but in the concentration of superior numbers on the field of battle. But if the best defence lies in a
vigorous offensive, to make victory complete it is necessary to carry the war into hostile territory. The Great
War has proved conclusively that even if a nation is
brought to the point of making terms by the defeat of
its armies beyond its own frontiers, it is never really conquered unless its capital is occupied, and the hideous suf-
ferings of war are brought directly home to the mass of
the population. " A single victory on Northern soil . . .

was far more likely to bring about the independence of the South than even a succession of victories in Virginia." [1]

Such were the ideas, advocated by General Lee, and accepted by President Davis, which led to the invasion of Maryland. Nevertheless, Lee himself had no great expectations of decisive results. He wrote Mr. Davis: " The army is not properly equipped for an invasion of the enemy's territory. It lacks much of the material of war, is feeble in transportation, the animals being much reduced; the men are poorly provided with clothes, and in thousands of instances are destitute of shoes. . . . What concerns me most is the fear of getting out of ammunition." At a later date (12 September), Lee wrote the President that the 1650 pairs of shoes obtained at Frederick, Williamsport, and Hagerstown, would " not be sufficient to cover the bare feet of the army." [2]

The captures made in the Peninsula, and especially at Manassas, had proved of the greatest value. Old muskets had been exchanged for new, smooth-bore cannon for rifled guns, tattered blankets for good overcoats. Their well-supplied foes had furnished the impoverished Confederates with tents, medicines, ambulances, ammunition wagons, and war material of every kind. Many of the soldiers were clad in Federal uniforms, and even the wagons at Lee's headquarters were marked with the initials U. S. A. [3]

Lee had been joined by the three divisions of D. H. Hill, McLaws, and Walker, and by Hampton's cavalry, and he should have had at this time about 65,000 effectives, but there were thousands of stragglers.

When Lee began his invasion of Maryland there were about 14,000 Union troops in the lower Shenandoah Valley: 3000 infantry and artillery at Winchester; 3000 cavalry at Martinsburg, and a garrison of 8000 at Harper's Ferry. Lee was aware of the presence of these forces, but he thought that they would all be withdrawn as soon as it was known that he had crossed the Potomac. If it had depended on McClellan this would have been done; but

[1] 2 Henderson, 248.
[2] 28 O. R., 590, 591, 605.
[3] 2 Henderson, 253.

Halleck gave orders for the commander at Harper's Ferry to hold that position.

Lee thus found his situation suddenly complicated. His line of communications, which ran from Manassas by Leesburg to Frederick, was too near to Washington, and in danger of being cut at any moment by the Federal cavalry. Arrangements had already been made, therefore, to transfer the line to the Valley; but this line also would be exposed so long as Harper's Ferry was garrisoned by the enemy. It was manifestly out of the question for Lee, with his small forces, to mask this post, and nothing remained but to capture it by a *coup de main*. Jackson, with 25,000 men, nearly half the Confederate army, was detailed for the expedition, and he was ordered to march at daybreak on the 10 September. Meanwhile, the remainder of the army was to move northwest to Hagerstown, twenty-five miles from Frederick, where it would threaten Pennsylvania with invasion, and be protected from McClellan by the parallel ranges of the Catoctin and South mountains.

When the army under Pope retreated within the lines of Washington, there was great alarm at the capital, and both the President and General Halleck feared that " it was impossible to save the city." At an early hour on the morning of the 2 September they called together on General McClellan, who had come up from Alexandria the previous day. The President stated, writes McClellan, that " the army was entirely defeated and falling back to Washington in confusion. He then said that he regarded Washington as lost, and asked me if I would, under the circumstances, consent to accept command of all the forces." [4] McClellan at once accepted, and this verbal order of the President was the only one by which he was reinstated in command. [5]

Making a virtue of necessity, Pope asked to be relieved, and was sent to a distant post in the Northwest where there were some Indian disturbances.

The reinstatement of McClellan was very popular with

[4] 2 B. & L., 549.　　　　[5] Palfrey, *Campaigns*, 5

the army, and did much to restore the *moral* of the troops. On his first appearance he was greeted with " frantic cheers of welcome that extended for miles along the column." Yet neither the President nor Halleck had any confidence in him, and the appointment was made with great reluctance. General McClellan himself says that he fought the campaign with a " halter around his neck," and if the Army of the Potomac had been defeated, he would have been condemned like General Porter, and perhaps executed.[6] This feeling undoubtedly influenced McClellan's actions during the campaign, and was most unfortunate.

The army which McClellan led from Washington was made up of the First Corps under Hooker; the Second under Sumner; of one division of the Fourth Corps under Couch; of the Sixth under Franklin; of the Ninth under Reno; and the Twelfth under Mansfield. Couch's division was attached to the Sixth Corps, and Cox's (Kanawha) division was at this time incorporated in the Ninth Corps.

The First and Ninth corps formed the right, under General Burnside; the Second and Twelfth, the centre, under General Sumner; and the Sixth Corps, with the division of Couch, constituted the left, under General Franklin.

General Banks was assigned to the " command of the defences of the capital," and had under him the Third Corps (Heintzelman), the Fifth (Porter), and the Seventh (Sigel).

At the time it left Washington, the army numbered on paper 84,000 men — in reality less than 70,000. About the same number (72,000) was left under Banks; but on the 12 September, at the urgent request of McClellan, Porter was sent to him, with the two divisions of Morrell and Sykes, about 13,000 men, thus raising his forces nominally to an aggregate of 97,000.

On the 7 September the corps of the Army of the Potomac occupied the following positions: Hooker and Burnside were at Leesboro; Sumner and Mansfield were

<hr />

[6] See page 179 *infra*.

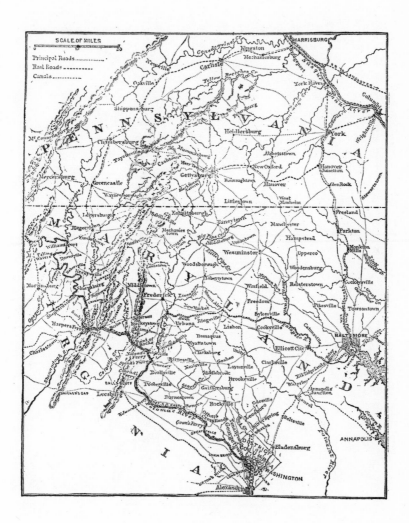

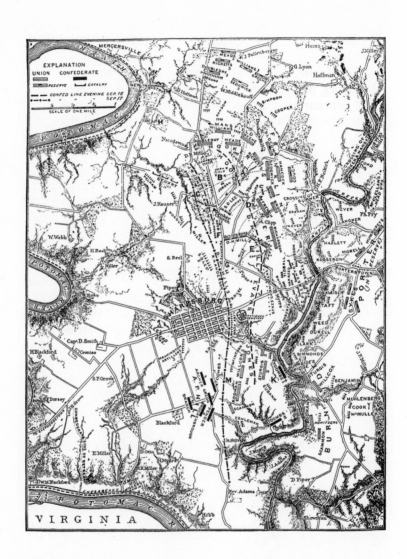

in front of Rockville; Franklin was at Rockville; and Couch was at Offutt's Cross Roads. The Union cavalry, under Pleasanton, was well in front, and in contact with Stuart, who formed a screen for Lee's army. From the 6th to the 15th, when Stuart finally retired behind the Antietam, there were daily engagements between the two cavalry forces.

Lee's army had crossed the Potomac by the fords near Leesburg on the 4th to the 6th, and on the 7 September was concentrated near Frederick. Here, on the 9th, he issued his famous order, known as " Special Orders No. 191," for the movement on Harper's Ferry. Jackson, with his corps (except D. H. Hill's division) was ordered via Williamsport to drive the Federals from Martinsburg into Harper's Ferry, which he would then attack from the south. Walker's division was to cross the Potomac below Harper's Ferry and occupy Loudoun Heights. McLaws, with his own division and Anderson's, was to march by the most direct route, and take possession of Maryland Heights, which command Harper's Ferry.

Harper's Ferry, at the junction of the Shenandoah with the Potomac, is nearly fifty miles northwest of Washington, in a straight line. Loudoun Heights, at the northern end of the Blue Ridge, are thirty miles from Washington, between Harper's Ferry and Leesburg, where Lee crossed the Potomac. Maryland Heights, on the north side of the river, opposite Harper's Ferry, are the hills at the southern end of Elk Ridge, the range next west of South Mountain. Frederick is in Maryland, forty miles north by west of Washington.

The Union army had moved very slowly, on account of the " fears of the authorities at Washington, and the necessity of reorganization." On the 9th, Couch's division, the extreme left, touched the Potomac, at the mouth of Seneca Creek. Franklin's corps was at Darnestown. The Second and Twelfth corps, constituting the centre, were at Middlebrook, and the First and Ninth, forming the right, were at Brookeville. Thus the army was still within twenty miles of the capital, on a front stretching from left to right of about twenty-five miles.

On the night of the 13th, having advanced only about twenty miles in four days, the army was concentrated near Frederick. In the meantime, Lee had crossed the mountains, and was at Hagerstown.

On his arrival at Frederick, on the 13th, an official copy of Lee's order No. 191, addressed to D. H. Hill, fell into McClellan's hands, and gave him an opportunity rarely presented to a general. This order told McClellan two things, both of great importance:

First, that Lee had divided his army, and sent Jackson to capture Harper's Ferry.

Second, where the remainder of the Confederate army was to march and to halt, and where the detached commands were to rejoin the main body.

This information placed the Army of Northern Virginia absolutely at the mercy of McClellan, provided he acted with the greatest celerity. If he despatched his left column through Crampton's Gap, it would fall directly upon the rear of McLaws at Maryland Heights. If he advanced his right, through Turner's Gap, he would interpose between Hill and Longstreet on the one hand, and Jackson's command on the other. These two Federal columns had less than twenty miles to march; the gaps were not held in any force before the morning of the 14th, and Harper's Ferry was not surrendered until 8 A.M. on the 15th. It must be admitted that, for him, McClellan acted with considerable energy: he almost grasped the opportunity, but not entirely.

Lee's movements, which were earlier in point of time, will be described first. Jackson left Frederick early on the 10th, and marched rapidly twenty-five miles through Middletown and Boonsboro, to Williamsport, where he crossed the Potomac the next morning. Hearing of the Confederate movement, the Union forces at Martinsburg abandoned that town on the night of the 11th and retreated to Harper's Ferry. Jackson followed, and on the 12th went into camp near Halltown, about two miles from the Union position on Bolivar Heights.

On the 10th, McLaws also moved, by way of Pleasant Valley, which separates South Mountain on the east from

Elk Ridge on the west. The southern extremity of the ridge, Maryland Heights, completely commands Harper's Ferry on the opposite bank of the Potomac. McLaws easily drove the small Union force from the heights, and gained full possession on the afternoon of the 13th. He at once placed his artillery in position, and opened fire at two o'clock the following afternoon.

The third Confederate column, under Walker, crossed the Potomac at Point of Rocks, on the night of the 10th, and on the 13th occupied Loudoun Heights, where he arranged his forces so as to prevent the escape of the garrison of Harper's Ferry down the right bank of the Potomac.

Harper's Ferry was now completely surrounded, and at the mercy of the enemy. At daybreak on the 15th, the Confederate guns opened fire, and at eight o'clock the Federal commander displayed the white flag. As the results of the expedition, Jackson captured over 12,000 men, with 73 pieces of artillery, many small-arms, and other stores.

The first part of Lee's program had been carried out successfully, although not quite as expeditiously as he had hoped, and the delay nearly proved fatal to him.

Leaving Hill to receive the surrender of the Federal troops and property, Jackson started at once to rejoin Lee in Maryland. By a severe night march of seventeen miles he reached Sharpsburg on the morning of the 16th. Walker's division followed closely, and also reported to General Lee the same morning.

To return now to General McClellan, whom we left at Frederick, on the 13th, with Lee's order in his hands. He decided not to move his left by the most direct road, through Jefferson and Knoxville, and thence up the river to Harper's Ferry, but by Burkittsville to Crampton's Gap, while the centre and right marched by Middletown to Turner's Gap. The Union left would thus debouch in rear of McLaws at Maryland Heights, and the remainder of the army between Longstreet and Hill on the right and Jackson's corps on the left.

The Blue Ridge Mountains cross Maryland from north to south in two distinct ranges six or eight miles apart, with a fertile valley between them. These ranges are known as the Catoctin and South mountains. The latter is a formidable obstacle, and can be crossed by an army only at two gaps, Turner's and Crampton's. There were several turnpikes in the region, of which the best known was the Old National Road, which passed westward through Frederick and crossed South Mountain at Turner's Gap. About a mile to the south, at Fox's Gap, the summit is passed by another route, known as the Old Sharpsburg, or Braddock, road, because it was used by General Braddock's army, in 1755. At about an equal distance to the north, still another road, the Old Hagerstown Road, finds a passage over the ridge. The National Road, because of easier grades and better engineering, was then, as now, the principal route, the others having remained rough country roads. The mountain crests are from 1000 to 1300 feet above the valley, and the gaps are 200 to 300 feet below the summits. There were other dirt roads in every direction, and all of them were in good condition at this season of the year. There were many small towns and villages, of which the most considerable was Frederick. It was on the whole a thickly settled farming country; the mountains were generally covered with woods; as also the valleys, except where cleared for cultivation.

General Lee's original plan had been for the main part of his army, under Longstreet, to halt at Boonsboro, with all the trains, and there await the return of Jackson, and the other detachments, while D. H. Hill's division formed the rear guard, and Stuart's cavalry covered the route. Learning, however, that a body of Pennsylvania militia had been collected at Chambersburg, Lee sent Longstreet forward to Hagerstown.

On the night of the 13th, Lee heard that a copy of his field order was in the hands of McClellan,[7] and that the advance of the Union army was at the eastern end of Turner's Gap. He immediately ordered Longstreet, who was thirteen miles away, to return; and directed D. H.

[7] Alexander, 230.

Hill, two of whose brigades were already at the gap, to proceed there with the remainder of his division.

The battle of South Mountain was opened on the morning of the 14th by the Union cavalry, under Pleasanton. About nine o'clock, Cox arrived with the Kanawha division, and took command of the attack. Three hours later the remainder of the Ninth Corps came up, under Reno, who was killed during the action. Later still, Hooker arrived with the First Corps, and all of the right wing was then on the field, under the immediate command of Burnside. The First Corps assaulted the Confederate left, and the Ninth attacked the right, at Fox's Gap, on the Braddock Road. The combat lasted until 10 P.M.; and at midnight the Confederates withdrew. The battle hardly admits of precise description, as it was a succession of sharp skirmishes rather than one connected action. The general result was a Confederate defeat.[8]

Franklin had been ordered to move the same day with the left wing by Crampton's Gap, to relieve the garrison at Harper's Ferry. As the distance from Turner's Gap is about six miles in a straight line, and the country between is very rugged, the action there was entirely disconnected from the other. Beginning about noon, after a spirited engagement of three hours Franklin, with his superior forces, easily carried the crest, and established his line in Pleasant Valley. On hearing of this, McLaws formed his troops in a strong defensive position across the valley, and made such a show of strength that Franklin believed he was outnumbered " two to one." After the surrender of Harper's Ferry, during the afternoon of the 15th McLaws skillfully and without molestation withdrew his command across the river to the town.

After his failure to hold the passes of South Mountain, Lee, who had only 19,000 men with him, decided to retreat to the south side of the Potomac.[9] About noon on the 15th, when his forces were on the way to the ford, he received at Sharpsburg a despatch [10] stating that Harper's Ferry had fallen, and Jackson was on his way to rejoin

[8] Palfrey, 33–40.
[9] Steele, 267.
[10] Paper by General George B. Davis, quoted by Steele, 267.

him. He at once recalled his troops from the ford, established a line of battle on the heights overlooking the Antietam, and ordered the batteries into position. By nightfall the divisions of Hood, D. H. Hill, and Jones, were in line of battle. After a hard night-march, Jackson arrived on the morning of the 16th, and McLaws, with his own division and Anderson's, twenty-four hours later. Lee's whole army was therefore reunited on the morning of the 17th, except the division of A. P. Hill, which Jackson had left behind to complete the arrangements for the surrender of Harper's Ferry.

Mr. Ropes speaks of Lee's decision to stand and fight at Sharpsburg as one of the " boldest and most hazardous " in his career, and is " bewildered that he should even have thought seriously of making it." [11]

General Alexander also expresses his amazement at the " audacity " of Lee in accepting battle " in the open field, without a yard of earthworks, against a better-equipped army of double his force, and with a river close behind him, to be crossed by a single ford, peculiarly bad and exposed, in case he had to retreat." [12]

General Longstreet was also of the opinion that the army should have recrossed the Potomac at once.[13] But Jackson, when he reached Sharpsburg on the morning of the 16th, heartily approved of Lee's decision. Colonel Henderson, as usual, agrees with his hero. He thinks that " the Army of Northern Virginia was so superior to the Army of the Potomac that Lee and Jackson " were warranted in believing that " they might fight a defensive battle, outnumbered as they were, with the hope of annihilating their enemy. . . . By retreating across the Potomac, in accordance with General Longstreet's suggestion, Lee would certainly have avoided all chances of disaster; but, at the same time, he would have abandoned a good hope of ending the war." [14]

[11] But Mr. Ropes apparently did not know that Lee had heard of the fall of Harper's Ferry, and of the return of Jackson. (See 2 Ropes, 348–350.)

[12] Alexander, 242.

[13] 2 B. & L., 666.

[14] 2 Henderson, 284.

ANTIETAM

McClellan's own words are the strongest justification of the views held by the Southern leaders. He says that the Army of the Potomac was so " thoroughly exhausted and depleted " by the last two campaigns; and its trains, administrative services and supplies, so disorganized, that " nothing but sheer necessity justified the advance . . . to South Mountain and Antietam." [15]

And in his official report he says: " One battle lost and almost all would have been lost. Lee's army might have marched as it pleased on Washington, Baltimore, Philadelphia, or New York; . . . nowhere east of the Alleghanies was there another organized force to avert its march." This apprehension goes far to explain, and to excuse McClellan's excessive caution during the campaign.

It is a curious fact that many battles of the Civil War bear double names. The Confederates generally named them for the town or place near the field of action: the Federals, for some natural object adjoining the scene of the conflict. Thus we have Manassas and Bull Run; Shiloh and Pittsburg Landing; Murfreesboro and Stones River; Sharpsburg and Antietam.

The village of Sharpsburg [16] is in the midst of a very irregular plateau which is almost enclosed by the Potomac River and the Antietam Creek. The Potomac bounds it on the south and west, and the Antietam on the east. In general outline, the plateau may be considered a parallelogram, four miles in length from north to south, and two and a half miles in width inside the bends of the river. From the village the ground descends in all directions, though a continuous ridge runs northward, on which is the Hagerstown Pike. The Boonsboro Turnpike crossed the Antietam on a stone bridge; entered the village from the northeast, and, continuing through Sharpsburg, ran southwest to the ford of the Potomac at Shepherdstown.

[15] 2 *B. & L.*, 554.
[16] LEGEND TO MAP: *A* — East Wood. *B* — Corn Field. *C* — Sumner's Attack. *D* — Roulette house. *E* — Sunken Road. *F* — End of battle on Lee's left. *G* — Piper house. *H* — Stuart's position. *J* — Boonsboro Road. *K* — Burnside Bridge. *L* — Lower Fords. *M* — End of battle.

[159]

The Hagerstown road entered the town from the north, passing the Dunker Church a mile out, and ran nearly due south, crossing the Antietam at its mouth, and continuing down the Potomac toward Harper's Ferry.

The Antietam is a deep creek, with few fords at an ordinary stage of water, and the principal roads, at the time of the battle, crossed it on solid stone bridges, which Lee did not have the time or the means to destroy. Within the field of battle there were three of these bridges: the upper one in front of Keedysville; the middle one upon the Boonsboro road; and the lower one, since known as Burnside's Bridge, on the road to Rohrersville.

Between Mercersville on the north and the mouth of the Antietam on the south, the Potomac flows in a series of remarkable curves, but its general course is such that a line of battle less than six miles long can be drawn from near Mercersville to a point just above the mouth of the Antietam, so as to rest both its flanks on the Potomac, to cover the town and the ford across the river, and to have its front covered by the creek.

To-day, the National Cemetery is situated upon the crest of a hill to the eastward of the town, and just beyond the houses. If one enters the cemetery and takes his position on the highest point, at the base of the flag-staff, he will be within the concave of the Confederate line as it stood at the beginning of the battle. Near this spot, on a small mass of limestone, which commands an extensive view, it is said that Lee stood to direct the battle. On the left, looking westward, is the town of Sharpsburg, with the road to Hagerstown partially in sight. In the border of a patch of woods, at the distance of about a mile, and in plain view, stood the famous Dunker Church. At the church two roads met the turnpike, almost forming a right angle with each other. To the west, northwest, and north of the church, were the so-called West Woods; and the woods to the east of the pike, separated from it by open ground, were called the East Woods. These two patches of timber, with the fields between, were the scene of the most desperate fighting of the 17 September.

To the northeast, at a distance of about two miles, on

the further side of the Antietam, could be seen a large brick building: this was the Pry house, the headquarters of McClellan during the battle. The creek itself cannot be seen, because of the depth of the ravine which forms its bed, but its course can easily be traced by the line of trees along its banks.

Further to the right, at the base of some hills, but concealed from view, is the Burnside Bridge, about a mile away. Practically the whole battle-field may be seen from this single point. To complete the description, it is to be added that the famous "sunken road" was almost directly opposite the centre of the Union position, looking west. It branched off from the northern side of the Boonsboro Pike, about halfway from the creek to Sharpsburg, and ran in zigzag fashion to the Hagerstown Pike, which it joined about mid-distance from the village to the Dunker Church, but nearer the latter.[17]

If troops moved on the field as chessmen are moved on the board; if corps and divisions went into action as complete wholes, the story of a battle could be told with more precision; but this is very far from being the case. "The combinations of a battle-field," writes General Palfrey, "are almost as varying, and far less distinctly visible and separable than those of a kaleidoscope." A great battle cannot be described in detail except at immense length, and even then imperfectly. Napoleon once said that no attempt should ever be made to narrate the events of a battle in smaller terms than army corps. If lesser units are used — "it is impossible to see the forest for the trees."

The Confederate position at Sharpsburg was in many respects a strong one, and could have been made even stronger with entrenchments, but these were not used, although there was ample time to dig them.[18] The flanks were reasonably secure. The right rested on the Antietam. The left was more open, but beyond the West Woods a

[17] The best view of the battle-field to-day is to be had from an observation tower erected at the northeasterly angle of the "Bloody Lane."
[18] See Steele, 281.

low ridge gave room for several batteries, while the Potomac was so close that there was but little space available for attack.

Jackson held the left, with Hood in second line. Next in order came D. H. Hill. Longstreet held the centre and right, with Walker in reserve. On the left flank, Stuart with Fitz Lee's brigade and his four guns, were between the West Woods and the river. On the right, Munford's two regiments of cavalry, with a battery, held the bridge at the Antietam Iron Works, and kept open the road to Harper's Ferry.

For the occupation of this front, of about three miles, Lee had at first only 23,500 men; and, even after the arrival of the absent divisions, no more than 35,000 infantry, 4000 cavalry, and 194 guns would be in line.[19]

On paper, McClellan's forces were far superior: [20]

	Men	Guns
First Corps — HOOKER	15,000	40
Second Corps — SUMNER	19,000	42
Fifth Corps — PORTER	13,000	70
Sixth Corps — FRANKLIN	12,000	36
Ninth Corps — BURNSIDE	14,000	35
Twelfth Corps — MANSFIELD	10,000	36
	83,000	259
Cavalry — PLEASANTON	4,000	16
TOTALS	87,000	275

The morning of Monday the 15 September found the Confederates retreating from South Mountain. It was only seven miles to Antietam Creek; the weather was fine; the roads were excellent and unobstructed. By noon the mass of McClellan's army might have been in contact with the enemy. With the First, Second, Fifth, and Twelfth corps, and the cavalry, in hand, he had over 60,000 men to the 25,500 of Lee. But McClellan never appreciated the value of time, and nothing was done that day. " Instead of making his reconnaissance at three in the afternoon of Monday," writes General Cox, " it might

[19] 2 Henderson, 298–299.   [20] 2 Henderson, 299.

have been made at ten in the morning, and the battle could have been fought before night. . . . Or if McClellan had pushed boldly for the bridge at the mouth of the Antietam, nothing but a precipitate retreat by Lee could have prevented the interposition of the whole National army between the separated wings of the Confederates." [21] Nothing was done, however, either on Monday or Tuesday, except reconnoitring, while Lee was straining every nerve to concentrate his forces.

On the afternoon of the 16th, McClellan completed his preparations for the battle which he proposed to deliver the next day. Sumner, with his own corps and that of Mansfield, was on the right, and Hooker, who had been removed from Burnside's command, was beyond Sumner, on the extreme right. The centre was occupied by the Fifth Corps, under Porter, and the left by the Ninth Corps, under Burnside. Franklin, who had been sent to watch McLaws, had been recalled on the night of the 16th, and on his arrival with the Sixth Corps McClellan proposed to place his troops in reserve.

McClellan's plan of battle, as stated by himself in his final and elaborate report, was to attack Lee's left with the corps of Hooker and Mansfield, supported by Sumner, and, if necessary, Franklin. Then, " as soon as matters looked favorably there," to carry the heights of Sharpsburg with Burnside's Ninth Corps. In case of success, with either or both these assaults, he proposed to advance his centre.

Whatever McClellan's plans may have been, his execution of them was very bad. It seems almost inconceivable that a commander of any military ability should have left a corps of four divisions idle for hours on his left, while he attacked on the right with three corps *in succession*, held the centre with a fifth corps, his cavalry and horse-artillery, and had another corps hastening up to the rear of his line. Yet this is precisely what he did do.

The three corps ordered to attack the Confederate left should have been under one commander, and should have moved together. The assault on Lee's right, which was the vulnerable part of his line, should have been made at the same time. If this had been done, it is hard to see how Lee's army could have escaped destruction.

As the first step in the execution of McClellan's plan, Hooker crossed the Antietam on the afternoon of the 16th and came in contact with Hood on the Confederate left. The action was sharp while it lasted, but the firing ceased at dark. About nine a light rain began to fall, and continued most of the night. When all was quiet, Hood's brigades were withdrawn to cook rations, and their position was filled by Lawton's division.

The morning of Wednesday, the 17th, broke crisp and clear. At early dawn the fight was renewed, and Hooker's three fine divisions advanced in columns of brigades in line: Doubleday on the right, Ricketts on the left, and Meade in reserve close behind. The attack fell principally upon Lawton, and the fighting was very severe. Hooker, in his report, says that he never witnessed a more bloody, dismal battle-field. Part of the Confederate line was exposed to the fire of the Union rifle batteries across the Antietam, at a range of about 3000 yards. Hooker handled his troops well, and conducted the attack with all the dash and energy which had earned him the soubriquet of "Fighting Joe." The Confederate resistance was desperate, and the losses great on both sides. Lawton was borne off wounded, and his brigades were put out of action for the day. He called on Hood for support, and the latter sent in his two brigades, about 2000 strong. Hooker was wounded, and his men driven back so far that they were forced to abandon some of their guns.

By this time the Twelfth Corps, under Mansfield, was coming on the field. He had crossed the Antietam during the night, and bivouacked more than a mile north of the First Corps. At daybreak he started to Hooker's support, but was so slow in deploying his troops that it was seven-thirty before he took any part in the action. His corps arrived just in time to save the First Corps from being routed by Hood's counter-stroke. Hooker's corps had lost 2500 out of the 9000 men who went into action, and Meade, who had succeeded to the command. withdrew from the field to a strong position about a mile in the rear. This ended the first phase of the battle.

The attack of Mansfield, which now followed, can scarcely be described in detail. Mansfield was killed at the start, and Williams took command of the corps. For two hours, the lines wavered backward and forward. Finally the Federals broke the Confederate line, and Greene's division was in possession of the Dunker Church, as well as a portion of the woods near it. By this time the Twelfth Corps had lost all of its *élan,* and for a period the firing ceased entirely. The casualties amounted to 1746 out of some 7000 men engaged. Here may be said to end in a draw the second phase of the battle.

But this truce was of short duration. The head of the Second Corps was now approaching. At 7:20 A.M., Sumner had at last received his needlessly delayed orders to advance. He immediately crossed the creek, and arrived upon the field about nine o'clock. " If his nine brigades of veterans," says General Alexander, " had been put into action along with Mansfield's five, they would have made decisive work upon Lee's left flank, and opened the road to Porter's corps to attack his centre. Here McClellan threw away another one of his many chances for a decisive victory, though it was by no means his last." [22]

Sumner reports that he found affairs in a " desperate state." The First Corps had been repulsed and forced to retire, and the Twelfth was barely holding its own. Sumner's corps had not fought at the Second Manassas, and consequently it was large, numbering on paper about 19,000 men, of whom some 15,000 were brought on to the field. Impatient at the three hours' delay imposed on his corps, Sumner ordered Sedgwick's division, with which he rode, to assault in close column of brigade front. He did not wait for his two other divisions, under French and Richardson, to come up; or stop to reconnoitre, or to inquire as to the enemy's position. Sedgwick advanced out of the East Woods, passed on his left the Dunker Church, where the remains of Greene's division were lying down,

[22] Alexander, 256.

and traversed the West Woods. His brigades were only between twenty and thirty yards apart — in too close order to be brought safely under fire.

Meanwhile, Lee had sent to the front his last reserves — the divisions of McLaws and Anderson, which after a weary night's march from Harper's Ferry had arrived about sunrise. Anderson's six brigades, about 3600 strong, were sent to D. H. Hill's division. McLaws's four brigades, some 3000 men, were directed to the woods behind the Dunker Church, under the guidance of Hood, who was familiar with the ground.[23]

In his march, Sedgwick passed, without being aware of it, Early's brigade upon his right, with the remnants of Jones's division; and on his left, he passed what was left of Walker's two brigades, who were holding in front of Greene's troops about the church. Early, unseen behind the ridge, moved parallel to Sedgwick's march, and opened fire on the flank of the Federal column as soon as it issued from the woods. At the same moment the column found itself presenting its left front angle to McLaws's division, which fired at close range. " Sedgwick had practically marched into an ambuscade." [24] Exposed to this deadly flank fire, " which it was impossible for the troops to return," Sedgwick's division lost over 2200 men " in a very few minutes." Sedgwick himself received three wounds, and his division was driven off the field. At the same time, Greene was forced to retire from the church, and the Confederate line rested where it had stood at the beginning of the battle, although very feebly held. This finished the third affair of the day.

The fourth, and last, assault upon this part of the field was made by the two remaining divisions of the Second Corps, under French and Richardson. Their combined strength amounted to about 10,000 muskets; and they were opposed by some 7000 Confederates " in good order and condition," besides three brigades " broken and much demoralized " by previous fighting. This struggle, the most terrible of the day, took place on new ground to the east of the scene of the previous combats. The field

[23] Alexander, 256–257.   [24] Alexander, 258.

was open and moderately rolling, with but one good feature for defence. This was the famous " sunken road," — an excellent thing under certain conditions, but a dangerous trap when enfiladed by the enemy.

After the second affair of the day, three of D. H. Hill's brigades had remained in position, holding advanced ground about the Roulette house, a few hundred yards in front of this sunken road. Here they were attacked by French, and after a stubborn resistance were driven back to the sunken road. In this position Hill received the united attacks of both French and Richardson. He was aided by Anderson's division of some 3000 or 4000 men, which had formed in his rear. After a brisk engagement of perhaps an hour, the Federals reached a position from which they could enfilade a portion of the sunken road. The road was soon filled with the dead and wounded, and has since borne the name of the " Bloody Lane." [25]

When the Confederates finally gave way and fled in confusion, leaving the Federals in possession of this part of the field, " Lee's army was ruined and the end of the Confederacy was in sight." [26] The rout was in plain sight of McClellan's headquarters at the Pry house, but he gave no orders to follow on the victory.

Franklin was now on the field, with his fine corps of 12,000 men, and was about to attack, when Sumner, his ranking officer, refused his consent. About the same time, McClellan came up, " on a visit to his right flank," and conferred with Sumner and Franklin. The latter urged a renewal of the attack, but Sumner advised against it, and McClellan ordered Franklin simply to stand on the defensive.[27]

This ended the battle on the left and centre of Lee's line. There was not a single fresh regiment in reserve: one more vigorous assault would have crushed Lee's army, but no attack was made. Yet, at that moment, McClellan had available the corps of Franklin and Porter — 25,000 men who had not fired a shot. All the morning, too, the Federal cavalry had stood idle. These fresh troops were

[25] 2 Ropes, 368.   [27] Alexander, 264.
[26] Alexander, 262.

almost equal to the forces that Lee had on the field at first.

It only remains to speak of the attack by the Ninth Corps on the Confederate right. At about nine in the morning, Burnside received an order to carry the bridge, since known by his name, and assault the Confederate lines posted on the bluffs above. There has been considerable controversy over the exact time at which this order was issued, but General Cox claims that it was not received until ten o'clock.[28]

The task of carrying this bridge was a difficult one, as the hills were higher than at other points, and the roads, on both sides of the creek, could not go up at right angles to the bank. The bluffs on the west side were wooded to the water's edge, while the assailants on the east side had no cover from the enemy.[29] The first two efforts to carry the bridge failed, but a third attempt, at one o'clock, was successful. The Confederates, under Tombs, withdrew to the right of the main line on the heights three-quarters of a mile from the bridge. Cox took command of the Union troops who had crossed the creek, and formed them to assault the enemy's line, which was held by four brigades of the division of D. R. Jones. The Confederates, only 2000 strong, were driven back up Cemetery Hill into the edge of the town.[30] This success, if properly followed up, would have cut off Lee's retreat, and insured the destruction of his army. But once more Fortune favored the side of the weakest battalions and the greatest brains. A. P. Hill, after a forced march from Harper's Ferry, came on the field, and threw his division against the left flank of the victorious Federals. Cox was driven back to the bridge, in some disorder, and there his troops bivouacked for the night. This ended the battle.

On the 18th, the hostile armies faced each other all day, but McClellan refused to attack. That night Lee crossed the Potomac, unmolested, and the invasion of Maryland was over.

[28] 1 Cox, 338.
[29] 1 Cox, 339.
[30] This was one of the few engagements of the war in which a village was included within the lines of battle. (Steele, 281.)

It is not easy to determine the exact numbers engaged on either side at the battle of Antietam. As stated above, Colonel Henderson estimates Lee's total, after the arrival of all his troops, at about 40,000. McClellan had over 87,000 men (nominally) on the field, but used less than 60,000. The odds against Lee were therefore about three to two, if we accept these figures.

Mr. Ropes makes the Confederate total 39,200 men; and he states that the First, Second, Ninth, and Twelfth corps, the only troops put in by McClellan, actually numbered only 46,000 men. These figures agree substantially with those given by General Palfrey, who says that the nominal totals of the four corps used by McClellan, about 58,000 men, should be reduced by 20 per cent., say 12,000, to ascertain the strength of these corps on the day of the battle.

Mr. Ropes states further that, based upon the official statement of the strength of the Confederate army on the 22 September 1862, five days after the battle, and allowing for losses in the battle, as well as the return of stragglers, he arrives at a total of 58,000 men present for duty on the morning of the 17 September.[31] But Longstreet says that the stragglers at Sharpsburg "reached nearly 20,000." [32]

In explanation of the discrepancies between the Confederate and Federal reports of men " present for duty," it may be stated that the former generally included *only* the combatants, while the latter included also all men on detached duty, such as, camp, dépôt, and train guards, and escorts; besides non-combatants, such as, cooks, servants, orderlies, and extra-duty men in various staff-departments. To make an exact comparison, therefore, of the number of men, on either side, available for combat, the Federal figures should always be reduced by one-fifth.[33] An equal allowance should also generally be made, on both sides, for straggling, which had reached enormous proportions.

[31] 2 Ropes, 382–383. Livermore (92) estimates Lee's effectives at 51,844.

[32] 2 B. & L., 674.

[33] 2 B. & L., 170. See also Palfrey, 70.

" The battle of Sharpsburg, or of the Antietam," says Mr. Ropes, " was one of the bloodiest battles of the war, and it is likely that more men were killed and wounded on the 17 September than on any single day in the whole war. The Confederate loss probably amounted to 8000 men or more; that of the Union army is given at 12,410 men. Each side lost about one quarter of the troops engaged." [34]

McClellan reported his losses for the 16th and 17th as, 2010 killed, 9416 wounded, and 1043 missing, a total of 12,469. He also stated that 2700 Confederate dead were buried by his officers. From these figures it is probable that their losses at least equalled those of the Federals.[35]

For the whole Maryland Campaign, General Alexander gives the losses as follows: [36]

	Federals	Confederates
Killed	3,273	1,924
Wounded	11,756	9,381
Missing	13,338	2,304
Totals	28,367	13,609

Tactically, Antietam was a drawn battle; but the prestige of victory rested with McClellan. Lee's invasion had terminated in failure — failure which could not but be admitted by the authorities and people of the South. Even Colonel Henderson concedes that the Confederates had not " drawn much profit from the invasion of Maryland." He claims, however, that the stake was well worth the hazard.[37]

" Of McClellan's conduct of the battle," writes General Palfrey, " there is little to be said in the way of praise beyond the fact that he did fight it voluntarily, without having it forced upon him."

[34] 2 Ropes, 376. Livermore (92) estimates Lee's losses at 13,724, including 2000 missing.

[35] In a detailed statement, Colonel Henderson places the Confederate grand total at 9550. (See 2 Henderson, 335.)

[36] Alexander, 275. He includes among the " missing " the 12,000 Federals captured at Harper's Ferry.

[37] Cf. Palfrey, 119; 2 Ropes, 379; 2 Henderson, 340–341.

Colonel Henderson is very severe in his comments. " The Federal attack," he says, " was badly designed and badly executed." There was nothing like close concert and aggressive energy; the principle of mutual support was utterly ignored; the army corps attacked, not simultaneously, but in succession, and in succession they were defeated. McClellan fought three separate battles: from dawn to 10 A.M. against Lee's left; from 10 A.M. to 1 P.M. against his centre; from 1 to 4 P.M. against his right. Only two-thirds of his army was engaged — 25,000 men hardly fired a shot; and from first to last there was not the slightest attempt at coöperation. " He had still to grasp the elementary rule that the combination of superior numbers and of all arms against a single point is necessary to win battles." [38]

Lee undoubtedly made a mistake in fighting at Sharpsburg.[39] Considering the great superiority of the Federals in numbers, and particularly in their artillery arm, a victory could have had no decisive results. On the other hand, owing to his dangerous position, a defeat would have involved the absolute destruction of his army. No commander is ever justified in voluntarily taking such chances. *C'est magnifique, mais ce n'est pas la guerre!*

In his comments on the battle, General Palfrey says: " If Lee had been in McClellan's place on the 17 September, and had sent Jackson to conduct the right attack and Longstreet to force the passage of the lower bridge and turn the Confederate right, the Army of Northern Virginia, though commanded by a second Lee, a second Jackson, and a second Longstreet, would have ceased to exist that day." [40]

The Confederate leaders on this day, almost without exception, were men who made great names in the Civil War, while the Federal commanders were generally men who never became conspicuous, except through failure. Hooker was brave, handsome, vain, insubordinate, untrustworthy; and he failed dismally when made com-

---

[38] 2 Henderson, 313–314.

[39] " Strategically, his position in this battle was as bad as could be." (Steele, 279.)

[40] Palfrey, 17–18.

mander-in-chief. Sumner was an old man, though still active and vigorous. He was a graduate of West Point, and had been a colonel of cavalry. His training in this arm seems to have done him positive harm as a leader of infantry. Of the unfortunate Porter it is unnecessary to add anything to what has already been said. Franklin had graduated at West Point at the head of his class in 1839, and was a brave and capable, but unfortunate, soldier. Burnside was also a graduate of the Military Academy, but he had been out of the service seven years when the war began. His large, fine eyes, his winning smile and cordial manners, won him friends on every side. Few men have ever risen so high as he on so slight a foundation. As commander of the army, he failed disastrously. Most of the men who later attained distinction, like Hancock, Humphreys, Griffin, Warren, and Barlow, in September 1862 were brigade or regimental commanders.

The strategical employment of cavalry, on both sides, was excellent in this campaign during the preliminary operations. But, during the battle, McClellan put his cavalry in the centre of his line, instead of on the flanks. This was all the more remarkable, because he had every reason to expect that Lee would be reënforced by A. P. Hill's division from Harper's Ferry, of whose approach the cavalry could have given notice, at least, even if it could not have held back the Confederates.

Major Steele sums up his comments on the battle in the words: " From beginning to end of the campaign the Confederate commander's conduct was characterized by boldness, resolution, and quickness; the Federal commander's, by timidity, irresolution, and slowness." [41]

[41] Steele, 283. It is fair to state, however, that McClellan's operations were much hampered by the contradictory orders which he received from Washington.

CHAPTER NINE

SEPTEMBER 1862 — JANUARY 1863

FREDERICKSBURG

Reorganization of the Confederate Army — Stuart's Raid — McClellan's Inaction — Lincoln Orders an Advance — The Union Army Crosses the Potomac — McClellan Relieved and Burnside Appointed — Relations of the Two Officers — Estimate of McClellan — Positions of the Hostile Forces — Burnside's Plan — Reorganization of His Army — The Movement to Fredericksburg — Lee Follows — Jackson Arrives — The Field of Fredericksburg — The Pontoon-Bridges Laid — Franklin and Sumner Cross — Franklin's Plan of Attack — Burnside's Orders — Franklin's Attack Fails — Sumner's Assaults Repulsed — The Federals Recross the River — Features of the Battle — A Barren Victory —Burnside Replaced by Hooker — Franklin Removed — Final Comments

AFTER crossing the Potomac on the night of the 18 September, Lee placed his army in camps in the fertile valley of Opequon Creek, near Winchester, where he could observe the movements of the Federals, while his men were recuperating from the late campaign.

On the 2 October, at the suggestion of General Lee, the Army of Northern Virginia was organized into two army corps, to the command of which President Davis appointed Longstreet and Jackson, with the rank of lieutenant-general. At the same time, major-generals and brigadiers were promoted to command the divisions and brigades into which the corps were divided.

It was while his army was resting near Winchester that Lee sent Stuart with about 1800 men across the Potomac, ostensibly " to ascertain the positions and designs of the enemy." The cavalry crossed the Potomac above Williamsport on the 10 October, went to Chambersburg, where some stores and horses were picked up, and forded the river on their return just above Poolesville. In a sense the raid was a success, but Stuart did his adversaries no harm, with the exception of wearing out the Union cavalry sent to chase him, and he secured no information of value to Lee.[1]

Lee's army gained rapidly in strength and efficiency. On the first day of November, the First Corps (Longstreet) reported a total of officers and men " present for duty" of 31,925, and the Second Corps (Jackson), of 31,794, while Stuart's cavalry numbered 7176; making an aggregate of 70,895.

Meanwhile, McClellan in his camp in Maryland was preparing for a winter campaign. He was determined not to make any movement until his ranks were recruited, his cavalry remounted, his army properly equipped, and his administrative service reorganized. " His obstinacy," says General Cox, " was of a feminine sort. He avoided open antagonism which would have been a challenge of strength, but found constantly fresh obstacles in the way of doing what he was determined from the first not to do."[2]

The first of October, Mr. Lincoln visited the camp at Sharpsburg and remained two or three days. He rode over the battle-field with McClellan, visited the Dunker Church, and returned by way of the Bloody Lane. He was very cordial in his praise of McClellan, and avoided any criticism of the campaign. But he showed plainly his apprehension that the delays of 1861 were to be repeated, and the fine October weather wasted. That General McClellan was aware of the President's anxiety is shown in his letters: " I incline to think," he wrote home, " that the real purpose of his visit is to push me into a premature advance into Virginia."[3]

The official correspondence proves conclusively that Mr. Lincoln returned to Washington fully determined to take drastic action if forced to do so. McClellan's private letters, at the same period, show that he was not ignorant of the situation, for he wrote that it was not improbable that he would be relieved from command.

[1] 2 Ropes, 438.
[2] 1 Cox, 367.
[3] McClellan's *Own Story*, 654.

During his visit Mr. Lincoln told McClellan plainly that his greatest fault was excess of caution; and he intimated that he should insist on an early advance. On his return to Washington, the President directed Halleck to send McClellan a peremptory order to cross the Potomac. This order, dated the 6 October, reads:

> The President directs that you cross the Potomac and give battle to the enemy or drive him south. Your army must move now while the roads are good. If you cross the river between the enemy and Washington, and cover the latter by your line of operations, you can be reënforced with 30,000 men. If you move up the valley of the Shenandoah, not more than 12,000 or 15,000 can be sent to you. The President advises the interior line between Washington and the enemy, but does not order it.

McClellan replied on the 7th that he would adopt the exterior line, because it would cover Maryland from a return of Lee's army, and indicated that he would move in three days. At the end of that time, he complained of lacking clothing; then, of horses for his cavalry; and so the discussion ran on until the 21st.

In a remarkable letter to McClellan on the 13th, Mr. Lincoln showed a grasp of the military situation and its strategic possibilities which place him "head and shoulders above both his military subordinates." [4] He argued in favor of the interior line, and pointed out its many advantages. The decisive vigor of this plan dismayed McClellan, but he finally adopted it as the means of getting larger reënforcements.

The advance began in the last days of October, the Sixth Corps, which was in the rear, crossing the Potomac on the 2 November. Lee, who had been closely following the movements of the Federal army, marched the same day from Winchester toward Culpeper, leaving Jackson in the Valley.

On the 7 November, the Army of the Potomac was concentrated in the vicinity of Warrenton. Late that evening, as McClellan sat in his tent near Salem, a special messenger from the War Department presented himself and

---

[4] 1 Cox, 373. The letter is quoted in full, Upton, 384–385.

handed the general a sealed envelope. It contained an order from the President relieving McClellan from the command of the Army of the Potomac, and appointing Burnside in his stead.

"McClellan ought not to have been removed," writes Mr. Ropes, "unless the Government were prepared to put in his place some officer whom they knew to be at least his equal in military capacity. This, assuredly, was not the case at this moment. No one, in or out of the service, had ever considered Burnside as able a man as McClellan." [5]

In the event of McClellan's removal, it was naturally to be expected that the selection of a new commander-in-chief would be made from the four senior corps-commanders — Burnside, Hooker, Sumner, and Franklin. The latter would have been decidedly the best appointment which the Government could have made, but the opposition to him on political grounds was too strong.[6]

McClellan and Burnside had been classmates at West Point, and had always kept up the intimacy which began at the Academy. They were "Mac" and "Burn" to each other, and their friendship was much closer than that with Fitz John Porter, Reno, and Hancock, who were in the same class. After Burnside had secured his first success in the Roanoke expedition, he was offered the command of the Army of the Potomac, but he refused it, and urged that his friend should be reënforced and allowed to continue his campaign against Richmond.

Before the Maryland campaign began, Mr. Lincoln again urged Burnside to accept the command, but he once more declined, and warmly advocated the reinstatement of McClellan.

These favors from his friend seem to have been too much for the vanity of McClellan, and during the Sharpsburg campaign every one noticed a marked coldness be-

[5] 2 Ropes, 442. No exception can be taken to these remarks; but Mr. Ropes is strangely in error when he says (441): "Nothing in the correspondence between Mr. Lincoln and General McClellan had indicated that such a crisis was at hand." For a clear and impartial review of McClellan's relations with the Administration at this time, see 2 Cox, 354–391.

[6] 2 Ropes, 442, and note.

tween the two former comrades. Hooker, who was under Burnside's command, was ordered to the right of the army at Antietam, and given an independent position, while Burnside was assigned to the left of the line. Although he did not waver in his loyal friendship to McClellan, Burnside was deeply grieved at many things which occurred during this campaign. There is the strongest evidence of his real unwillingness to supersede McClellan when the final order came in November. He was also sincere in feeling that he was not equal to the command; and the chief reason for his acceptance was his reluctance to see it go to Hooker, who would have been the next choice.

Regarding none of the leading generals of the Civil War has there been such a difference of opinion as in the case of General McClellan; and after the lapse of three score years the controversy is not yet settled. As Cicero said of Julius Cæsar, " coming generations will dispute over him." To some, McClellan is the " prince of egoists, the grand procrastinator, the timid and doubting captain "; to others, he is a " military genius of the first order," who was " thwarted by an incapable administration and the intrigue of politicians." [7]

The character and abilities of General McClellan have been so freely commented on in the course of this narrative that it is unnecessary to repeat those criticisms here. His capacity and energy as an organizer are universally acknowledged. " Had McClellan never done anything else but organize the Army of the Potomac, and bring order out of chaos after the battle of Bull Run," writes Dr. Macartney, " his service to the nation would have been not far behind that of any of the Union generals. The weapon which Grant finally used to strike down the Confederacy was the finely tempered sword of McClellan, the Army of the Potomac." [8]

McClellan was a good strategist, and in many respects an excellent soldier. He was a courteous gentleman, and his private character was above reproach. No orgies disgraced headquarters while he was in command.

[7] Macartney, 68.   [8] Macartney, 71.

It is manifestly unfair to judge McClellan, as so many writers seem inclined to do, by his *Own Story*. This work, printed after his death, " is one of the most lamentable publications that family piety ever produced, and has made it exceedingly difficult to treat McClellan with fairness." [9]

Notwithstanding all of the faults of McClellan's military operations, General Palfrey expresses the opinion that " he was the best commander that the Army of the Potomac ever had." [10]

This opinion is endorsed by so great an authority as General Lee.[11] " His failure to accomplish more," adds General Palfrey, " was partly his misfortune and not altogether his fault." [12]

McClellan, as a general, was certainly far superior to Pope, or Burnside, or Hooker; and, in many respects, to Meade or Grant. No commander since Napoleon has ever aroused such enthusiasm among his soldiers, or inspired them with such personal devotion.

Colonel Henderson, one of the ablest military critics of our times, says: " McClellan was not a general of the first order; but he was the only officer in the United States who had experience of handling large masses of troops, and he was improving every day. Stuart had taught him the use of cavalry, and Lee the value of the initiative. He was by no means deficient in resolution, as his march with an army of recently defeated men against Lee in Maryland conclusively proves; and although he had never won a decisive victory, he possessed, to a degree which was never attained by any of his successors, the confidence and affection of his troops." [13]

Few students of the war to-day will deny that the withdrawal of McClellan's army from the Peninsula was a great blunder — the first of the many errors for which Halleck was to be responsible. McClellan's protest was not heeded at Washington, and he was condemned where, two years later, Grant was supported.

[9] 6 Channing, 451, note.
[10] Palfrey, 134.
[11] See Hosmer, *Appeal to Arms*, 166; 2 Barton's *Lincoln*, 89; and **Long**, 233.   [12] Palfrey, 135.   [13] 2 Henderson, 368.

That McClellan's apprehensions regarding his fate, if he had failed in the Antietam campaign, were not groundless is proved by the *Diary* of Secretary Welles. " It was evident," he writes, " that there was a fixed determination to remove, and, if possible, to disgrace McClellan. Chase frankly stated that he deserved it; that he deliberately believed that McClellan ought to be shot, and should, were he President, be brought to summary punishment." [14]

The restoration of McClellan to command, in September 1862, in the face of the almost unanimous opposition of the Cabinet and Congress, was " one of the most important and patriotic acts of Lincoln's administration of the war." It was the only step which could have restored the shattered *moral* of the army, after its defeat under Pope, and it enabled the Army of the Potomac to repel Lee's invasion of the North. Blair states that Stanton and Chase " actually declared that they would prefer the loss of the capital to the restoration of McClellan to command "; and Welles describes the meeting of the Cabinet as " the most agitated and despondent ever held." But the splendid reception which the army gave McClellan when he returned to take command proved that Lincoln was right and his Cabinet wrong.

However, if the reinstatement of General McClellan was one of the finest acts of President Lincoln's administration, his removal after Antietam was perhaps the most unfortunate and inexcusable. It certainly prolonged the war for many months.[15]

At the same time that McClellan was removed, Fitz John Porter, the gallant soldier of Gaines's Mill and Malvern Hill, " probably the best officer in the Army of the Potomac," [16] was ordered to resign command of the Fifth Corps, and to appear before a court-martial on charges growing out of the Second Manassas, already mentioned.

On the 7 November, Lee was at Culpeper with Long-

---

[14] Cited, Macartney, 88. See also, 1 Smith, 241, where Garfield states that Chase made the same remark to him.

[15] *Cf.* Macartney, 88–93.

[16] 2 Henderson, 369.

street's corps, the reserve artillery, and two brigades of cavalry under Stuart, about 45,000 men; while Jackson's corps, some 40,000 strong, was near Millwood in the Valley.

On this date the Federal army was distributed as follows: the First, Second, and Fifth corps, with the reserve artillery, were at Warrenton; the Ninth Corps at Waterloo; the Sixth at New Baltimore; the Eleventh en route for the same place; and one division of the Third Corps was between Manassas and Warrenton Junction. Pleasanton with two brigades of cavalry was at Amissville and Jefferson, and the front and flanks of the army were covered by cavalry pickets and patrols. The Twelfth Corps was at Harper's Ferry, and General Morrell with a division of infantry was on the upper Potomac.

The Federal army concentrated about Warrenton was therefore within twenty miles of Longstreet's corps, and still nearer the direct road to Millwood in the Valley, where Jackson was stationed, at a distance from Lee of forty miles in a direct line. There was never a better opportunity for the Federal army to attack and defeat the Confederates in detail, or force them to concentrate as far back as Gordonsville, which had been McClellan's plan. But this was not to be. McClellan was removed and Burnside adopted an entirely different plan. The day he took command, the 9 November, he forwarded a letter to Halleck explaining his project. This, in brief, was to abandon his line of communications by the Orange and Alexandria Railroad, and transfer his base to Aquia Creek; to " impress upon the enemy the belief that he was to attack Culpeper or Gordonsville; . . . then to make a rapid move of the whole force to Fredericksburg, with a view to a movement upon Richmond from that point."

This was poor strategy, as it made Richmond, instead of Lee's army, his objective; and it was not until the 14th that President Lincoln gave his reluctant assent to Burnside's plan.

A feature of Burnside's plan, which was not made very prominent in his statement, was that pontoon trains enough to span the Rappahannock with two tracks should be sent at once to Falmouth. To Halleck's delay in complying promptly with this request, Burnside attributed his failure at Fredericksburg.

Burnside's first step on assuming command, on the 9 November, was to reorganize the Army of the Potomac into three Grand Divisions and a Reserve Corps.

The Right Grand Division, under General Sumner, was formed of the Second Corps (Couch) and the Ninth (Willcox).

The Centre Grand Division, under General Hooker, comprised the Third Corps (Stoneman) and the Fifth (Butterfield).

The Left Grand Division, under General Franklin, was made up of the First Corps (Reynolds) and the Sixth (W. F. Smith).

The Reserve Corps, under General Sigel, was composed of his own corps, the Eleventh, and the Twelfth, under General Slocum. These two corps did not arrive at Fredericksburg until after the battle.

It will be noticed that nearly all of the corps had new commanders. Among the division-commanders were many officers who subsequently gained great distinction.

In sending Mr. Lincoln's approval of Burnside's plan, General Halleck wrote: " He thinks that it will succeed, if you move very rapidly; otherwise not." Burnside, however, made no unnecessary delay. Sumner marched on the morning of the 15th, and reached Falmouth on the 17th. Hooker and Franklin followed, and arrived a day or two later. But the pontoons were not there, and in fact did not come until the 25th. Sumner wanted to cross by the fords, and seize the heights opposite, but Burnside would not consent, as he feared that any troops sent over to the south side might be overwhelmed before they could be reënforced or withdrawn. At that time the Confederate forces holding Fredericksburg were so weak that they could have offered but feeble resistance to Sumner's Grand Division. But on the 18th, as soon as he learned of Burnside's movement, Lee sent McLaws's division to Fredericksburg, and the remainder of Longstreet's corps followed immediately, arriving on the 21st, or a day or two later.

Lee had not definitely decided, however, to stand at Fredericksburg. On the 19th, he wrote Jackson from Culpeper that he did not anticipate making a determined stand above the North Anna River. This explains his reason for leaving so small a garrison in the city, and his delay in ordering Jackson to join him. Even after his arrival at Fredericksburg, on the 23rd, Lee still abstained from giving the commander of the Second Corps any order. When it became apparent, however, a few days later, that the Federals were preparing to cross the river, Lee finally decided to fight at Fredericksburg, and wrote Jackson to join him at once, as he feared the roads might become bad later. Jackson accordingly joined the main army on the 30 November.

The two armies now confronting each other across the Rappahannock were very unequal in point of numbers, the Union forces consisting of about 122,000 officers and men of all arms of the service, while Lee had only about 78,500 men. But the strength of the Confederate position went far to equalize the discrepancy in numbers.

The river at Fredericksburg is about 400 feet wide and unfordable. The hills on the north side, known as Stafford Heights, are closer to the river, and higher, than those on the opposite bank, which they command. On the south bank nestles the little city of Fredericksburg, surrounded by fertile fields. At a point just above the town, a range of hills begins, and extends around the valley somewhat in the form of a crescent, at a distance of about a mile from the river. The first elevation on the west was known as Taylor's Hill; the next, Marye's Hill; then came the highest point, called Telegraph Hill, but later known as Lee's Hill, as General Lee had his headquarters there during the battle. Beyond this was a ravine, through which ran Deep Run Creek; and then the gentle elevations at Hamilton's Crossing, not dignified with a name, where Jackson massed his corps during the battle. The range of heights is broken by ravines and small streams, and covered in parts with woods.

FREDERICKSBURG

The gently sloping ground between the city and the heights was crossed by a ditch that carried off the waste water from a canal. The railroad crossed the river at Fredericksburg, and followed down it for about four miles to Hamilton's Crossing, where it turned south. Another line, unfinished, led out of the town and through the hills by Hazel Run Valley. There were numerous roads running out from the town, of which the most notable were the Plank Road and the Telegraph Road. At the base of Marye's Hill there was a sunken road, with a stone retaining-wall, about breast-high, on either side. This was to play a very important rôle in the battle.

The left of the Confederate line was held by Longstreet's corps: Anderson's division was on Taylor's Hill, near the river; Ransom's and McLaws's divisions, on Marye's Hill; Pickett's, on Lee's Hill; and Hood's, about Deep Run Creek.

On the hill occupied by Jackson's corps, at the right of the line, were the divisions of A. P. Hill, Early, and Taliaferro, that of D. H. Hill being in reserve on the extreme right.

After some tentative movements at places down the river, which resulted in nothing, Burnside decided to force a crossing in front of the Confederate position. On the night of the 10 December arrangements were made to span the river with five pontoon-bridges, three opposite Fredericksburg, and two just below the mouth of Deep Run. Sumner was to cross by the upper, and Franklin by the lower bridges. Hooker was to remain in reserve on the left bank.

The two lower bridges were thrown across without much trouble, but the construction of those opposite the town was impeded for a time by Confederate sharpshooters in the houses along the bank of the river. Finally, a call was made for volunteers, who crossed the river in boats and dislodged the enemy. Then the bridges were soon completed. Franklin's troops had already crossed by the lower bridges; Sumner's men now went over, and occupied the town.

The Federal left wing, under Franklin, was opposite

Jackson's position at Hamilton's Crossing. Its only line
of supply and retreat was over the bridges which had been
laid south of Deep Run, behind the extreme right of his
line. Jackson's front, which did not rest on any natural
obstacle, had been protected by earthworks and abattis,
and Franklin thought that the best chance of success lay
in a strong attack on the extreme Confederate right. As
Hamilton's Crossing was two miles below the bridges,
this operation called for important changes in the disposition of the Union troops.

General Franklin says that he strongly advised General
Burnside to make this attack upon the enemy's right with
a column of at least 30,000 men, and that it be supported
by two divisions of General Hooker's command, which
were on the north side near the two bridges he had crossed.
He urged also that the orders should be issued as early
as possible, so that he might arrange his troops before
daylight.

The orders, promised by Burnside before midnight at
the latest, finally came at seven-thirty in the morning;
but they were as far as possible from the plan suggested
by Franklin. They directed him: (1) To keep his whole
command in position for a rapid movement down the
Old Richmond Road; and (2), to send out at once a
division, at least, to pass below Smithfield, to seize, if
possible, the height near Captain Hamilton's, on this side
of the Massaponax, taking care to keep it well supported
and its line of retreat open.

Attention should be called to the word *seize*, which in a
military sense is used to refer to an unguarded position, or
one weakly held, to be taken by a sudden rush. When a
point is to be gained by hard fighting, the word *carry* is
generally used. The peculiar wording of this order shows
conclusively the state of Burnside's mind. " One rises,"
says Mr. Ropes, " from the perusal of this famous order
with a feeling of hopeless amazement that such a wild
and absurd plan of battle should ever have been enter-
tained by any one." [17]

Burnside's one chance of winning a victory was to

[17] 2 Ropes, 461.

recognize the impregnable character of Lee's left, and to attack Jackson on the right with more than half the Federal army, as advised by Franklin. This he did not do; and it only remains to sketch the events of the day.

Meade, who commanded a division of Reynolds's corps, was entrusted with the task which Burnside's order directed should be performed by " a division, at least, well supported," namely, that of " seizing " the height near Captain Hamilton's; and he was supported by the division of Gibbon on his right, and that of Doubleday on his left and rear. Meade succeeded in penetrating the enemy's lines at a weak point, and capturing several hundred prisoners. Gibbon was also successful, but not to the same degree. But the Confederates soon rallied, and were reenforced; the Union divisions were driven back in confusion, with heavy loss; and the pursuit was only checked by the resistance of other Federal troops. Franklin's loss amounted to nearly 5000 men.

Burnside states in his Report that he did not intend to move Sumner until he had " learned that Franklin was about to gain the heights near Hamilton's," and it would have been wiser if he had adhered to this plan. But about eleven o'clock, " feeling the importance of haste," he ordered Sumner to begin his attack.

The Federal attack on the right had but little chance of success. As the corps of Couch issued from the town, the troops found themselves in an open plain, with the Confederate works in their front only 600 or 700 yards distant. From the hills on their right the Confederate artillery poured upon them an enfilading fire. At the foot of Marye's Hill, the stone wall, already described, made an entrenchment which was practically impregnable. On the summit above were other lines of infantry, and powerful batteries. The Union troops advanced in column, until they passed the ditch or canal, which could only be crossed by the bridges, and then deployed for the assault, at a distance of only 300 yards from the enemy's front line. They advanced to the attack in the most gallant fashion, but the fire was too strong for them. Two other divisions, under Hancock and Howard, were ordered up to support

French, who had led the attack, but all in vain. The sunken road could not be carried. After suffering terrible losses, the men were withdrawn.

This failure ought to have satisfied General Burnside that the Confederate position was too strong to be carried, but he insisted on several more efforts. The division of Sturgis, with one brigade of Getty's division from the Ninth Corps, and the divisions of Griffin and Humphreys of the Fifth Corps, were sent in. These troops were also repulsed with terrible slaughter before they could reach the stone wall. The Federal losses at this point were nearly 8000 men.

The total losses, on both sides, were reported as follows: [18]

	Federals	Confederates
Killed	1,284	608
Wounded	9,600	4,116
Missing	1,769	653
Totals	12,653	5,377

General Burnside wished to renew the battle the next day, and even proposed to lead his old Ninth Corps in column of regiments to the assault of the stone wall; but he was dissuaded by the unanimous remonstrance of his officers. The two armies remained facing each other for two days, but there was no more fighting. On the morning of the 15th, Burnside admitted his defeat by sending a flag of truce with a request that he might be allowed to bury his dead, and remove the wounded, who for forty-eight hours had been lying untended between the hostile lines.

The same night a fierce storm swept the valley of the Rappahannock; under cover of the elements the Army of the Potomac recrossed the river and returned to its old camps at Falmouth. The retreat was effected with a skill which did much credit to the Federal staff. Within fourteen hours 100,000 troops with all their trains passed the river without attracting the observation of the Confederate patrols.[19]

[18] 3 B. & L., 145, 147.   [19] 2 Henderson, 403.

FREDERICKSBURG

No attempt was made by Lee to follow the Federals across the Rappahannock. The upper fords were open, but the river was rising fast, and the Army of the Potomac, closely concentrated, was too strong to be attacked. Burnside's escape, says Colonel Henderson, demonstrated the fallacy of one of the so-called rules of war. The great river which lay behind his army at the battle of Fredericksburg had proved his salvation, instead of his ruin, as theoretically it should have done. The five bridges across the river provided more lines of retreat than is usually the case when only roads are available; these lines of retreat also were protected by the river from the Confederate cavalry, and from the infantry and artillery by the powerful batteries on Stafford Heights. The result might have been very different if the battle had been fought on the North Anna, thirty-six miles from Fredericksburg.

There was a striking resemblance between the situation of Lee at Fredericksburg and that of Napoleon at Austerlitz in December 1805. Napoleon wanted a decisive victory, and not " only an *ordinary* battle," as he expressed it. With this object in view, he allowed the Allies to seize without opposition the commanding heights of the Pratzen, which almost any other general would have held in force. Then, on the day of battle, he rested on the defensive until the Allies had weakened their centre, in the endeavor to turn his right flank and cut off his line of retreat. As soon as the turning movement was fully developed, he easily pierced the enemy's centre, and then destroyed his wings in detail.

The Confederate position at Fredericksburg possessed two of the requirements for an ideal battle-field, but it lacked two others. It afforded (1) good cover to the troops, and a good field of fire; and (2) was not so strong as to deter the enemy from attacking; but (3) it gave no facilities for a counter-stroke, or (4) any opening for a pursuit in case of victory.[20]

For the two reasons last named, Jackson, on his arrival,

[20] 2 Henderson, 406.

objected to the position, and thought that the army should retire behind the North Anna. This was also Lee's design in the first instance, but he yielded to the wishes of President Davis, who was almost as poor a strategist as General Halleck. The Confederate authorities objected to allowing the Army of the Potomac to approach any nearer to Richmond, and were also unwilling to open more of their country than necessary to depredation.[21]

For these inconclusive reasons, Lee accepted battle at Fredericksburg, and, at the loss of 5000 valuable lives, gained a victory which was absolutely barren of any decisive results.

After the battle General Lee went to Richmond to suggest further operations, " but was assured that the war was virtually over." On the news of Fredericksburg gold had advanced in New York to 200, and the Confederate authorities were confident that peace would be proclaimed within thirty or forty days. General Lee was far from sharing this belief.[22]

" In reviewing this bloody defeat of the Army of the Potomac," writes Mr. Ropes, " one is moved to wonder at the fact that General Burnside made the attempt at all. He had practically no chance of success in assaulting the Confederate left; and even if he had given Franklin *carte blanche* as respects the attack on the Confederate right, and had that able officer done what he told Burnside he proposed to do . . . the issue of the battle would have been far from certain. . . . Nothing short of a complete rout of Jackson's extreme right — which was hardly to be expected — would have answered Franklin's needs." [23]

Undeterred by his defeat, Burnside immediately decided on another forward movement, to be made the latter part of December, but was checked by a telegram from President Lincoln enjoining him not to take any further steps without first informing him. Burnside then went to Washington, where he had a conference with the President, General Halleck, and the Secretary of War, Mr.

[21] 3 *B. & L.*, 71–72, and note. See also 2 Ropes, 451.
[22] 3 *B. & L.*, 84.
[23] 2 Ropes, 467–468.

Stanton. He was informed that certain general officers were of the opinion that his movement would end in disaster; and it was formally disapproved by the authorities.

Burnside finally resolved to act on his own responsibility: on the 20 January 1863 he moved up the river, and was preparing to cross in force when the whole operation was stopped by a storm of unusual violence. The army returned from this " Mud March " to its camps at Falmouth, tired, discouraged, and absolutely convinced of the incompetency of Burnside for his high command.[24]

Burnside went directly to Washington and made the issue boldly with the Government. He gave Mr. Lincoln the choice of accepting his resignation, or approving an order, which he had prepared, relieving from further duty with the army, Hooker, Franklin, and other high officers. Mr. Lincoln met the situation by relieving Burnside himself from command, and appointing in his place " Fighting Joe " Hooker, who had gained much popularity in the army and with the public by his dashing bearing and frank manners. At the same time Mr. Lincoln declined to accept Burnside's resignation from the service, and gave him a leave of absence for his home in Providence. In March 1863, Burnside was appointed to the command of the Department of the Ohio, where he relieved General Wright.

The order of the 25 January 1863, appointing General Hooker to the command of the Army of the Potomac, relieved Sumner and Franklin from further duty with that organization. The reasons for this action are not clear. Sumner was old for active service, but apparently hale and hearty, although he died within the year. There was dissatisfaction with Franklin's conduct at Fredericksburg, and a general feeling that, with the large force under his command, he did not accomplish what might have been expected. He " had contributed the only valuable suggestion for winning the battle "; and his failure to accomplish anything under Burnside's ridiculous orders in no way justified " the removal from the service of so intelligent and capable an officer." [25] This is also the

---

[24] 2 Ropes, 470.   [25] 2 Ropes, 472.

opinion of General Palfrey, who says: " General Franklin was practically ruined as a soldier by the battle of Fredericksburg, and his connection with it, but so far as the accessible evidence enables one to judge, he was most unjustly blamed." [26]

It is a sad reflection upon the Administration of Mr. Lincoln that, from one cause or another, the Union lost, long before the close of the war, the services of four of its ablest officers — Buell, McClellan, Porter, and Franklin. With the exception of President Davis's unjust treatment of General Joseph E. Johnston, the Confederacy made few, if any, mistakes of this kind. It does not make the matter any better that several of these removals were made by Mr. Lincoln mainly for political reasons, and largely growing out of the Emancipation Proclamation, which he issued just after the battle of Antietam.

In commenting on the Fredericksburg Campaign, General Longstreet says: " Burnside made a mistake from the first. He should have gone from Warrenton to Chester Gap. He might then have held Jackson and fought me, or have held me and fought Jackson, thus taking us in detail. . . . By interposing between the corps of Lee's army, he would have secured strong ground and advantage of position. With skill equal to the occasion, he should have had success. This was the move about which we felt serious apprehension." [27]

Other critics, however, think that the movement to Fredericksburg was right, and that it failed, through no fault of Burnside's, on account of Halleck's neglect to send the pontoons in time. In that event, General Longstreet states that the Confederates would have concentrated behind the North Anna, in a much stronger position. In either position, the Union army would probably have been defeated under a commander as incompetent as General Burnside, and at the North Anna might have met with a greater disaster. As in previous campaigns, the best of Lee's strategy appears to have been his comprehension of the character of the Federal commander, and the use he made of it.[28]

[26] Palfrey, 154.   [27] 3 B. & L., 85.   [28] Steele, 303.

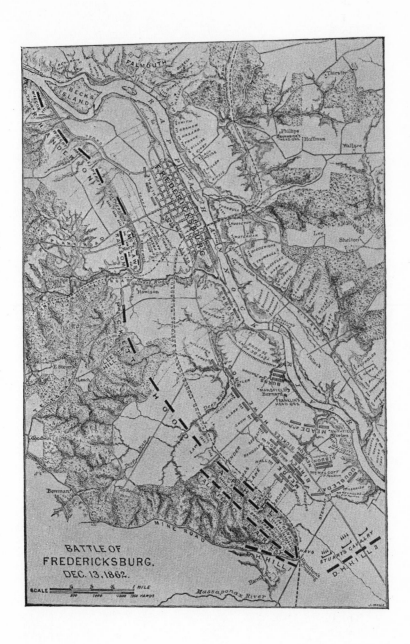

BATTLE OF
FREDERICKSBURG.
DEC. 13, 1862.

SCALE — 1 MILE
500   1000   1500   2000 YARDS

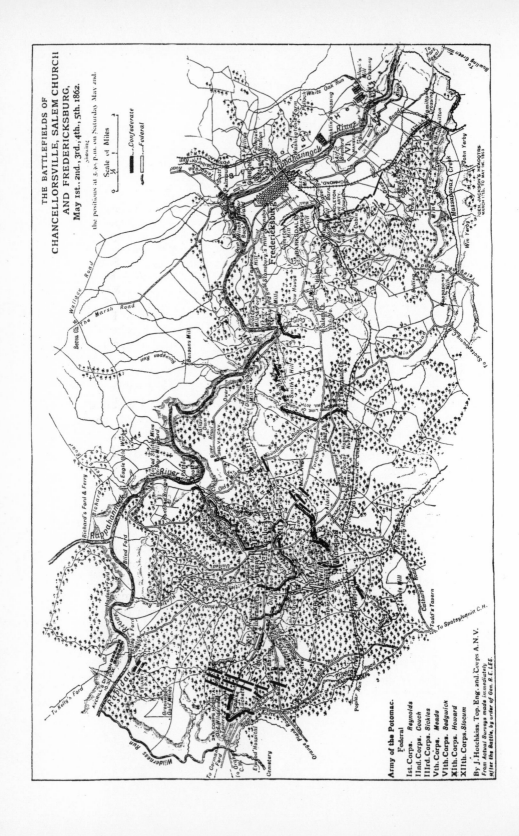

THE BATTLEFIELDS OF
CHANCELLORSVILLE, SALEM CHURCH
AND FREDERICKSBURG,
May 1st., 2nd., 3rd., 4th., 5th. 1862.

showing
the positions at 5. p. m. on Saturday May 2nd.

Scale of Miles

......Confederate
......Federal

Army of the Potomac.
Federal

Ist. Corps.	Reynolds
IInd. Corps.	Couch
IIIrd. Corps.	Sickles
Vth. Corps.	Meade
VIth. Corps.	Sedgwick
XIth. Corps.	Howard
XIIth. Corps.	Slocum

By J. Hotchkiss. Top. Eng. and Corps A. N. V.
From Actual Surveys made immediately
after the Battle, by order of Gen. R. E. LEE.

GEN. JACKSON'S HEADQUARTERS.
MARCH. TO. TO. MAY. 1st. 1863.

CHAPTER TEN

APRIL — DECEMBER 1862

MURFREESBORO

Halleck's Advance to Corinth — Beauregard Retires to Tupelo —
Buell Moves on Chattanooga — Halleck's Forces Dispersed
— Bragg Succeeds Beauregard — He Occupies Chattanooga —
Buell's Communications Cut — Bragg Takes the Offensive —
Buell Returns to Kentucky — Movements of Bragg and Smith
— Battle of Perryville — Bragg Retires to Chattanooga — Buell
Relieved — His Career — Rosecrans in Command — He Moves
on Bragg at Murfreesboro — The Field of Battle — The Hos-
tile Lines — The Plans for the Battle — The Union Right
Broken — The Afternoon Battle — Final Attacks Repulsed —
Bragg Withdraws — Losses — Comments — General Disappoint-
ment — Cavalry Operations

ON the 11 April 1862, four days after the battle of
Shiloh, General Halleck arrived at Pittsburg
Landing and took command in person of the
Union forces. On the 21st, he was joined there by General
Pope, who had successfully terminated on the 8 April his
operations against New Madrid and Island No. 10 on the
Mississippi River. He brought with him some 30,000
troops, and other reënforcements soon raised Halleck's
army to about 120,000 men.[1]

After the battle, the Confederate army, under General
Beauregard, had retired to Corinth, where it was joined
about the first of May by General Van Dorn with upwards
of 15,000 men. Beauregard's forces were then estimated
at about 70,000, but in reality they were much smaller,
and the men were demoralized from their recent defeat.

The last of April, Halleck began a slow and cautious
advance toward Corinth. His army was organized into a
right wing, commanded by Thomas; centre, under Buell;
left, under Pope; and a reserve, under McClernand.
Grant was second in command — a position more honor-

[1] 1 Grant, 376.

able than useful, as no specific duties were assigned to him.

General Grant says in his *Memoirs* that, " the movement was a siege from the start to the close." The army would construct corduroy roads, move forward a mile or two, then halt and entrench. Nearly a month was consumed in covering the twenty miles from Pittsburg Landing to Corinth! Finally, on the 30 May, Beauregard evacuated the place. He withdrew with 52,000 men, carrying off all his artillery, and the greater part of his stores. The army retired to Tupelo in Mississippi, a place about fifty miles south of Corinth, which Beauregard had selected as possessing healthful surroundings and a good water supply. In a very short time the Confederate army was as large and formidable as ever.

On the 30 May, the Federal army reached Corinth, and took possession of the town almost without bloodshed. Although the Confederate army had been allowed to escape intact, the occupation of Corinth was nevertheless an event of great importance. It gave the Federals possession of the only railroad which directly connected the Mississippi with the Atlantic seaboard. It turned the Confederate positions at Fort Pillow and Memphis, which were occupied a week later, thus opening the river as far down as Vicksburg.

Instead of pursuing the Confederate army, which should have been his first objective, Halleck now made the terrible mistake of dispersing his army of over 100,000 men. While he himself remained at Corinth, and undertook the impracticable task of repairing the railroads, he sent Wallace's division to Curtis in Arkansas, and ordered Buell to proceed to Chattanooga. Buell, who had resumed command of the Army of the Ohio, now about 31,000 strong, began his march on the 10 June. He was instructed by Halleck, as he proceeded toward Chattanooga, to repair and rebuild the Memphis and Charleston Railroad, on which he was to depend for his supplies. Nothing could more distinctly show Halleck's military incapacity than this order.[2] This line, which ran

2 2 Ropes, 385.

on the boundary between the territory just conquered, and the hostile region to the south, was everywhere exposed to interruption by the Confederate troopers. Buell protested against this order, but Halleck for several weeks insisted upon it.

The remainder of Halleck's army, about 65,000 strong, was stationed at various points between Memphis and Decatur. It consisted of the Army of the Tennessee, once more under the command of Grant, and the Army of the Mississippi, commanded by Pope until he was ordered East, and then by Rosecrans. Halleck remained at Corinth until early in July, when he too was ordered to Washington to assume the position of commander-in-chief. Grant then took the command of the two armies of the Tennessee and the Mississippi. The force left with him by Halleck was not large enough to undertake an offensive campaign against the Confederates at Tupelo, and his army was practically useless during the entire summer.

In his movement on Chattanooga, Buell had with him the four divisions of McCook, Nelson, Crittenden, and Wood. His first division, under Thomas, was not allowed to join him until the end of July. In the opinion of General Grant, if Buell had had his whole army at the outset, and been allowed to move on Chattanooga with all despatch, he would have had a good chance of success.[3] But the delay, occasioned by the repairs to the railway, gave the enemy notice of his intentions, and ample time to thwart his plans.

On the 27 June, Beauregard, whose health had broken down, was succeeded in command by Braxton Bragg, who immediately sent McCown's division to Chattanooga, for the defence of that post. On the 21 July, Bragg started for the same place with the greater part of his forces, sending his infantry by rail by way of Mobile. The remainder of his army was left in Mississippi under Price and Van Dorn. The force thus assembled at Chattanooga numbered about 30,000. At the same time there was another Confederate army of 18,000 men under General Kirby Smith at Knoxville in eastern Tennessee.

[3] 1 Grant, 383, 401.

The last of June, Buell finally secured Halleck's consent to abandon the effort to keep open the Memphis and Charleston in his rear, and he adopted for his line of communications the Louisville and Nashville, and Nashville and Chattanooga railroads, with Louisville as his primary base, and Nashville as his secondary base of supplies. But on the 13 July, Forrest, wth some 1400 troopers, captured the Union garrison of over 1000 men at Murfreesboro, and broke up the railway so thoroughly that it was not repaired until the 28th. Buell's march was thereby brought to a full stop for over two weeks. Later, he was again halted by the destruction of a tunnel on the Louisville and Nashville at Gallatin, Tennessee, by another Confederate cavalry raid under John Morgan.

" Cavalry-raids like these," says Mr. Ropes, " made in a friendly country, upon the communications of a hostile army which has advanced far into this country, are justifiable on the plainest principles of warfare, and ought always to be distinguished from those cavalry-raids which are made in a hostile territory, and are intended either to intimidate and harass its inhabitants, or cut the communications of a hostile army operating in its own country." [4]

Chattanooga was one of the most important strategic points in the Confederacy. If it were lost, the direct line of communication between the Atlantic and the Mississippi would be cut, and there would be no connection between the sections east and west of the Alleghanies except by a long détour by way of Atlanta. General Kirby Smith, who commanded the Department of East Tennessee, seems to have had a clear and comprehensive view of the whole situation. He urged Bragg in several letters to bring the main body of his army to East Tennessee, and undertake an offensive campaign, offering cheerfully to serve under him. He pointed out that there was yet time for a brilliant summer campaign, with a chance of regaining middle Tennessee, and perhaps Kentucky.

Bragg, as we have seen, issued orders for the movement; and he came to Chattanooga the last of July for a conference with Smith, at which their plans were arranged.

[4] 2 Ropes, 392-393.

His infantry arrived by rail early in August, but his cavalry and artillery, being compelled to march over the hilly country of northern Alabama and Georgia, did not get there until later.

The plan proposed that Kirby Smith, with his 18,000 men, should turn the Union position at Cumberland Gap, held by a Federal force under General Morgan, while Bragg, with the main column of some 30,000 troops, should move directly on Munfordville, where he would be squarely on Buell's line of communications. The two forces were to unite in Kentucky.

On the 6 August, Buell's headquarters were at Huntsville, Alabama, where he wrote Halleck that he was preparing to concentrate his divisions for an advance on Chattanooga. He had learned of the arrival of Bragg, with some of his troops, and expected to find the place occupied in force. The next day, in a fuller letter to Halleck, he gave his strength, exclusive of garrisons and railway-guards, as about 35,000 men, and the forces under Kirby Smith and Bragg at about 15,000 and 30,000 respectively. These estimates were substantially correct. In this letter he reiterated his intention of marching at once on Chattanooga, unless he learned that " the enemy's strength rendered it imprudent "; and on the 12th he asked General Grant to send him the two divisions for which General Halleck had authorized him to call in case of emergency.

But, before Buell could concentrate his forces, the destruction of the tunnel at Gallatin effectually broke his line of communications, and compelled him to modify his plans. Toward the last of August he renounced his project of an advance on Chattanooga, and hurried back to repel the invasion of his Department by the enemy.

It was late in August before Bragg could complete all his arrangements for the movement. He sent Smith at Knoxville McCown's division and some other troops, thereby increasing Smith's forces to 20,000 men. Bragg's original intention had been to operate only in Tennessee, but he was later influenced to change his plans, by Smith's views of the political results of an invasion of Kentucky;

and he " ended by practically subordinating the military management of his campaign to political projects." [5]

There were no railroads or rivers running in the direction of the proposed Confederate advance, and the roads, over which their stores must be transported in wagon trains, were mountainous and generally poor. The distance from Chattanooga to Munfordville, in a straight line, was about 160 miles. Very little forage and subsistence could be obtained in the country; and Bragg's march presented many other peculiarly trying features. He had to cross the river Tennessee; traverse Walden Ridge, some 1200 feet above the level of the sea; descend into the valley of the Sequatchie River; and then ascend the plateau of the Cumberland Mountains, somewhere about 2200 feet above the sea level, before he could possibly concentrate his army for the invasion proper.[6]

Kirby Smith crossed the mountains about the middle of August, and cut Morgan's line of communications. Leaving one of his divisions to watch the Federals, he pressed on to Lexington, where he arrived on the 2 September, and established his headquarters. He met no opposition en route, except at Richmond, where he routed a small Union force on the 30 August.

Bragg began his advance the first of September, and arrived at Sparta on the 5th. Up to this time his movements had been screened by the Cumberland Mountains, and Buell could not obtain any definite information regarding them. That same day Buell concentrated his army at Murfreesboro, where he could cover Nashville, and could easily be joined by the reënforcements he was expecting from Grant. Here he heard of Smith's victory at Richmond, and concluded that Bragg was intending to effect a junction with him. So he left a sufficient force to protect Nashville, and marched north with the remainder of his army.

On the 14th, Buell was at Bowling Green, and Bragg at Glasgow. On the 17th the Federal commander at Munfordville surrendered to Bragg, with 4000 men. Bragg, who was now squarely across Buell's line of communications, remained at Munfordville several days, hoping that Buell would attack him. He then started for Bardstown to connect with Kirby Smith, and Buell marched to Louisville, where he arrived on the 25th.

Buell remained only a week at Louisville, where his army was largely reënforced. On the 30 September, just as he was ready to move against the enemy, there came an order from Halleck removing him from command, and appointing Thomas in his place. But Thomas was magnanimous enough to protest against this injustice, and the order was revoked.

The first day of October, Buell began his advance. Bragg's forces were at Bardstown, and Smith's at Lexington, where the two generals were amusing themselves with inaugurating a Confederate governor. Both Bragg and Smith were deceived as to Buell's movements, and thought he was advancing toward Frankfort. They therefore moved to Harrodsburg and Versailles in order to cover the large dépôt of stores collected at Lexington. These manœuvres brought on an engagement at Perryville between Bragg's left wing, under Hardee, and the Federal left under McCook. The Federals were driven back in disorder, and lost some fifteen guns. Later in the day they rallied, and drove back the enemy. In the counter-attack, a young Union brigadier showed brilliant leadership, and the name of Philip H. Sheridan first became known to fame. Although the Federal centre and right were hardly three miles away, through some strange atmospheric condition the cannon were not heard, and the remainder of Buell's army was not aware of the combat. The Union losses were 845 killed, 2851 wounded; Confederate, 510 killed, 2635 wounded.

The battle of Perryville, on the 8 October, was a tactical success for the Confederates, but for all practical purposes it was a drawn battle.[7] At night Bragg's forces retired to Harrodsburg, where, on the 10th, they were joined by Kirby Smith's.

Bragg waited a day or two, to see if Buell would attack him; then passed through Cumberland Gap, and returned

[7] Steele, 312.

to Chattanooga. After following the Confederates as far as the mountains, Buell gave up the pursuit, and stationed his troops at Bowling Green and Glasgow, with the intention later on of moving to some point on the railroad to Chattanooga, as a base for a new campaign. But on the 30 October he was relieved from command and succeeded by Rosecrans.

Rosecrans, as already stated, had served under Grant in western Tennessee; and he had recently fought two bloody actions against the forces under Van Dorn and Price. The battle at Iuka, on the 19 September, was not a brilliant success, although the Confederates retired after it. The second action, fought at Corinth on the 3 and 4 October, was a decisive victory, and established Rosecrans's reputation as a hard fighter and an able officer.

Don Carlos Buell was a graduate of West Point; he was an excellent soldier, brave, able, and accomplished. Mr. Ropes considers him " as able a general as any in the service." He also expresses the rather extravagant opinion that if Buell had been placed in chief command in the West in November 1861, " it is not too much to say that the Confederate army of the West would have ceased to exist before June 1, 1862, and that thereafter a regiment of Union troops could have marched without opposition from Nashville to Chattanooga and Knoxville." [8]

In several respects Buell much resembled McClellan. He was a good organizer, and to him the Army of the Cumberland owed its efficiency. He had the same dislike of moving until he was entirely prepared. He was equally lacking in political tact, and his removal was due partly to his having gained the enmity of the war governors of Illinois, Indiana, and Ohio, and partly to his failure to carry out Mr. Lincoln's impracticable plans for the occupation of East Tennessee.

As a strategist, Buell was superior to McClellan, and he handled his men better in the field; but he was entirely devoid of the personal magnetism which made McClellan so popular with his troops. He, too, was unfortunate in being placed prematurely in a position of extraordinary

[8] 2 Ropes, 414.

responsibility and difficulty. His retirement was a distinct loss to the Union cause.

By the end of November, Rosecrans had concentrated his entire army at Nashville. From this point he refused to move, in spite of urgent and even threatening letters from Halleck, until he had collected two million rations, to make him independent of the railroad back to Louisville. The wisdom of this course was proved by the fact that his communications were broken by Morgan's cavalry on the 26 December.

In the meantime, Bragg had advanced from Chattanooga to Murfreesboro, a station on the railroad thirty miles southeast of Nashville, and on the morning of the 26 December, Rosecrans set out to meet him. The Union army marched in three columns, designated as the Right Wing, Centre, and Left Wing, commanded respectively by McCook, Thomas, and Crittenden. As soon as the army left Nashville, it encountered Wheeler's cavalry, which reported the movement to Bragg, and opposed it at every step. Aided by fogs and heavy rains, the cavalry so impeded the progress of the Federals that it took them four days to cover the thirty miles from Nashville to Murfreesboro. The Union cavalry seems to have accompanied the infantry on the march, and not to have taken its place in front of the columns until the 29th. Rosecrans was kept so poorly informed by his cavalry concerning the position of the Confederate army that he ordered Crittenden, whose wing was in advance, " to occupy Murfreesboro with one of his divisions on the night of the 29th, and encamp the other two miles outside." [9] But Bragg's army at that time was drawn up in front of the town!

The battle-field of Murfreesboro, or Stones River [10] as it is generally called by the Federals, is situated west of the river, about two miles from the town. The river, which flows in a winding course slightly west of north, at the time of the battle was spanned by several bridges, and was fordable in various places; hence it was not a serious

[9] Van Horne.
[10] This name is variously written *Stone*, *Stone's*, and *Stones*, but the latter form is generally used locally. (See Steele, 308, note.)

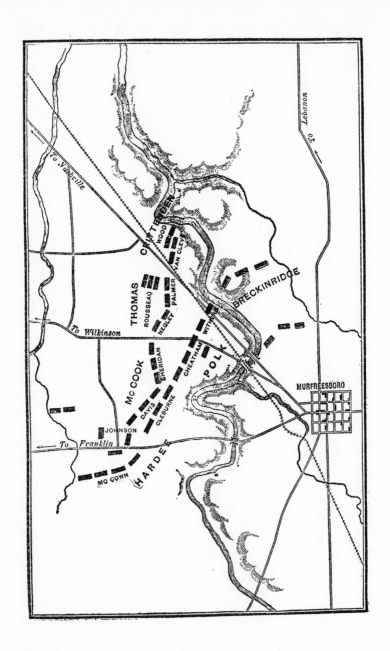

military obstacle. The turnpike and railway from Nashville traversed the northern part of the field, and, after intersecting at an acute angle, passed the river by separate bridges. The centre of the field was crossed from east to west by the Wilkinson Turnpike, and the southern part by the road to Franklin. The country was generally flat, with occasional hills which afforded good artillery positions. There were a number of farmhouses, in the midst of cultivated fields; and many patches of cedar woods, which could be traversed easily by infantry, but formed an obstacle to artillery. The thickets were dense enough to conceal troops within them.

The Confederate army was drawn up in line of battle nearly parallel to the general course of the river and mostly to the west of it. The left wing under Hardee and the centre under Polk were west of the river, while on the east side was the right wing, composed of Breckinridge's division of Hardee's corps, separated from its fellows. The general direction of the line west of the river was north and south, with the left wing somewhat advanced toward the west. Breckinridge's division was refused to the northeast, to ward off any flank attack upon the town. If Murfreesboro had been located in hostile territory, Bragg would probably have taken up a position on the east side of Stones River, in front of the town, but he wished, so far as possible, to protect the place. Under the circumstances, but little fault can be found with his arrangements.

The Union army was drawn up in a somewhat irregular line, but generally parallel to the enemy's front. The right under McCook stretched from the Franklin to the Wilkinson road. It consisted of three divisions, commanded by Johnson, Davis, and Sheridan. The centre under Thomas comprised the two divisions of Negley and Rousseau, but in the plan of battle Palmer's division of the left wing practically formed part of the centre. The remainder of the left wing under Crittenden, made up of the divisions of Wood and Van Cleve, reached from the Nashville Pike across the railroad, and rested its left on the river. The two lines, Union and Confederate, were each about three miles in length, and the two armies were practically equal in numbers, aggregating about 40,000 each.[11]

By a curious coincidence, as at the first Manassas, the two plans of battle were exactly the same. At Manassas, both McDowell and Beauregard had proposed to turn the enemy's left flank; at Murfreesboro, also, Rosecrans and Bragg had planned to turn their adversary's left. On both occasions, the course of the battle was determined by the party who secured the initiative: at Manassas, by the Federals, and at Murfreesboro by the Confederates.

Rosecrans's plan of attack was bold and brilliant. It was, to throw the two divisions of Wood and Van Cleve across the river, crush the single division of Breckinridge, and place their artillery upon a commanding ridge from which the entire Confederate line could be enfiladed. Aided by this galling fire, Rosecrans then expected to break the Confederate centre with the three divisions under Thomas, while his right under McCook would carry Murfreesboro, occupy the Franklin road, and cut off the enemy's retreat. It was for this purpose that Rosecrans massed his troops so heavily on his left, where he had nearly two-thirds of his forces. But for the success of this plan it was essential that the Federal right should be so strong, and so well placed, that it could hold Bragg while the attack on his right was carried out. In this particular, Rosecrans failed; and his error not only spoiled his plan of battle, but nearly resulted in the defeat of the Union army. McCook's line was too long and too thin, and faced too much to the east. It should have been refused nearly to the Wilkinson road, so as to face more to the south. In this position, the enemy would have had to move farther to attack it, and it could have been more easily reënforced from the centre. Rosecrans had realized this weakness, and called McCook's attention to it. But McCook, who was over-confident, stated that he could hold out for three hours, and Rosecrans did not press the matter, as he should have done.

[11] In 3 *B. & L.*, 613, Rosecrans's force is given as 43,400, and Bragg's as 37,712.

As above stated, Bragg's plan of battle was practically identical. He had massed his troops on the left, and proposed to overlap and crush the Union right; then, swinging to the north, with Polk's right as the pivot, he would take the Union centre in reverse, fold it back against the river, seize the Nashville road, and cut off the Federal line of retreat. The position favored Bragg's plan, as there was no natural obstacle in the way, and the woods on the Union right formed a screen for his movement. On the other hand, Rosecrans had to throw his two divisions across the river, which, although easily fordable, would cause considerable delay.

Soon after dawn on the morning of the 31 December, Hardee with nearly half the Confederate infantry attacked the Federal right, which was at once thrown upon the defensive. Johnson, who commanded the First Division, was at his headquarters a mile and a half in the rear, with one of his brigade commanders, and there was no one at the front to direct the troops. The Confederate attack, led by Patrick Cleburne, the ablest division-commander in the West, was absolutely irresistible, and Johnson's whole division was forced to flee in wild disorder toward the Wilkinson road. This disaster uncovered the right of Davis's division which was immediately refused, forming with Sheridan's line a salient to the enemy. Here, two assaults of the Confederates were repulsed, but a third was more successful, and Davis was forced back. This left Sheridan's right exposed, but he ordered his left brigade to charge the Confederates, and thus gained time to form a new line facing south, parallel to the Nashville Pike, and forming a right angle with Negley's division. At the same time, Rousseau's division, which had been held in reserve, formed on Sheridan's right. The new Federal front, held by the divisions of Rousseau, Sheridan, Negley, and Palmer, arranged in order from right to left, was now assaulted by the entire Confederate force west of the river. The attacks at first were repulsed, but finally Sheridan's ammunition was exhausted, and he was forced to fall back. This necessitated the withdrawal of Rousseau and Negley, also of Palmer's right; but his left, under Hazen, stood fast, and was the only part of the original Union line to hold its ground. The entire right, centre, and right of the left wing, had been forced back about this point as a pivot, " like a knife blade half-shut."

Early in the morning, pursuant to his original plan, Rosecrans had sent Van Cleve's division across the river, and these troops were actually deployed in front of Breckinridge's position before Rosecrans realized the extent of the disaster on his right. He then recalled the division to reënforce his line west of the river. It arrived just in time to hold the Confederates after Rousseau and Negley were driven back.

By noon, Rosecrans had formed a strong new line on high ground along the Nashville Turnpike, and here for four hours he resisted the continued assaults of the Confederates. The offensive movement against Bragg's right, although a failure, had nevertheless a decided effect upon the result of the battle, as it prevented Breckinridge from obeying Bragg's first order to send assistance to Hardee, which might have enabled him to break the Union line.

The final Confederate assaults had been repulsed with great slaughter, and " at four o'clock it became evident to the Confederate commander that his only hope of success lay in a charge upon the Union left, which, by its overpowering weight, should carry everything before it." [12] But there were no fresh troops left except those of Breckinridge, and he was again ordered to send them across the river. As soon as the first two brigades arrived, Polk hurled them against the Union left, where Hazen had been strongly reënforced. The attack failed, as did another made later when the other Confederate brigades had arrived. This ended the day's battle.

The two hostile armies bivouacked on the field within musket-range of each other. There was no fighting on the following day; in the afternoon Crittenden moved a division across the river, and formed line of battle in front of Breckinridge, who had returned to his former position.

[12] 3 B. & L., 628.

On the 2 January, Bragg was disappointed to find the
Federal army still in front of him. He ordered Breckinridge to dislodge the enemy from his position east of the
river. The Union troops were driven back at first, but
were soon reënforced, and recovered the position, which
they entrenched.

There was some fighting on the 3rd, but of little consequence, and that night Bragg began his retreat to Tullahoma. Rosecrans occupied Murfreesboro, but made no
pursuit of the Confederates. Like Antietam, Murfreesboro was practically a drawn battle; but the Federals remained in possession of the field of battle, in both cases.

The total losses during the campaign were as follows: [13]

	Federals	Confederates
Killed	1,730	1,294
Wounded	7,802	7,945
Missing	3,717	1,027
Totals	13,249	10,266

The outcome of the campaign in Kentucky was a distinct disappointment both to the North and to the South.
The Government at Washington thought that Buell
should not have allowed Bragg to escape, and he was removed from command. Mr. Davis felt that Bragg should
have fought Buell and defeated him, instead of allowing
him to retreat to Louisville, where he secured supplies and
reënforcements for his army.

After the battle of Murfreesboro, Bragg's corps-
commanders scarcely concealed their lack of confidence
in him, and General Polk wrote Mr. Davis that another
commander should be appointed. The feeling against
Bragg finally became so strong, both inside and outside
the army, that Mr. Davis sent General Joseph E. Johnston to Chattanooga, with authority to relieve General
Bragg from command. After a full investigation of the
conditions, however, General Johnston decided not to
remove Bragg, and returned to Mobile.[14]

[13] 3 B. & L., 611.
[14] 3 B. & L., 608; Johnston, 162.

The excellence of the work of the Confederate cavalry during the campaign has already been noticed. In Forrest, Morgan, and Wheeler, Bragg possessed three of the best cavalry commanders of the time. As Major Steele says: " It would be hard to find in the annals of modern warfare any better cavalry work." [15]

On the other hand, the Federal cavalry was so lacking in numbers and efficiency that both Buell and Rosecrans were at a great disadvantage. Buell had again and again urged the Government to remedy his deficiency in this respect, but in vain.

The tactics were good on both sides, at Murfreesboro. " Few battles have been fought," says Mr. Ropes, " which have better exhibited the soldierly virtues. The Confederate assaults were conducted with the utmost gallantry and with untiring energy. They were met with great coolness and resolution. . . . The Confederates had a right to claim a victory, for they had taken 28 guns and about 3700 prisoners. Still, the Federal army was, for all practical purposes, as strong as ever. The truth is, the Confederates were not numerous enough to complete their victory." [16]

[15] Steele, 326.   [16] 2 Ropes, 431.

CHAPTER ELEVEN

JANUARY — MAY 1863

CHANCELLORSVILLE

The Union Army Reorganized — Lee's Forces — Hooker's Plans — His Troops Cross the River — Lee Assumes the Offensive — The Wilderness — Lee Attacks — Hooker Falls Back — The Federal Position — Lee Resolves to Turn Hooker's Right — Jackson's March — His Last Despatch —·Howard's Fatal Negligence — His Corps Overwhelmed — Hooker's Perilous Position — Jackson Mortally Wounded — Battle of the 3 May — Sedgwick Carries the Fredericksburg Lines — Lee Forces Him to Retreat — Hooker Recrosses the River — Numbers and Losses — Comments — Mistakes of Hooker and Howard

AFTER the disaster of Fredericksburg, the Union army went into winter quarters on the north bank of the Rappahannock. The new commander, General Hooker, was a man of fine presence, of great personal magnetism, and had the reputation of being one of the most efficient and successful of the corps commanders.[1] He at once instituted some excellent reforms, which did much to restore the badly shaken *moral* of the troops. He adopted a system of furloughs, which remedied to a great extent the evil of desertion, which had assumed enormous proportions.[2] He abolished the clumsy grand divisions of Burnside, and reorganized the army corps. He consolidated the scattered squadrons of cavalry into a corps, under General Stoneman. The Cavalry Corps comprised three divisions, under Pleasanton, Averell, and Gregg, and a reserve brigade of regulars under Buford.

The infantry now consisted of seven corps: First (Reynolds), Second (Couch), Third (Sickles), Fifth

[1] Doubleday, *Campaigns*, 1.

[2] When he took command, Hooker reported that nearly 85,000 officers and men were absent from the colors, the majority for causes unknown.

[207]

(Meade), Sixth (Sedgwick), Eleventh (Howard), and Twelfth (Slocum). Burnside's old corps, the Ninth, was sent to Newport News.

By the end of April 1863, Hooker had the largest, the best organized and equipped army ever assembled on the continent. It numbered on paper about 120,000 infantry and artillery, with more than 400 cannon, and nearly 12,000 cavalry. From these aggregates, the usual deductions should be made, so that it is doubtful if Hooker had over 105,000 men for combat.

On the opposite side of the river, the Army of Northern Virginia, under General Lee, numbered about 60,000 men, including 3000 cavalry. Although so near Richmond, the army was poorly clothed, shod, and fed, in spite of Lee's earnest efforts. The corps occupied approximately the same positions as at the time of the battle of Fredericksburg — Longstreet's on the left and Jackson's on the right. Lee's headquarters were in a camp near Hamilton's Crossing; Jackson's at Moss Neck, eleven miles below Fredericksburg.[3]

The great need of rations for the coming campaign had led the Confederate War Department to send Longstreet with two divisions for a campaign toward Suffolk, to collect provisions and forage from the territory near the Union lines. This had reduced Lee's available forces by about a quarter, and was poor policy.[4] At the opening of the campaign, therefore, Lee had only the two divisions of Anderson and McLaws, of Longstreet's corps; and those of A. P. Hill, Rodes, Early, and Colston, of Jackson's corps.

Hooker's plan of campaign was to force Lee to come out from behind his breastworks and fight in the open. To turn his right was very difficult, owing to the width of the Rappahannock toward its mouth, the swampy character of the country, and the practical impossibility of concealing the movement. Hooker therefore decided to turn Lee's left. Stoneman was to start upon a raid against the Confederate line of communications with all the cavalry except Pleasanton's small brigade. Sedgwick, with his own

[3] Alexander, 317–318.   [4] Alexander, 319.

corps and that of Reynolds, was to cross the river below Fredericksburg and make a demonstration against Lee's right. The three corps of Meade, Howard, and Slocum, under the personal command of Hooker, would cross the Rappahannock at Kelly's Ford; then the Rapidan at Germanna and Ely's fords, march down the river, and reopen Banks's Ford, thus reuniting the two wings of the army. Sickles was to remain on Stafford Heights, ready to reenforce either wing. Couch was to leave one division of his corps on outpost at Falmouth, and place two divisions on the north bank of the river opposite Banks's Ford.

This plan was simple, and should have been successful: the only error was in sending away so large a proportion of the Union cavalry. Stoneman was detained two weeks by a heavy storm, which made the river unfordable, and did not get across until the 28 April. The result was that he did little harm to Lee's communications, and his absence from the battle-field made possible Jackson's turning movement which defeated the Union army.

Hooker felt no apprehension in thus dividing his army in the face of the enemy, as either wing was practically equal to the whole Confederate force. Sedgwick would have about 40,000 men, with the Third Corps (Sickles), about 19,000, on Stafford Heights, and one division of the Second Corps (Couch) at Falmouth. The main turning force under Hooker would also be about 40,000 strong, with two divisions of the Second Corps, say 10,000 men, at Banks's Ford. If Lee detached any considerable part of his force toward Chancellorsville, Sedgwick was ordered to carry the Fredericksburg works at all hazards, and establish his force on the Telegraph Road. The right wing, if not strongly resisted, was to advance far enough to uncover Banks's Ford; but, in case the Confederates were found in force, it was to select a strong position and await attack, while Sedgwick, coming up from Fredericksburg, would assail the enemy in flank and rear. It thus appears that Hooker's ambitious program aimed at nothing short of surrounding Lee and forcing him to surrender! Let us now see how it was carried out.

After making several demonstrations at various points,

with a view of confusing the enemy, Hooker began his grand movement on the 27 April. The Fifth, Eleventh, and Twelfth corps started for Kelly's Ford under the command of Slocum. The small Confederate guard at the ford was easily dispersed, and by the morning of the 29th the three corps had crossed the Rappahannock on pontoon bridges. On the afternoon of the 30th, they reached Chancellorsville, the Fifth Corps having crossed the Rapidan by way of Ely's Ford, and the two other corps by Germanna Ford. As soon as these troops had crossed the Rapidan, the two divisions of the Second Corps joined them at Chancellorsville, by way of United States Ford. Hooker himself arrived at Chancellorsville on the night of the 30th. Meanwhile the Fifth and Sixth corps, under Sedgwick, had laid four pontoon bridges below Fredericksburg, and crossed the river there on the 29th.[5]

No resistance, except that of picket forces, had been encountered anywhere, and the first part of Hooker's program had been carried out successfully. In three days and a half, he had covered forty-five miles, crossing two rivers, and established a force of 45,000 men on Lee's flank at Chancellorsville. Hooker was naturally elated at his success, and issued a congratulatory order to his troops, in which he said that, " the enemy must ingloriously fly, or come out from behind his defences and give us battle on our own ground, where certain destruction awaits him."

But Lee had no idea even of a " strategic retreat." Manœuvre was to be met by manœuvre, blow by counter-blow! At first he had been in doubt as to the meaning of Hooker's movement, and even suspected that it was an advance against Gordonsville and the Virginia Central Railroad. It was not until the evening of the 29th that he received word from Stuart that the Federals had crossed the Rapidan at two fords that afternoon. Anderson's division was at once despatched to Chancellorsville.

During the morning of the 30th, Lee learned that

---

[5] From the point where Sedgwick crossed, to Kelly's Ford is 27 miles; to Ely's Ford, 19 miles, and to Chancellorsville, 11 miles.

Hooker had divided his army, and that one-half of it was at Chancellorsville, while most of the remainder was in his front. He at once resolved to attack one of the wings. As his army was concentrated in front of Sedgwick, Jackson at first favored a movement against the Federal left; but, after a careful reconnaissance, he came to the same conclusion as Lee, that the position was impregnable. A force of 10,000 men under Early was left, therefore, to hold the Fredericksburg lines, and contain Sedgwick; the rest of the army was ordered to march to Chancellorsville. Jackson's three divisions, under Hill, Rodes, and Colston, numbered about 25,000; Anderson's division of Longstreet's corps about 8000, and McLaws's three brigades of the same corps about 6000. Thus Lee had in hand less than 40,000 troops, to meet Hooker's 72,000 men. To any general but Lee the outlook would have seemed hopeless.

The field upon which the battle of Chancellorsville was to be fought was in the midst of a forest of second-growth pine and black oak, the original forest having been cut for charcoal many years before. This tract, well named the " Wilderness," was about fourteen miles long from east to west, toward the Rapidan, by some ten miles wide from north to south. It was drained by many crooked brooks, with marshy borders; the soil was poor, farms were scarce, and the few clearings were not more than a rifle-shot in width. A *terrain* less suitable for the manœuvring of a large army would be hard to find. Infantry could move only with difficulty, and cavalry nowhere, except along the roads. There were few good positions for artillery, and there was no range for the guns.

Chancellorsville was merely a brick mansion, situated at an important junction of roads, on high ground, about a mile back from the eastern edge of the Wilderness, with a considerable clearing to the westward. From the house, three roads ran toward Fredericksburg: the Plank Road to the right; the more direct Old Turnpike in the centre — these two roads joining about midway to the city near the Tabernacle Church; and, to the left, the roundabout River Road, which passed near Banks's Ford.

East of the Wilderness, the country was more open, and it was there that Hooker expected to fight his battle. Accordingly he ordered his columns to move forward on the morning of the first day of May. Slocum, followed by Howard, took the Plank Road on the right. Sykes's division of Meade's corps, followed by Hancock's division of Couch's corps, went by the Turnpike in the centre. The two other divisions of Meade's corps, under Griffin and Humphreys, took the River Road. French's division of Couch's corps was ordered to march to Todd's Tavern.

Before the advance began, Sickles came up with the Third Corps, and was left at Chancellorsville as a general reserve, with one brigade guarding United States Ford, and another at Dowdall's Tavern, watching the approaches in that quarter.

Hooker's line of battle ran about two miles in a northeasterly direction from Chancellorsville to the river, covering United States Ford. To the west, it covered the Plank Road for about three miles, ending in a short offset to the north. The front was protected by entrenchments, hastily constructed.

Anderson, on his arrival the previous day, had taken a strong position at Tabernacle Church. When Jackson, marching since midnight, arrived about eight o'clock on the morning of the 1st, he found that Anderson had entrenched his whole front, from near Duerson's Mill on the right, to the unfinished railway on the left, about three miles. The position effectually blocked all of the roads by which the Federals would have to advance beyond the forest, and there were 40,000 Confederates to hold it, with 100 guns, and Fitz Lee's brigade of cavalry.

But Lee could not afford to rest on the defensive: only Early's small force of 10,000 men was in the lines at Fredericksburg to keep the Federal left wing under Sedgwick from falling upon the Confederate rear at Tabernacle Church. Therefore, at the same hour that Hooker began his advance, Lee's army also moved forward. Anderson was in advance, with one brigade on the Turnpike, and two on the Plank Road; his two other brigades and McLaws's division followed on the Turnpike; and Jackson's corps of three divisions marched on the Plank Road.

The fronts of the two armies soon came in contact on both roads. The Federals, says Doubleday, were almost out of the thickets, and the general line, on the whole, was a good one, for there were large open spaces where the artillery could move and manœuvre.[6] Sykes, however, had been directed to advance only to the first ridge beyond the forest; and there he maintained his line until ordered to withdraw to his original position. Slocum's corps had not become seriously engaged, when he, too, was directed to fall back. Griffin and Humphreys had advanced nearly five miles along the River Road, entirely unopposed, and were within sight of Banks's Ford when the orders for the countermarch reached them.

" Up to the moment of the withdrawal of his troops," says General Alexander, " Hooker's campaign had been well planned and well managed, and its culmination was now at hand in the open field — as he had desired. . . . By all the rules of the game a victory was now within his grasp." [7] Yet, at this early stage of the engagement, " Fighting Joe " seems for once to have lost his nerve; and, in spite of the protests of his amazed and indignant corps-commanders, he ordered his forces to withdraw to Chancellorsville. For this Hooker has been very severely blamed, and it is not too much to say that these orders lost him the campaign.

The Confederates felt that there was something mysterious about so easy a victory, and pursued with great caution, fearing a trap. At length, late in the afternoon, Hooker's tactics became clear: it was evident that he was standing fast on the defensive, in a position of great natural strength. As the nature of the country rendered a night attack hazardous, Lee halted his troops, and formed line of battle in front of Chancellorsville, at right angles to the Plank Road, extending on the right to the Mine Road, and to the left in the direction of Catherine Furnace.

[6] Doubleday, 13.   [7] Alexander, 326.

Hooker's position at Chancellorsville was about five miles in length, reaching from Scott's Dam on the Rappahannock to Talley's farm on the Turnpike. The left of the line was held by Meade; then, at an angle, and facing more nearly east, came Couch's corps, — French's division covering the junction of the roads at Chancellorsville, and Hancock's division in an advanced position several hundred yards in front. Next came the Twelfth Corps (Slocum), formed around the crest of Fairview Hill, and facing south. Then there was a gap in the line of about 800 yards, beyond which Howard's corps, *en échelon* along the Plank Road, held the right of the line. The Third Corps (Sickles) was kept in reserve back of the mansion. On the morning of the 2d, two brigades of Birney's division of this corps, and two batteries, were placed in the gap between Slocum and Howard, with a strong line of skirmishers thrown out in front. The 8th Pennsylvania cavalry picketed the roads and kept the enemy in sight.[8]

Although the Federal position was very strong in some respects, it had several marked defects: the almost impenetrable thickets made manœuvring difficult, and gave little scope to the artillery; besides, and most important of all, the right of Howard's line was " in the air," that is, it rested on no obstacle. Hooker was aware of this weakness, and sent one brigade of the Third Corps, with a battery, to strengthen the line; but Howard declined this assistance, as being a reflection on the bravery of his troops, or on his own military skill. As Howard had recently been appointed to the command of the Eleventh Corps, Hooker did not like to offend him, by any action which might imply lack of confidence, so the order was countermanded.[9]

During the night of the 1st, a council of war was held at Hooker's headquarters. Some of the generals favored an early assault; others, a strictly defensive attitude. Hooker himself wished to contract, and thus strengthen, his lines, but was deterred by Howard's opinion that his position was impregnable against any assault: " he would

[8] Doubleday, 16.   [9] Doubleday, 16–17.

send his compliments to the whole rebel army, if they lay in front of him, and invite them to attack him." [10]

Three miles down the Plank Road, under a grove of oak and pine, Lee and Jackson, for the fourth and last time, laid their plans for the overthrow of their enemy. If Hooker was still in position in the morning, he was to be attacked: the situation admitted of no other course. The Federal army was divided, the right wing involved in a difficult country, and so favorable an opportunity might never occur again. [11]

News had come from Fitz Lee, who commanded the cavalry on the extreme Confederate left, that Hooker's right wing was in the air. Lee's only chance was to cross the enemy's front and get in the rear of this exposed flank. The attempt would be both difficult and hazardous, and failure meant absolute destruction: if defeated, retreat would be impossible. " But no risks appalled the heart of Lee, either of odds, or position, or of both combined. His supreme faith in his army was only equalled by the faith of his army in him." [12]

The decision once made, immediate preparations were begun for the movement. Wilcox was sent with his brigade to hold Banks's Ford. This was a wise precaution, for after midnight on the 1st Hooker ordered Reynolds to leave Sedgwick and march with his corps to Chancellorsville. It will be remembered that the divisions of Griffin and Humphreys, after arriving within sight of Banks's Ford, on the afternoon of the 1st, had been recalled. Therefore, Reynolds, on reaching the ford after sunrise on the 2d, found Wilcox's brigade occupying the trenches, and was forced to continue his march to United States Ford, where he crossed.

The four remaining brigades of Anderson, and the three of McLaws, of Longstreet's corps, were ordered to entrench during the night. The turning movement was to be made by Jackson, with his three divisions, his own artillery, and Alexander's battalion of Longstreet's corps. Fitz Lee, with his cavalry, was to precede the infantry and

[10] Doubleday, 17.   [12] Alexander, 329.
[11] 2 Henderson, 528.

cover the flank. Lee himself was to remain with Anderson's and McLaws's troops, and contain the enemy while the long march of fourteen miles was made.

Two hours after sunrise, Lee, standing by the roadside, watched the head of the column march by, and exchanged with Jackson the last few words ever to pass between them. The division of Rodes led the column, Colston followed, and A. P. Hill brought up the rear.[13]

The sun rose on this day, the 2 May, about five o'clock, and set a little before seven. There was a full moon that night. Moving in a southwesterly direction, Jackson struck the Brock Road, a narrow track which runs nearly due north, and crosses both the Plank Road and the Pike about two miles west of Howard's position. The Brock Road, which would have been strongly held by the Union cavalry if Stoneman had been present, was free and unobstructed. Couriers brought word that the trains in the rear had been attacked and forced off the direct road; that some of Hill's brigades had turned back to save them, and that the enemy in great strength had poured into the gap between the two Confederate wings, but still Jackson pressed on, without a look behind him.

About two o'clock, just as the rear brigades, after checking Sickles's attack on the trains, were leaving the Welford house, six miles distant, Jackson himself reached the Plank Road, where he purposed to turn eastward against the Federal flank. Here he was met by Fitz Lee with the important information that by attacking down the Turnpike, instead of the Plank Road, he could take the Union line in reverse. Having satisfied himself by a personal reconnaissance that this was correct, Jackson at once changed his plans. The cavalry, supported by the Stonewall Brigade, was sent a short distance down the Plank Road, to mask the march of the column. At four o'clock, Rodes was on the Pike, where he was joined by Jackson. Marching down the road about a mile, in the direction of the enemy, the troops were ordered to halt and deploy for battle. Meanwhile, seated on a stump near the Brock Road, Jackson wrote his last despatch to General Lee:

[13] Alexander, 329.

CHANCELLORSVILLE

Near 3 P.M., May 2, 1863

GENERAL — The enemy has made a stand at Chancellor's [Dowdall's Tavern], which is about two miles from Chancellorsville. I hope as soon as practicable to attack. I trust that an ever-kind Providence will bless us with great success.

Respectfully

T. J. JACKSON,
Lieutenant-General

The leading division is up, and the next two appear to be well closed.

T. J. J.

GENERAL R. E. LEE

Without their presence being suspected by a soul in the Federal army, 25,000 Confederates were now deploying in the forest directly in the rear of the Union lines, and overlapping them both to north and south.

At Chancellorsville, the day had passed quietly. Early in the morning, Hooker had ridden around his lines. Expecting to be attacked only in front, he was well satisfied with their location and construction. To Howard, he exclaimed, " How strong! how strong! " When he heard about ten o'clock that a large Confederate column had been seen marching westward past Catherine Furnace, he was uncertain as to the meaning of the movement. As the hours went by, however, and there was no further news, he became convinced that Lee was retreating on Gordonsville. At four o'clock he sent orders to Sedgwick to " capture Fredericksburg with everything in it, and vigorously pursue the enemy." He added, " We know that the enemy is fleeting, trying to save his trains." At this very moment, the Confederate avalanche was about to descend on his unprotected flank and rear!

Howard, in charge of the Union right, seems to have been as blind as Hooker. During the morning some slight preparations were made to defend the Pike to the westward, but even when his only reserve, Barlow's brigade, was sent to reënforce Sickles's attack on Jackson's trains, no change was made in the disposition of the other troops.

Every one was convinced that Lee was retreating. No attention was paid to the reports of the pickets that the enemy was massing in the forest, and no attempt was made by a reconnaissance in force to ascertain what was actually going on in the thickets.

This neglect was the more remarkable because Howard's position was very weak. He had twenty regiments of infantry, and six batteries, but his force was completely isolated. Devens's division was along the Pike on the right, with two regiments facing west and the balance south. Next came the division of Schurz, deployed along the Pike, and to its north. At Dowdall's Tavern, one brigade of Steinwehr's German division held a line of rifle-pits at right angles to the Pike. There were batteries in the road and near the Wilderness Church.

It was now six o'clock, and less than two hours of daylight remained. Jackson sat on his horse, watch in hand, awaiting the formation of his lines.

" Are you ready, General Rodes? " he asked.

" Yes, sir," Rodes replied.

" You can go forward, sir."

The signal for the advance was given by a bugle, taken up and repeated for each brigade by bugles to the right and left through the woods. But no mention is made in the Federal reports of these sounds, which seem to have been deadened in the forest. The first warning to the Union troops came from the wild rabbits, foxes, and deer, which ran scuttling through their lines. Then came shots from the pickets, followed by the onrush of the Confederate line, which charged with the famous rebel yell. For the second time in the Civil War, the Federals were taken completely by surprise. They were not " bayoneted in their beds," as at Shiloh, but the soldiers, " scattered in small groups, laughing, cooking, smoking, sleeping, and playing cards," with " their arms stacked in the rear," were taken entirely unawares. Devens's division, struck in flank, was driven back against that of Schurz, before the latter had time to deploy, and the whole mass ran pell-mell toward Chancellorsville, where they streamed in wild disorder past Hooker's head-quarters.

" Much undeserved obloquy," says General Alexander, " was heaped upon the Eleventh Corps for their enforced retreat. No troops could have acted differently." [14]

The pursuit was kept up for some distance, but was finally ended by the fading daylight. The Confederate troops were much fatigued and entirely disorganized. The loss of the Federals was 1438 killed and wounded, 974 missing — the total of 2412 being only about 20 per cent. of Howard's corps. This loss would certainly have been much larger but for the fact that only one-third of Jackson's force took part in the attack and pursuit. Five brigades did not reach the field in time, and four of A. P. Hill's brigades were not in line until after six o'clock.

Owing to some peculiar state of the atmosphere, as happened at Perryville, the firing was not heard at Chancellorsville, only two miles away. At half-past six, Hooker was sitting on the veranda of the mansion in entire confidence that Lee was in full retreat, when an aide, looking down the road with his glass, exclaimed, " My God! here they come! " All sprang to their horses, and, riding down the road, soon met the fugitives from Howard's corps. If the hour had not been so late, Hooker's situation would have been desperate, as he had only two divisions at hand to confront Lee and Jackson, who were then only two miles apart. But, as so often happened in the Peninsula, darkness robbed the Confederates of the full fruits of their victory. Hooker acted promptly and on the whole judiciously, and the night restored nearly all the advantages lost during the day. Even with the moon at its full, offensive operations could not be continued by night in such a wooded country.

Sickles was recalled, and reached the field with his corps at ten o'clock. The artillery of the Twelfth Corps (Slocum) was placed in a commanding position, known as Fairview, along the western brow of the plateau south of the Plank Road, and this now became the key-point of

[14] Alexander, 337.

the Union line. In front of it the open ground extended about 600 yards to the edge of the forest, and a small stream at the foot of the plateau offered shelter for a strong body of infantry in front of the guns. During the night parapets were constructed, and a powerful battery of 34 guns was established. The forest in front offered no single position for a Confederate gun.[15]

About eight o'clock in the evening, Jackson was at Dowdall's Tavern. There was a lull in the battle, and he was planning a further advance, to cut Hooker off from United States Ford. After issuing his orders, about 8:45 he rode forward to join his advanced line. He was followed by several staff officers and couriers. The party rode slowly forward upon an old mountain road, now almost obliterated by the forest, which ran toward Chancellorsville, parallel to, and about 80 yards distant from the Plank Road. After advancing some 100 or 200 yards, they halted and listened awhile to the axes of the Federals, who were cutting abattis in the woods beyond. Suddenly firing began between the skirmishers of both armies, and spread rapidly along the lines. Jackson was slowly retracing his way back to his line, when Major Barry of the 18th North Carolina ordered his men to fire on the group of horsemen, whom he took to be a squadron of Federal cavalry. Two of the party were killed, and Jackson received three wounds, one of which proved fatal. During the night it was found necessary to amputate his left arm, which had been shattered between shoulder and elbow. The next day he was taken in an ambulance via Spottsylvania to a small house called Chandler's, near Guinea Station. For several days his recovery was expected, but pneumonia set in, and he died on the 10 May.

As A. P. Hill, the next in rank, was soon afterwards wounded, Stuart took command of Jackson's corps.

At dawn on Sunday, the 3d, Stuart renewed the attack. Hooker had made the mistake of withdrawing Sickles from the heights of Hazel Grove, which were seized by

---

[15] Alexander, 337–338.

the enemy. Here, Stuart placed thirty guns, which enfiladed a part of the Union line, and reached the space
around the mansion.

During the night Hooker had readjusted his line.
Howard's corps had been sent to the left to reorganize;
the right was held by Couch, Sickles, and Slocum. The
Union line, about a mile and a quarter long, extending
northward from Fairview to beyond the Plank Road,
was held by some 25,000 men — about as many as Stuart
had. The position was strongly entrenched. The roads
toward Fredericksburg were covered by Hancock's division of the Second Corps, and a part of the Twelfth
Corps (Slocum). Meade was near Howard, on the left,
on the road to United States Ford; and Reynolds, in the
rear, covered the road to Ely's Ford.

After several hours of hard fighting, Stuart forced the
Federals back, and occupied Fairview Hill, to which he
moved his batteries. At the same time, Anderson and
McLaws were assaulting the centre and left of the Union
line, which were also compelled to fall back. Finally the
flanks of Stuart's and Anderson's forces came together
at Fairview. At ten o'clock Lee had possession of the
mansion, now only a smoking ruin.

Just before this Hooker had been knocked down and
disabled by a brick torn by a shell from one of the columns
of the front porch of the house. Couch succeeded temporarily to the command, and directed the withdrawal of
the Union forces to a new line in the rear, which had been
selected and prepared by the engineers. The right rested
on the Rapidan and the left on the Rappahannock, the
position covering the line of retreat by United States
Ford.

Lee was preparing to assault the new position when he
was forced to turn his attention to the Federal movement
on his rear.

At nine o'clock on the evening of the 2d, Hooker had
sent Sedgwick an order to carry the works at Fredericksburg; then move on Chancellorsville, and attack Lee from
the rear. As Reynolds was gone, Sedgwick now had only
his own corps, of about 22,000 men. The works were

held by Early's division, of some 10,000 men, but he was soon reënforced by Wilcox, who brought his brigade from Banks's Ford.

Sedgwick reached Fredericksburg about three o'clock on the morning of the 3d, and attacked at daybreak. During the morning three separate assaults were repulsed, and an effort to turn Marye's Hill failed. But a fourth attack carried the strong position in the sunken road, and the Federals soon reached the crest of the hill. Early's troops retreated by the Telegraph Road, leaving the roads to Chancellorsville protected only by Wilcox's single brigade.

This was the news which reached Lee just as he was preparing for a final attack. He at once sent four brigades under McLaws to meet Sedgwick. Wilcox formed his brigade across the Plank Road, and fell back slowly to Salem Church, where he was joined by McLaws, about three o'clock. When Sedgwick came up, about an hour later, a desperate combat ensued, which lasted until dark. Sedgwick could make no further progress; since morning, he had lost nearly a fourth of his force.

Finding that Hooker did not attack the next morning, the 4th, Lee sent Anderson's division to join McLaws, leaving only what remained of Jackson's old corps in front of Hooker. Meanwhile Early had retaken Marye's Hill, and then advanced on the rear of Sedgwick, who found himself surrounded on three sides, with only the road to Banks's Ford open. Fortunately for the Federals, it was six o'clock before the Confederates were ready to make a vigorous attack, and Sedgwick was able to reach the river at Banks's Ford, where he crossed during the night on a pontoon bridge which had been laid after the departure of Wilcox the previous day.

Tuesday morning, the 5th, Lee concentrated all his forces in front of Hooker, and prepared to assault the Union lines at daybreak on the 6th. When morning came, however, it was found that, during the night, the Army of the Potomac had retreated across the river, leaving behind the killed and wounded; fourteen guns, and twenty thousand stand of arms.

The losses on both sides during the few days of the campaign were: [16]

	Federals	Confederates
Killed	1,606	1,649
Wounded	9,762	9,106
Missing	5,919	1,708
Totals	17,287	12,463

According to the official returns of the 30 April, Hooker had about 130,000 men, including 11,000 cavalry, most of which was not present at the battle. Lee's army was some 60,000 strong.

After the disaster of Fredericksburg, there was a strong demand from the army for the recall of McClellan, but the authorities at Washington seemed to fear that a military dictatorship might result from the return of the "young Napoleon." General Halleck and Secretary Stanton favored the transfer of Rosecrans; but at this time it was thought unwise to put another Western man in command. The choice being narrowed to the Army of the Potomac, a process of elimination began. Franklin was under a cloud owing to his alleged misconduct at Fredericksburg; Sumner was considered too old and too feeble; Couch was a possible second choice. Finally the selection was found to be restricted to Reynolds, Meade, and Hooker. The latter had strong popular and political support, but his appointment was violently opposed by Halleck and Stanton, who thought that he was unfit for a position of such responsibility. Reynolds, when sounded on the subject, refused to accept the command unless given complete liberty of action, which at that time the Administration was not willing to grant. Finally, as the result of an obscure political intrigue, connected with the aspirations of Secretary Chase to be elevated to the Presidency at the end of Mr. Lincoln's term, the President overruled Halleck and Stanton, and directed the appointment of Hooker.[17]

In making the announcement of his selection, Mr.

[17] 3 B. & L., 239–240. See also, 2 Barton, 170 et seq.
[16] 3 B. & L., 237.

Lincoln wrote Hooker a most remarkable letter, in which he said, among other things: " I have heard, in such a way as to believe it, of your recently saying that both the army and the Government needed a Dictator. Of course it was not for this, but in spite of it, that I have given you the command. Only those generals who gain successes can set up dictators. What I now ask of you is military success, and I will risk the dictatorship. . . . And now beware of rashness. Beware of rashness, but with energy and sleepless vigilance go forward and give us victories." [18]

During a visit to Hooker's camp, in April, Mr. Lincoln gave him another bit of good advice: " I want to impress upon you in your next fight — *put in all of your men!* "

The Campaign of Chancellorsville began with the crossing of the Rappahannock on the 28 April, and ended with the return of the Union army to the north side of the river on the night of the 5 May. It will be hard to find in the annals of the Civil War a greater series of blunders than those made by the Federal commander **during** this brief period of eight days!

Hooker's first mistake was in sending Stoneman with 10,000 sabres against Lee's communications, while he retained with his army only Pleasanton's small brigade of 1500 men. It would have been better if the arrangement had been exactly reversed. Nearly all of the successful cavalry raids during the war were made with comparatively small bodies of men. During this same month of April, Grierson rode the whole length of the State of Mississippi with only a thousand troopers, and destroyed an immense amount of Confederate property. Stuart's brilliant rides around the Union army were generally made with less than two thousand horsemen.

It was an essential part of Hooker's plan that the cavalry should begin operations two weeks before the infantry. Stoneman started on the 13 April, but a heavy storm made the river unfordable until the 28th. Although this delay had entirely altered conditions, Hooker was too impatient to wait longer, and all — infantry, artillery,

[18] 8 Lincoln, 206–207.

and cavalry — were sent over together. The result was that the battle was fought before Stoneman had time to carry out the plan of cutting Lee's communications.

If Stoneman's 10,000 men had been on the Union right, where they should have been, on the 2 May, Jackson's famous turning movement would not have been made; [19] or, if attempted, it would have been a disastrous failure, instead of a brilliant success.

Another great mistake was made by Hooker in withdrawing his troops on the afternoon of the 1st. "The position thus abandoned," says General Couch, "was high ground, more or less open in front, over which an army might move and artillery be used advantageously; moreover, were it left in the hands of an enemy, his batteries, established on its crest and slopes, would command the position at Chancellorsville." [20]

It was also of the utmost importance to secure Banks's Ford, then almost within the grasp of the Federals, which would have greatly shortened the distance between the two wings of the army.

When the order to retire was received, the Union officers at the front — Couch, Hancock, Sykes, Warren, and others — agreed that the ground should not be abandoned. An aide was sent to General Hooker, to protest against the withdrawal; but he returned in half an hour with positive orders to fall back. Even so loyal an officer as General Warren suggested that they should disobey; and he then rode back to see the general. Later, about two o'clock, when nearly all the regiments had been withdrawn, there came a third order from Hooker: "Hold on until five o'clock." Disgusted at the general's vacillation, General Couch sent back the rather impertinent reply: "Tell General Hooker he is too late, the enemy is already on my right and rear. I am in full retreat." [21]

The Army of the Potomac was in no sense defeated by the disaster to Howard's corps. By a vigorous combined assault, Lee might still have been driven off the field. Hooker failed to comply with Lincoln's order, "to put

---

[19] *Cf.* Maurice, 184.   [21] 3 *B. & L.*, 159.
[20] 3 *B. & L.*, 159.

in all his men." He employed little more than half his force. The two corps of Reynolds and Meade — over 30,000 strong — were not allowed to go into action, though the generals were eager to do so. In the opinion of General Alexander, Hooker's decision to retreat, on the night of the 5th, was "the mistake of his life." He then had his whole united army, upwards of 90,000 men, behind "probably the strongest field-entrenchment ever built in Virginia." [22] Lee was preparing to attack this position with only 35,000 men, worn out with seven days' marching and fighting! Hooker's retreat saved Lee from a disastrous repulse.

General Couch alludes to the "charge that the battle was lost because the general was intoxicated." By implication, he denies this, but insinuates that it might have been better for the Union army if the charge had been true! He says that Hooker "probably abstained from the use of ardent spirits when it would have been far better for him to have continued in his usual habit in that respect." [23]

Howard was principally responsible for the disaster to the Union right on the 2d, and should have been cashiered, but he got off with a mild censure. The whole blame was laid on the Germans, who did not deserve it.

In spite of all his precautions, Jackson's column was seen to pass over a bare hill about a mile and a half from Birney's front, and the number was almost exactly estimated. Birney immediately reported this important fact to headquarters, and at 9:30 A.M., General Hooker issued an order, addressed to Slocum and Howard, warning them to guard their flanks, and be prepared for the enemy "in whatever direction he advances."

Notwithstanding this order to Howard, *he took no precautions against the impending danger.* His apathy and indifference can only be explained on the supposition that

[22] Alexander, 344, 359, 360.

[23] 3 B. & L., 170. In answer to an inquiry from General Doubleday, during the Gettysburg campaign, as to what was the matter with him at Chancellorsville, Hooker replied: "I was not hurt by a shell, and I was not drunk. For once I lost confidence in Hooker, and that is all there is to it." (Cited, Macartney, 154.)

he really believed Jackson was retreating to Gordonsville, although on what grounds, it is difficult to imagine. During the eight hours, from 10 A.M., when Hooker's order was received, to 6 P.M., when the assault came, Howard had ample time to render his line impregnable, but he did nothing. The few precautions taken were due entirely to the initiative of two of his division commanders — Schurz and Devens.

All the blame for the rout was thrown upon the Germans, but it is only fair to state that when a force, not deployed, is struck suddenly and violently on the flank, resistance is impossible. Napoleon's Old Guard, the best and bravest troops that ever existed, could not have held together in such a case.

Howard scouted the reports which came in all day long, and fairly insulted the informants, saying that their stories were the result of their imaginations or their fears. Apparently nothing could vanquish his incredulity; he could not be made to believe that there was any force of the enemy near him. In his official report the pious Howard writes as though he believed that his corps was overwhelmed by the act of God! [24]

The two greatest commanders of modern times — Frederick and Napoleon — both played a good game of chess, and every student in the Army War College should be taught the game; for it is *the* game, above all others, in which one must constantly play his opponent's hand as well as his own, in order to achieve success. Otherwise, he will continually find that his most brilliant combinations fail, because his adversary is not considerate enough to make the moves that he desires or expects.

In the first Italian campaign of 1796, the Austrian commanders — Beaulieu, Alvinzy, and Wurmser — all complained bitterly that the young Bonaparte did not play the game according to the rules of war! Lee and Jackson had the same disagreeable habit. According to all prec-

[24] See Doubleday, 22–32. General Doubleday says that the subsequent inquiry was "very much of a farce." As Hooker and Howard were both left in high command, "it was absurd to suppose their subordinates would testify against them."

edents, when Lee found himself outnumbered two to one at Fredericksburg, with the Federal hosts massed on both his flanks, and Stoneman's 10,000 horsemen riding against his communications, he should have retreated precipitately. But Lee did nothing of the sort. In defiance of all the rules of war, he left Early with 10,000 men behind the breastworks of Fredericksburg, to hold back Sedgwick's two corps of 40,000 troops, and with the balance of his forces marched to Chancellorsville to meet Hooker. Then he had the even greater audacity to divide his army once more, and remain with 25,000 men in front of Hooker while he sent Jackson with the other half of his available forces by a roundabout march of fourteen miles to fall upon the Federal flank and rear!

The power of striking like a " bolt from the blue," says Colonel Henderson, is of the very greatest value in war. Surprise was the foundation of almost all the grand strategical combinations of the past, as it will be of the future. Success is seldom to be won without incurring risks. " The very course which appeared to ordinary minds so beset by difficulties and dangers as to be outside the pale of practical strategy has, over and over again, been that which led to decisive victory." [25]

" The battle of Chancellorsville," says Colonel Livermore, " although faulty in respect to the flank march of Jackson, is nevertheless one of the most instructive to the military student of any in ancient or modern times, from the succession of kaleidoscopic changes of position from day to day and from hour to hour, in which superior tactical skill on the part of one or more of the commanders on either side might have changed the fate of the campaign; and this faulty move, which did in fact partially succeed through the stupendous blunders of Hooker and especially through the persistent negligence and blind credulity of Howard, gave rise to situations of great dramatic interest, in one of which the picturesque and noble Jackson was stricken down at the moment when he thought that all Hooker's army would soon be within his grasp." [26]

[25] Henderson, *Science of War*, 35.   [26] 3 Livermore, 151.

CHAPTER TWELVE

JUNE — JULY 1863

GETTYSBURG

The Military Situation — Lee Rejects Longstreet's Plan — Changes in His Army — Inferiority of the Federal Organization — Lee Starts North — Hooker's Orders — Brandy Station — Hooker Follows the Confederates — He Is Superseded by Meade — Positions of the Two Armies — Chance Collision at Gettysburg — The Battle-field — The First Day — Confederate Success — The Federals Occupy Cemetery Ridge — Meade Decides to Fight There — Lee Determines to Attack — The Union Line — Sickles Occupies a Dangerous Position at the Peach Orchard — The Federals Driven Back — Meade Decides Not to Retire — Lee Plans to Assault — The Famous Pickett Charge — Its Failure — Cavalry Engagements — Numbers and Losses — Lee Retreats — Meade's Failure to Attack — The Confederates Re-cross the Potomac — Comments — Errors of Lee — The Cavalry in the Campaign — Stuart's Fatal Raid

AFTER the battle of Chancellorsville the two armies resumed their former positions on the opposite sides of the Rappahannock. The *moral* of the Union army had suffered from another defeat, while the Confederate *hopes*, in the words of General Alexander, reached the highest point attained during the war. Under the system of obligatory service,[1] Lee's army was at once increased by a large force of conscripts. He was also re-joined by Longstreet with his two divisions which had been absent during the Chancellorsville campaign. On the 31 May, Lee had an army of over 76,000 men, and 272 guns. At the same date, the Army of the Potomac was reduced by loss in battle and by expiration of the terms of service to less than 105,000 effectives.

Although there were few men then endowed with the foresight to realize the fact, the next five weeks were to

[1] Under the acts of 16 April and 27 September 1862.

mark the turning point of the war; and the fate of the Confederacy was to be decided by the policy adopted by the Southern leaders at this time. Grant, with 75,000 men, had Pemberton, with 30,000, securely invested at Vicksburg, while Johnston, with less than 25,000, was at Canton, powerless to raise the siege. Unless Johnston could be heavily reënforced, or some measure taken to force the Washington Government to recall a part of Grant's army, Vicksburg was doomed, and the Mississippi would be lost to the Confederacy.

On the 15 May, Beauregard suggested to Johnston a plan to submit to the War Department for a " brilliant " summer campaign; and about the same date, Longstreet, when passing through Richmond on his way to rejoin Lee, outlined to Mr. Seddon, the Secretary of War, a very similar project. This plan, in brief, was to take advantage of the interior lines of the Confederacy to transfer Longstreet's two veteran divisions, 13,000 strong, via Lynchburg, Knoxville, and Chattanooga, to Murfreesboro, Tennessee, where Bragg, with some 45,000 Confederates, confronted Rosecrans with about 60,000 Federals; to send Johnston's 25,000 from Mississippi, and Buckner's 5000 from Knoxville to the same point; then for Lee to go West, take command in person, defeat Rosecrans, and march on Louisville and Cincinnati. " If anything could have caused Grant's recall from Vicksburg," says General Alexander, " it would have been this. Surely the chances of success were greater, and of disaster less, than those involved in our crossing the bridgeless Potomac, into the heart of the enemy's country, where ammunition and supplies must come by wagons from Staunton, nearly 200 miles, over roads exposed to the raids of the enemy from either the east or the west. In this position, a drawn battle, or even a victory, would still leave us compelled soon to find our way back across the Potomac." [2]

But foreign intervention was the ruling idea with President Davis, and he declined to entertain the proposition. After reporting to General Lee, Longstreet made him

[2] Alexander, 365.

the same suggestion. " He reflected over the matter several days," says Longstreet, " and then fell upon the plan of invading the Northern soil, and so threatening Washington as to bring about the same hoped-for result." [3]

What might have been the result of the acceptance of this plan, which was strategically sound, is a problem of great interest; but it is doubtful whether the result for the Confederacy would have been any more satisfactory than the campaign which Lee actually conducted in the East. At that time Mr. Davis was very sanguine that a victory on Northern soil would bring about foreign recognition; and Lee himself was averse to leaving Virginia, — also to any division of his army. Ever since the failure of the invasion of Maryland, both Lee and Jackson had longed to try it once more, and during the winter and spring, the latter had had prepared a remarkable large-scale map of the country from Winchester to the Susquehanna, on which even the farm-houses were noted, with the names of the owners. [4]

In preparation for the coming campaign, Lee decided to reorganize his army, making three corps, instead of two. General James Longstreet, a native of South Carolina, remained in command of the First Corps. He had the unbounded confidence of his troops, who called him " Old Pete," and was considered the hardest fighter in the Confederate service. Jackson's old corps, the Second, was assigned to General Ewell, who was entitled to the command by reason of his rank, services, and ability. Lee wished to place the new third corps under the command of a Virginian, although this made it necessary to disregard the claims of two officers who had been very efficient. He accordingly selected for the command of the Third Corps, General Ambrose P. Hill, passing over the two generals next in rank, D. H. Hill, a native of North Carolina, and McLaws, a Georgian, against whom there was no objection, except that they were not Virginians. General Longstreet thinks that this reorganization somewhat impaired the *moral* of the troops. General Alex-

[3] Longstreet, 327–331.   [4] See Alexander, 322, 365.

ander also states that D. H. Hill had strong claims for promotion, and that Stuart would have made a more active and efficient corps-commander than Ewell.[5]

Each corps consisted of three divisions, and each division of four brigades, except Anderson's and Rodes's, which had five each, and Pickett's, which had three at Gettysburg, — in all thirty-seven infantry brigades.

The cavalry, which comprised the select troops of the Confederacy, were now organized as a division, consisting of six brigades, under Stuart.

At this time, the general artillery reserve, commanded by Pendleton, was broken up, chiefly due to the lack of guns, and was never reëstablished. Pendleton, however, was retained as chief of artillery. The new artillery organization, of a few batteries with each division, and a reserve with each corps, but with no general reserve for the army, was the first of the kind ever adopted, and it was subsequently copied by all the principal nations of Europe. But General Alexander thinks that the fine service of the Federal reserve of 110 guns, under Hunt, at Gettysburg demonstrates the advantage of such an organization in every large army.[6]

The three Confederate army corps, of from 21,000 to 23,000 men, approximated in numbers what is to-day considered the proper strength of an army corps, that is 30,000 men; and each corps only lacked a complement of cavalry to make it a complete little army in itself, which is also the approved organization of to-day.[7]

Lee was a full general; his corps were commanded by lieutenant-generals, his divisions by major-generals, and all but two of his forty-two infantry and cavalry brigades by brigadier-generals. Nearly all of these officers were veterans of proved ability, and many had served in the Mexican War.

In the Army of the Potomac, on the other hand, the average strength of the army corps and divisions was about half that of the Confederates. At the battle of Gettysburg the seven army corps consisted of nineteen

[5] 3 B. & L., 245. Alexander, 367.   [7] Steele, 354.
[6] Alexander, 370.

infantry divisions, of which seven had two brigades, eleven had three, and one had four — in all fifty-one brigades. The army and the corps were commanded by major-generals, the divisions by three major-generals and sixteen brigadiers, the infantry brigades by twenty-two brigadiers and twenty-nine colonels. It is impossible to understand or explain the aversion of the Congress to bestowing proper rank upon the general officers in the United States Army. Since the Revolutionary War, there have been only four full generals in our service — Grant, Sherman, Sheridan, and Pershing. Washington was only a lieutenant-general, and Scott, until after his retirement, held the same rank only by brevet. During the four short years of the existence of the Confederacy, eight full generals, and twenty-three lieutenant-generals were commissioned: their armies were always commanded by full generals, and their army corps by lieutenant-generals.

" It will be perceived by comparison," says General Hunt, " that the organization of the Army of the Potomac was at this period in every way inferior to that of its adversary. The army corps and divisions were too numerous and too weak. They required too many commanders and staffs, and this imposed unnecessary burdens on the general-in-chief, who was often compelled to place several army corps under the commander of one of them, thus reproducing the much abused ' grand divisions ' of Burnside, under every possible disadvantage. Had the number of infantry corps been reduced to four at most, and the divisions to twelve, the army would have been more manageable and better commanded; and the artillery, without any loss, but rather a gain of efficiency, would have been reduced by a dozen or fifteen batteries." [9]

Lee's movement began on the 5 June, and on the 8th the corps of Longstreet and Ewell were concentrated at Culpeper. Hill remained at Fredericksburg to watch Hooker, and keep him quiet as long as possible. On the 5th, Hooker wrote the President that he thought Lee was

[9] 3 B. & L., 261.

[233]

contemplating another invasion of the North, and asked instructions. In their replies both Mr. Lincoln and General Halleck advised Hooker to attack Lee's column on the north side of the river, and by no means to cross the Rappahannock to assault his entrenchments. In the President's letter he uses the famous illustration of the " risk of being entangled upon the river, like an ox jumped half over a fence and liable to be torn by dogs front and rear, without a fair chance to gore one way or kick the other."

As a matter of fact, the Army of the Potomac, under a competent commander, stood in no danger of being caught " half over the fence," and could have attacked Lee's movable column, or assaulted his entrenchments, with equal impunity. But the Administration had lost all confidence in Hooker since the battle of Chancellorsville.

Since Lee took command of the Army of Northern Virginia in June 1862, his career had been one of almost uninterrupted success. His victories on his own soil had been extraordinary, and he had become convinced, like nearly all of his officers and men, that he and his army were invincible. Over and over again — in the Peninsula, at Second Manassas, at Chancellorsville — he had showed contempt of his foe. In his second invasion of the North he displayed the same contempt. No other construction can be placed on the stretching of his line from Fredericksburg to Winchester in the face of an opponent who greatly outnumbered him. On the 14 June, President Lincoln wrote Hooker: " If the head of Lee's army is at Martinsburg and the tail of it on the plank road between Fredericksburg and Chancellorsville, the animal must be very slim somewhere. Could you not break him? "

" War," says Colonel Henderson, " is more a struggle between two human intelligences than between two masses or armed men." [10] The great general does not give his first attention to numbers or position, but puts himself in his opponent's place, and observes the situation with that commander's eyes, taking into consideration his weakness,

[10] Henderson, *Science of War*, 283.

tactical, strategical, and political; detecting the points for the security of which he is most apprehensive; divining what his action will be if attacked here or threatened there. Looking at things thus from his enemy's point of view, he decides whether or not apparent risks can be taken with impunity.

It was through his knowledge of the character and position of Mr. Lincoln, the Commander-in-Chief of the Armies of the United States, that General Lee well knew that a threat against Washington was morally certain to result in the recall of Hooker's army for the protection of the capital, and that there was little danger of an attack on Hill. This is why he ventured to distribute his army corps along so wide a front.[11]

In order to obtain information as to the enemy's position and proposed movements, Hooker ordered Pleasanton, who was now in command of the cavalry, to beat up Stuart's camps at Culpeper, and gave him two small brigades of infantry, 3000 men, which raised his total force to about 11,000. These troops were in échelon along the railroad, which crosses the river at Rappahannock Station, and runs thence ten miles to Culpeper. About midway is Brandy Station, and here the two cavalry forces came in contact on the 9 June. After an indecisive battle, lasting all day, Pleasanton withdrew, but not until he had secured sufficient information to report to Hooker that two-thirds of the enemy were at Culpeper preparing to move on Washington. The affair was of importance chiefly from the fact that it was the first true cavalry battle fought during the war, and that " it enabled the Federals to dispute the superiority hitherto claimed by, and conceded to, the Confederate cavalry." [12]

On the 10 June, Ewell left Culpeper for Winchester, where he arrived on the 13th. He then pushed on to the Potomac, crossed the river, and occupied Hagerstown and Sharpsburg. The Union forces in the Valley withdrew before the enemy's advance, the garrison at Harper's Ferry being the last to cross the river, to Maryland

[11] *Cf.* Maurice, 139 and 199.   [12] 3 *B. & L.*, 263.

Heights; and on the 17th the Shenandoah Valley was cleared of Federal troops.

On the night of the 13th, Hooker started for Manassas Junction, on his way to the Potomac, which he expected to cross near Leesburg. A. P. Hill's corps immediately followed toward the Valley, crossed the mountains to the south of Longstreet, who had left Culpeper on the 15th; then marched down the Shenandoah, and reached Shepherdstown on the 23d. Longstreet marched along the east side of the Blue Ridge, to cover the passes; but finally crossed to the Valley, and followed Hill to the Potomac. Their columns united at Hagerstown on the 25th. These movements were all screened by the cavalry thrown out on the flanks of the two armies, so that it was impossible for either commander to obtain much information.

Hooker crossed the Potomac at Edwards Ferry on the 25th and 26th. On the 27th, the First and Eleventh corps, under Reynolds, occupied Middletown and the South Mountain passes; the Twelfth Corps was near Harper's Ferry, and the four other corps were at Frederick.

Lee's objective was Harrisburg, and Ewell, continuing his march, reached Carlisle and York on the 28th. The same day, Hooker ordered Slocum, with the Twelfth Corps, to march to Harper's Ferry, there unite with the force at Maryland Heights, cut Lee's communications, and, in conjunction with Reynolds, operate on his rear.

In a council held after the battle of Chancellorsville, Mr. Lincoln, Stanton, and Halleck had decided that Hooker should not be entrusted with the conduct of another battle. He could not be removed immediately, however, as he still had the strong support of the Chase faction, who refused to consent to a change in the command of the Army of the Potomac unless Hooker should *voluntarily resign.*

Halleck now interposed and refused to allow the withdrawal of the troops from Maryland Heights, although Hooker pointed out that the position was of no possible importance. Hooker appealed in vain to the President and Secretary Stanton. Finding that he had lost the support of the Government, and that he was "not to be allowed to manœuvre his own army in the presence of the enemy," on the 27 June Hooker tendered his resignation. This was just what Stanton and Halleck had been scheming to bring about, and his request to be relieved was immediately granted. Major-General George G. Meade was appointed in his place, and took command at Frederick on the 28th.[13] Meade was an excellent corps-commander, and a safe choice, but he was too lacking in aggressiveness to make a good general-in-chief. He had a disagreeable disposition, and was not popular with his fellow-officers.[14] Meade was succeeded in the command of the Fifth Corps by Major-General George Sykes, a veteran of the Mexican War and a distinguished soldier.

The Union army was now organized as follows: First Corps, Reynolds; Second, Hancock; Third, Sickles; Fifth, Sykes; Sixth, Sedgwick; Eleventh, Howard; and Twelfth, Slocum. The seven corps averaged about 12,000 men, making a total of 84,000 infantry; there were about 5000 in the artillery, and 15,000 cavalry — an aggregate of 104,000.

Lee had about 66,000 infantry, divided almost equally between the three corps of Longstreet, Ewell, and Hill; and about 10,000 cavalry, under Stuart, who were not present at the opening of the battle of Gettysburg.

With the consent of Lee, on the 24 June, Stuart had started on another of his famous rides around the Union army; but this time his raid was a total failure, and his absence probably lost Lee a victory at Gettysburg. He finally rejoined the army on the second day of the battle, with his horses worn out and his men utterly exhausted.

At the time Meade assumed command the situation was briefly as follows: The advance of Lee's army, under Ewell, was at Carlisle and York, threatening Harrisburg; Longstreet's corps was at Chambersburg, and Hill's be-

---

[13] He was the *fifth* commander assigned to this army within ten months. (Steele, 360.)

[14] Alexander, 377–378.

tween that place and Cashtown. Meade's army was in and around Frederick.

Owing to the absence of Stuart, and the failure of his " scouts " to report, Lee did not yet know that the Federal army was across the Potomac. But about midnight on the 28th, the famous spy, Harrison, appeared at headquarters, with the news that Hooker had crossed the Potomac, and had been superseded by Meade. He was able also to give the approximate positions of five of the seven Federal corps.[15]

This news caused an immediate change in Lee's plans. On the 29th, orders were sent recalling Ewell, and directing a concentration of the three corps at Cashtown, eight miles west of Gettysburg, where he hoped the enemy would be forced to attack him. At the same time, Meade was laying out a line behind Pipe Creek, in northern Maryland, where he, too, hoped to fight on the defensive.

The Administration at Washington at last seemed to have learned some wisdom from experience. Halleck wrote Meade that he would " not be hampered by any minute instructions from these headquarters "; and that he was " intrusted with all the power and authority " which the Government could confer on him. Accordingly, as soon as Meade took command, he had abandoned Hooker's plan of operating against Lee's rear, and selected the line Emmitsburg-Hanover for the front of his army, with Westminster as his base, in order to force Lee to battle before he could cross the Susquehanna. This line covered both Baltimore and Washington.

On the 30 June, the Union troops occupied the following positions: Buford's cavalry division was at Gettysburg; Reynolds was at Marsh Run; Sickles at Bridgeport; Slocum at Littlestown; Howard, behind Reynolds, at Emmitsburg. These troops, with Kilpatrick's cavalry division at Hanover, composed the first line. In second line were Hancock at Uniontown, Sykes at Union Mills, and Sedgwick at Manchester, with Gregg's cavalry division covering the rear at Westminster.

[15] Alexander, 378–379.

On the same day, Lee's army was thus situated: two of Ewell's divisions were at Heidlersburg, and the third at Greenwood; two of Longstreet's were at Fayetteville, and the third (Pickett) at Chambersburg, guarding the trains; one of Hill's divisions (Anderson) was back at the mountain pass on the Chambersburg Road, and the two others had reached Cashtown and Mummasburg.

On the 30 June, Heth, in command of one of Hill's divisions, heard that shoes could be obtained at Gettysburg, and ordered Pettigrew's brigade to go there and get them. But on approaching Gettysburg, Pettigrew found Buford's cavalry just occupying the town, so he withdrew about five miles and bivouacked. This chance collision suddenly precipitated a battle, unforeseen and undesired by either party.[16]

Buford realized the importance of Gettysburg as a strategic centre, and made his dispositions to hold it if possible. He established his outposts to the west and north of the town, and sent word to Reynolds and Meade.

The town of Gettysburg lies in a small valley surrounded by low hills. From the town twelve roads run to every point of the compass. Ten miles to the west the horizon is bounded by the South Mountains, through which lay Lee's line of retreat in case of defeat. About a half mile west of the town is an elevation called Seminary Ridge, from the Lutheran Seminary standing on it. This ridge begins at a commanding knoll, nearly a mile and a half north of the Seminary, called Oak Hill; from this point the ridge runs in a southerly direction, and is covered with open woods. The Chambersburg Pike and the Hagerstown Road pass over the ridge, and meet at an acute angle at the end of one of the streets on the western edge of the town. Parallel to the Pike, and 200 yards north of it, was an unfinished railway.

Directly north of the town the country is low and flat, and is traversed by Rock Creek. About a half mile south of the town, facing Seminary Ridge, is Cemetery Hill, rising 80 feet above the level of the valley below. The

16 Alexander, 380.

position which was occupied by the Union army on the second and third days of the battle is shaped like a fishhook. The shank is formed by Cemetery Ridge, which connects the Round Tops on the south with Cemetery Hill on the north. The line then curves to the east and again to the south to Culp's Hill, which corresponds to the point of the hook. The total length is about three miles, and the distance from Seminary Ridge is from 1400 to 1600 yards. Round Top rises about 330 feet, and Little Round Top about 220 feet above the bed of Plum Run on the west, Culp's Hill about 170 feet above Rock Creek on the east. Both of the extremities of the line were strong, and capable of defence against superior numbers. Cemetery Ridge is not high, and the slopes are gentle. The distance of the point of the hook from the shank was little more than a mile, so that any point attacked could be readily reënforced. Troops could move from one part of the line to another out of view of the enemy; and the reserves were sheltered by the rocks and hills. So long as Culp's Hill on the north and the Round Tops on the south were held, the position could not be outflanked. The weak point of the position was Cemetery Hill, which presented a salient where the line could be enfiladed, and the enemy could approach from the north and west under shelter to within a few hundred yards of the entrenchments. Of this part of the line General Alexander says: " Briefly, the one weak point of the enemy's line, and the one advantage possessed by ours, were never apprehended." This salient " *offered the only hopeful point of attack upon the enemy's entire line.* . . . It would not be too much to say that an attack here on the morning of the 2 July *would have succeeded.*" [17]

Some 500 yards west of Seminary Ridge the land rises gradually to another ridge, which is wider, smoother, and lower than Seminary Ridge, and which also begins at Oak Hill. Beyond this second ridge, Willoughby Run flows south to Marsh Creek. The roads to Chambersburg and Hagerstown cross the run about a mile apart.

[17] Alexander, 388, 418. The italics are General Alexander's.

About five o'clock on the morning of the 1st, Hill, with the divisions of Heth and Pender, started from Cashtown for Gettysburg, eight miles distant. At dawn, Buford had made arrangements to " entertain " the enemy until General Reynolds could reach the scene. He dismounted his two cavalry brigades, 3100 men, and deployed them beyond the second ridge along Willoughby Run. About ten o'clock Heth advanced to the attack, with Pender close behind. Although greatly outnumbered, Buford kept the Confederates back for half an hour, until Reynolds arrived on the ground, with Wadsworth's division, of his corps, which was immediately deployed along the ridge; the cavalry then took post on the flanks. Almost at the beginning of the engagement, Reynolds was shot through the head and instantly killed. " The death of this splendid officer," writes Fitz Lee, " was regretted by friend and foe "; and, borrowing the words of another, he adds, " No man died on that field with more glory than he; yet many died, and there was much glory! " [18]

About eleven o'clock, the two other divisions of the First Corps came up, with four more batteries. Rowley's division and the guns were placed in the line, which was thus extended to the right along Seminary Ridge. The third division (Robinson) was posted in reserve at the Seminary.

Howard arrived at noon, ahead of his corps, and assumed command by virtue of his rank. When the Eleventh Corps came up, an hour later, Schurz, who was in temporary command, was ordered to prolong the line of the First Corps to the north on Seminary Ridge with his own division and that of Barlow, and place the third division (Steinwehr) at Cemetery Hill in reserve.

Before these arrangements were completed, Buford's cavalry brought word that Ewell's Confederate corps was approaching by the Heidlersburg Road, directly on the right flank and rear of the Federal position. Thereupon, Howard ordered the Eleventh Corps to change front to the right, and take up a line across the valley to the north of the town, in order to hold back the enemy. At the

[18] *Life of General Lee,* 272.

same time he called for aid from Slocum and Sickles, whose corps were between Gettysburg and Emmitsburg, from five to ten miles away.

Up to this time, the Federals had been quite successful, as they were superior in numbers at the actual points of contact. "Whether from discipline, or the inspiration of home," writes General Alexander, "the fighting done by the Federal brigades was of the best type." [19] Archer was captured, with several hundred of his men, and two regiments of Davis's brigade were cut off and made prisoners.

Ewell's two leading divisions were soon at hand, and he deployed his troops facing south on a line about two miles and a half long, from the Hunterstown Road on his left to the Mummasburg Road on his right. He had been directed by Lee not to bring on an engagement, if the enemy was in force at Gettysburg, until the remainder of the Confederate army was up.

Howard's dispositions were bad, as he attempted to hold a line too long for his small forces, and his right was in the air. Ewell placed a battalion of artillery [20] on Oak Hill, which opened fire on both angles of the Union line, enfilading the left wing, and forcing the right end back to Seminary Ridge. The reserve of the First Corps, Robinson's division, was ordered to reënforce this part of the line, one brigade facing west and the other north. [21]

By this time, Hill's corps was coming up on the Chambersburg Road, and attacking the Union left, while Ewell was assailing their right with overwhelming numbers. Schurz called on his reserve (Steinwehr) for assistance, and tried to cover the town; but the Confederate attack was overpowering. About three o'clock the whole Union right gave way, and the troops were driven back to Cemetery Hill, with the loss of some 5000 prisoners. This retreat uncovered the Federal left, and made its position untenable. Doubleday accordingly gave the command for

[19] Alexander, 384.

[20] He had two Whitworth breach-loading guns, the only ones on the field, and they were very effective.

[21] It was here that General Paul, who commanded the First Brigade, received a shot which put out both of his eyes.

the First Corps to fall back to Cemetery Hill. Wadsworth's division went to Culp's Hill, and the two other divisions were posted on the left of Steinwehr, whose position became the rallying point of the Union troops. The two other divisions (Schurz and Barlow) of the Eleventh Corps were placed at the right of Steinwehr. Barlow himself had been severely wounded, and fallen into the hands of the Confederates.

About three o'clock, Hancock arrived on the scene, and took command, under orders from General Meade. He at once gave orders to establish a line of battle on Cemetery Hill.

Soon after two o'clock General Lee arrived on Seminary Ridge. Seeing the flight of the Federals through the town, he sent a staff-officer to Ewell with orders to press the pursuit, and " if possible " secure possession of the heights; but he took no steps to see that the order was obeyed. Sunset was about 7:30; twilight was long, and the moon was full; but Ewell, for some unknown reason, failed to continue the pursuit, and made no attempt to carry the heights. As General Alexander remarks: this was another striking illustration of the danger of giving conditional orders, and then failing to follow them up.[22] If the Confederates had been prompt, they might have carried Cemetery Ridge, before the Federals were able to occupy it in force. Nevertheless the battle of the first day at Gettysburg was a Confederate success.[23]

About one o'clock, Meade at Taneytown, hearing that Reynolds was killed or badly wounded, ordered Hancock to go in person to the front, assume command of the First (Reynolds) and Eleventh (Howard) corps, and of the Third (Sickles), then at Emmitsburg; also, if he thought the position better than Pipe Creek to fight a battle, so to advise him (Meade), and he would order up all the troops.

General Warren, the chief engineer on Meade's staff, arrived soon after Hancock, and, going over the ground together, they came to the conclusion that if the position could be held until night, it would be the best place for the army to accept battle if attacked. The Twelfth Corps (Slocum) arrived between four and five o'clock, and was placed in line with the other troops already on the ground. Hancock then sent an aide to Meade to say that he could hold the position until night. He added that, " the position at Gettysburg was a very strong one," and he left it to Meade to decide whether the battle should be fought there or at Pipe Creek. Between five and six, Slocum himself arrived, and Hancock, after transferring the command to him, returned to Taneytown.

During the afternoon, Longstreet had joined Lee on Seminary Ridge, and surveyed the Union position. He said to Lee: " We could not call the enemy to a position better suited to our plans. We have only to file around his left and secure good ground between him and his capital." To his surprise, Lee replied: " If he is there to-morrow, I shall attack him." Longstreet answered: " If he is there to-morrow, it will be because he wants you to attack him." [24]

Late in the afternoon, Lee had a long conference with Ewell, Early, and Rodes. Ewell obtained permission to send Johnson's division to occupy Culp's Hill, a half-mile to the east of the town. But Johnson found the Federals in possession of the hill, and was not strong enough to attack this almost impregnable position. Nevertheless, says General Alexander, " *the division was allowed to remain until the end of the battle, and, as long as it remained absent, the task before the remainder of the army was beyond its strength.*" [25]

The field of the second and third days of battle at Gettysburg has already been described. The key-points of the strong defensive position occupied by the Union army were Culp's Hill, Cemetery Ridge, and the two Round Tops. The line as finally occupied was about four miles long. Its convex form gave it the advantage of interior lines of operation. The only weak point was the salient,

[24] Alexander, 387. Maurice (207) thinks that Lee was right in rejecting Longstreet's plan.

[25] Alexander, 386. The italics are General Alexander's.

already mentioned, where the apex of the line rested on Cemetery Hill, which was exposed to an enfilading fire from the town and its flanks and suburbs.

Meade arrived in person about one o'clock on the morning of the 2d, and at daybreak rode over the field, assigning his troops to position. By noon, all of his army was on the field except the Sixth Corps (Sedgwick), which arrived during the afternoon, nearly exhausted after a continuous march of thirty-four miles from Manchester.

As finally arranged the Union line was formed as follows: One division (Wadsworth) of the First Corps held Culp's Hill, with the Twelfth Corps (Slocum) to the right; along Cemetery Ridge were the Eleventh Corps (Howard), the two other divisions of the First Corps (Reynolds — now commanded by Newton), the Second (Hancock) and the Third (Sickles), which prolonged the line to the Round Top on the left. The Fifth Corps (Sykes) was in reserve near the point where the Baltimore Pike crossed Rock Creek. On its arrival the Sixth Corps (Sedgwick) was also held in reserve back of the Round Tops. The artillery reserve and the ammunition trains were parked in a central position from which roads radiated to various sections of the line. The right flank was covered by the cavalry divisions of Gregg and Kilpatrick, and the left by Buford. But on the morning of the 2d, Buford was sent to Westminster to escort the trains, and the left of the line, through some error, remained uncovered until Kilpatrick was sent over from the right the next morning.

At the base of the steep western slopes of the Round Tops flows a small marshy stream, Plum Run, beyond which, at a distance of some 500 yards, rises another wild and steep hill, known as the Devil's Den. From Cemetery Hill, the Emmitsburg Road runs southwest along a low ridge past the Peach Orchard, which lies just at the foot of the slope from Devil's Den, about a half-mile west of the lowest part of Cemetery Ridge.

Sickles, on finding the part of the line assigned him, just north of Little Round Top, to be lower than the ground in front of it at the Peach Orchard, asked leave to move his corps forward to the higher position. While General Hunt was examining the forward position, Sickles, without awaiting an answer to his request, took the grave responsibility of ordering his line to advance to the Emmitsburg Road. He placed Humphrey's division along the road, with its left at the Peach Orchard, and Birney's division on the ridge from the orchard to Devil's Den. No troops were posted on the Round Tops.

On the afternoon of the 2 July, the forces were practically all up on both sides, and the two armies faced each other across the valley between Cemetery Hill and Seminary Ridge. Meade had nearly 90,000 men and Lee about 70,000. " Except in equipment," writes General Alexander, " I think a better army . . . never marched upon a battle-field." [26] " With such soldiers," says Mr. Rhodes, " if Lee had been as great a general as Napoleon, Gettysburg had been an Austerlitz; Washington and the Union had fallen." [27]

It was Lee's intention to attack the enemy as early as practicable on the morning of the 2d, but much time was consumed in reconnoitring the Union position, and it was eleven o'clock before his orders were issued: " Anderson's division of Hill's corps was directed to extend Hill's line upon Seminary Ridge to the right, while Longstreet with Hood's and McLaws's divisions should make a flank march to the right and pass the enemy's flank, which seemed to extend along the Emmitsburg Road. Forming then at right angles to the road, the attack was to sweep down the enemy's line from their left, being taken up successively by the brigades of Anderson's division as they were reached. Ewell's corps, holding the extreme left, was to attack on hearing Longstreet's guns." [28]

Pickett's division was still at a distance, but Longstreet's other divisions (Hood and McLaws), with the exception of one brigade (Law) had bivouacked only four miles from the field. Longstreet set his men in motion at daybreak, but they halted on the way, and lost time in trying to find a route out of sight of the Union Signal·Corps on

[26] 3 B. & L., 358.
[27] 4 Rhodes, 285.
[28] Alexander, 391.

Little Round Top, also in waiting for Law to come up. These incidents caused the loss of two or three hours, and " it was about 3 P.M. when Hood's division, in the advance, crossed the Emmitsburg Road about 1000 yards south of the Peach Orchard." [29]

The centre of Lee's line was held by Hill's corps, with Anderson at the right, Pender on the left, and Heth in the rear, acting as a general reserve. Ewell's corps was on the left: Rodes's division in the town, Early's between the town and Rock Creek, and Johnson's east of the creek, under Culp's Hill.

Stuart was still absent, and Lee had only a few squadrons of cavalry, on the extreme left.

The Confederate artillery opened fire at three o'clock against the two sides of the angle at the Peach Orchard, but it was after four o'clock when Hood advanced to the attack. The fault of Sickles's position was now obvious. No force can hold its ground when attacked on both sides of a right angle; Sickles's force had both its lines enfiladed by batteries, to the south and west, and had to yield: each side of the angle was taken in flank, and the position was untenable. [30]

About this time Warren, who was inspecting the Union left, discovered that there were no troops on Little Round Top, the key of the position. He sent a request to Meade for a division to hold that point, and also asked Sykes, whose corps was moving to the support of Sickles, to detach two brigades and a battery to Little Round Top. The two brigades arrived just in time to drive back the right of Hood's line, which, after seizing Round Top, was on the point of occupying the other elevation.

A fierce combat now ensued for the possession of the Peach Orchard. Hood was wounded, and Law, who took command of the division, finally got possession of Devil's Den. Longstreet and Meade both hurried up reënforcements; the Federals were driven back with severe loss, and followed across the Wheat Field up the slopes of Little Round Top. Then other forces, sent by Meade, came to the rescue of the imperiled Union line, and the

[29] Alexander, 394.   [30] Doubleday, 163.

enemy was slowly driven back. Several other Confederate attacks were repulsed, although one brigade (Wright) actually gained the crest of Cemetery Ridge, before it was forced to retire from lack of prompt support. This ended the battle of the second day on the right end of the Confederate line.

The faulty salient of Sickles at the Peach Orchard had been crushed in, and the defenders driven back to the main Federal line, which was still intact. Only eleven Confederate brigades — eight of Longstreet's and three of Hill's — had been engaged, while Meade had sent twenty brigades to reënforce that part of his line. Hill and Ewell, although ordered to coöperate with Longstreet's attack, had confined themselves mainly to an ineffective long-distance cannonading of the Federal entrenchments in their front. Johnson made a demonstration against Culp's Hill, but refrained from attacking; two brigades of Early's division carried a part of the Union line on Cemetery Hill, but were not supported, and were soon forced to withdraw.

The result of the day is accurately summed up by Lee: " We attempted to dislodge the enemy, and, although we gained some ground, we were unable to gain possession of his position." At 8 P.M., Meade telegraphed Halleck: " The enemy attacked me about 4 P.M. this day, and, after one of the severest contests of the war, was repulsed at all points." In brief, the small success of the Confederates was due to a succession of tardy, isolated, unsupported attacks, which showed very poor management on the part of Lee and his three corps-commanders.[31] On the Union side, Warren and Humphreys distinguished themselves. Sickles was struck by a cannon ball that caused the loss of a leg, and was borne from the field.

General Alexander finishes his account of the day with the words: " Thus ended the second day, and one is tempted to say that thus ended the battle of Gettysburg. For of the third day it must be said, as was said of the

[31] " The story of the second of the three days' battle presents a picture of mismanagement that is almost without parallel." (Henderson, *Science of War*, 222.)

charge of the Six Hundred at Balaklava, ' Magnificent, but not War! ' " [32]

Nevertheless, in the Union camp that night the feeling was one of gloom. On the first day, the First and Eleventh corps had been badly shattered; on the second day, the Third, the Fifth, and part of the Second, had been used up and were not in good condition to fight; only the Sixth and Twelfth corps were fresh. The army had lost nearly 20,000 men.

Soon after the fighting had ceased, Meade called a council of war, and put the question in writing, " Should the army remain in its present position or take up some other? " All voted to remain and await another attack. As the council broke up, Meade said to Gibbon, who was in temporary command of the Second Corps: " If Lee attacks to-morrow it will be on your front; because, he has made attacks on both our flanks and failed, and if he concludes to try it again, it will be on our centre." Meade has been very unjustly criticised for directing his chief-of-staff to prepare orders for retiring to Pipe Creek in case it should become necessary. [33]

About midnight, Geary's division of the Twelfth Corps, which had been withdrawn from the extreme right of the line, returned to its former position, and was surprised to find its trenches occupied by a part of Johnson's Confederate division. This position enabled the Confederates to take the Federal line in reverse. Before dawn, Ewell reënforced Johnson with one of Early's brigades and two of Rodes's. Some other changes were made on both sides during the course of the night, but on the whole the two armies occupied about the same positions as at the close of the battle on the second day. Longstreet held the rocks and woods of the Devil's Den, the bases of the Round Tops, and the Wheat Field; and had possession of the Emmitsburg Road, at this point.

Lee believed that, with proper concert of action, and with the increased support that the artillery could give the columns from the positions gained on the right, ultimate success was possible. He accordingly decided to con-

[32] Alexander, 412.   [33] 4 Livermore, 468.

tinue the attack. The general plan was unchanged. Longstreet, reënforced by Pickett's three brigades, was to assault the Union centre, while Ewell was to attack the right at the same time.

General Lee was aware that Cemetery Ridge was strongly held from one end to the other, but, after a careful reconnaissance of the enemy's position, he concluded that the weakest point of the line was at the angle where it approached nearest to the Emmitsburg Road, about half a mile south of the intersection of that road with the Taneytown Road. If the Confederate assaulting column could pierce the Union line at this point, it would take the entire right of the position in reverse: owing to the convexity of their line there, the Federals could not support the position by a cross artillery-fire either from the right or the left, and their troops could not fire into the backs of the victorious Confederates without endangering their comrades on the right as much as their foes. So Lee decided to make his assault at this point, and directed Longstreet to carry it out.

Longstreet, who had not been in full accord with Lee since the opening of the campaign, protested against this plan of a frontal attack. He said that, " the column would have to march a mile under concentrating battery fire, and a thousand yards under long range musketry; . . . that the 15,000 men who could make successful assault over that field had never been arrayed for battle." [34] But Lee was " impatient of listening and tired of talking," so nothing remained but to obey orders.

Before telling the story of the celebrated assault, known as " Pickett's charge," which was the event of the last day at Gettysburg, it may be well, however, to give here briefly the outcome of Johnson's battle. The effect of sending him the three brigades from Rodes and Early, says General Alexander, was " to emasculate the centre of our line and to concentrate seven brigades where they were utterly useless." [35] Johnson had been ordered to attack at daylight, but was himself attacked by the Federals at that hour. He repulsed the assault, and attempted

[34] Longstreet, 385, 386.   [35] Alexander, 414.

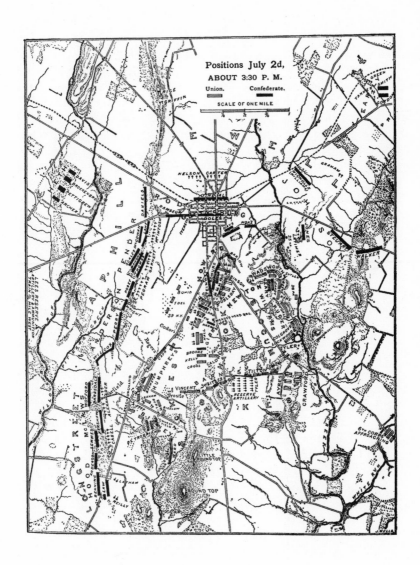

Positions July 2d,
ABOUT 3:30 P. M.
Union.   Confederate.
SCALE OF ONE MILE

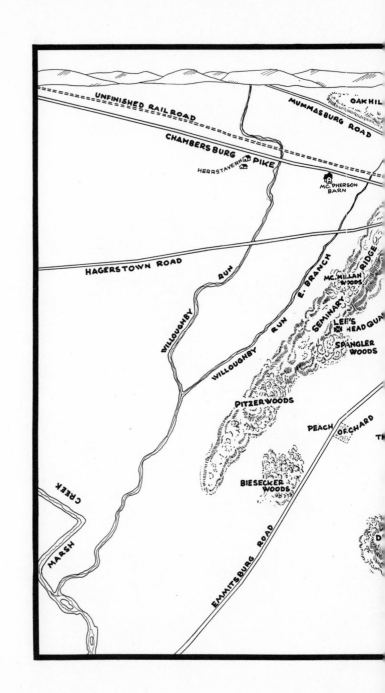

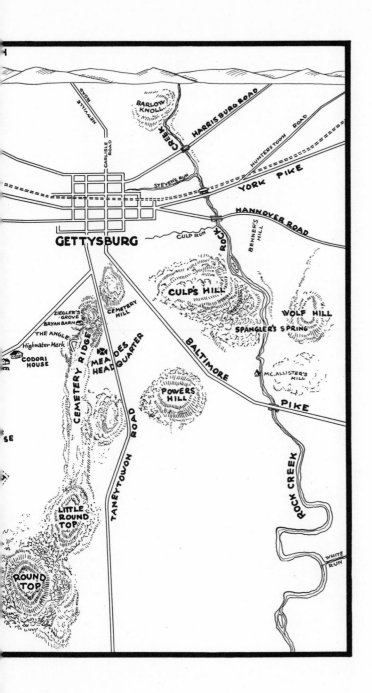

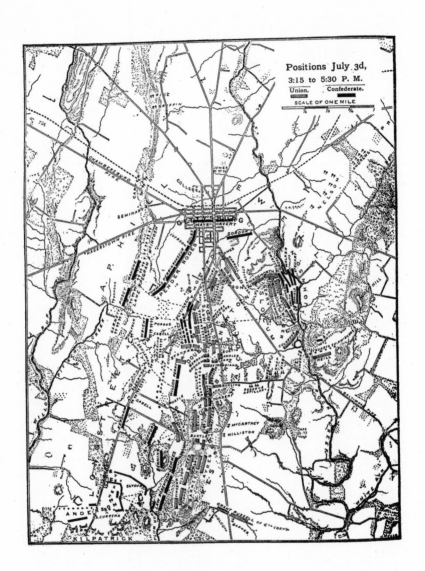

Positions July 3d,
3:15 to 5:30 P. M.
Union. Confederate.
SCALE OF ONE MILE

to follow up his success, but was in turn driven back. Heavy firing was kept up until noon, when he retired to the foot of the hill; in this position, he remained unmolested until night, and was then recalled to the west of the town. He lost 1873 men, which shows the severity of the fighting.[36]

The formation of the infantry lines for Pickett's assault consumed a long time, and then the arrangement was one not suited for such a heavy task. For the attack, in addition to Pickett's three brigades, Lee assigned to Longstreet six brigades of Hill's corps; and one more, Wilcox of Anderson's division, was added later, making ten brigades in all. None of these brigades, except Wilcox's, had taken part in the battle of the previous day. The brigades of Garnett and Kemper formed Pickett's first line, with Armistead in second line. In the first line, on the left of Pickett's men (from right to left), were the four brigades of Archer, Pettigrew, Davis, and Brockenbrough, of Heth's division, which was commanded by Pettigrew. Behind the right of these four brigades were Scales and Lane, in second line. The six brigades in the first line comprised about 10,000 men; the three in second line about 4000, and the third line about 1000 — or 15,000 men in all. There was a distance of about 200 yards between the first and second lines. The brigade of Wilcox, which alone formed the third line, was posted in the rear of the right of the column; it was not put in motion until twenty minutes after the rest of the column — too late to be of any assistance whatever. " Both flanks of the assaulting column were in the air, and the left without any support in the rear: it was sure to crumble away under fire." [37]

---

[36] Alexander, 415. See also 4 Livermore, 470–471; 3 *B. & L.*, 316 and 369. The statement, made by many writers, that the Confederates took Culp's Hill is an error. They only succeeded in occupying "part of the entrenchments of the Twelfth Corps," abandoned by Geary's division. (See 3 *B. & L.*, 369, also Doubleday.)

[37] Alexander, 419. But Lee's intention was for the rest of Hill's corps to support the assault on the left, and the divisions of Hood and McLaws were to support it on the right. (Steele, 380.)

The arrangement may be represented thus: —

Brockenbrough Davis Pettigrew Archer Garnett Kemper
                        Lane   Scales   Armistead
                                         Wilcox

The front line was more than a mile long; its right was near the Peach Orchard, and its left near the southern end of an old sunken road leading out of the southwestern angle of the town.

The charge was preceded by a heavy cannonading by 115 guns on the Confederate side, replied to by 80 guns of the Federals, whose convex line did not admit of bringing into action a large part of their artillery. At the end of an hour and a half of this bombardment, which did little harm on either side, Hunt, the Union chief-of-artillery, gave the order to cease firing, as his ammunition was running low.

In the morning, Longstreet had taken Pickett to the crest of Seminary Ridge, and pointed out to him what was to be done. Alexander, in charge of the Confederate artillery, was directed to note carefully the effect of his fire, and when the favorable moment came, to give Pickett the order to advance. When the Federal fire ceased, Alexander sent word to Pickett: " For God's sake come quick, . . . or my ammunition will not let me support you properly." The note reached Pickett in Longstreet's presence. He read it, and handed it to Longstreet, who read it without comment.

" General, shall I advance? " said Pickett.

Longstreet was unwilling to give the order; he turned in his saddle, and looked away.

" I am going to move forward, sir," said Pickett, as he saluted, and galloped off.

It was now about two o'clock, and Longstreet, leaving his staff, rode over to join Alexander. " I do not want to make this charge," he said, slowly and with great emotion. " I do not see how it can succeed. I would not make it now but that General Lee has ordered it and is expecting it." Alexander felt that on a word of acquiescence from him, Longstreet, even then, would have countermanded the order, but he was too conscious of his youth and inexperience to express an opinion not directly asked.[38]

At this moment Pickett at the head of his troops rode over the crest of Seminary Ridge and began his descent down the slope. " As he passed me," writes Longstreet, " he rode gracefully, with his jaunty cap raked well over on his right ear, and his auburn locks, nicely dressed, hanging almost to his shoulders. He seemed a holiday soldier." [39]

Meade still held the line of the " fishhook ": Slocum at Culp's Hill; Howard at Cemetery Hill; Hancock, and Newton now commanding the First Corps, along Cemetery Ridge; Sykes and Sedgwick at the Round Tops; Birney, with Sickles's corps, in reserve behind Hancock and Sykes.

The point of attack, marked by a clump of trees which has since become famous, was held by Hancock's corps. From a point on the Emmitsburg Road about half a mile from the outskirts of Gettysburg, his line extended about 500 yards along Hay's front, the southern half along a stone wall, which continued westward 100 yards, and then ran south again, along Gibbon's front, forming the " bloody angle." Here the wall was lower, and surmounted by a country rail-fence for about 100 yards to a point directly in front of the clump of trees; south of this there was an ordinary rail-fence, which had been thrown down to form the revetment of a shallow shelter-trench.

Pickett's men had nearly a mile to go to cross the valley. They moved at a walk, keeping their lines accurately, as though on parade. Midway, they halted for a short rest in a ravine, which gave some shelter from the enemy's fire, and then moved on.

The infantry had no sooner debouched on the plain than all the Federal batteries opened fire. As the troops drew nearer, they were exposed to the front and slant fire of the Union infantry and artillery, as well as the enfilade fire of the batteries from Cemetery Hill to the Round Tops. Both flanks of the advancing line were shot

[38] Alexander, 423–424.   [39] 3 B. & L., 345.

to pieces, but the survivors crowded in toward the centre, and continued to advance. The groans from the battle-field were heard amidst the storm of combat. The slaughter was terrible, but still they pressed on. Stannard's brigade of the First Corps wheeled to the right and attacked the Confederates in flank and rear, adding to the confusion. Armistead leaped the stone wall, waved his sword with his hat on it, shouted, " Give them the cold steel, boys! " and laid his hand upon a gun. A hundred of his men followed; the Confederate battle-flags were planted on the crest among the cannon they had captured and for the moment held. Armistead was shot down; Garnett was killed; and their men lay literally in heaps beside them.

> " A thousand fell where Kemper led;
> A thousand died where Garnett bled;
>   In blinding flame and strangling smoke,
>   The remnant through the batteries broke,
> And crossed the works with Armistead." [40]

When Armistead fell, the wavering troops " seemed appalled, broke their ranks, and retired." The Federals attacked them on all sides, and drove the remnants back on the Confederate lines. " The conflict," writes General Alexander, " hardly seemed to last five minutes before they were melted away, and only disorganized stragglers . . . were coming back." [41]

One of Pickett's brigade commanders, Kemper, was desperately wounded, and the two others were killed. Eleven field officers were slain, nine wounded, and only one escaped. Pickett himself was not injured, and no member of his staff was killed or wounded. Although he set forth so bravely at the head of his troops, he stopped part way, and never reached the Union lines. [42]

Twenty colors were captured within a space one hundred yards square, and nearly 2000 prisoners were taken.

[40] Thompson, *The High Tide at Gettysburg.*
[41] 3 *B. & L.,* 347.
[42] This fact, which seems to have been well known in both armies, is mentioned by only one historian (Rhodes, *Civil War,* 243). ⁊

Out of 5000 men who went into action, Pickett's division lost nearly 1400 killed and wounded, and 1500 prisoners — the total loss being about sixty per cent. The casualties in the seven other brigades were not reported separately, but were probably nearly as large.

Hancock displayed the same reckless courage as the Confederate brigadiers, and seemed to be everywhere, directing and encouraging his men, until he was struck by a ball and fell from his horse. Lying on the ground, he shouted, " Go in, Colonel, and give it to them on the flank! " [43]

" It is a popular belief," says Colonel Livermore, " that if the gap where Armistead entered had not been closed, Meade's line would have been shattered and the battle lost. But this is far from probable. About 30,000 men were closing around the 3000 of Pickett's shattered division. . . . If they had forced their way into the mass of troops that was awaiting them, what could they do? Where could they go? . . . Penetrating a hostile line like that on Cemetery Ridge was like entering the jaws of a monster." [44]

While Wilcox's brigade was making its charge, General Lee, entirely alone, rode up to Alexander's position near the Emmitsburg Road, and remained about an hour. After the charge, he seemed apprehensive of a counterstroke by the Federals, and endeavored to rally the fugitives. He spoke to nearly every man who passed, using such words as: *Don't be discouraged. It was my fault this time. Form your ranks again when you get under cover. All good men must hold together now.*[45]

While this great battle was raging on the field of Gettysburg, there was a fight between the horsemen of

[43] Walker, *Hancock*, 143. Since his graduation at West Point in 1844, Hancock had had wide and thorough military experience; and through able and faithful service he had climbed from colonel to corps commander. At this time, there was no better all-round officer in the Army of the Potomac than Winfield Scott Hancock, whose dash and magnetism in the field had earned him the title of " The Superb." His vigor, moreover, was tempered by judgment.

[44] 4 Livermore, 482.

[45] Alexander, 425–426.

the two armies about two miles and a half east of the town. Stuart with four brigades of cavalry and four horse-batteries endeavored to reach the rear of the Union line, between the York and the Hanover roads. Here he was met by the Federal cavalry, and a combat ensued which "swayed from side to side" about the Rummel farm. Afterwards the hostile batteries engaged in an indecisive duel, "and at nightfall each side held substantially its original ground." [46]

About an hour after this fight, Kilpatrick ordered Farnsworth, with two regiments of cavalry, to charge the rear of Longstreet's line on the slopes of Round Top. The men rode, as best they could, over rocks and creeks, stone walls and rail fences, and were shot down helplessly by the Confederate infantry. Farnsworth was killed, and a large part of his brigade was sacrificed in what has been termed a "hopeless and useless" struggle,[47] which, however, may have prevented Longstreet from supporting Pickett's charge. As soon as the Pickett assault was repulsed, Meade went to the left of the Union line with the determination to attack the enemy. Under his orders three brigades dashed across the Wheat Field, cleared the woods in front, and captured many prisoners. Longstreet's right fell back to Seminary Ridge. It was then so late in the evening that Meade abandoned the attack which he had contemplated.

The next day, which was the Fourth of July, Lee concentrated his army on Seminary Ridge in a position nearly parallel to Meade's centre and left. Slocum's corps advanced, and Howard occupied Gettysburg. It rained very heavily during portions of this day, "so violently," says Meade, "as to interrupt any very active operations if I had designed making them." During the night he learned that the enemy had retreated through the Fairfield and Cashtown passes.

The losses on both sides at Gettysburg were very heavy: [48]

---

[46] Hunt, 3 *B. & L.*   [47] Steele, 383.

[48] 3 *B. & L.*, 437, 439. Livermore (102–103) makes the Federal losses 26,000.

	Federals	*Confederates*
Killed	3,072	2,592
Wounded	14,497	12,709
Missing	5,434	5,150
Totals	23,003	20,451

No complete returns were ever made of the Confederate losses. Comte de Paris estimates them at 22,728, and Livermore at the much higher figure of 28,063.

Meade probably had about 85,000 combat troops on the field; and Lee some 70,000 men of all arms, after making all allowances.

On the night of the 3d, Lee decided that he could save his army only by a retreat across the Potomac. His ammunition was nearly exhausted, no supplies of food or forage could be obtained where he was, and there was danger of his line of retreat being cut off by the enemy. On the 4th, he started his ambulances by the Chambersburg Pike under escort of a brigade of cavalry. At dark the other trains set out by the Hagerstown Road, guarded by Hill's corps. Longstreet started next, and Ewell formed the rear-guard. The withdrawal was delayed by the heavy storm, and the wounded suffered terribly.

As soon as Meade was sure that Lee had begun his retreat, on the 5th, he started Gregg's cavalry brigade in pursuit by the Pike, and Sedgwick's corps by the Hagerstown Road. The next day, the other corps marched by the Emmitsburg Road. Finding the Confederate rear-guard entrenched in the Fairfield pass, Meade gave up the direct pursuit, and moved toward the lower passes.

On the 8th, Lee's army was near Hagerstown, and the Union forces were between Frederick and Boonsboro.

On his arrival at Williamsport, Lee found that the pontoon-bridge had been destroyed by Federal cavalry, and the river was so high from the recent rains as to be impassable. He therefore took up a strong position, and began to build a bridge with what material he could find, while waiting for the river to fall. He was in daily expectation of being attacked by Meade.

On the 13th, the Union army was in front of Lee's position, but Meade spent the day in reconnoitring, instead of attacking. That night Lee's army crossed the river, partly by fording, partly by the new bridge. The second invasion of the North had ended in failure, and Lee had again escaped through excess of caution on the part of the Union commander. It is difficult to see how he could have avoided capture if he had been vigorously pursued and attacked by his adversary.

Meade's excessive caution after the battle, for which he has been so severely criticised, is perhaps explained by these words of Colonel Livermore: " In the dread silence which followed the result of the great charge," he writes, " it was hard for the men of the Army of the Potomac to realize that some fearful ordeal was not awaiting them. The memory of Fredericksburg and Chancellorsville was fresh in their minds; the great captain had at times been checked before, but never defeated in so great a battle. . . . A false move on Meade's part . . . might turn his victory into defeat." [49]

If Lee had been victorious, the result might have been, the capture of Baltimore and Washington, foreign intervention, the recognition of the independence of the Confederate States. Meade stood in such awe of Lee, even in defeat, that he was unwilling to take any chances. By remaining on the defensive, and forcing Lee to strike again, or to retreat, he insured the safety of the North.

There are many striking points of resemblance between the battle-fields of Gettysburg and of Waterloo. On both fields the hostile armies were drawn up on two parallel ridges, separated by a shallow valley, about three-quarters of a mile wide. The Federal salient at the Peach Orchard, occupied by Sickles on the second day, corresponds to the farm of Hougomont, held by the British at Waterloo. The Codori buildings, near the centre of the field, are similar to the farm of La Haie-Sainte.

The chief point of dissimilarity is, that the main highway at Waterloo ran perpendicular to the two lines of

[49] 4 Livermore, 497.

battle, while at Gettysburg the Emmitsburg Road was nearly parallel to the lines. This road was bordered on either side by a five-bar rail fence which proved almost as formidable an obstacle to the charge of Pickett's men as did the famous " sunken road " at Waterloo to the assaults of Napoleon's Old Guard. When the Confederates reached these fences, they tried to knock them down with the butts of their muskets, but the construction was too solid, and they were forced to climb over, under a heavy short-range musketry fire, before continuing their advance.

Pickett and his staff rode through the gates into the Codori barn-yard on the easterly side of the road, and there they remained until the troops came back in defeat twenty or thirty minutes later. This point was not over 200 or 300 yards from the front of the Union line at the " bloody angle."

It will always be a mooted question whether Lee was right in deciding to attack the front of the Union position, instead of outflanking it by a move to his right as advocated by Longstreet. General Maurice, in his recent biography of General Lee, expresses the opinion that Lee was correct in rejecting Longstreet's plan. But there are many reasons for thinking that Sir Frederick is wrong.

The most vulnerable point of the Union position was not the angle which Lee selected for his assault on the third day, but the Round Tops, at the extreme left of the line. There were no Federal troops on Little Round Top until after four o'clock on the afternoon of the second day, and none on Round Top until the following morning. Moreover, Buford's cavalry division, which had been posted near Round Top, to guard the left flank, had been ordered on the morning of the 2d to Westminster, to escort the trains, and had not been replaced by Gregg's division " as General Meade had understood." [50] The left of the line was therefore entirely uncovered. If Lee had gained possession of the Round Tops on the morning of the 2d, as he might easily have done, he would have

---

[50] Fiebeger, cited by Steele, 374.

won a great victory. Not only would the Union position on Cemetery Ridge have been untenable, but the Confederates would have commanded the roads to Taneytown and Littlestown by which the Federals would have to retreat in order to cover Washington and Baltimore. The Taneytown Road runs at the very foot of the Round Tops, and the Baltimore Pike only a short distance to the east. The only routes available for withdrawal would then have been the roads to Hanover and York, running to the east and northeast.

Lee's decision to make a frontal attack was all the more remarkable because his two greatest victories — Second Manassas and Chancellorsville — had been won by turning movements; but on both of these occasions he had owed his success largely to the energy and skill of his great lieutenant, Jackson; and he had lost his " right arm " at Chancellorsville. It has often been remarked that after the death of Jackson, Lee never again employed these tactics. If Stonewall Jackson had been in command of the right wing at Gettysburg, instead of Longstreet, the result might have been very different. " Had I had Stonewall Jackson at Gettysburg," Lee said to his nephew, " I should have won a great victory." [51] " In war," said Napoleon, " *men* are nothing, *a man* is everything."

The victory of Gettysburg demonstrated two things: First, that the previous defeats of the Army of the Potomac were due to its leaders, and not to its troops; Second, that the great commander who had so often beaten it was not invincible. As a military genius, Meade cannot be compared with Lee; but his success in this campaign was due mainly to his fine generalship. Lee's repeated victories had led him to believe that he could take great risks in dealing with the Army of the Potomac, and his defeat may be attributed largely to over-confidence. " With that wonderful magnanimity which Lee so fully possessed," writes his nephew, " he took all the responsibility on his own broad shoulders." [52]

[51] See Fitzhugh Lee, 281; also J. W. Jones, 237.
[52] Lee's *Lee*, 297.

GETTYSBURG

Wellington is reported to have said that the best general is not the one who makes fewest mistakes, but the one who takes most advantage of the mistakes of his opponent. Like Napoleon, Lee made some mistakes in his campaigns, but no commanders, in ancient or modern times, were more prompt than these two to take advantage of the errors of their adversaries. During the first parts of their military careers they were therefore almost invariably successful; but, later, when their opponents had profited by experience, their success was not so marked.

At Gettysburg, Lee seems to have been below his usual form: his military genius was under an eclipse. His plan of battle appears to have been dictated by chance, rather than due to mature reflection. Ewell's corps had arrived by the northerly roads, from Carlisle and York, and it was left during the battle in and around the town, where it was of little use in deciding the issue of the conflict. Hill and Longstreet, who came up by the Chambersburg Road, were placed on Seminary Ridge. Lee's line, concave in form, was fully six or seven miles long, and was held by only 70,000 men; whereas the Union line, convex in shape, was manned by 90,000, and was only about half as long.

Then, as stated by Colonel Henderson, Lee's conduct of the battle " presents a picture of mismanagement that is almost without parallel," in the career of this great commander. On the first day, he gave Ewell an order to carry Cemetery Hill " if possible," and then failed to see that his command was obeyed. If the Confederates had gained this strong position before it was held in force by the Federals, there would have been no second and third days at Gettysburg: Meade would have retired to his Pipe Creek line, and the decisive battle would have been fought there.

When Lee decided to attack the Union army in its strong position on Cemetery Ridge, he should have concentrated all of his forces on Seminary Ridge, instead of leaving Ewell in the town, and giving Johnson seven brigades to assault the impregnable Union position on Culp's Hill. As General Alexander well says: in the absence of these troops, " the task before the remainder of the army was beyond its strength."

On the second day, too much time was wasted in reconnoitring, and getting the troops into position. Then the attacks which followed were isolated, and were not properly supported. While Meade sent twenty brigades to reënforce the menaced end of his line, only eleven Confederate brigades were engaged. The three divisions of Heth, Pender, and Rodes, and four brigades, scarcely fired a shot. Nothing was really accomplished except the destruction of the faulty Federal salient at the Peach Orchard, leaving the main Union line intact.

The famous assault on the third day, known as " Pickett's charge," was certainly a mistake, as Lee himself admitted later: it had little chance of success, in any event, and none at all as made, without proper formation, and with no support. After this useless sacrifice of ten thousand of his best men, Lee had no alternative except to retreat, to save his army from destruction: his ammunition was nearly exhausted, and no supplies of food or forage could be obtained where he was.

The Federal cavalry performed excellent service during this campaign. It constantly covered its own army, and kept in touch with the Confederates, until the two forces joined battle at Gettysburg. On the first day of the battle, it held back the enemy at Willoughby Run until the infantry came up. In the opinion of Major Steele, " This was the most valuable day's work done by the cavalry in the Civil War."

On the third day, a part of the Union cavalry defeated Stuart on the right, and prevented him from molesting the Federal rear; while on the left, another part so menaced Longstreet's flank and rear as to prevent him " from assailing Round Top with vigor, or detaching a force to aid Pickett." [53]

After the battle, the cavalry led the pursuit; it destroyed the bridge over the Potomac, and thus delayed Lee's crossing six days; it captured wagon-trains, and

[53] Doubleday.

hindered the retreat; and two divisions attacked the Confederate rear-guard just before it passed the river, killing General Pettigrew, and capturing about 1000 prisoners.

On the other hand, the Confederate cavalry was allowed, if not ordered, by Lee, to make a useless raid around the Union army. Leaving two brigades to guard the gaps of the Blue Ridge Mountains, Stuart started on the night of the 24 June with the three brigades of Fitz Lee, Hampton, and W. H. F. Lee. He expected to make the circuit and rejoin General Lee in Maryland, but the movements of the Federal army forced him so far east that he was obliged to ford the Potomac within twenty miles of Washington on the night of the 27th. Marching northward to Rockville, where he captured a wagon-train, he pushed on to Westminster. Finding that the Union cavalry was still between him and Lee, he proceeded across country on the 30th to Hanover, where he had an engagement with Kilpatrick.

Encumbered by a useless wagon-train, with his men and horses nearly worn out, Stuart was now in a perilous position. He made a night march to York, only to learn that Early had left the previous day; then he pushed on to Carlisle, to find once more that Early had gone, and that the town was held by a force of Pennsylvania militia. That night he learned that Lee's army was concentrating at Gettysburg, and he set out for that place the next morning (2 July).

Thus ended a useless raid, which probably cost the Confederates a victory at Gettysburg. Deprived of " the eyes of his army," Lee had been groping in the dark from the time that he started for the Potomac. He told Colonel Long that Stuart's absence " had materially hampered the movements, and disorganized the plans of the campaign."

During the retreat, however, the cavalry did good work, in guarding the flank and rear of the Confederate army, and protecting its trains.[54]

[54] See Steele, 362–363, 393.

CHAPTER THIRTEEN

SEPTEMBER 1862 — JULY 1863

VICKSBURG

Situation in the West — Battles of Iuka and Corinth — Grant Moves
on Vicksburg — McClernand's Intrigues — Valley of the Missis-
sippi — Strength and Strategic Importance of Vicksburg —
Grant's Line of Communications — Sherman Repulsed at
Haynes's Bluff — Grant Retreats — He Relieves McClernand —
Failure of His First Projects — His Final Plan — His Army
Crosses the River — The Confederate Forces — Grierson's Raid
— Battle of Port Gibson — Grant Abandons His Base — Jackson
Occupied — Battle of Champion's Hill — Vicksburg Invested —
Pemberton Capitulates — Comments — Numbers and Losses

IN September 1862, the situation in the West was as
follows: After capturing Corinth, and dispersing his
army, Halleck had gone to Washington to assume
the position of general-in-chief, leaving Grant in command of the troops in the vicinity of Memphis and Corinth. Grant's forces had been reduced to 42,000 men, to
reënforce Buell, who was on his way to Kentucky to oppose Bragg's invasion. He was required by Halleck to
guard the railway from Memphis to Decatur, 200 miles
in length, and keep communications open with Buell.
This, for a time, constrained him to adopt a passive attitude.

Opposed to him in Mississippi were two independent
commands, each about 16,000 strong. One, under Van
Dorn, scattered from Holly Springs to Vicksburg, was
charged with the defence of the river; the other, under
Price, near Tupelo, was to guard the Mobile and
Ohio south of Corinth. Learning that Rosecrans was to
be detached from Grant's army, to join Buell, Bragg asked
Price to attack Rosecrans, and prevent this movement.
Price accordingly moved on the 14 September to Iuka,
where he expected to be joined by Van Dorn for an

[264]

advance to Corinth. Grant resolved to attack Price before the Confederate forces were united, and ordered Rosecrans and Ord to march on Iuka. The troops advanced by two different roads, and the movement was not well coordinated. The result was that Rosecrans attacked alone. Darkness ended the battle, and during the night Price escaped.

Rosecrans and Ord then returned to Corinth. On the 28 September, Van Dorn and Price joined forces at Ripley, and the former took command by virtue of his rank. The Confederates advanced to Corinth, where they attacked Rosecrans on the morning of the 3 October. By sunset they had driven the Federals into the works at the edge of the town. Van Dorn renewed the assault the next morning, but by noon was defeated, after a furious combat, and forced to retreat. Rosecrans made no pursuit until the next day, and the Confederates retired to Holly Springs. General Pemberton was then sent to take the general command of the Confederate forces in Mississippi, and General Rosecrans relieved Buell of the command of the Army of the Ohio.

General Grant was now reënforced, and toward the end of October he felt strong enough to attempt the advance on Vicksburg, which he had long had in mind. His headquarters were then at Jackson, Tennessee. His right wing at Memphis, under Sherman, consisted of 7000 men; his centre at Bolivar, under Hurlbut, of 19,000; his left at Corinth, under Hamilton,[1] of 17,500; with about 5000 more at Columbus, his base, under Dodge — a total of 48,500 men.

Pemberton had made his headquarters at Jackson, Mississippi, where he had 2000 troops; Van Dorn, at Holly Springs, had some 24,000 men, in two divisions under Price and Lovell; Vicksburg was garrisoned by 6000, and Port Hudson by 5500 — in all 37,500 men.

Grant's plan was to abandon Corinth, after destroying the railroads around it; concentrate his forces at Grand Junction, and move upon Vicksburg by way of the Mississippi Central Railroad. But his letter of 26 October to

[1] General Hamilton had succeeded Rosecrans at Corinth.

Halleck remained unanswered, and it was a full month before he got started.

Unknown to Grant, McClernand was then in Washington working out a secret scheme with the President, and the Secretary of War, to raise a volunteer army in Indiana, Illinois, and Iowa, and lead it down the Mississippi to capture Vicksburg. Although he had had no military training, McClernand had handled his division very creditably at Donelson and Shiloh. As an Illinois politician, he had long been known to Mr. Lincoln, and he succeeded in winning the President and Mr. Stanton to his plan. To the credit of General Halleck, it must be said that he was not in favor of this scheme. As a professional soldier he realized the defects of a plan which proposed an advance against the same point by two independent expeditions: it was contrary to military principles, ruinous to discipline, and full of the seeds of disaster. To make matters worse, Grant was kept ignorant of the whole scheme, and was so puzzled by Halleck's brief enigmatical telegrams that his own movements were embarrassed.

The Mississippi is the most crooked of all the great rivers of the world. In many places it is necessary for a boat to traverse thirty miles to reach a point ten miles distant from its starting place. The river flows through a soft alluvial soil, in which it cuts new channels to the right or left on meeting the slightest obstacle to its direct course. It is lined by natural dikes, created by the deposits of sediment along the banks, and by artificial " levees " constructed by the people who live along the stream. For twenty miles on either side of the great river the land is intersected by a network of " bayous," or sluggish streams as crooked as the Mississippi itself. The river basin is covered with dense forests of cypress and other trees. In such a country it is manifest that armies could not operate, and that, upon these low, flat shores, fortifications could not be erected.

But to this rule there were a few notable exceptions. At points like Columbus, Memphis, Vicksburg, Grand Gulf, and Port Hudson, there are bluffs rising from 80 to 200 feet sheer above the turbid stream. Fortifications erected at such points were unassailable from the river. A ship's guns could not be elevated sufficiently to inflict any damage, and the vessels were subjected to a destructive plunging fire.

Of all these points along the river, Vicksburg was the strongest. To a fleet it was inaccessible, and to an army nearly so. The city crowns the bluffs at a height of 200 feet above the river, which washes the cliffs for a distance of eleven miles below the place. Grand Gulf is 60 miles, and Port Hudson 250 miles further down the river, but much nearer in a direct line.

Between Vicksburg and Port Hudson, the Mississippi was joined on the west by the Red River, the great highway by which the states of Texas, Louisiana, and Arkansas were connected with the central and eastern sections of the Confederacy. Vicksburg and its outpost Port Hudson were therefore places of the highest strategical importance. Their capture would cut off the great granary from which the Confederacy was largely supplied with food, and destroy nearly half its power of resistance.

The Mississippi between these two points was entirely in the hands of the enemy. The Federal fleet at New Orleans could not pass above Port Hudson, nor the one at Helena go below Vicksburg. No Union army could land on the eastern bank of the river between these two fortresses without being cut off from its source of supplies.

Above the city the bluffs swerve in a northeasterly direction, and away from the Mississippi, but near to its tributary, the Yazoo. Here, twelve miles above Vicksburg, the Yazoo washes the base of Haynes's Bluff, which commands all the river approaches. This position, which had been strongly fortified by the Confederates, rendered the city inaccessible from the north.

Vicksburg, therefore, could only be assailed from the rear; and here, too, the rugged country, broken by deep ravines, presented formidable obstacles to an enemy. No more arduous task had ever confronted a general than the reduction of this " Gibraltar " of the Confederacy.

By the 5 November, Grant had reached Oxford, and

Van Dorn, under orders from Pemberton, had fallen back to Grenada. As Grant's line of communications, by a single-track railway back to Columbus, Kentucky, was now more than 200 miles long, he established a secondary base at Holly Springs.

The first movement of Grant against Vicksburg was a continuation of the same strategy which had been so effective in the previous campaigns in the West. By moving south on a line parallel to the Mississippi, the river had been conquered all the way from Cairo to Vicksburg. One after another, the series of Confederate strongholds, at Columbus, Island No. 10, Fort Pillow, and Memphis, had become untenable, and had been abandoned. But now the conditions were different, for reasons which will be explained presently, and the length of the line of communications made a further advance almost impossible.

As Napoleon once said, every army, like a serpent, moves on its belly. In the densely populated centres of Europe an army can often live off the country, but this was seldom the case in the South. The food, forage, and ammunition, had to be brought to the armies. While the lines were near the great rivers — the Mississippi, the Tennessee, and the Cumberland — the problem was a very easy one, but the insecurity of the railroads rapidly increased with the length from the base, as it was impossible to guard them from the raids of the enemy's cavalry. The weight of food, ammunition, and other supplies, required by each soldier, averaged four pounds daily. The animals necessary for the cavalry, artillery, and trains, consumed twenty-five pounds of forage. In the present century, the problem of keeping an army supplied has been much simplified by the use of motors, but in December 1862, it required 1900 wagons, drawn by 11,000 animals, to keep Grant's army supplied at three days' march from its base. The army could not travel more than three days without shifting its base along the line of some river or railroad; and this base must be securely connected by river or rail with some permanent base established in a region entirely under Federal control.[2]

[2] Fiske, 191–192.

VICKSBURG

After considerable correspondence, it was finally arranged with Halleck that Sherman should return with one division to Memphis; there pick up the newly arrived troops, and organize an expedition to move down the river to Haynes's Bluff, under escort of Porter's gunboats, while Grant marched his army along the left bank of the Yazoo to the same objective point. Sherman arrived at Memphis on the 12 December, and started down the river on the 20th.

But Grant was prevented from carrying out his part of the program. Forrest's cavalry tore up sixty miles of the railway north of Jackson, Tennessee, and another mounted force captured the Union garrison at Holly Springs and destroyed all the Union supplies at that base. Grant was forced to place his army on short rations, and fall back along the railway to a point where he could open communications with Memphis.

In the meantime Sherman had descended the river with his force of 32,000 men, and landed at Milliken's Bend, twenty-five miles above Vicksburg. On the 29th he assaulted the Confederate works at Haynes's Bluff, but was repulsed with heavy loss. The position was held by 12,000 troops sent there by Pemberton, and was too strong to be carried. On the 2 January, Sherman reëmbarked his men, and returned to the mouth of the Yazoo. Here he was met by McClernand, with an order assigning that general to the command of the expedition. Thus ended in failure Grant's first movement against Vicksburg.

Upon assuming command of the Union force near Vicksburg, which he called the "Army of the Mississippi," McClernand divided it into two corps, under Morgan and Sherman. He then moved his army about fifty miles up the Arkansas River, and attacked Fort Hindman, which surrendered on the 11 January, with 5000 prisoners. There he was contemplating what General Grant called a "wild-goose chase" further into Arkansas, when he was recalled by a peremptory order from Grant. Halleck, when informed of McClernand's operation, authorized Grant to relieve McClernand, and supersede him by the next in rank, or to take command of the Vicksburg expedition in person. Grant thought that the easiest way of solving the problem was to assume the command himself, which he did on the 30 January. He then reorganized the expeditionary force in four corps, under the command of McClernand, Sherman, Hurlbut, and McPherson.[3] McClernand protested bitterly over his removal from the command of the Vicksburg movement, but the Washington authorities paid no attention to his complaints.

We do not propose to relate here in minute detail the history of Grant's work during February and March. His plans were foredoomed to failure, and except as showing the tenacity of the man — his grim determination to succeed in the face of the most appalling difficulties — the story possesses but few points of interest.

A little below the mouth of the Yazoo, the Mississippi turns sharply to the northeast, and after flowing five miles in that direction, it makes another equally abrupt bend to the southwest, enclosing a peninsula less than two miles in width, nearly opposite Vicksburg. McClernand and Sherman were ordered to set their men to digging a canal across this narrow neck of land. By this passage Grant hoped to transfer his army south of Vicksburg, there cross the river, and attack the town from the rear.

This plan was the simplest, and apparently the most promising of all. The distance was not much over a mile, but as the canal was designed to admit vessels of sixty feet beam and nine feet draught, considerable excavation was required. The chief problem, however, was to keep the water out during the progress of the work. After six weeks of hard labor, success seemed assured, when, on the 8 March, a sudden rise in the river broke the dam, and flooded not only the bed of the canal but also the surrounding country. From the first, Grant had had but little confidence in this plan, as he had observed that the lower end of the canal would enter the river just opposite the bluffs at Warrenton, a few miles below Vicksburg. Indeed, just before the break occurred, the enemy planted batteries on these heights, which completely commanded

---

[3] Hurlbut's corps remained at Memphis, to guard the bases and lines of communication. (Steele, 399.)

the southern end of the canal, so that even if finished it would have been of little use.

Grant's second experiment was carried on simultaneously with the canal work. About seventy miles above Vicksburg, on the west side of the river, there is a remnant of one of the numerous deserted beds of the stream, known as Lake Providence. This lake connected with the Red River, by a tortuous system of waters, navigable almost the entire distance. By this roundabout route of 400 miles, the ships could avoid the guns of Vicksburg, and bring supplies and reënforcements to the army below the city. McPherson's men were ordered to clear a passage through Bayou Macon, the only point at which the channel was obstructed. As soon as this work was completed, it was proposed to break the levees east of the lake, and let in the waters of the Mississippi; but all the obstacles had not been overcome when Grant abandoned the plan for the one which finally proved successful.

The third plan was, to find a passage for the army down the east side of the river, so as to turn the enemy's strong position at Haynes's Bluff. Just south of Helena, about 150 miles above Vicksburg in a straight line, there is a winding bayou, some 80 feet wide by 30 feet deep, known as the Yazoo Pass. This route, in former times, had been used by vessels plying between Vicksburg and Memphis. Later, it had been closed by a strong levee, 18 feet high and 100 feet thick, because the waters from the river overflowed so much land that they became a nuisance. On the 2 February this levee was destroyed by a mine, and the river let in to its old channel. But this route was obstructed by the enemy, who felled large trees across the stream, so as to make a formidable barricade. Before this obstacle could be removed, the Confederates constructed a strong earthwork, called Fort Pemberton, in a commanding position on a peninsula where two rivers unite to form the Yazoo. Here they mounted several heavy guns, and completely barred the descent of the river. So this experiment also failed.

One more attempt was made, on the east side of the river, to outflank Haynes's Bluff by utilizing the Big Sun-

flower River, which empties into the Yazoo 100 miles
below Fort Pemberton. But the stream was obstructed by
the Confederates, and the transports were attacked by a
considerable force. The situation became so perilous that
Sherman was obliged to back out.

Almost any other commander, except Grant, would
have been entirely disheartened by these repeated fiascos,
and have abandoned further efforts. The press was calling for his removal, and he had to do something. Only
three plans seemed feasible: (1) To assault the Confederate batteries at Vicksburg, which would have been suicidal;
(2) to return to Memphis and renew his attempt along
the line of the railway, which presented no greater promise of success than before; or (3), to find some way of
transporting his army to a point below Vicksburg, cross
the river there, and attack the town from the rear, without
any base of supplies. He chose the third plan.

The idea of Grant's final plan was suggested by the success of the gunboats, on several occasions in February and
March, in running by the dreaded batteries at Vicksburg
and Port Hudson. On the 2 February Porter sent a ram
down; and ten days later a gunboat also made the passage without any damage. On the 14 March, Farragut, in
his flagship the *Hartford*, with one consort, succeeded in
passing the batteries at Port Hudson, although four other
vessels were disabled and one destroyed. From this time
forth, the Federals were able to close the mouth of the
Red River.

Having decided upon his course, Grant went ahead regardless of the opinions of his generals. Every one of
them, including even the sanguine Sherman, thought that
it was sheer madness to cross south of Vicksburg. Having
concentrated his army at Milliken's Bend, on the 29
March McClernand's corps was ordered to lead the way
to New Carthage, twenty-seven miles below. By construct-
ing corduroy roads Grant was able to move his troops and
a large part of his supplies by land. On the night of the
16 April, ten shiploads of rations and forage, under convoy of the gunboats, made the passage of the forts without serious damage. Ten days later another squadron ran

the gauntlet successfully; and now at last Grant was ready to cross the river.

The point selected for crossing was Grand Gulf, opposite the hamlet of Hard Times where the army was concentrated. The fortress of Grand Gulf, on a bluff twenty-five miles below Vicksburg, formed the extreme left of the defences of the city. On the 29 April, the works were bombarded for five hours by Porter's fleet, but no impression was made. It was therefore necessary to select another point for the crossing. During the night the fleet, convoying the transports and supply ships, ran by the batteries, and the army marched farther down the right bank.

Grant was now informed by a slave that there was a good road from Bruinsburg, six miles below Grand Gulf, to Port Gibson twelve miles inland. The next day McClernand's corps was ferried over on the transports, and McPherson's corps immediately followed. In the meantime the attention of the enemy was completely absorbed by a demonstration made by Sherman in front of Haynes's Bluff. He now received orders from Grant to follow the other troops and cross at Bruinsburg.

Before continuing the story of the Vicksburg campaign, let us see what the Confederates were doing at this time. At the end of March, Pemberton had in Mississippi about 50,000 troops, scattered at different points. The line from Haynes's Bluff to Grand Gulf was held by 22,000; Port Hudson had a garrison of about 16,000; at Fort Pemberton and neighboring points there were some 7000; and in the northern part of the state perhaps 5000 more. All the cavalry had been sent to Bragg, and there was none in the state.

On the 17 April, Grierson left Lagrange, on his famous raid, and reached the Union camp at Baton Rouge on the 2 May. With 1000 men he rode the entire length of the state of Mississippi, covering 600 miles in 16 days, and destroying many miles of railway and telegraph lines, besides much other property. The Confederates were kept in a wild state of alarm, and, far more important than this, their attention was distracted at the most critical mo-

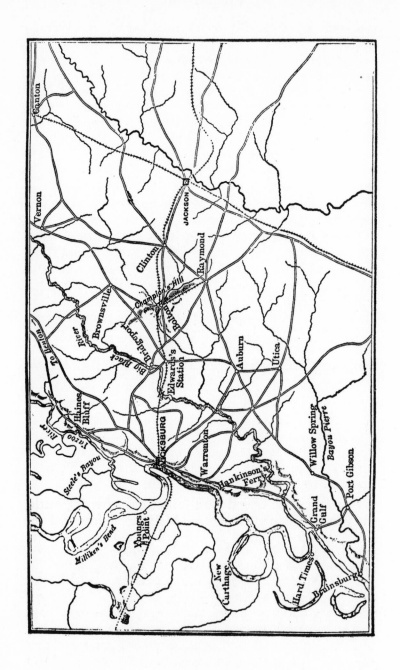

ment of the campaign — while Grant was crossing the river. " In its strategic effect," says Major Steele, " this was perhaps the most successful cavalry raid of the Civil War." [4]

As soon as Pemberton, who was at Jackson, heard of the attack on Grand Gulf, he ordered reënforcements sent there from Vicksburg. By night two brigades had arrived, and one of these marched on toward Port Gibson. By daybreak on the first of May, this brigade, with one other which McClernand had encountered on his march, was in position in front of the Union corps. The combat opened at dawn. McClernand's whole corps, of 18,000 men, was soon on the ground, but the country was so difficult to manœuvre on, that it was not easy to beat the Confederates, although they were outnumbered three to one. They finally gave way about five o'clock, and retreated to Grand Gulf, by two different routes, burning all the bridges behind them.

Pemberton hastened to Vicksburg, where he spent the following day in sending telegrams in every direction to collect his scattered forces. The Confederates, fleeing from the field of Port Gibson, stopped at Grand Gulf long enough to blow up the magazines and dismount the guns, and then started for Vicksburg by way of Hankinson's Ferry. At the ferry they met three brigades sent to their assistance, and were also joined by some troops from Jackson. The whole body then marched to Vicksburg, which the soldiers reached in a more or less demoralized condition.

Grant occupied Grand Gulf on the day after the battle, and established his base there. McPherson followed the retreating Confederates to the ferry, and halted there; McClernand bivouacked at Willow Spring. The two corps remained in these positions for three days, awaiting the arrival of ammunition and rations. Sherman crossed at Grand Gulf on the 7th, and Grant then had his entire force of 43,000 men concentrated on the east side of the river.

As previously stated, the forces of Pemberton were

[4] Steele 404.

very badly dispersed. About 15,000 men were at Port Hudson, a place almost as important to hold as Vicksburg. Over 20,000 men were posted at Vicksburg, and this left only about 15,000 troops available to oppose Grant in the field.

Halleck had notified Grant that he was expected to co-operate with Banks in the reduction of Port Hudson and Vicksburg, but that officer was then absent from his head-quarters at Baton Rouge in an expedition against the Confederates on the Red River. After crossing the river Grant received a letter from Banks, stating that he could not get back before the 10 May. Under all the circumstances, Grant decided that he could not wait. He resolved to advance at once against the railway from Vicksburg to Jackson, so as to place his army between the Confederate garrison in the fortress, and the army which it was rumored that the enemy was assembling at the state capital. This was the critical moment in Grant's career, upon which his whole future turned. " To face the difficulties in the way of such a movement," says Mr. Fiske, " required the stoutest of hearts and the coolest of heads." [5]

Grant was ignorant of the numbers and the exact positions of his adversaries. Unlike many Union commanders, he was apt to underrate, rather than to overestimate, the enemy's strength, but he assumed that there were about 30,000 men at Jackson. He had heard that Joseph E. Johnston was on his way from Chattanooga to take command in person, and he anticipated that troops would be rushed from every point to oppose him. His plan was to beat the two hostile forces in detail: first driving Johnston eastward, then turning upon Pemberton, defeating him, and pushing him back into Vicksburg. In order to do this, he must keep his army together; he could not spare any forces to guard his line of communications, and must cut loose from his base altogether, relying for supplies only upon what the men could carry with them or what they could find in the country. No general ever adopted a more daring scheme: there was no precedent for it in modern warfare. It seemed like defying Fortune

[5] Fiske, 232.

outright.[6] None of his generals approved of the plan, and Halleck forbade it as soon as the news reached Washington; but Grant was fortunately beyond the reach of the telegraph, and the order did not reach him until success was achieved.

Grant began his advance on the 7 May, as soon as Sherman arrived. His force consisted of the three corps of McClernand, McPherson, and Sherman — about 43,000 men. He had a train of 120 wagons, and the men carried five days' rations. Foraging parties were sent out every night to scour the country for food and forage.

Grant's movements were admirably calculated to mask his purpose. Small detachments were sent west of the Big Black to threaten Vicksburg and keep Pemberton in the city. The left wing under McClernand marched up the eastern bank of the Big Black toward Edwards's Station on the Vicksburg and Jackson railway, about midway between the two cities. The right wing under McPherson was directed toward Jackson by way of Bolton, and, after destroying the railroad and public stores, was to rejoin the main army. Sherman was to follow in the rear of McClernand, or midway between him and McPherson if he could find a road, and within supporting distance of the two wings. It was Napoleon's favorite movement of two wings with a central reserve column.

On the 12 May, McPherson encountered about 5000 Confederates in a strong position at Raymond and routed them after a sharp fight of about two hours. He then continued his advance on Jackson, supported by Sherman.

On the 9 May, Johnston had received orders at Tullahoma to proceed at once to Jackson, and take command of the forces in Mississippi. On his arrival there four days later, he found the brigades of Gregg and Walker. Two more brigades, Gist's and Maxey's, were expected to arrive on the 14th. This would give him 15,000 men, but Grant was too quick for him.

On the morning of the 14th, Sherman and McPherson were before Jackson. The flank of Gregg's brigade was enveloped by Sherman, and it was forced to retreat.

[6] Fiske, 233.

Walker occupied a very strong position, and made more of a fight; but he could not resist the charge of McPherson's troops, and his brigade was soon driven from its trenches. The Confederates escaped by the Canton Road, and Sherman and McPherson entered Jackson between three and four o'clock in the afternoon. That night Grant slept in the house which Johnston had occupied the night before.

On receiving Pemberton's telegram, stating that Grant had crossed the river, Johnston replied: " Unite all your troops to beat him — success will give you back what was abandoned to win it." [7] Pemberton should have advanced to Clinton, and attacked Grant in the rear; but he thought that sound strategy required him to seize Grant's line of communications to Grand Gulf. It never entered his head that Grant had done anything so rash as to abandon his base! Accordingly, he wasted his time in marching down toward Raymond.

Grant did not tarry long at Jackson. He faced his army to the westward, and started for Vicksburg, leaving Sherman to burn the bridges, factories, and arsenals at Jackson, and destroy the railroads for twenty miles in every direction. Johnston had retreated to Canton thirty miles north of the capital. From that place he telegraphed Pemberton, on the 16th, to march to Clinton, where he expected to unite all his forces. But Grant's army was already at Bolton, ten miles west of Clinton, and it was impossible for Pemberton to comply with the order.

On the 15th, Grant marched by the different convergent roads on Edwards's Station, where Pemberton was posted with three divisions, about 23,000 men; his two remaining divisions were at Vicksburg. On the night of the 15th the lines of the two armies were only about four miles apart, but neither commander seems to have been aware of the nearness of the other.

On the morning of the 16 May, the Confederates were found in line of battle in a strong position a little south of the railway, about three miles west of Bolton. Their left wing occupied the crest of an elevation some 70 feet in height, known as Champion's Hill. The knoll was steep

[7] Johnston, 170.

and rugged and covered with timber on the northern side, but gentler and partly cleared on the eastern and southern slopes. The bald crest was covered with artillery. Pemberton had about 18,000 men to hold his line, which stretched for two miles south of the hill. Grant had the two corps of McClernand and McPherson. The fighting was almost all done by McPherson's corps and one division (Hovey's) of McClernand's, on the Union right, directed by Grant in person. The possession of the hill was stubbornly contested: it was taken and retaken several times. It required eight hours of severe fighting to dislodge the Confederates. McClernand, on the Union left, practically did nothing. If he had attacked as vigorously as McPherson, the defeated Confederates would have been cut off from the ford over Baker's Creek, on the Raymond road, and been captured.

Grant lost about 2500 men. The Confederate losses were 1400 killed and wounded, 2500 prisoners, and all their artillery; while one division of 4000 men, cut off from the rest of the army, fled to the southeast many miles beyond Jackson. Practically half of Pemberton's army had been destroyed, and the rest retreated in disorder toward Vicksburg. That evening Grant received Halleck's telegram! He had staked everything, but he had won: Vicksburg was doomed.

Sherman arrived at Bolton on the night of the battle. Grant took up the pursuit with his entire army at daylight on the 17th. The railway crossing was in a deep bend of the Big Black, and this point was defended by about 5000 of the retreating Confederates. The head of Grant's column came up about eight o'clock, and drove the enemy from this position after a fight of less than an hour. The Confederates abandoned 18 pieces of artillery, and 1750 men were captured. They succeeded however in burning the bridge, which delayed the Federals for a whole day.

Next day, the 18th, while the two other corps marched directly on Vicksburg, Sherman occupied the Benton Road, in the rear of Haynes's Bluff, thus rendering that stronghold untenable. It was immediately abandoned by the Confederates, with all its guns and stores, and Sherman had the satisfaction of occupying this fortress which had defied him only a few months before.

On the 18th, Pemberton received an order from Johnston to evacuate Vicksburg, if not too late, and save his army. Pemberton called a council of war, which decided that it was too late to withdraw, thus exemplifying Napoleon's maxim that these meetings always " terminate in the adoption of the worst course, which in war is ever the most timid." Pemberton therefore made no effort to obey Johnston's order.[8]

Before two o'clock on the afternoon of the 19th, Grant's three corps were in position in front of the city — Sherman's on the right, McPherson's in the centre, and McClernand's on the left. Grant thought that the works might be carried by a vigorous assault, before the Confederates had recovered from their demoralization; he therefore ordered an immediate attack, but it failed all along the line.

Anxious to avoid the long and dreary work of a siege, Grant ordered another assault on the 22d, which also was repulsed. The attack was continued after Grant was satisfied that it could not succeed, because of McClernand's mendacious reports of success on his part of the line. Grant lost over 3000 men, due largely to these misleading reports of McClernand's.

It was now plain that Vicksburg could only be taken by a regular siege, and preparations were begun at once. The ground about the city is much cut up by ravines and small streams, and is admirable for defence. The line of the enemy was about seven miles long; that of Grant, more than fifteen miles, extending around the city from Haynes's Bluff on the north to Warrenton on the south. He also had a second line to the east, as a defence against attacks by Johnston in the rear. He had not troops enough at first to man all these works, but Halleck forwarded reenforcements at once.

Grant had no siege-guns except six 32-pounders, but Admiral Porter supplied him with a battery of navy-guns of large calibre, and with these, and the field-artillery,

[8] See Johnston, 187–188.

the siege began. Within a short time, Grant had 248 guns in his line, and about 75,000 men in his investing force. Approaches were dug, and mines and counter-mines set off. On the first of July the approaches were all within a few yards of the enemy's works. Orders were issued for a final assault on the 6th. But this was not to be: on the 4 July Pemberton capitulated, after a siege of forty-seven days.

Grant at first demanded his usual terms of " unconditional surrender," but, for reasons stated in his *Memoirs*,[9] later agreed to release the Confederates under parole, and also granted them the privilege of marching out with flying colors to stack arms.

With the single exception of Napoleon's capture of the Austrian army at Ulm in 1805, where he took 23,000 men and 60 cannon, there had been no such surrender in modern history. Over 29,000 men laid down their arms, and 172 cannon were taken. Sedan and Metz were in the future.

To find a parallel to this campaign, we must go back to Napoleon's first campaign in Italy in 1796. In eighteen days Grant marched 200 miles, and with a loss of 4000 men defeated two armies in five engagements, taking nearly 100 cannon, and destroying or capturing 12,000 of the enemy. Including the capture of Vicksburg, he put *hors de combat* 40,000 Confederates, and took nearly 300 cannon. This achievement by itself is sufficient to put Grant in the foremost rank of the second-rate captains of history, in the same class with Turenne, Marlborough, Wellington, and the Archduke Charles.

The capture of Vicksburg, with the simultaneous victory at Gettysburg, marked the turning-point of the Civil War. There were still many gloomy days to come, but the final outcome was no longer in doubt. Port Hudson surrendered to Banks five days later, and on the 16th a merchant vessel tied up to the wharf at New Orleans after an eight days' run from St. Louis. In the striking words of President Lincoln, " the Father of Waters rolled unvexed to the sea."

[9] 1 Grant, 561.

At the end of June, Johnston, who had finally succeeded in collecting an army of 25,000 men, advanced as far as Edwards's Station. But on the night of the 4 July, on hearing of Pemberton's surrender, he retreated rapidly to Jackson, with Sherman in hot pursuit. Sherman, who had about 30,000 men, refused to attack, but prepared for a siege. Johnston was not to be caught in a trap like Pemberton; on the night of the 16th he skillfully made his escape, and went into camp midway between Jackson and Meridian.

"Not a mistake of strategy can be pointed out in Grant's operations," says Major Steele, "and scarcely a mistake of tactics was made by his subordinate commanders." [10] Grant was fortunate in having two such able corps-commanders as Sherman and McPherson. During the siege of Vicksburg, McClernand issued a congratulatory address to his corps, full of inuendoes against the other troops and their commanders. It was published in the Illinois papers, and was evidently intended for political effect. In flat defiance of army regulations, no copy was sent to headquarters, and for this act of insubordination, Grant sent him home to Illinois, appointing Ord to succeed him. So ended the stormy military career of McClernand.

Grant's effective forces during the campaign ranged from 43,000 at the beginning to 75,000 at the close.

According to Johnston's reports, his forces at no time exceeded 24,000. Pemberton's greatest available force probably numbered over 40,000.

The losses on both sides during the last two months of the campaign were as follows: [11]

	Federals	Confederates
Killed	1,514	1,260
Wounded	7,395	3,572
Missing	453	4,227
Totals	9,362	9,059

According to the parole-lists on file at the War Department the number surrendered at Vicksburg was 29,491.

[10] Steele, 417.   [11] 3 B. & L., 549–550.

CHAPTER FOURTEEN
JANUARY — SEPTEMBER 1863
CHICKAMAUGA

Rosecrans at Murfreesboro — Cavalry Raids — Halleck's Prize —
Reorganization of the Army — The Tullahoma Campaign — The
Advance on Chattanooga — Theatre of the Campaign — Rose-
crans's Plan — Bragg Reënforced — Chattanooga Evacuated —
The Union Army Scattered — Concentrated at Chickamauga —
Bragg's Order of Battle — The Field of Chickamauga — Battle
of the 19 September — The Confederate Attacks All Repulsed
— The Second Day's Battle — Lines of the Two Armies — The
Fatal Order to Wood — The Union Right Annihilated —
Thomas Occupies the " Horseshoe " — Granger Marches to the
Cannon — The Last Stand — Rosecrans Rides to Chattanooga —
He Orders Thomas to Withdraw — The Federals Abandon the
Field — The Terrible Losses — Comments

AFTER the battle of Murfreesboro, during the first
days of January 1863 Rosecrans occupied the town,
and kept his headquarters there until the last week
in June. During the same period, Bragg was strongly
fortified at Shelbyville and Tullahoma, with his headquarters at the latter place. His cavalry was thrown well
north of Duck River, and extended from Spring Hill on
the west to McMinnville on the east. Polk's corps was at
Shelbyville; Hardee's headquarters were at Wartrace,
and his infantry held Hoovers, Liberty, and Bellbuckle
gaps, passes in a range of rough rocky hills which covered
his front toward Murfreesboro.

Although the two armies remained practically immobile
during this half-year, the cavalry on both sides were very
active. Each general was striving to cut the other's communications, and the cavalry operations almost assumed
the proportions of campaigns. In January, an attempt of
the Confederates to capture Fort Donelson was repulsed,
and their cavalry lost 1000 men. In April, a Union force

penetrated far into Georgia, and burned the important Round Mountain Ironworks, but the whole force of 1500 men was finally captured by Forrest.

The Union cavalry was greatly outnumbered by the squadrons of Forrest, Morgan, and Wheeler, and Rose-crans appealed, but in vain, to the War Department for an adequate force. He finally mounted Wilder's infantry brigade on captured horses, and it did good work during the campaign. The efficiency of the Confederate cavalry is shown by the report of the Louisville and Nashville Railroad for the year ending 30 June 1863. During this period, there were but seven months and twelve days when trains could run over the whole length of the road. Every bridge had been destroyed and rebuilt within the year — many of them several times. The tunnel at Gallatin was choked with rubbish for a distance of 800 feet, and could not be used for days. At times the Federal troops were on half rations; vegetables could not be had in quantity sufficient to keep off scurvy; and forage was scarce.[1]

Although possessed of many amiable traits, Rosecrans was very irascible, and was constantly wrangling with Lincoln, Stanton, and Halleck. They were continually urging him to move against Bragg, and drive him out of Tennessee, but he always complained that something was wrong which should be righted at Washington.

In the spring Halleck hit on a new device for hastening matters. He wrote Grant and Rosecrans offering the rank of major-general in the regular army as a prize to the first commander who should win an important success. Grant treated the offer with a quiet disdain which was more elo-quent than words; but the fiery Rosecrans replied that he felt "degraded at such an auctioneering of honors," and thereby incurred the enmity of the incompetent Halleck, as well as of the despotic and passionate Stanton.[2]

Meanwhile, by orders of the War Department, the Army of the Cumberland had been organized into three corps: the Fourteenth under Thomas, the Twentieth under McCook, and the Twenty-first under Crittenden,

[1] See Fiske, 253–254.   [2] Fiske, 254–255.

comprising practically the same divisions which had made up the Centre, Right Wing, and Left Wing, during the Murfreesboro Campaign. In addition Rosecrans formed a Reserve Corps of three brigades under General Gordon Granger. The army numbered some 60,000 men, while Bragg had about 43,000. At the same time, East Tennessee was occupied by a Confederate corps under Buckner; and Burnside, at Cincinnati, was organizing the Army of the Ohio, for an advance into East Tennessee from Kentucky by way of Cumberland Gap.

The last week in June the general situation in both theatres of the war was as follows: In the East, Lee was on his way to Gettysburg; in the West, Grant had Pemberton's army invested at Vicksburg, Burnside was advancing on Cumberland Gap, and Rosecrans at last was ready to move.

On the 23 June Rosecrans issued his orders for the advance. As the Confederate position at Shelbyville was nearly impregnable in front, Rosecrans made only a feint against this point with Granger's Reserve Corps and most of his cavalry, while he massed his three main corps against Bragg's right at Wartrace. There was some fighting at the gaps, but the Confederate right was forced back from one position to another, and the left had to retire to keep from being cut off. On the 30 June the Union army was concentrated at Manchester, and Bragg was forced to abandon his position at Tullahoma. By the end of the first week in July the Confederate army was back in Chattanooga.

In a period of nine days of continuous rain, by brilliant strategy, with the loss of only 583 men, Rosecrans had manœuvred the Confederate army out of its natural and artificial strongholds, and forced it across the Tennessee. Up to this time there had been no strategic campaign so brilliant in plan and execution, and General Rosecrans was warmly congratulated by all his corps-commanders, under the lead of General Thomas.[3]

[3] This operation, which General Cox says "is reckoned one of Rosecrans's chief claims to military renown" (1 Cox, 484), was begun against the almost unanimous protest of the general officers, who said that it was "a rash and fatal move." (See 1 Smith, 304.)

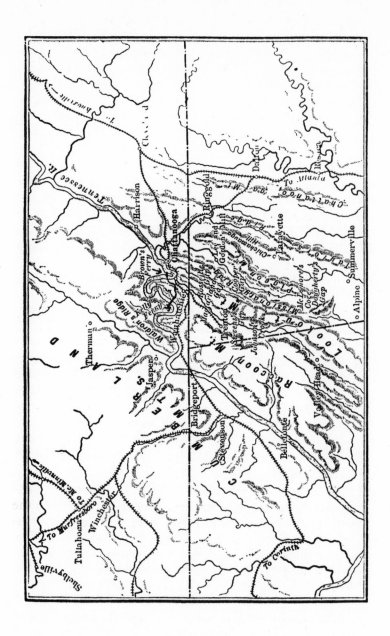

CHICKAMAUGA

At the end of the short Tullahoma campaign the two armies occupied nearly the same positions as the previous year, when the Army of the Cumberland, then under Buell, was preparing for an aggressive campaign against Chattanooga. The Union army was encamped along the western base of the Cumberland Mountains from Winchester to McMinnville, a distance of forty miles. As usual, there was soon a feeling at Washington of irrational impatience over what seemed to be the lack of energy on the part of the Union commander. But time was needed to accumulate the supplies of every kind necessary for the campaign; also to acquire information regarding the mountain passes by which the army must move. The railroad by which supplies reached the army also had to be repaired, and this work was not completed until the last week in July.[4] On the 14 August the advance began.

The most direct approach to Chattanooga was by the left over Walden Ridge, a spur of the Cumberland Mountains. The principal objection to that route was that it would necessitate a long line of communications over steep and narrow roads. The only other feasible route was by the right through Bridgeport and Stevenson, and over the mountains of northern Alabama and Georgia. This was finally adopted, because it would keep the army near the railway and its base of supplies, although there stood in the way a number of mountain ranges, hard to climb, and passable only at a few narrow defiles.

After crossing the Cumberland range west of the Tennessee, and the river itself, there is a series of mountain ridges, valleys, and streams, generally parallel to the river, on the eastern side. First, there is Raccoon Mountain, which ends in a mass of rough ridges and gorges, enclosed in a deep bend of the Tennessee, about four miles west of Chattanooga. Next comes Lookout Valley,

[4] It was at this time (27 July) that Garfield wrote Secretary Chase to express his disappointment over Rosecrans's slowness. This letter was subsequently used by Dana as the basis of his charges in *The Sun* that Garfield was responsible for Rosecrans's removal after the battle of Chickamauga. As a matter of fact, the Official Records show that *Dana himself was responsible.* (See 2 Smith, 868 *et seq.*)

beyond which is Lookout Mountain, which ends abruptly four miles south of Chattanooga in a commanding point of rock, rising from the edge of the river. From the summit of its steep palisades, 1400 feet above the swift current of the Tennessee, on a clear day parts of seven states can be seen, spread out in a magnificent panorama. Below, on the easterly side, is the valley of Chattanooga, through which flows Chattanooga Creek. Near the mouth of the creek stands the city, superbly situated in the midst of a great amphitheatre of hills. On the further side the valley is enclosed by Missionary Ridge, which also extends up to the river. Four miles south of the town this ridge is traversed by Rossville and McFarland's gaps, beyond which lies Chickamauga Valley, the scene of the battle.

At their upper or southern ends the valleys of Chattanooga and Chickamauga unite in a single valley known as McLemore's Cove. Beyond Pigeon Mountain and Taylor's Ridge, to the east, are the towns of Ringgold and Dalton, stations on the railroad from Chattanooga to Atlanta, where Bragg had his base of supplies.

The valleys were generally covered with timber, but there were some farms, and a few villages. There were no turnpikes, but good country roads through the valleys and the gaps in the mountains. The theatre was somewhat similar to that of Tullahoma, but different from any other in which a campaign had been carried on in this war.

The plan finally adopted by Rosecrans was to move his army directly across these formidable mountain barriers, and aim straight at Dalton, where he would be squarely on Bragg's line of communications. This would compel the enemy to evacuate Chattanooga or stand a siege there. The more effectually to mask his movements, Rosecrans kept his left wing under Crittenden thrown out so as to menace Chattanooga from the north. While still keeping up this demonstration, between the 29 August and the 4 September, he moved the remainder of his army across the Tennessee, and began his march over Raccoon Mountain. The left under Crittenden took position at Wauhatchie in Lookout Valley; the centre, under Thomas, went to Trenton; the right, under McCook, crossed from Stevenson and Bellefonte to Valley Head, whence cavalry demonstrations were made as far south as Alpine.

Meanwhile, the advance of Burnside on Knoxville had caused Bragg to order Buckner to Chattanooga; and he was also reënforced by Walker's corps from Mississippi. At the same time Lee sent him two divisions of Longstreet's corps, and Alexander's battalion of artillery, from the Army of Northern Virginia. Owing to Burnside's occupation of Knoxville, these troops had to make a long détour by way of Atlanta, and some of them did not arrive until after the battle. Hardee was detached about this time, and D. H. Hill was sent from Virginia to command his corps.

At first Bragg had been deceived by Rosecrans's feints, and was convinced that he intended to cross Walden Ridge, so as to join hands with Burnside. When the Federal plan was finally disclosed, Bragg evacuated Chattanooga on the 9 September and marched twenty-five miles south to Lafayette. But he had no idea of retreating, although he took great pains to give the impression that his army was fleeing in utter demoralization. His object was to cover his communications, and defeat the Union corps in detail as they debouched from the mountain passes.

Rosecrans, in turn, was absolutely deceived. He ordered Crittenden to leave a brigade in Chattanooga to garrison the town, and to pursue by the road to Ringgold. Thomas was directed to advance from Trenton on Lafayette, and McCook from Valley Head to Alpine and Summerville. These orders were issued on the 9th, and it was three days before Rosecrans realized his terrible mistake. The two wings of the Union army were then nearly sixty miles apart, and Bragg was concentrated opposite the centre under Thomas.

Bragg was aware of the isolated positions of the Federal corps, and made some efforts to cut them off, but his plans were frustrated by the neglect or incompetency of his subordinates. As already stated, his relations with his officers had not been very cordial since the battle of Murfreesboro.

As soon as he understood the situation, Rosecrans acted very promptly. Crittenden was moved from Ringgold to Lee and Gordon's Mill in Chickamauga Valley. Here he was joined by Thomas, who had withdrawn with great skill from the enemy's front, marched along the west side of Missionary Ridge, and passed through Cooper's Gap. McCook, however, was deceived by local guides, who assured him that there was no direct road practicable for his troops to McLemore's Cove; so he retraced his steps over Lookout Mountain to Valley Head, and did not reach the field until the 18th, after a tiresome march of five days. If it had not been for this delay of McCook's, Rosecrans would have withdrawn to Chattanooga instead of making a stand at Chickamauga. The delay also gave time for one of Longstreet's divisions to arrive. Therefore Rosecrans was forced to fight, not only in the wrong place, but also against larger numbers.

On the 18 September the Union corps were finally united along the west bank of Chickamauga Creek. The same day Hood's division of Longstreet's corps arrived, and Bragg was informed that McLaws was following closely. He accordingly issued his orders for an attack on the 19th.

The order of battle was of the progressive or *échelon* type, and prescribed that the attack should be begun by Hood on the right, who was to cross at Reed's Bridge, turn to the left oblique, sweep up the creek, and be joined as he proceeded by Walker and Buckner, who were to cross by Alexander's Bridge and Tedford's Ford. Hill was to cover the left flank; but to cross and attack the enemy's right if he attempted to reënforce his centre. The cavalry was to protect the flanks, Wheeler on the left and Forrest on the right.

The order contemplated turning the left of the Federals, and cutting off their retreat to Chattanooga; with this end in view, it was simple and well conceived, but it was based on wrong premises. Bragg thought that the Union centre was at Lee and Gordon's Mill, while in fact it was much further north, opposite Alexander's Bridge; and the left, under Thomas, greatly overlapped the Confederate right. The execution of the order therefore departed widely from the course prescribed, as will appear later.

Four miles south of Chattanooga the highway passes Missionary Ridge at Rossville Gap, where it forks, one branch running east to Ringgold, the other south to Lafayette. About three miles south of Rossville, the ridge is crossed by another gap, McFarland's. The battle-field of Chickamauga is an irregular parallelogram, bounded on the west by Missionary Ridge and on the east by Chickamauga Creek. From the Ringgold Road on the north to Crawfish Spring on the south the distance is about seven miles in a straight line; from McFarland's Gap on the west to Alexander's Bridge on the east is approximately four miles. The road to Lafayette traverses the field from north to south, and crosses the creek at Lee and Gordon's Mill. This road is intersected, at a point just north of the Union left, by the road from McFarland's Gap, which crosses the creek at Alexander's Bridge. The country is rolling, with some considerable elevations, and at the time of the battle was thickly wooded. There were no villages, but a number of farmhouses. The creek, which runs from south to north, is very winding in its course. Opposite the Federal position there were three bridges, Reed's, Alexander's, and Lee and Gordon's, and there were numerous fords. About three miles north of the Union left wing, the road to Ringgold crossed the creek at still another bridge, which did not figure in the battle.[5]

On the evening of the 18 September, Colonel McCook, of Granger's Reserve Corps, made a reconnaissance as far as Reed's Bridge, which he burned.[6] Meeting Thomas the next morning, he reported that there was an isolated brigade of the enemy on the west side of the creek, which

[5] " The Union army had few and incomplete maps; the topography of the actual battle-field was but dimly comprehended by most of the generals, including the commander-in-chief and his staff." (1 Smith, 325.)

[6] Steele (432) says: " The advance of the Confederate columns on the 18th was slow due to . . . the resistance offered by Minty's cavalry " which " was finally driven across the creek; it managed to burn the bridge [Reed's] after one of the Confederate brigades had crossed." This was doubtless the brigade referred to here.

might be cut off and captured. Thomas accordingly ordered Brannan to reconnoitre the road to Reed's Bridge in search of this brigade. Baird, under orders from Thomas, threw forward his right wing, so as to get in line with Brannan, and a part of Palmer's division, which came up a little later, was placed in position on the right of Baird. Thomas, who occupied the critical point of the line, on the left, had been ordered to hold the road to Rossville at all hazards, and had been assured by Rosecrans that he would be reënforced, if necessary, by the entire army.

Under Bragg's orders, Walker's corps forded the creek, on the morning of the 19th, a little below Alexander's Bridge, and then moved up the creek opposite this point. At the same time, Johnson, of Buckner's corps, crossed at Reed's Bridge, and marched up the stream some three miles. About ten o'clock, Brannan's advance movement encountered the enemy, being the cavalry of Forrest and two brigades of infantry, and drove them about half a mile, when it met with obstinate resistance. This reconnaissance of Brannan, therefore, developed the relative positions of the hostile forces, which had previously been unknown to the two commanders. Realizing for the first time that his right was greatly overlapped, and his flank in danger of being turned by the Federals, Bragg halted Walker on his march, and ordered him to retrace his steps. This movement brought on the battle of Chickamauga, before Bragg had his troops in position.

Under orders from Thomas, the two divisions of Brannan and Baird now attacked the enemy in their front and drove him back with great loss, taking many prisoners. Here the Union line was halted and readjusted; but, before this was completed, Walker assaulted in overwhelming numbers, and drove the Federals back in disorder.

Early on the morning of the 19th, McCook was in position at Crawfish Spring beyond the extreme left of the Confederate army. A little after ten o'clock, he was ordered by Rosecrans to send the two divisions of Johnson and Davis to Thomas. On Baird being driven back, Thomas ordered Reynolds's division of his own corps, and Johnson's division — both of which had opportunely arrived at the same time — to advance and repel the enemy. Walker's corps was attacked on the flank with great vigor, by these troops, and driven back to its first position, while Brannan also advanced in front and recaptured the artillery lost when Baird was forced back.

Bragg then sent Cheatham to the assistance of Walker, and the two united commands, charging with the " rebel yell," seemed on the point of sweeping everything before them. But, at the critical moment, Davis reported with his division, and, assisted by Wood, checked the Confederate advance. The Union line was reformed, and the divisions of Wood and Davis, reënforced by Sheridan, who came up from the right, then drove the Confederates back again to their first line.

Finding that Rosecrans was massing his troops on his left, to hold the road to Rossville and Chattanooga, Bragg placed Polk in command of his right, and ordered up Hill from Lee and Gordon's Mill.

At about half-past two o'clock, the Confederates made another furious assault on the Union line, which pierced the right centre and gained the Lafayette Road, opposite the Widow Glenn house, three-quarters of a mile west of the road, where Rosecrans had his headquarters. At this moment, Negley's division came up from the right, and was sent into the fight, with Brannan from Thomas's left. Advancing with loud cheers, these two divisions hurled back Hood and Johnson, and pursued them until darkness ended the combat, the Union troops reoccupying their old positions.

After dusk, Thomas prepared to reform his lines for the engagement to be renewed on the morrow, and placed the divisions of Baird and Johnson on his left, with Palmer and Reynolds next, and Brannan to the rear and right of Reynolds as reserve. While these arrangements were being made, the Confederates assaulted with tremendous force, but were repulsed, with heavy losses on both sides. Minty's cavalry was now ordered to report to

Granger, who with his reserve corps protected the road toward Rossville, and guarded the left flank.[7]

When the fighting finally ceased, some time after dark, the troops slept on their arms, awaiting the more terrible conflict of the morrow. On the 19th, only Hood with three of Longstreet's veteran brigades had reached the field, but a little before midnight Longstreet himself arrived, closely followed by two more brigades, in time to take part in the second day's battle. The four remaining brigades, of McLaws, and Alexander with the reserve artillery, were just behind, but did not reach the field in time to turn the evenly balanced scale of the battle.[8]

Bragg ordered the battle renewed at daybreak, but under a different organization. The army was now divided into two wings, the right under Polk, and the left under Longstreet. To Polk was assigned Cheatham's division of his corps, and the corps of Hill and Walker, with Forrest's cavalry on the right. Longstreet had under him the division of Hindman of Polk's corps, Johnson's division, Buckner's corps, and the five brigades of Hood and McLaws, with Wheeler's cavalry on the left. This arrangement was adopted to avoid changing the positions of the troops, but it led to a delay of some hours in opening the battle.[9]

Bragg's plan of battle was the same as on the previous day: the whole army was to wheel on Longstreet's left as a pivot, to crush the Federal left, and gain possession of the road to Chattanooga.

During the night the Union troops threw up temporary breastworks of logs and rails. At daybreak Rosecrans rode along his lines and spent some time in rearranging his troops, particularly in strengthening Thomas on the left. A heavy fog hung over the battle-field during the early morning.

Bragg was also up at sunrise, and took position with his staff just in the rear of the centre of his line, where he

[7] Cist, *Campaigns*, 193–199.   [9] Alexander, 457.
[8] Alexander, 455.

waited impatiently for the attack to begin. Owing to unavoidable delays, two hours were consumed in getting the
troops even approximately into position, and the first assault was not made until half-past nine o'clock.

For the second day's battle, on Sunday the 20 September, the lines of the two armies were arranged as follows: [10]

Baird's division, of Thomas's left wing, extended
around the northeast corner of Kelly Field, his left refused. Bordering this field on the east, next came the
divisions of Johnson, Palmer, and Reynolds, the right
brigade of the latter being in échelon, west of the Lafayette Road, its right reaching the Poe Field. Brannan's
front covered the latter field at its western edge. Next
came Negley, along the western line of the Brotherton
Field; then Davis and Sheridan, in front of the Widow
Glenn house, with Wood and Van Cleve in reserve, the
latter reaching to Vittetoe's.

During the night, however, Thomas received word
from Baird on his extreme left that his line did not extend to the road to Reed's Bridge, as had been anticipated;
so Rosecrans, at Thomas's request, hurried Negley over
to the extreme left, and sent Wood's division to occupy
the position thus vacated. As will appear later, this
change led to the catastrophe which overwhelmed the
Federals.

The Confederate line was wholly east of the Lafayette
Road, the right and centre being in close contact with the
Union line. In order from right to left it was arranged
as follows: Breckinridge confronted Baird, extending beyond his left; then in succession in the front line came the
divisions of Cleburne, Stewart, Johnson, Hindman, and
Preston. In reserve, in rear of Breckinridge, were the
two divisions of Walker's corps; in rear of Cleburne and
Stewart, the five brigades of Cheatham; and in column
just behind Johnson, opposite Brotherton's, the divisions
of Hood and Kershaw. The divisions of Hindman and
Preston prolonged the line beyond the right of the Fed-

[10] From the *Campaign for Chattanooga*, published by the Military
Park Commission (1902).

[295]

erals, who were thus overlapped on both flanks. Bragg had therefore five divisions, fifteen brigades, of infantry in reserve; besides two divisions of cavalry, who were between the Union left and Granger's reserve corps at McAfee Church. Rosecrans had in reserve only Wilder's brigade, and two brigades of Van Cleve.

The first Confederate assault, made by the divisions of Breckinridge and Cleburne, fell on Negley and Baird at the extreme Union left, and was delivered with tremendous force. Thomas hurried up reënforcements from the right of his line, which checked the assault and finally drove the enemy back. The attack on Baird was followed by assaults which successively struck Johnson, Palmer, and Reynolds, with equal fierceness, but all were gallantly repulsed. At last Bragg abandoned the attempt, and his troops fell back to their first positions.

About eleven o'clock, Longstreet appealed to Bragg for permission to attack with his entire wing, and, consent being given, prepared for a general advance. At nearly this same hour, an aide on Thomas's staff, who had been riding the lines, reported that there was a long gap in the line between Reynolds and Wood. This was not correct, as Brannan's division, although not in front line, was still in position, retired a short distance back, and concealed by the thick woods. This information was sent to Rosecrans, who dictated a message to Wood: "*The general commanding directs that you close up on Reynolds as fast as possible and support him.*"

The order to Wood was dictated by General Rosecrans to Bond of his staff, and handed to Colonel Starling, Crittenden's chief of staff, for transmission. That officer, in his own words, "hesitated, not understanding the object of the order, when General Garfield called out that the object of the order was that *General Wood should occupy the vacancy made by the removal of Brannan's division, Brannan having been ordered to Thomas's left.*" [11]

If Garfield had written the order, he would, after his almost invariable custom, have included the explanatory

[11] 50 O. R., 983.

phrase, but, as it was, the order was absolutely peremptory.[12]

Wood could not understand this order, which it was impossible for him to execute literally, but he did not ask for any explanations, and undertook, in spite of the staff-officer's protest, to carry it out as well as he could. The withdrawal of his command from the front left a gap of two brigades in the line of battle. Into this gap, which he would have sacrificed a division to create, Longstreet poured the divisions of Stewart, Johnson, Hindman, Hood, Kershaw, with Preston's large division in support. The Union right, already depleted to sustain Thomas, was almost annihilated. Several thousand prisoners were lost, with forty guns, and a large number of wagon-trains. Davis, overpowered by numbers, was compelled to retire to save his command. One of Van Cleve's and two of Sheridan's brigades had already been sent to Thomas, but five brigades on the right were entirely cut off.[13]

Davis returned to the field at sundown. Sheridan rallied part of his command, moved by way of McFarland's Gap to Rossville, and thence marched back toward the battle-field. As Rosecrans, McCook, and Crittenden, were caught in the break of the right, and went to Chattanooga, Thomas was left in command on the field.

A part of the remnants of the Union right rallied at Snodgrass Hill, which should more properly be designated as " Horseshoe Ridge." It is not a single hill, but a ridge composed of three distinct hills, jutting out eastward from Missionary Ridge, and lying athwart the valley of the Chickamauga, with the concavity of its crescent-shaped curve opening directly toward the south. It is situated west of the Lafayette Road, about two-thirds of a mile from Kelly Field, and just south of the present military post of Fort Oglethorpe in Chickamauga Park.

---

[12] 1 Smith, 332. In a history of his military record, written in 1873, on the request of the War Department, Garfield states that he " wrote every order save one from the Army headquarters during the two days of the Battle of Chickamauga." From this statement, it would appear that the " fatal order " to Wood was the only order not written by Garfield. (See 2 Smith, 861.)

[13] Cist, 201–207.

The distance from the Horseshoe to McFarland's Gap is about two miles and a half, and by this gap to Rossville nearly six miles.

About one o'clock, Brannan withdrew his line to this position, and Stanley's brigade, of Negley, rallied on his left, these two commands occupying the two westerly hills of the Horseshoe Ridge. Harker's brigade, of Wood, after repulsing part of Longstreet's column which was moving toward the ridge, finally took position on the easterly hill in front of the Snodgrass house, on Stanley's left.

Soon after one o'clock, Longstreet began his assaults on the Horseshoe with the brigades of Anderson (Hindman) and Kershaw (McLaws). By two o'clock the Confederates had passed over the hill on Brannan's right and gained the valley in his rear.

Three miles away, near Rossville Gap, Gordon Granger was stationed with three brigades of the reserve corps. He had listened all the morning to the heavy firing to the south, which seemed to increase in intensity as the day wore on. Judging that Thomas was being hard pressed, he now decided, against orders, " to march to the sound of the cannon." Placing Dan McCook's brigade at the McAfee Church to protect the Ringgold road, he started for the front with his two remaining brigades. Marching at double-quick, Granger arrived about two o'clock, at the most critical hour of the day, when Longstreet was forming the divisions of Hindman and Johnson in heavy columns for an assault on the right flank and rear of the Union position. Granger promptly hurled his two brigades, under Whitaker and Mitchell, against the threatening force. After a terrific conflict, which lasted only about twenty minutes, the Confederates were put to flight. The victory was won at fearful cost, but the army was saved.[14]

The enemy was driven from Brannan's right and rear, and the Union line was extended south three-quarters of a mile to the heights overlooking Vittetoe's. Immediately after, Van Derveer's brigade of Brannan's division came

[14] Cist, 209–210.

up from the Kelly Field and strengthened his right, and Hazen's brigade, brought from Palmer's line, took position on Harker's left.

The Kelly Field line, where the four divisions still stood fast, now formed Thomas's left; the Horseshoe, with five brigades and some remnants of regiments, his right. Dan McCook's brigade, left by Granger, was on the high ground northwest of and overlooking Baird's left. On his way to the Horseshoe, Steedman, in command of Whitaker's and Mitchell's brigades of the reserve corps, had retaken the Union hospital at Cloud's Spring, captured about noon by Forrest's cavalry.

Longstreet had eleven brigades for his assaults on the Horseshoe. The final charges covered a period of nearly two hours. At three o'clock, he asked Bragg " for some troops of the right wing, but was informed by him that they had been beaten back so badly that they could be of no service."

In the meantime, Bragg had personally superintended the preparations for another assault on the Kelly Field line, in even greater force. This attack, which was made with Walker's corps and the divisions of Breckinridge and Cleburne, was repulsed by the divisions of Baird, Johnson, and Palmer. But later in the afternoon Bragg succeeded in reaching the Lafayette Road at McDonald's, in the rear of the Union army.

In the *débâcle* of the right, two brigades of Davis's division, one of Van Cleve's, and two of Sheridan's, were cut off from any communication with Thomas except by a long détour by way of the Dry Valley Road to Rossville, and thence back by the Lafayette Road. A part of these troops tried to join Thomas, and were placed along the road from Rossville to the battle-field.

When Longstreet's men poured through the gap in the Union line, Rosecrans was on the right, near the rear of Davis. He was swept away with the tide of defeat, and finally reached Rossville with Garfield, his chief of staff. There, after a consultation with Garfield, he decided to send the latter back to Thomas, while he went himself to

Chattanooga to make preparations for his troops as they came back in rout. This act practically ruined the fine reputation of Rosecrans.[15] In this campaign, from Tullahoma to Chickamauga, Rosecrans had shown great ability, and but for the unfortunate order given to Wood during the battle he would doubtless have defeated Bragg, and won undying fame. It was a sad ending to a glorious career.

During the whole afternoon there was a gap of nearly half a mile between Thomas's right on the Horseshoe and his left at Kelly's Field, which was a constant anxiety to him and his generals.[16] Longstreet, who was directing the Confederate assaults from his headquarters in the Dyer Field, entirely neglected this opportunity to move directly forward along the Lafayette Road and cut the Union line in two. His object seems to have been, not so much to drive an entering wedge between the two wings, as to prevent the Federal left at the Kelly Field from reënforcing that part of the army posted on the Horseshoe Ridge.[17]

During the afternoon of the second day, three important despatches were sent, which have excited much controversy. These are given below in their chronological order: —

Garfield to Rosecrans [18]

GENERAL THOMAS'S HEADQUARTERS

BATTLE–FIELD, FIVE MILES SOUTH OF ROSSVILLE

September 20, 1863, 3:45 P.M.

GENERAL ROSECRANS: —

I arrived here ten minutes ago, via Rossville. . . . I hope General Thomas will be able to hold on here till night, and will not need to fall back farther than Rossville; perhaps not any. . . .

[15] General Daniel H. Hill writes that, at the outbreak of the Civil War, it was thought that Sherman, McClellan, and Rosecrans, were the three Federal officers who were most to be feared. Grant was not once thought of by any one.

[16] See Hazen's *Narrative*, 131; also his Report, 50 O. R., 764.

[17] 51 O. R., 290.

[18] 50 O. R., 141.

This despatch was sent from the headquarters of General Thomas near the Snodgrass house on Horseshoe Ridge.

At about 4:30 P.M.,[19] Thomas received the *first* order from Rosecrans to withdraw his troops. Up to that time, as the ranking general on the field, he had resolutely maintained his position.

This order, which was received " soon after Garfield had reported," read as follows: —

Rosecrans to Thomas [20]

HEADQUARTERS DEPT. OF THE CUMBERLAND

CHATTANOOGA, September 20, 1863, *12:15* P.M.

MAJOR-GENERAL THOMAS: —

Assume command of all the forces, and with Crittenden and McCook take a strong position and assume a threatening attitude at Rossville.

W. S. ROSECRANS, *Major-General*

When General Thomas was preparing his Official Report of the 30 September, he called the attention of General Rosecrans to the alleged sending-time of this order (*12:15* P.M.), and the latter said that it was an error, that he " did not leave the battle-field until after that hour, nor reach Chattanooga before 3:40 P.M." [21]

We know that Rosecrans was on the battle-field until after midday. He then rode to Chattanooga, over ten miles, stopping en route at Rossville for a long conference with Garfield. It would therefore seem physically impossible for him to have reached Chattanooga before three-thirty or four o'clock. He afterwards stated that the despatch " must have been written as late as 4:15 P.M." This hour, however, seems too late, as Thomas began his withdrawal about 4:30.

[19] One of the most difficult historical points to establish in any battle is that of *actual* time. This is particularly true of Chickamauga. In the Official Reports, the terms *sunset, dark, dusk, nightfall, close of the day*, and so on, are used in a most confusing way. At Chattanooga, on the 20 September 1863, the sun set at six o'clock, twilight lasted one hour and twenty-five minutes, and night fell at 7:25 P.M.

[20] 50 O. R., 140.   [21] 50 O. R., 256, 257.

Rosecrans's *second* despatch, of the same purport, was addressed to Garfield, and read as follows: —

Rosecrans to Garfield [22]

CHATTANOOGA, September 20, 1863

BRIGADIER-GENERAL GARFIELD: —

See General McCook and other general officers. Ascertain extent of disaster as nearly as you can and report. Tell General Granger to contest the enemy's advance stubbornly, making them advance with caution. Should General Thomas be retiring in order, tell him to resist the enemy's advance, retiring on Rossville to-night.

According to Thomas's Report,[23] this second despatch was given him by Garfield at a point beyond the Ridge Road (which runs from the battle-field to McFarland's Gap) on his way from the field, whence he " proceeded to Rossville, accompanied by Generals Garfield and Gordon Granger." From other Reports it seems certain that the exact point was the Cloud house, near the Lafayette Road, about two miles from the Snodgrass house, and the time " a little after sunset," that is to say, soon after six o'clock.

Soon after Thomas received Rosecrans's *first* despatch, addressed to himself, ordering withdrawal, he sent an aide to Reynolds to direct the beginning of the movement. At the same time orders were despatched to the other left wing division commanders for their withdrawal successively.

Reynolds, who was in danger of being cut off, had already begun to retire before receiving Thomas's order. He was joined on the Lafayette Road by Thomas, who had left the Snodgrass house a little before five.[25] Thomas then took personal charge of the movement, and directed the troops to withdraw by way of McFarland's Gap.

Misunderstanding Thomas's order, Reynolds marched directly along the Lafayette Road toward Rossville Gap,

[22] 50 O. R., 140. The wording of this despatch shows that it was sent before McCook reached Chattanooga " about 4.30 or 5 P.M." (50 O. R., 941.)

[23] 50 O. R., 254.   [25] 1 Smith, 343.

until checked at Cloud Church by Forrest's cavalry, while Thomas, separating King's brigade from the rest of the division, wheeled to the left near McDonald's and took the Ridge Road to McFarland's Gap. Here he halted and sent orders for the withdrawal of the troops on the Horseshoe, who, however, had been driven from their positions before the order arrived.

The most direct line of retreat would have been by Rossville Gap, but Thomas obeyed literally the order of Rosecrans, and withdrew via McFarland's, in order to join his forces " with Crittenden and McCook," whose troops were in that vicinity. As directed, he also " assumed a threatening attitude," by forming a line from the gap to the Lafayette Road, to protect the withdrawal and check pursuit. This alignment was completed about 5:30, and shortly thereafter he received Rosecrans's *second* despatch ordering him to retire on Rossville.

The assaults by Anderson and Kershaw ceased about four o'clock, and Preston's two brigades of Buckner's corps made their final and successful attacks about five. An hour later, the whole of the Horseshoe was in the possession of the Confederates — the last Federal stand being, not on the main ridge, but over 300 yards north of it, on the bare hill near the Snodgrass house. " At the end of the battle, at the hour of sunset [6. P.M.]," says General Buckner, " the enemy was retreating hastily from every part of the field." [26]

About six o'clock, General Longstreet, in command of the Confederate left wing, halted the pursuit. A few minutes later, the sun went down, and the moon rose; it was a bright moonlight night.

After nightfall, Thomas skillfully withdrew his command to Rossville, where ammunition and rations were sent him by Rosecrans from the city. Some attempts by the Confederates to interfere with this movement were repulsed without serious difficulty. So quietly was the army withdrawn that Bragg did not discover the retirement until the next morning.

[26] Letter from General Buckner to Colonel Gracie, quoted by the latter (page 37). *Cf.* 51 O. R., 417–434.

There was no object to be gained in holding the line at Rossville Gap beyond securing time to make the final arrangements for the withdrawal of the troops to Chattanooga, which was accomplished on the 21st. The following morning found the Army of the Cumberland in position before the city, and too strong to be attacked by the enemy with any chance of success.

The name " Chickamauga " in the Indian tongue is said to mean " Valley of Death," and the place had now fairly earned that sombre epithet. Chickamauga was the most bloody battle of the Civil War, and also, with few exceptions, of modern times. The losses, as given by General Alexander, were as follows: [27]

	Federals	Confederates
Killed	1,657	2,074
Wounded	9,754	12,797
Missing	4,753	1,328
Totals	16,164	16,199

It is hard to determine the exact numbers engaged on each side. Cist says: " The largest number of troops Rosecrans had of all arms on the field during the two days' fighting was 55,000 effective men "; and that " Bragg, during the battle, when his entire five corps were engaged, had about 70,000 effective troops in line."

The figures given in *Battles and Leaders* are substantially the same: Federals, 56,965 of all arms; Confederates, 71,551 of all arms.

Livermore estimates the Union effectives at 58,000, and the Confederates at 66,000.

General Alexander gives the following figures:

Federals, 55,799 infantry and artillery, and 9842 cavalry; total 65,641; Confederates, 47,520 infantry and artillery, and 14,260 cavalry; total 61,780.

There were probably about 125,000 men, on both sides,

[27] Alexander, 463. In 3 *B. & L.*, 675, the Confederate losses are estimated at 17,804; in Livermore (106) at 18,454; and in Cist (228) at 20,950. A full report of their losses was never made.

engaged in the battle, and the total losses, in killed, wounded, and missing, were about 32,000. If we deduct from the total forces the 24,000 cavalry, in which the casualties were very light, we find that the losses in the two other arms were about 32 per cent., or nearly one-third of those engaged. If we exclude prisoners, the losses in killed and wounded were about 27 per cent.[28]

To paint a battle, says Victor Hugo, would require one of those powerful artists who has chaos in his brush. The historian narrates the features which strike him in this *pêle-mêle*. The line of battle floats and twists like a rope stretched across a swift current; the fronts of the armies move forward and back; regiments advancing or retiring make promontories or indentations. There always arrives a certain moment when a battle degenerates into a combat, becomes particularized, and is resolved into innumerable details, which, to borrow the expression of Napoleon, " belong rather to the biography of regiments than to the history of the army." In this case, the historian evidently has the right to give a résumé. He can seize only the outstanding features of the combat: no narrator, however conscientious, has the gift to fix absolutely the form of that horrible haze which we call a battle. This, which is true of all great combats, is applicable particularly to Chickamauga.

" Chickamauga," says Judge Tourgee, " was a battle almost unparalleled in modern times. Volumes have been written to prove how those who fought were marshalled.

---

[28] In 2 Henderson, 614–617, it is stated that the losses (excluding prisoners) in the great battles of the Civil War, and in Napoleon's campaigns were:

CIVIL WAR		NAPOLEON'S CAMPAIGNS	
Battle	Per cent.	Battle	Per cent.
Shiloh	20	Rivoli	30
Second Manassas	17	Marengo	22
Antietam	17	Eylau	33
Chickamauga	27	Friedland	23
Gettysburg	24	Aspern	26
Murfreesboro	24	Borodino	28
Wilderness	14	Leipzig	20
Spottsylvania	16	Waterloo	24

Such efforts are mostly vain. . . . Confusion grows more confounded with each attempt to reduce order out of impenetrable chaos." [29]

Other authors have also had to confess the impossibility of making up a clear and true account from the published material. But, although the details of the battle are very complicated, the salient points are not difficult to understand. The trouble has been that nearly all of the earlier histories were based, not upon official authority, but upon unreliable newspaper stories, and that until recently no true and complete account of the battle has been written. None of the histories published prior to 1889 was based on official facts, as the Official Records had not then been published. The reports written by 215 Federal and 199 Confederate officers have since been printed, and fill nearly four volumes of about 1000 pages each. [30]

The misinformation began in the "complimentary orders" issued to his troops by General Rosecrans on the 2 October 1863. He wrote:

When the day closed you held the field, from which you withdrew in the face of overpowering numbers, to occupy the point for which you set out — Chattanooga.

Here are recorded three statements of alleged fact, not one of which is supported by the records.

(1) "When the day closed," the field was abandoned by the Federals.

(2) The records show that Rosecrans had about 60,-000 men in the battle, and Bragg about 65,000.

(3) The battle was *not* fought to gain possession of Chattanooga, which Rosecrans might have occupied on the 9 September without opposition.

The facts are more correctly stated in Rosecrans's telegram to President Lincoln from Chattanooga at 9 A.M. on Monday the 21 September: —

[29] Tourgee, *A Story of a Thousand*, 228.
[30] *War of the Rebellion Official Records of the Union and Confederate Armies*, vol. XXX, parts I, II, III, and IV, more conveniently designated as Serial Nos. 50, 51, 52, and 53.

After two days of the severest fighting I ever witnessed our right and centre were beaten. The left wing held its position until sunset [six o'clock]. . . . We have no certainty of holding our position here.

Thomas received about 4:30 the order from Rosecrans to withdraw his troops from the battle-field. He was then holding the Horseshoe with some remnants from the right wing, and the Kelly Field with the divisions of Reynolds, Palmer, Johnson, Baird, and Barnes's brigade, of Van Cleve. He began the movement at once by despatching orders to Reynolds and his other left wing division commanders for their withdrawal successively from right to left. Thus General Thomas " quit when ordered and because he was ordered."

Through a misunderstanding of Thomas's orders, as stated above, Reynolds moved straight along the Lafayette Road toward Rossville, while the other divisions took the Ridge Road, as intended, toward McFarland's Gap.

Thomas formed his divisions to resist pursuit in a line from the head of McFarland's Gap to the Lafayette Road and the Cloud house, nearly to Rossville Gap. This formation was completed about 5:30. *At that hour the Horseshoe Ridge was in the possession of the enemy.*

At this same hour, in the vicinity of the Cloud house, Sheridan reported his arrival on Thomas's left.[31] This brave general had accomplished a feat almost unique in the annals of war. After the dispersal of his division by the onslaught of Longstreet on the Union right, and the loss of thirty per cent. of his command, he had gathered and rallied together in the woods more than half of the scattered remnants, about 1500 men, and brought them into line again at the extreme left flank, ready for action, before sunset.

It thus appears that there is little or no truth in the three popular fallacies regarding Thomas's connection with the battle, which may be specified as follows: —

(1) That the troops who remained with him were all members of his own Fourteenth Corps.

[31] 50 O. R., 581.

(2) That he used his own discretion, and did not immediately withdraw his men on receiving Rosecrans's order.

(3) That he held Horseshoe Ridge until nightfall (7:30), and then marched his men from the battle-field in perfect order.

The facts, as conclusively proved by the Official Records, are: —

(1) That the troops under Thomas's orders, who held the Kelly Field and the Horseshoe, were composed of all the different corps of the Army of the Cumberland.

(2) That on the receipt of Rosecrans's order, about 4:30, Thomas immediately issued his orders for the withdrawal.

(3) That his troops were so much " disorganized " he considered it futile to attempt to make a stand in front of the two gaps.[32]

What is said above is not meant in any sense as a criticism of General Thomas. He did his full duty; he inspired his men with courage and confidence, and his conduct deserves only words of praise. He was in no way responsible for the Federal defeat, and was powerless to avert the disaster. He took no steps to withdraw his men until he received direct orders from the commander-in-chief to retire. Although he did not retreat to the famous Horseshoe Ridge, and there stand at bay " for six weary hours," while with "25,000 men " he " hurled back again and again the furious onset of 60,000 rebels mad with desire to clutch the prize they had so nearly won," [33] he none the less deserved his title of the " Rock of Chickamauga." He could not prevent the Federal defeat, but he saved the army from destruction.

General Cist says that the campaign of Chickamauga, taking everything into consideration, was " the most brilliant one of the war." [34] Up to the time of Bragg's withdrawal from Chattanooga, Rosecrans's manœuvres were masterly, but then he was utterly deceived. Bragg never intended his retirement to be permanent: all the indica-

---

[32] Sheridan, 1 *Memoirs*, 284.　　[33] Fiske, 274.　　[34] Cist, 215.

tions he left behind him proved that. No bridges were destroyed; all hospitals, storehouses, and other buildings used by his army were left standing. Yet Rosecrans was duped by one of the oldest and most common *ruses de guerre*, and believed the tales of "deserters" that the Confederate army was retreating in utter demoralization. His first mistake was in scattering his army in pursuit before this fact was definitely determined, and the difficulty in again concentrating his troops forced him to fight at Chickamauga. Had Bragg received his promised reënforcements at the date he expected them, the Union army would have been completely crushed in detail.

While the Confederates gained some slight advantages in the battle of the 19th, there was nothing to indicate that they could finally defeat the Federals. Their victory on the second day was due mainly to Rosecrans's order to Wood, given under a misapprehension, and which so experienced a soldier should never have executed without question. General Wood was a graduate of West Point, had been in the army all his life, and knew the full meaning of all technical terms used to describe military movements. He must have realized that there was some error in the order to "close up on Reynolds," for he carefully put away the order in his note-book, with the remark that he "was glad the order was in writing, as it was a good thing to have for future reference." He was apparently irritated over a reprimand received from Rosecrans earlier in the day, and undertook the execution of an impossible order rather than ask an explanation of it from the general in command. To this extent he was responsible for the disaster which overwhelmed the Union army.[35] In justice to General Wood, however, it should be added that after he reported to Thomas "there was no more splendid fighting done . . . than was done by Thomas J. Wood and his division. To the last he aided Thomas in holding Horseshoe Ridge, and his was one of the last divisions to retire." [36]

Rosecrans's final error was in not returning personally

[35] Cist, 220–223.   [36] *Ibid.*, 223.

[309]

to the battle-field, instead of sending Garfield. As at Murfreesboro, he might have done much to restore the *moral* of his troops, and pluck victory from defeat. Thomas was a stubborn fighter, but he lacked the personal magnetism of Rosecrans. " That was the turning-point," says Cist, " and his hour had arrived."

The hero of Chickamauga was George H. Thomas, and well was it for the Army of the Cumberland that he was in command of the left on that day. Carefully posting his troops, he stood at bay, " with his back to the wall," and refused to be driven from the field. Here he stayed, repulsing every attack until ordered to withdraw. He fully earned his glorious title of the Rock of Chickamauga!

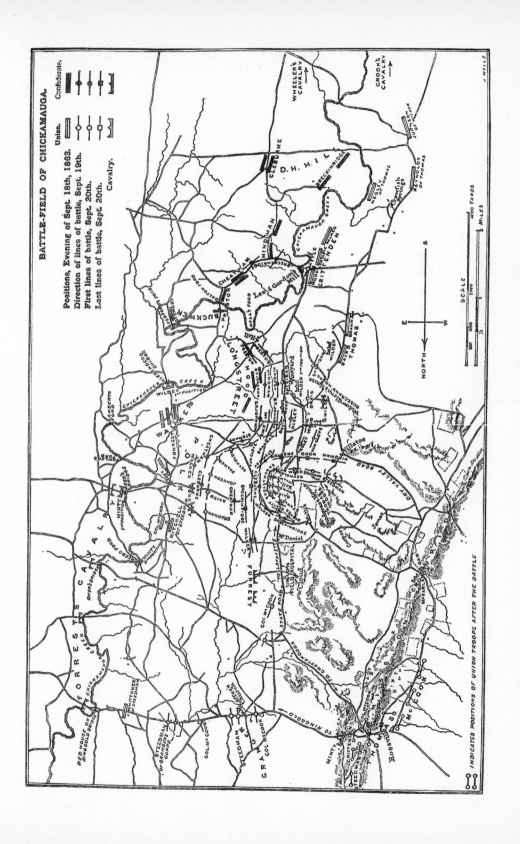

BATTLE-FIELD OF CHICKAMAUGA.

Positions, Evening of Sept. 18th, 1863.
Direction of lines of battle, Sept. 19th.
First lines of battle, Sept. 20th.
Last lines of battle, Sept. 20th.

Cavalry.

Confederate.

Union.

INDICATES POSITIONS OF UNION TROOPS AFTER THE BATTLE

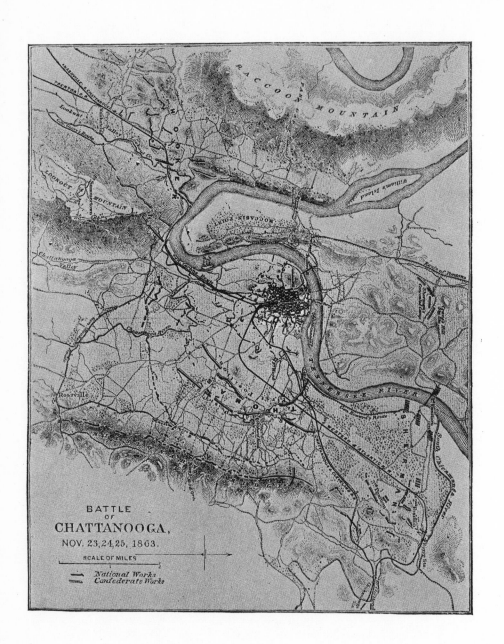

BATTLE
OF
CHATTANOOGA,
NOV. 23, 24, 25, 1863.

SCALE OF MILES

National Works
Confederate Works

CHAPTER FIFTEEN

SEPTEMBER — DECEMBER 1863

CHATTANOOGA

HAVING retired to Chattanooga after the battle of
Chickamauga, the Union army formed a line in
front of the town from the river above to the
river below. The troops occupied as salients the strong
unfinished works left by the Confederates, which they
connected by rifle-pits. Within two days the position was
made practically impregnable.

In the meantime the Confederates had advanced from
Chickamauga and taken up position in front of the Federals. Their line began on the right at a point near the
railway tunnel east of the town, ran along the western
side of Missionary Ridge to a point about two miles south
of Orchard Knob, then turned westward across the valley
to Lookout Mountain.

At Chattanooga the course of the Tennessee River is
due west; after passing the town it flows south to the foot
of Lookout Mountain, and then makes a great bend to
the north, enclosing a peninsula some three miles in length
by less than a mile in width, known as Moccasin Point.

Crossing the river at the town, a road leads southwest across this point to Brown's Ferry, and thence continues in a southerly direction along a deep gorge between a narrow range of hills, close by the water's edge, and the base of Raccoon Mountain until, as it enters Lookout Valley, it curves westward and passes over a depression in the mountain to Kelly's Ferry. The railroad from Chattanooga to Bridgeport runs along the south side of the river, passes close under the point of Lookout Mountain, and crosses Raccoon Mountain by this same depression, as does also the wagon-road from Wauhatchie in the valley to Bridgeport. At the extreme northern angle of the bend in the river, the water rushes through the mountains with such velocity that steamers in high water cannot stem the current. This necessitated the landing of supplies at Kelly's Ferry, and then hauling them overland across the bridge at Brown's Ferry to Chattanooga.[1]

On retiring to Chattanooga, Rosecrans withdrew a small force which had been stationed on the point of Lookout Mountain, as he did not think it practicable to keep up communication between this force and his army in the town. Bragg immediately occupied the mountain, and placed batteries commanding the railroad and the river. He also sent Longstreet's corps into Lookout Valley, and the Confederate sharp-shooters stationed along the river prevented the use of the wagon-road to Bridgeport. From water to water the Union army was invested in a semicircle. The only route by which supplies could come was a narrow and winding wagon-road from Bridgeport through Jasper and over Walden Ridge,[2] a distance of sixty miles. Bragg sent Wheeler's cavalry to cut this line also, and sat down to await the starvation of the Union army. Longstreet, indeed, advocated the bolder course of crossing the river above Chattanooga, so as to cut off Rosecrans's line of retreat and compel him to come out and fight at a disadvantage, but Bragg felt that he would make sure of his prey by simply waiting.

[1] Cist, 233.
[2] This name is spelled *Waldron's* and *Walling's* by some writers, but *Walden* is the form given in the *Century Atlas*.

Rosecrans had placed his cavalry on the northern side of the river to protect his trains; but they were eluded by Wheeler, who struck the line at Anderson's Cross-Roads in the Sequatchie Valley, where he burned 300 wagons and captured 1800 mules. He was closely pursued, however, by the Federal cavalry, and finally driven across the Tennessee into Alabama in a very shattered condition.

Then, early in October, heavy rains set in, and proved a worse foe than the Confederate troopers. The roads became almost impassable; the remaining mules were pressed beyond endurance; each successive trip from Bridgeport was made with fewer wagons and lighter loads. The artillery horses died by the score from starvation, and finally it was impossible to move the guns for lack of animals. It began to look as if the Union army would be starved into surrender, or forced to retreat with great peril, and certain loss of all *matériel*. But the Government at Washington had become thoroughly aroused concerning the dangerous situation of the army at Chattanooga, and prompt measures were taken for its relief. Hooker was sent West with the Eleventh and Twelfth corps, under Howard and Slocum, from the Army of the Potomac; and General Grant, at Vicksburg, was ordered to despatch large reënforcements to Rosecrans.

Grant himself was directed to go to Louisville, and was met en route at Indianapolis on the 17 October, by Mr. Stanton. The secretary handed him two orders, identical in all but one particular, and told him that he might take his choice. Both gave him the command of all the territory between the Alleghanies and the Mississippi River, but one left the department commanders as they were, while the other assigned Thomas to the command of the Army of the Cumberland in place of Rosecrans. Grant accepted the latter, and a copy was telegraphed to Rosecrans.[3]

While Grant and Stanton were at Louisville, a telegram was received from Charles A. Dana, a representa-

---

[3] See 2 Smith, 845–885, for a very full statement of the reasons for Rosecrans's removal.

tive of the War Department then at Chattanooga, saying that Rosecrans was preparing to retreat. This information was incorrect, but Grant telegraphed Thomas, now in command, that he " must hold Chattanooga at all hazards "; and that brave soldier replied, " We will hold the town till we starve."

Meanwhile, there had been several important changes in the organizations of the two hostile armies. McCook and Crittenden had been relieved, and ordered before a Court of Inquiry for their conduct at the battle of Chickamauga; and their two corps, the Twentieth and Twentyfirst, had been consolidated into a single corps, numbered the Fourth, which was placed under the command of Gordon Granger. In the Confederate army, Polk had been relieved, under charges for failure to open the battle of the 20 September at daybreak; Hill and Buckner were gone, but Hardee had returned. The army was now organized in three corps, under Longstreet, Hardee, and Breckinridge.

The right of the Confederate line was held by Hardee, the centre by Breckinridge, and the left by Longstreet, whose line extended from Chattanooga Creek to Mount Lookout. Although the outposts of the two armies were so close together that the sentinels could " swap yarns and tobacco," there was practically no fighting. Occasionally the Confederates threw a few shells into the town, but they did no harm.

On the 3 October, Hooker arrived at Stevenson. On the 21st, after dark, Grant reached the same place on his way to Chattanooga. Rosecrans, who was there on his way north, saw Grant, and they had a " brief interview in which he [Rosecrans] described very clearly the situation at Chattanooga, and made some excellent suggestions as to what should be done." Grant adds, very sarcastically, " My only wonder was that he had not carried them out." [4] This slur was absolutely uncalled for, as Grant, when he reached Chattanooga two days later, had nothing to do beyond approving the plan proposed by General Smith, for reopening the line of communications

[4] 2 Grant, 28.

to Bridgeport, which Rosecrans had accepted, and Thomas was arranging to carry out. It is necessary to make this point clear, because some writers have shown a disposition to give all the credit to Grant.

There was universal regret among the troops when they learned that Rosecrans had been relieved. Every soldier in the army felt that he had a friend in " Old Rosy." Although Rosecrans was frequently irascible with his superiors, to his subordinates he was one of the most genial of men. He was one of the finest strategists of the Civil War, and the Union cause suffered a great loss when he went to join so many other able generals in retirement.

On the 24 October, the morning after his arrival, General Grant ordered pushed to completion the admirable plan conceived by the chief engineer of the Army of the Cumberland, General William F. Smith — familiarly known to the soldiers as " Baldy " Smith. This plan was to throw a pontoon bridge across the river at Brown's Ferry; get control of the country south of the Tennessee and west of Lookout Mountain; then reopen the line of communications by the wagon-road to Kelly's Ferry, and by boat from there to Bridgeport. As Hooker's troops were not required in Chattanooga, they had been kept near Bridgeport since their arrival on the 3 October, until arrangements could be made for their coöperation. Hooker was now ordered to cross the river with the Eleventh Corps and one division of the Twelfth, and march up via Wauhatchie to Brown's Ferry. Palmer, with a division of the Fourteenth Corps, was ordered to move down the river on the north side, by a back road, until opposite Whiteside's, then cross and hold the road in Hooker's rear, after he had passed. At the same time 4000 men were detailed to act directly under Smith from Chattanooga: 1800 of these troops, under General Hazen, were to float down the river in pontoon boats to Brown's Ferry, under cover of night, land on the south side, and capture or drive away the enemy's pickets. Smith was to march with the remainder of his force, also by night, by the north bank to Brown's Ferry, taking with him all the material for laying the bridge as soon as the crossing was secured.[5]

This project was carried out exactly as planned: the Confederate pickets were driven off, up the valley; the bridge was promptly laid; the position entrenched, and held until the arrival of Hooker's troops the next day.

Hooker marched into Lookout Valley by the road along the base of Raccoon Mountain. Howard's corps, which was in the lead, met a part of Law's brigade, which was supporting the Confederate sharp-shooters along the river, and drove it up the valley. This detachment, in its retreat, destroyed the railway bridge over Lookout Creek. Geary's division was left at Wauhatchie to guard the road to Kelly's Ferry, and at six o'clock Howard halted for the night within two miles of Brown's Ferry. Bragg, at first, could not credit the report of his signal officers, but hurried to Lookout Mountain with Longstreet, and from the summit watched the Federal column " marching quietly along the valley toward Brown's Ferry." Longstreet continues: " Presently the rear guard came in sight and made a bivouac immediately in front of the point where we stood." This was Geary's division at Wauhatchie.

It was arranged to make a night attack upon Geary with four brigades, but the Confederates were repulsed, with heavy casualties on both sides. General Alexander terms this night attack " one of the most foolhardy adventures of the war."

No further attempts were made by Bragg to molest the " cracker line," as the soldiers called it, and the supply problem was solved. The siege of Chattanooga was raised, and the reënforcements from the Army of the Potomac made Grant's strength equal to that of Bragg. A Richmond paper said: " The admirably conceived and perfectly executed *coup* at Brown's Ferry . . . has robbed the Confederacy of all its dearly earned advantages gained at Chickamauga." [6]

It seems almost inconceivable that Bragg should have chosen this moment to weaken his forces by sending

[5] 2 Grant, 35–36.   [6] Quoted in Hazen's *Narrative*, 164.

Longstreet, his ablest corps-commander, with one-third his army, to attack Burnside at Knoxville. He apparently underrated the energy of his opponent, and thought that Longstreet could chase Burnside out of East Tennessee and return before Grant was ready to assume the offensive. Bragg has been very severely criticised for his action. " It ought to have been clear to him," says Professor Fiske, " that if he won the battle Knoxville would be at his mercy, while if he lost it, Knoxville would be relieved." [7]

But Bragg was no fool. He knew the deplorable condition of the Army of the Cumberland at this time. When Grant suggested to Thomas an assault on Missionary Ridge, in the hope of causing Bragg to recall Longstreet, Thomas reminded him that the artillery horses were all dead, and the cannon could not be moved.

Immediately after the defeat at Chickamauga, Halleck had ordered Sherman to start for Chattanooga. Sherman accordingly left Vicksburg on the 27 September, with his command in steamboats, and reached Memphis, 400 miles up the river, five days later. With his usual fatuity, Halleck had directed Sherman to repair the railroad as he advanced toward Chattanooga. Thus hampered, it was nearly a month before Sherman could reach Iuka, still 200 miles distant from Chattanooga. As soon as Grant arrived at Chattanooga he telegraphed Sherman to " drop everything," and hurry to Stevenson with his entire force. The result was that Sherman got his army up to Stevenson and Bridgeport by the 14 November, and the following day reported in person to Grant at Chattanooga. With his arrival, and the army again well supplied with everything necessary, Grant was at last ready to strike. His plan of battle was as follows:

Sherman with his four divisions was to cross to the north bank at Brown's Ferry, march east behind the hills, out of view of the Confederates, and take a position under cover of the woods opposite the mouth of Chickamauga Creek. Here he was to recross the river by a pontoon bridge, and seize the north end of Missionary Ridge

[7] Fiske, 293.

before the enemy could occupy it in force. As soon as he was astride the ridge at the tunnel, Thomas was to move the Army of the Cumberland to the left and connect with Sherman; then their united forces were to move southward, driving the Confederates up the valley of Chattanooga Creek and away from their base of supplies at Chickamauga Station. Howard's corps was to be in reserve on the north bank, ready to aid Sherman or Thomas as circumstances might require. Hooker, with Cruft's division of Granger's corps, sent him from Chattanooga, was to hold Lookout Valley. This plan, as will appear later, was modified in its execution.

Sherman's movement was much delayed by heavy rains which raised the river, and he did not cross east of the town until the morning of the 24 November. Even then, a break in the bridge at Brown's Ferry prevented Osterhaus's division from joining him, and it was ordered to report to Hooker.

Bragg was completely deceived by Sherman's movements, and thought that he was going to the relief of Burnside at Knoxville. He, therefore, on the very eve of the battle, despatched two more divisions to reënforce Longstreet, and was able to get only one of them back in time to be of service.

On the 20th Bragg sent Grant a most extraordinary letter, which it is not easy to understand. " As there may still be some non-combatants in Chattanooga," he wrote, " I deem it proper to notify you that prudence would dictate their early withdrawal." This may have been intended to deter Grant from detaching any more troops to aid Burnside, but Grant was more inclined to regard it as a ruse to prevent him from attacking before the enemy had time to withdraw. Accordingly, on the afternoon of the 23d, he ordered Thomas to make a demonstration in force. His line, in the centre, facing Missionary Ridge, was made up of the corps of Granger and Palmer, of the Army of the Cumberland, and Howard's corps, of the Army of the Potomac, about 30,000 men in all. After advancing a short distance with such deliberation that the enemy thought they were on parade, these troops made a sudden rush and captured Orchard Knob, a prominent knoll about a mile in front of the western base of Missionary Ridge.

The results of this demonstration were three-fold: It was developed that Bragg's army was present in force, and meant to stay; it gained an excellent position, when strengthened by artillery, from which to make the final assault two days later; and it caused Bragg to weaken his left on Lookout Mountain by transferring Walker's strong division to his right. This division took position on Missionary Ridge, half a mile south of the tunnel, and was the first Confederate detachment to occupy the crest. This withdrawal greatly lightened Hooker's task of assaulting and carrying Lookout the following day.

Grant's original plan was only for Hooker to hold Lookout Valley and guard the line of communications with Bridgeport. But the addition of Osterhaus's division gave him a force of some 10,000 men, and Grant thought that he was strong enough to do more. Hooker was therefore ordered to try to take the point of Lookout Mountain. This position was almost impregnable by nature, but since the withdrawal of Walker's division it was held only by three weak brigades: one on the slope where Hooker made his assault, and two at the summit — about 1700 men in all.

The side of Lookout Mountain rises from the valley below in a natural slope, covered with a scrubby growth of wood, and of bowlders of all sizes which have fallen from the cliffs. Beyond this slope, a precipice, of solid, bare, jagged rock, rises several hundred feet straight to the plateau of the mountain, 1400 feet above the waters of the Tennessee. At the northern end of the mountain, however, beyond the foot of the precipice, was the Craven farm, a comparatively smooth piece of land under cultivation. Between the farm and the base of the palisades there were wooded and rocky slopes; as also on the river side, where they ended in another cliff which drops straight to the railway track at the water's edge. The narrow road from Chattanooga to Lookout Valley passes over the nose of the mountain just above this cliff. Another road from the town ran up the eastern face of the mountain to Summertown on the plateau. The military road, winding up the north face of Lookout, was built by Hooker after the battle. The Summertown road was then the only way by which troops on the plateau could reach the slopes of the mountains or the valley below. The Confederates had entrenchments at the Craven farm; also near the base of the western slope, covering the railway and wagon bridges over Lookout Creek, and down the northern slope, so arranged as to meet attacks from either Lookout or Chattanooga valleys.[8]

On the morning of the 24 November there was a mist over the mountain, which later settled down into a dense fog. At eight o'clock, Geary's division of the Twelfth Corps crossed Lookout Creek from Wauhatchie; it was joined on the left in the valley by Osterhaus's division of the Fifteenth Corps, and Cruft's division of the Fourth Corps. These troops, supported by artillery placed in commanding positions on the left bank of the creek, drove the enemy out of his entrenchments at the bridges, and crossed near that point. Aided by the fire of batteries on Moccasin Point, the Union forces pushed up the rocky slope, driving the Confederates from one position after another. By noon Hooker had possession of the Craven farm. Here the Confederate brigade which had defended the slope was joined by the two brigades from the plateau, and a stand was made about 400 yards beyond the Craven house. This line was held until midnight, when the Confederates withdrew from the mountain. On account of the fog, and the exhaustion of his ammunition, Hooker halted his line and entrenched.

Late in the afternoon, a supply of ammunition was brought from Chattanooga by Carlin's brigade, which took post on the right of the line. Early the next morning, the 25th, some men from the 8th Kentucky scaled the heights and hoisted the Stars and Stripes on the summit, where, at sunrise, the flag floated in full view of the Union and Confederate troops in the lines below.

[8] Steele, 455.

While the " battle above the clouds " was taking place, Sherman, at the other end of the line, was endeavoring to carry out his part of the program. His pontoons had been concealed in North Chickamauga Creek, which enters the Tennessee on the north side two miles above the mouth of the Chickamauga on the opposite side. During the night of the 23d, these were quietly floated down the stream, and by daybreak 8000 men had crossed. Little opposition was encountered, and the troops immediately threw up a bridge-head. As soon as the bridge was finished, at one o'clock Sherman crossed with his three divisions, and Davis's division of the Fourteenth Corps which had been sent him to take the place of Osterhaus's. At four o'clock, Sherman seized the north end of Missionary Ridge, which was occupied only by Confederate outposts. Then, to his surprise, he found that the ridge was not continuous, but was separated by a wide depression from Tunnel Hill, his objective on the south. Viewed from below and at a distance this break in the crest of Missionary Ridge was not apparent. Sherman also found Cleburne's division in position at Tunnel Hill, and strongly entrenched. He therefore made no attempt to carry the hill that afternoon.

During the night of the 24th, Bragg drew in all his troops from Lookout Mountain and Chattanooga Valley, and formed his line along Missionary Ridge from Tunnel Hill to Rossville Gap, a distance of over six miles. Hardee commanded the right wing, and Breckinridge the left.

On the morning of the 25th, Grant stationed his headquarters at Orchard Knob, from which the whole field was in full view. The day was clear and bright, and Bragg's headquarters on the ridge could be plainly seen — with the staff officers coming and going constantly.

Grant's orders for the day were as follows: " Sherman was directed to attack at daylight. Hooker was ordered to move at the same hour, and endeavor to intercept the enemy's retreat if he still remained; if he had gone, then to move directly to Rossville and operate against the left and rear of the force on Missionary Ridge. Thomas was not to move until Hooker had reached Missionary Ridge." [9]

Sherman's assault, the main attack, was a complete failure. Although he had six divisions against Cleburne's one, the position was too strong to be carried by frontal assault, and all his attacks were repulsed with heavy losses. " Such is the strength of field-works against frontal assault; and Sherman does not appear to have tried to outflank Cleburne's position." [10]

On the right, Hooker had marched at daybreak, but he found the bridge over Chattanooga Creek destroyed and the roads obstructed; he was thus delayed four or five hours. From his central position at Orchard Knob, Grant watched in vain " to see Hooker crossing the ridge in the neighborhood of Rossville." He saw that Sherman's assault had failed, and judged incorrectly, from some movements of the Confederate troops, that Bragg was weakening his centre to reënforce Cleburne on his right. So, to relieve Sherman, he ordered Thomas to move out the four divisions he held at the centre, assault the first line of the enemy's rifle-pits in front, and there to halt and await orders. Baird was on the left, Wood next, then Sheridan, with Johnson on the extreme right — in all eleven brigades and four field-batteries, on a front two miles and a half long. The men had been under arms all day, and when the order to attack came at three-thirty, they advanced with a rush, eager to redeem their defeat at Chickamauga. Three lines of entrenchments were in front of them, one at the foot of the ridge, another near the middle of the slope, the third and strongest at the crest. Through an error of the Confederate engineers, the upper line of works had been placed on the natural instead of the " military " crest, which " left numerous approaches up ravines and swales entirely covered from the fire of the breastworks." Bragg had also made the fatal mistake of dividing his forces, already too small, putting one-half in their skirmish line at the bottom of the hill, and the other half at the top. Private instructions were given the superior officers, if attacked by more than

[9] 2 Grant, 75.   [10] Steele, 457.

a single line of battle, to await the enemy's approach within 200 yards, then to deliver their fire, and retire to the works above.[11]

The ridge here was some 200 feet high, with steep slopes broken by many ravines and swales, and obstructed at the time by the stumps of recently felled timber. The line was held by four Confederate divisions — eleven and a half brigades, and sixteen batteries.

The Federals charged at double-quick, and carried the first line at the point of the bayonet, killing and capturing large numbers of the defenders, and putting the rest to flight. Here the troops halted as ordered; but, finding themselves exposed to a galling fire from the enemy, by an almost spontaneous impulse the line resumed its advance up the ridge, which was carried in six places at the same moment. Wood and Sheridan both claimed the credit of reaching the top first.

Bragg's centre was broken, and his troops, after a feeble resistance, gave way and fled from the field in a panic. Thirty-seven guns and 2000 prisoners were taken. Bragg, with his entire staff, narrowly escaped capture. Sheridan and Wood followed the fleeing enemy for a short distance, but the hour was too late for a general pursuit.

Meanwhile Hooker had reached Rossville and driven in the Confederate left. He then advanced northward, with one division on top the ridge, and one on either side, until he connected about sunset with Thomas's right. During the night Cleburne withdrew from the position he had so valiantly held in front of Sherman.

The following morning, Sherman, Hooker, and Palmer, took up the pursuit and pressed it as far as Ringgold, where the enemy made a stand on the 27th. Bragg then withdrew to Dalton, where a few days later he was relieved of the command, at his own request. He was called to Richmond by President Davis, and given the position of chief-of-staff, his duties being to control military operations under the direction of the President. He did not see any more active service until the final days of the war. He was a good strategist and tactician, with

[11] Alexander, 475, 476.

great powers of organization and discipline. Grant considered him a man of the highest character, and Sherman also speaks well of him. But he had a most irritable temper, due largely to ill health, and was disliked by his officers and men. His failure to crush Rosecrans at Chickamauga was caused mainly by the disaffection of his subordinates.

Owing to various reasons, Longstreet was not ready to attack Burnside at Knoxville until the 29th, and then he was repulsed with a loss of over 800 men. He was about to renew the assault when he heard of Bragg's defeat, and of the approach of large Federal reënforcements. On the 4 December he raised the siege, and returned to Virginia.

In the battles around Chattanooga Grant had about 60,000 men and Bragg 40,000. The losses were not heavy:[12]

	Federals	Confederates
Killed	752	361
Wounded	4,713	2,180
Missing	350	4,146
Totals	5,815	6,687

Both Bragg and Alexander attribute the sudden panic, which seized the veteran Confederate troops, to the sight of the "enemy marshalling his immense forces in plain view." General Alexander says: "The sight was a grand and impressive one, the like of which had never been seen before by any one who witnessed it." This was the only battle of the Civil War in which the topographical conditions were such that the defenders, in a position "which ought to have been held by a line of skirmishers against any assaulting column," could look down upon the hosts of the enemy forming for the attack,[13] and it was too much for the nerve of the Confederate soldiers, who were as brave as any on earth.

Among the great battles of the Civil War, Chattanooga was unique in many respects: First, it was a series of three

[12] 3 B. & L., 729, 730.
[13] Bragg's Report; Alexander, 476. See also 2 Cox, 182.

distinct actions, fought by the Union troops at different points on a line thirteen miles in length. Second, for the first time, corps of the three great armies, of the Potomac, the Cumberland, and the Tennessee, fought together under one commander. Third, it was the only battle of the war in which the four most famous Union generals — Grant, Sherman, Sheridan, and Thomas — were all engaged. Fourth, unlike most of the battles, the fighting was nearly all in full view of both armies. Finally, the immense length of the line, the grandeur of the scenery, the dizzy heights scaled, all combined to make it a wonderful spectacle.

Owing to unforeseen obstacles, the attack of Sherman on the left was almost a complete failure; but Hooker's " battle above the clouds," and the assault of Missionary Ridge by the Army of the Cumberland, were both brilliant victories, owing to the irresistable *élan* of the soldiers rather than the plans of the commander-in-chief. It is therefore absurd for Grant to claim that the battle effectually carried out his orders.[14] Grant's orders to Thomas on the 25th were only to make another " demonstration " in behalf of Sherman, so that he could take the tunnel in accordance with the original plan. When the soldiers of the Army of the Cumberland, who were " so demoralized that they would not fight," pressed on up the ridge, without orders and even against orders, Grant was very angry, and told Thomas that " some one would suffer " if the movement failed. But it won for General Grant the battle of Missionary Ridge! In his official report, after narrating the events of the 23–25 November, General Thomas quietly says: " It will be seen by the above report that the original plan of operations was somewhat modified to meet and take the best advantage of emergencies which necessitated material modifications of that plan." [15] And Professor Fiske remarks: " Now if anything in this world can be said to be clear, it is that the battle of Chattanooga was not fought as Grant had planned it." [16]

In many respects Chattanooga was the most brilliant victory of the war: remarkable not only for its picturesque

[14] 2 Grant, 80.　　[15] Cist, 261, 262.　　[16] Fiske, 308.

features and interesting tactics, but also for its strategic importance. The Confederate line of communications between the Atlantic seaboard and the Mississippi was severed at the centre, and there was no longer any connection between the sections east and west of the Alleghanies except by a long détour by way of Atlanta. It completed the recovery of the valley of the Mississippi, begun by the capture of New Orleans and Vicksburg. With the exception of Hood's rash advance to Nashville at the end of the following year, the remaining campaigns of the war were fought within the limits of the original thirteen states of the Union.

The exultation at the North, after the great victories of Gettysburg and Vicksburg in July, had been changed almost to despair by the terrible reverse at Chickamauga. Now, when the people sat down to their dinners on this Thanksgiving Day, as Halleck said in his telegram of congratulations, Grant had indeed given them cause for thanksgiving!

It is a general rule of modern warfare that an army which allows itself to be shut up within fortifications is lost. But the Army of the Cumberland was never entirely invested, although for a time its line of supplies was over a long and difficult road. Nevertheless, the army would ultimately have been starved into surrender, or have been forced to retreat, with the loss of most of its artillery and equipage, if means had not been found to open the short piece of road, about five miles long, from Brown's Ferry across Raccoon Mountain to Kelly's Ferry. Neither Bragg, nor Longstreet who commanded the Confederate left, appears to have appreciated the great strategic importance of this road. It was guarded only by a small brigade, which was sent around the toe of Lookout Mountain for the purpose. "A full division at least," says General Alexander, "should have guarded so important a point, and one so exposed." Bragg lost his campaign primarily when he allowed the enemy to reopen the short line of his communications.[17]

[17] Alexander, 466, 480.

CHAPTER SIXTEEN

JULY 1863 — MAY 1864

THE WILDERNESS

Meade Follows Lee Across the Potomac — Longstreet and Hooker Sent West — A Campaign of Manœuvres — Grant Made General-in-Chief — His Plan of Campaign — Organization of the Two Armies — Theatre of the Campaign — Grant's Plans Anticipated by Lee — The Federals Cross the Rapidan — Lee Moves to Attack Them in Flank — Battle of the 5 May — Grant Surprised — The Wilderness — The First Day Indecisive — Battle of the 6 May — The Union Left Turned — Longstreet Wounded — Lee Also Turns the Federal Right — Numbers and Losses — Comments

TEN days after the battle of Gettysburg, on the night of the 13 July 1863, Lee crossed the Potomac, and then continued his retreat slowly up the Shenandoah Valley. The last week in July, Meade also passed the river, and marched south along the east side of the Blue Ridge. Lee thereupon left the Valley and took position near Culpeper. Meade continued his advance, and placed his army on the north side of the Rappahannock.

The end of July, Lee withdrew across the Rapidan to Orange Court House, where he could receive supplies by rail. At this time Longstreet again called attention to the plan suggested by him the previous May, of taking advantage of the interior lines of the Confederacy to transfer troops to the West. About the 23 August, Lee was called to Richmond, and was detained there by President Davis for nearly two weeks. During this time, it was decided to send Longstreet, with the divisions of Hood and McLaws, to reënforce Bragg at Chattanooga.[1]

As soon as Lee withdrew behind the Rapidan, Meade again advanced, and posted his army along the north bank

[1] Alexander, 447–448.

of the river. Learning of the departure of Longstreet, the authorities at Washington detached the Eleventh and Twelfth corps from the Army of the Potomac, and sent them West, under the command of Hooker, to reënforce Rosecrans. This reduced Meade to the defensive; and there then ensued a " campaign of manœuvres," marked by much marching and strategy, but little fighting or tactics. Meade was gradually forced back until he took a strong position on the heights of Centreville, almost in sight of the defences of Washington, behind which he could retire within a few hours. As Lee was now a long way from his base, he fell back again to his former position at Culpeper. Meade immediately followed, crossing the Rappahannock at Kelly's Ford on the 7 November, and turning the Confederate right; thereupon Lee retired once more to the south side of the Rapidan.

The last week in November, Meade crossed the river at Germanna Ford, with the object of surprising the Confederates in their extended winter quarters, but Lee was warned of the movement by his cavalry, and Meade found him so strongly entrenched along Mine Run that he did not deem it prudent to attack. He quietly recrossed the river, and both armies resumed their quarters along the Rapidan. Here Meade and Lee were content to watch each other across the river until the following May.

In February 1864, Congress revived the grade of lieutenant-general which had first been conferred on Washington in 1798. President Lincoln, as was generally expected, immediately appointed Grant to the office, and made him general-in-chief of all the armies of the United States. Grant was personally assured by the President that he would be allowed full freedom of action, and be supported by all the resources of the Government.

Grant states that it was his first intention to remain in the West, but he soon realized that this was not practicable. He accordingly recommended the appointment of Sherman to his former command. Early in March, Grant visited Meade at his headquarters at Brandy Station, and at that time requested him to remain in command of the

Army of the Potomac. This proved to be a cumbersome arrangement, as it made it necessary to transmit all orders through Meade, instead of giving them direct to the corps commanders, and was often embarrassing to Grant.[2]

At this time the South had left in the field only two considerable forces: Lee's Army of Northern Virginia, and the two western armies of Tennessee and Mississippi, now consolidated under General Joseph E. Johnston, at Dalton, Georgia. For the first time since the beginning of the Civil War, a definite plan was now adopted by the Union Government for a simultaneous and concentrated movement of all the Federal forces toward a single objective — the destruction of these two remaining organized bodies of Confederate troops.

Before this time the various Union armies had acted separately and independently of each other, giving the enemy an opportunity often of depleting one command not pressed, to reënforce another more actively engaged. Grant was determined to stop this. He regarded the Union forces as one large army, of which the Army of the Potomac was the centre, Sherman's army the right wing, and the Army of the James, under Butler, the left wing.

There was to be a " simultaneous movement all along the line." Sherman was to move from Chattanooga; Crook, in West Virginia, was to move against the Virginia and Tennessee Railroad; Sigel was to advance up the Shenandoah Valley; Butler was to move by the James River on Petersburg and Richmond.[3]

So far as the main armies under Grant and Sherman were concerned, this plan was carried out successfully, but some of the details did not work out as expected. Butler allowed his army to be " bottled up " by Beauregard, and Sigel did nothing but retreat.

Grant established his headquarters at Culpeper on the 26 March. The First and Third corps had been suppressed, and their divisions transferred to the Second, Fifth, and Sixth corps, which were retained. Upon the reorganization of the army, General Hancock, who had

[2] 2 Grant, 117.   [3] 2 Grant, 127–132.

been absent, owing to wounds received at Gettysburg, resumed command of the Second Corps; General Warren
was appointed to the command of the Fifth Corps; General Sedgwick continued at the head of the Sixth Corps;
and General Sheridan was brought on from the West to
command the Cavalry Corps.

The Ninth Corps, under General Burnside, joined the
army on the 6 May, but was not formally incorporated in
the Army of the Potomac until the 24 May.

Longstreet had rejoined Lee with his two divisions
which took part in the Chickamauga campaign, and the
Confederate army was still organized the same as at
Gettysburg, except that Pickett was absent.

The organizations of the two armies at the beginning
of the campaign were as follows:[4]

ARMY OF THE POTOMAC

Second Corps, HANCOCK	27,000
Fifth Corps, WARREN	24,000
Sixth Corps, SEDGWICK	23,000
Ninth Corps, BURNSIDE	19,000
Cavalry Corps, SHERIDAN	12,000
Total	105,000

ARMY OF NORTHERN VIRGINIA

First Corps, LONGSTREET	15,000
Second Corps, EWELL	17,000
Third Corps, HILL	22,000
Cavalry Corps, STUART	8,500
Artillery and Miscellaneous	6,500
Total	69,000

Pickett's division of 5000 men did not join Lee until
the last of May; he therefore had only 64,000 men at
the beginning of the campaign.

The Union army had 15 divisions, 40 brigades, of Infantry; 3 divisions, 6 brigades, of Cavalry; and 242 guns.

The Confederate army had 9 divisions, 40 brigades, of

4 Doubleday, 13–17; Alexander, 494–495.

Infantry; 3 divisions, 7 brigades, of Cavalry; and 224 guns.

That part of the Union army not engaged in guarding the lines of communication was on the northern bank of the Rapidan. It was confronted, on the opposite side of the river, by the Confederate forces in a strongly entrenched position, which was almost impregnable against direct attack. The country back to the James River was cut up with many streams, generally narrow, deep, and difficult to cross except where bridged. The region was heavily timbered, the roads narrow, and almost impassable after the least rain. It would be hard to find a country more difficult for manœuvring and supplying a large army.

As already stated, Grant's main objective was Lee's army, and, as it was practically unassailable in front, he decided to turn its right flank. He hoped by concealment and celerity to cross the Rapidan and traverse the Wilderness on the south side before Lee could discover his movement, or at least before Lee could have time to oppose it.

On the second day of May 1864, General Lee, surrounded by his corps and division commanders, stood at the Confederate signal station on Clark's Mountain, south of the Rapidan, and examined through his field-glass the position of the Federal army across the river. Although several demonstrations had been made in the direction of the upper fords, General Lee expressed the opinion that the Union army would cross at Germanna or Ely's. Thirty-six hours later the Army of the Potomac began its march to the fords indicated by him.[5]

Grant issued his orders for the movement on the 2 May, and the troops began their march at midnight on the 3d. Sheridan with two of his cavalry divisions led the way, and the third was left to cover the rear. Two pontoon bridges had been laid at Germanna, and two more at Ely's ford, where Hooker crossed twelve months before, and a fifth was laid between, at Culpeper Mine Ford. Hancock's corps, preceded by Gregg's cavalry division,

[5] 4 B. & L., 118.

after crossing the river, took the road from Ely's Ford to Chancellorsville, where it arrived at nine o'clock on the morning of the 4th, followed by the reserve artillery. The corps remained there all day, waiting for the trains to come up, and bivouacked that night on the old battle-field. The cavalry pushed on to Piney Branch Church, and from there threw out patrols on all the roads.

Warren's corps, preceded by Wilson's cavalry division, marched by way of Germanna Ford, and bivouacked the night of the 4th at the Old Wilderness Tavern, at the junction of the road from the ford with the Turnpike, just about a mile west of the point where Jackson's turn-ing-column struck the pike on the afternoon of the 2 May the previous year. Sedgwick's corps followed the same route, and passed that night along the road, just south of the ford. The cavalry moved on to Parker's Store, throwing out patrols on all the roads from that point.

Up to this time the movement had been carried out successfully: the three corps were all south of the Rapi-dan, and no opposition had been encountered. But for the great train of 5000 wagons, the army might have moved further south, and been out of the Wilderness on the morning of the 5th. Although the baggage had been cut down to the smallest limit, the ammunition, ten days' rations, and three days' forage, filled a train which, in Grant's words, " would have extended from the Rapidan to Richmond, stretched along in single file." The army could not move on until the trains were up, and they did not finish crossing at Culpeper Mine and Ely's fords until after five o'clock on the afternoon of the 5th. Thus a whole precious day was lost, and Grant, much against his will, was forced to fight a battle in the Wilderness.

As already stated, Lee had not been deceived by the feints made on his left, and had anticipated Grant's move-ment. As usual, he took no steps to prevent the passage of the river, but made his plans to strike the Union army in flank before it could get out of the Wilderness.

Lee's headquarters were two miles northeast of Orange Court House; Ewell's corps was on and near the Rapidan; Hill's, higher up the river on the left; and Longstreet's, in the rear, near Gordonsville. Two roads led from Lee's position down the Rapidan toward Fredericksburg, both following the general direction of the river, and almost parallel to each other: the Old Turnpike, nearest the stream, and the Plank Road, a short distance south of it. The route of the Federal army lay directly across these two roads, along the western borders of the famous Wilderness.[6]

About noon on the 4 May, Ewell's corps was put in motion along the Turnpike, while Hill with two divisions started by the Plank Road. The two divisions of Longstreet's corps, at Gordonsville, were ordered to march rapidly across country and follow Hill on the Plank Road.

As Ewell's corps advanced along the Turnpike on the morning of the 5th, a Federal column was seen crossing it from the direction of Germanna Ford. Ewell promptly deployed his troops across the Turnpike, and sent word to Lee, who was with Hill on the Plank Road. Lee ordered him to avoid bringing on a general engagement until Longstreet could come up, and to regulate his movements by the head of Hill's column, whose progress he could tell by the firing in its front. But his position was so near the flank of the Federal column that a collision soon occurred which opened the campaign in earnest.

Warren, whose corps was passing when Ewell came up, halted, formed line of battle, and vigorously attacked Johnson's division, posted across the Turnpike. The Confederates were driven back; but Rodes's division was thrown in on Johnson's right, south of the road, and the Federal attack was finally repulsed. The fighting was severe while it lasted, and the losses quite heavy.

Ewell's entire corps was now up, and Sedgwick soon joined Warren, on his right. Early's division was sent to meet Sedgwick, while the two other divisions continued to confront Warren. The Federals kept up their attacks until nightfall, but could not drive off the enemy.

Although the heads of the two Confederate columns had bivouacked on the night of the 4th within five miles of the Union camps, Grant does not seem to have been

[6] 4 *B. & L.*, 120.

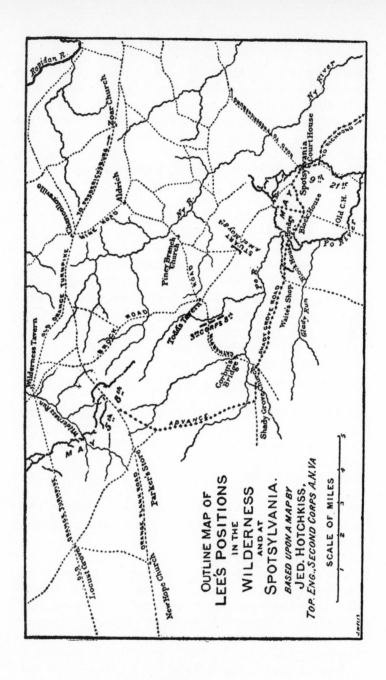

OUTLINE MAP OF
LEE'S POSITIONS
IN THE
WILDERNESS
AND AT
SPOTSYLVANIA.

BASED UPON A MAP BY
JED. HOTCHKISS,
TOP. ENG., SECOND CORPS A.N.VA

SCALE OF MILES
1 2 3 4 5

aware of the nearness of the enemy. When Warren was attacked the next morning, Meade is said to have remarked, " They have left a division to fool us here, while they concentrate and prepare a position on the North Anna." [7]

If General Meade had any such idea, he must soon have been undeceived by Hill's attack along the Plank Road, which struck the Federal outposts at Parker's Store soon after Ewell became engaged on the Turnpike. The Union patrols were driven in, and followed up to their line of battle, which covered the junction of the Plank Road with the Stevensburg and Brock roads, by which the Federals were marching. The fight began between Heth's division, at the head of Hill's column, and Getty's division of the Sixth Corps. Hancock's corps, which was already two miles beyond Todd's Tavern, was recalled, and was ordered to drive Hill " out of the Wilderness."

The character of the Wilderness has already been described in connection with the Chancellorsville campaign.[8] For more than one hundred years iron mines had been worked within it, and the great trees of the primæval forest had been cut as fuel for the furnaces. The land was now covered with a dense second-growth of cedar, pine, and black oak. In his report Hancock says that the forest was " almost impenetrable by troops in line of battle," and " manœuvring was an operation of extreme difficulty and uncertainty. The undergrowth was so heavy that it was scarcely possible to see more than one hundred paces in any direction. The movements of the enemy could not be observed until the lines were almost in collision."

General Law writes: " It was a battle of brigades and regiments rather than of corps and divisions. Officers could not see the whole length of their commands, and could tell whether the troops on their right and left were driving or being driven only by the sound of the firing. It was a fight at close quarters, too, for as night came on, in these tangled thickets . . . the approach of the opposing lines could be discerned only by the noise of their

[7] 4 B. & L., 121.   [8] See *ante*, page 211.

passage through the underbrush or the flashing of their guns." [9]

At two o'clock the head of Hancock's column reached the Plank Road. As his divisions came up they were formed on Getty's left, in front of and along the Brock Road, by which Jackson had made his turning movement the year before. Instead of engaging the enemy at once, as ordered, Hancock spent about an hour in completing the entrenchments begun by Getty, which gave Hill time to select and prepare his ground.

At a quarter past four, Getty advanced to the attack. He met with such stubborn resistance that Hancock sent two divisions to his assistance. The lines were very close, and a most desperate combat now ensued. Another Federal division was sent in, but Heth had been reënforced by Wilcox, and the Confederate line held fast. The fighting did not cease until after dark.

Late in the afternoon Grant sent Wadsworth's division of the Fifth Corps to Hancock's assistance, but it was so much delayed by the tangled underbrush that night fell before it got in position. As soon as the fighting ended on the night of the 5th, Grant issued orders to renew the battle at five o'clock the next morning.

It was near midday on the 4th, says General Alexander, when Longstreet, at his camp six miles south of Gordonsville, received news that Grant was crossing the Rapidan, and orders from General Lee to march to Todd's Tavern on the Brock Road. He was directed to march all night, only stopping to feed and water. At four o'clock he was on the way, and kept it up until near sundown the next day, when his corps bivouacked near Craig's Church, on the Carthapin Road, having marched about 36 miles. Longstreet at this time had with him only Hood's old division, under the command of Field, and McLaws's division, under Kershaw, about 10,000 men. Pickett's division, of 5000 men, was with Beauregard, and did not return until the last of May. The troops were ordered to rest until 1 A.M. before resuming their march; but,

[9] 4 B. & L., 122.

before starting, orders came from Lee to cross over to
Parker's Store on the Plank Road, about six miles.[10] It
was after sunrise on the 6th before Longstreet reached
this position, three miles in the rear of Hill's front line.

During the night both armies strengthened their field-
works, and made preparations for the coming struggle.
All day long, on the 5th, there had been a wide gap between the two wings of the line of battle — between
Warren and Hancock on the Union side, and between
Ewell and Hill on the Confederate side. In fact two distinct battles had been fought on fields more than a mile
apart. Early in the afternoon of the 4th Grant had telegraphed Burnside at Brandy Station to make a forced
march to Germanna Ford, and by the night of the 5th
three of his four divisions were across the river. He was
now ordered to place two of his divisions (Potter and
Willcox) in the gap between Warren and Hancock, and
to be in position to advance at five o'clock in the morning
with the rest of the army. The third division of his corps
(Stevenson), then south of the river, was to remain in
reserve at the Wilderness Tavern.

At dawn on the 6th Hancock's troops advanced to the
attack. The blow fell with greatest force on Wilcox's division south of the Plank Road. The whole Confederate
line was " rolled up " from the right, and the troops fell
back in disorder along the Plank Road until they reached
the position of Poague's artillery, which now opened on the
attacking force. The Federals pressed on, until abreast
of the battery, and their musketry-fire reached the guns,
where General Lee himself stood. Matters looked very
serious for the Confederates, but Lee sent messengers to
hurry the movement of Longstreet's corps, which soon
appeared swinging down the Plank Road at double-quick.
Kershaw's division took the right of the road and moved
obliquely south to meet the Federal left, which had
pivoted toward the north. The Union advance was
checked, and the troops driven back to their breast-works,
which were soon carried by the Confederate rush.

[10] Alexander, 498.

At the same time, Field's division deployed along the left side of the road, and advanced to the attack. As they passed General Lee, the men gave a rousing cheer for " Marse Robert," who spurred his horse forward to take part in the charge. As soon as the troops realized that he was " going in " with them, there was a general cry of, " We won't go on unless you go back! " One of the men seized the bridle and turned the general's horse around, and he reluctantly rode over to join General Longstreet on the Plank Road.[11]

Field's troops struck the right of Hancock's line, and after a bloody combat finally succeeded in carrying the entrenchments. Here the storm of battle swept to and fro for more than two hours, and the works were taken and retaken several times. General Wadsworth was killed as he rode up close to the front of his line on the Plank Road.

About ten o'clock, Longstreet ascertained that the Union left south of the Plank Road was in the air, and sent Mahone with his own and three other brigades to make a turning movement. The Federal line, attacked in flank and rear, and in front, at the same time, was rolled up in confusion toward the Plank Road, and then back upon the Brock Road.

Mahone's turning column was now in position facing north on the south side of the Plank Road, and parallel to it. General Longstreet prepared to press his advantage, and ordered Jenkins's fresh brigade, supported by Kershaw's division, to move forward on the Plank Road and renew the attack. As Longstreet rode forward with Jenkins and Kershaw along the road, a sudden volley from Mahone's men killed Jenkins, and wounded Longstreet in the neck. The Confederates had failed to recognize their friends through the intervening thickets, and this unfortunate volley practically lost them the fruits of the success they had just won. It was almost an exact repetition of the killing of Jackson on this same field the year before.[12]

Lee came up in a few minutes, and took personal charge

[11] 4 *B. & L.*, 124.   [12] 4 *B. & L.*, 126.

of the attack. But, although Longstreet explained to him
the situation and his plans, Lee " did not care to handle
broken lines, and ordered a formation for parallel
battle." [13]   This delayed the attack until after four
o'clock. Then a part of Hancock's front line was carried;
but by five o'clock the Confederates had been repulsed,
and driven back with heavy loss.

Meanwhile Burnside's corps had taken but small part
in the battle. The divisions of Willcox and Potter, which
were ordered to enter the gap between Ewell and Hill,
did not get into position before two o'clock; by that time
Heth and Wilcox had closed the gap, and the Union
attack was repulsed.

Late in the afternoon, under the personal direction of
General Lee, Ewell made an attack on the Union right,
similar to that by which Longstreet had rolled up Hancock's left in the morning. Two brigades, under General
Gordon, took the Federal line in reverse, and Sedgwick's
corps was driven from a large portion of its works, with
the loss of 600 prisoners — including Generals Seymour
and Shaler. Night closed the combat, and the battle of the
Wilderness was over.

The losses on both sides were as follows: [14]

	Federals	Confederates
Killed	2,246	2,000
Wounded	12,037	6,000
Missing	3,383	3,400
Totals	17,666	11,400

Livermore estimates the numbers engaged as 102,000
Federals, 61,000 Confederates.

Grant's main objective in this campaign was Lee's army
and not Richmond. In its entrenchments behind the Rapidan this army was unassailable in front, and it was neces-

[13] Alexander, 507.
[14] The Union casualties are as given in 4 *B. & L.*, 182. Humphreys
(53) gives the total as 15,387. Alexander estimates the Confederate
losses at 7750. We have used the detailed estimate of Humphreys's (54),
based on the *Medical and Surgical History of the War.*

sary to turn one or the other of its flanks. To accomplish this object, three plans were possible: (1) To transport the Union army by water to the near vicinity of Richmond; (2) To move by the Federal right against Lee's left flank; (3) To move by the Federal left against the enemy's right flank. The latter plan was adopted. In his *Memoirs*, Grant states his reasons as follows: [15]

" At this time I was not entirely decided as to whether I should move the Army of the Potomac by the right flank of the enemy, or by his left. Each plan presented advantages. If by his right — my left — the Potomac, Chesapeake Bay and tributaries, would furnish us an easy line over which to bring all supplies to within easy hauling distance of every position the army could occupy from the Rapidan to the James River. But Lee could, if he chose, detach or move his whole army north on a line rather interior to the one I would have to take in following. A movement by his left — our right — would obviate this; but all that was done would have to be done with the supplies and ammunition we started with. All idea of adopting this latter plan was abandoned when the limited quantity of supplies possible to take with us was considered. The country over which we would have to pass was so exhausted of all food or forage that we would be obliged to carry everything with us."

From the above it is evident that Grant did not even consider McClellan's plan, of moving his troops by water to the neighborhood of Richmond. The reason for this may have been political, rather than military. " Many of us thought," writes Mr. Everett P. Wheeler, " that politics had something to do with the plan that was adopted. McClellan had been removed from command and was at his home in Trenton, subject to order but receiving none. He was a conspicuous figure in the political debates, and many at the North still believed in him. Naturally the leaders of the Democratic party looked to him as an available candidate in the Presidential election of 1864. Many felt that McClellan's plan of assaulting Richmond from the south, on the line of the James River, was the

[15] 2 Grant, 134–137.

true plan; and that the nature of the country between Washington and Richmond was such that the Confederates could not be defeated if assailed on that line. Therefore, when Grant undertook to march directly across that rugged and broken country, which was aptly called the Wilderness, and to attack Lee in the front, many thought that the wiser plan of campaign had been given up because to adopt it would have been to reflect credit upon the discarded leader. Certain it is that Grant's frontal attacks on Lee were bloody and unsuccessful." [16]

On this same point General Humphreys says: [17]

"The question has been asked why the Army of the Potomac was not . . . moved by water to the near vicinity of Richmond, where, by taking possession of the lines of supply of that great military dépôt, the force defending it would be obliged to assume the offensive and attack the enveloping army in its entrenchments. But it is not to be supposed that Lee would have withdrawn to and remained within the carefully prepared fortifications enclosing Richmond while this transfer was being made, but that . . . he would have advanced beyond the city; . . . and that by his entrenching and continuing to extend and entrench, the Army of the Potomac would have been forced to attack constantly in order to gain possession of those lines of supply at a suitable distance from Richmond, and while extending its enveloping lines would have been subject to attack on the extending flank under unfavorable circumstances."

As this is exactly what finally occurred, it is difficult to see much point to this argument.

The overland route to Richmond had been tried five times — by McDowell in 1861, by Pope and Burnside in 1862, by Hooker and Meade in 1863 — and had proved a failure every time. Under Grant in 1864, it again proved a failure. At every turn he found Lee across his path, and was unable to drive him off. Finally, after six weeks of the hardest fighting in the Civil War, and the loss of 55,000 men — a number nearly equal to Lee's

[16] Wheeler, *Sixty Years of American Life*, 43.
[17] Humphreys, *Campaigns*, 7–8.

whole army — Grant was to find himself on the James River, with Fortress Monroe as his base, where his fleet might have landed him at the beginning, and without losing a man. " Here at last," says General Alexander, " literally *driven* into the location in front of Petersburg, Grant found himself in a position of rare strategic advantage: certain to give him possession of Richmond if properly utilized." This position was literally " the key to Richmond. For it would force Lee to hold an exterior line of such enormous length — nearly 30 miles — that it could not be long maintained." [18]

A move by Grant's *right* flank had the apparent advantages that the rivers were smaller and more easily passed in that quarter, and the country was more open and better suited for the manœuvring of large forces. But he would have been operating on a front parallel to his line of communications, the Orange and Alexandria Railway, which would require a large force for its protection; while Lee would have operated on a front perpendicular to his communications with Richmond.

On the other hand, in moving by his *left* flank, Grant had short lines of supply, entirely protected, to navigable waters connected with his main dépôts. The only drawback was the unfavorable character of the country for the distance of ten or fifteen miles south of the Rapidan; but Grant hoped, by concealing his movements, to cross the river, and traverse the Wilderness, before Lee had time to attack. In this expectation he was disappointed, owing to the necessity of waiting for his trains to come up, and it is difficult to understand why he had any such hopes. " It was well known," writes General Humphreys, chief-of-staff of the Army of the Potomac, " that daylight would divulge our movement to Lee's signal officers on Clark's Mountain, . . . and it was believed that he would at once move by the Orange and Fredericksburg pike and plank roads to oppose us." [19]

" No poorer cavalry work was done in the Civil War," says Major Steele, " than that done by the cavalry of

18 Alexander, 60–61. 19 Humphreys, 11.

Sheridan and Stuart in the afternoon and evening of the 4 May and the early morning of the 5 May 1864." [20]

In excuse of Stuart, however, it should be explained that Lee had sent him over to Fredericksburg to obtain forage for his lean horses, and he did not rejoin the army until the 5th. For Sheridan, and two of his division commanders, Torbert and Wilson, it may be said that they had had practically no cavalry experience before they were given their high commands in the Army of the Potomac. Wilson was an engineer officer, and the service of Sheridan and Torbert had been with the infantry. Later, both Sheridan and Wilson learned their lesson, and performed most efficient service.

Lee again showed his sublime audacity in attacking a Union army of twice his strength. His only error was in not calling up Longstreet sooner: he had 42 miles to march, while Hill had 28, and Ewell only 18. If Longstreet had been close behind Hill on the Plank Road on the morning of the 5th, Hancock's corps might have been cut off and overwhelmed.

The bad tactics of the Wilderness can be attributed to the difficult character of the country. There was no plan of battle on either side — no simultaneous, concerted effort either to turn the enemy's flank or pierce his centre. The first day, there were two distinct battles — one on the Plank Road and the other on the Turnpike. On the second day, the Confederates turned the left of the Federals in the morning and their right in the evening. Either of these flank attacks might have given decisive results; but the first failed on account of the wounding of Longstreet, and the second was made so late in the day that there was no time to gather the fruits of the victory.

The Wilderness is unique among battles as presenting the novel spectacle of an army of 60,000 men enveloping both flanks of an army of 100,000!

[20] Steele, 484.

CHAPTER SEVENTEEN

MAY — JUNE 1864

SPOTTSYLVANIA AND COLD HARBOR

Grant Moves on Spottsylvania Court House — His Determination to Win — Difficulty of His Task — " On to Richmond! " — Lee Reaches the Court House First — The Hostile Lines — Battle of Spottsylvania — Desperate Assault on the " Bloody Angle " — Its Final Failure Due to the Bad Formation — Grant Moves to the Left — Robbed of Success by the Weather — Fails in Second Attack on the Salient — Losses at Spottsylvania — The Movement to North Anna — Sheridan's Raid — Lee's Position Too Strong to Attack — Battle of Cold Harbor — Grant's Rash Assault — Numbers and Losses in the Wilderness Campaign — Comments

AFTER the bloody, but indecisive, battle of the Wilderness, Lee expected that Grant would retreat, as his predecessors in command of the Army of the Potomac — Pope, Burnside, and Hooker — had invariably done under similar circumstances; and probably this expectation was shared by every man in the Union army. But when Grant arose at dawn the next morning, thoroughly refreshed after a sound sleep, the first thing he did, at 6:30 A.M. on the 7 May, was to issue his orders for a night march of the entire army toward Spottsylvania Court House, on the direct road to Richmond.[1]

The Federal situation is well summed up by Colonel Henderson in these words: [2]

" Now, here was Grant, a stranger to his troops, face to face with the hero of the war, the man before whom so many generals had gone down. He had fought him for two days in the Wilderness, and if he had escaped defeat he had lost a great many more men than Lee, and the fighting all through had certainly not been in the Federal

---

[1] Porter, *Campaigning with Grant*, 74.
[2] Henderson, *Science of War*, 320.

favor. The morning after the battle they brought in a list of losses — 15,000 men — and the enemy was still there: still there, and not retreating! Grant had to decide what to do; it was little use attacking the enemy in his entrenchments; there seemed no hope of success, and the army would not have been surprised had he followed the example of his predecessors and retreated. But despite his losses, despite the demoralization of his troops, despite the fact that he had not won one inch of ground, he determined to move forward, to follow out his original plan, and, if possible, to cut Lee off from Richmond, or at all events to force him to battle in a less impregnable position than the one he now held. This was the turning point in the campaign."

As a commander, Grant can not be compared with General Lee, " undoubtedly one of the greatest soldiers, if not the greatest, who ever spoke the English tongue," [3] but he possessed the determination, the perseverance, the fixed resolve to conquer, which enabled him to triumph over obstacles before which men of weaker fibre would have turned aside. He was endowed with that almost indefinable force which Napoleon declared was three times more effective than physical means, that is, than numbers, armament, and position. In other words, Grant relied far more on the moral effect of his manœuvres than on the mere fighting qualities of his troops, and it was this which finally brought him success. It was perhaps to this that Napoleon referred when he said that reading and meditating on the wars of the greatest captains is the only way of learning the science of war.

In order to appreciate fully Grant's difficulties, and his strength of character, we must remember that, with strange troops, who had far more dread of Lee than confidence in himself, he was to continue his campaign against that formidable adversary, in a most difficult country, which was far better known to Lee and his officers than to any one in the Union army. The few maps available were not reliable. The theatre of war was covered with pri-

[3] Henderson, 314.

mæval forest, and very thinly populated. There were immense tracts of swamp and jungle which were *terra incognita* to all but a few farmers and their negro slaves. The roads were as scarce and as indifferent as the maps. There were many unfordable streams, crossed by few bridges, at long intervals. The country produced but little food or forage, and the invaders had to carry both their supplies and their ammunition.

Under Grant's orders, Hancock's corps, on the left of the line, was to remain in position until the trains and the other army corps marched by his rear. The trains were started in the afternoon of the 7th, and the troops moved at eight-thirty. Warren marched by the Brock Road; Sedgwick, followed by Burnside, moved by way of Chancellorsville, Aldrich's, and Piney Branch Church. Hancock was ordered to follow Warren to Todd's Tavern. The cavalry preceded the infantry columns, and covered the flanks and rear.

The troops began their march in a state of great discouragement, under the impression that they were to retire once more behind the Rapidan. But when they came to the cross-roads, the command was, " Column right! "

" Soon after dark," writes General Porter, " Generals Grant and Meade, accompanied by their staffs, . . . rode along the Brock Road toward Hancock's headquarters, with the intention of waiting there till Warren's troops should reach that point." Then occurred an unexpected demonstration which was one of the most memorable scenes of the campaign. In spite of the darkness, Grant was recognized. The men then understood that the watchword was to be, " On to Richmond! " " Wild cheers echoed through the forest, and glad shouts of triumph rent the air. . . . The night march had become a triumphal procession for the new commander." [4] Grant sent his staff-officers along the line to urge the men to keep quiet so as not to attract the enemy's attention.

On the afternoon of the 7th, Lee was informed by Stuart of the movement of the Federal trains, and he was

[4] Porter, 78–79.

convinced that Grant's objective was Spottsylvania Court House. He at once ordered Anderson, now commanding Longstreet's corps, to make a night march for the same point, and sent Stuart's cavalry to retard the Federals as much as possible, in order to enable Anderson to reach Spottsylvania first and take up position.

In the race for the Court House, Grant had a little the worse of the luck. His route was somewhat the longer of the two, but his troops started at 8:30 P.M. on the 7th, while the Confederate corps was not to march until 3 A.M. on the 8th. Luckily for Lee, however, Anderson took the responsibility of starting at an hour before midnight, in order to escape from the blazing woods, which had been set on fire by the battle. This enabled Anderson to win the race.

The Confederate cavalry felled trees across the Brock Road, and disputed every foot of ground, so that the progress of Warren's column was much delayed. It was half-after eight the next morning before the leading division (Robinson) emerged from the woods into open ground at Alsop's, about two miles and a half from the Court House. As the division advanced across the clearing, toward a dense pine thicket on the further side, it was met by a staggering musketry and artillery fire from the Confederate breast-works, and driven back to the shelter of the woods in the rear.

Robinson was badly wounded; Griffin came up on his right, but was also forced back, until the two other divisions (Crawford, and Wadsworth now under Cutler) of the Fifth Corps arrived and took part in the engagement. Warren then advanced, and entrenched a position from 200 to 400 yards in front of the Confederate line.

Several roads came together at the Court House, from Chancellorsville, and Fredericksburg, now the Union base, as well as from the east and south. This gave the place a strategic value, and made it the field of the battle.

The troops on both sides now came up rapidly. Sedgwick joined Warren, and in the afternoon his corps vigorously assaulted Anderson's right wing, which, assisted by the timely arrival of Ewell's corps, repulsed the attack

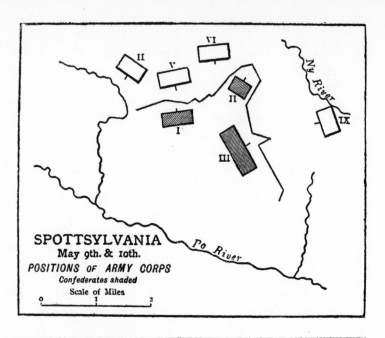

SPOTTSYLVANIA
May 9th. & 10th.
POSITIONS OF ARMY CORPS
Confederates shaded
Scale of Miles
0   1   2

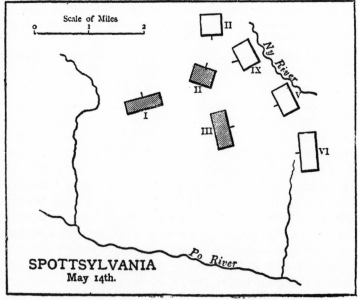

Scale of Miles
0   1   2

SPOTTSYLVANIA
May 14th.

with great slaughter. Hill's corps, now under the command of General Early, did not arrive until the next morning, the 9th.

General Lee's line now covered the Court House, with its left, Longstreet's corps, resting on a small stream called the Po River; Ewell's corps was in the centre, north of the Court House, and Hill's on the right, covering the Fredericksburg Road. These positions were generally maintained during the battle, although troops were frequently shifted from one point of the line to another.

The sketches show how skillfully Lee had made his dispositions. Like Napoleon, he had an extraordinary eye for ground, and relied largely on natural features in his defensive tactics. Throughout this campaign — in the midst of woods, jungle, and streams — with very little time at his disposal, he always seems to have selected positions of great strength. His eye for ground had much to do with his successful resistance to Grant's overwhelming numbers.

At Spottsylvania, Lee's front, between the Po and the Ny,[5] was well adapted to his smaller forces, and his line was far stronger than that held in the Wilderness. In order to turn his position Grant would have to cross one of the streams, and so divide his army, giving Lee an opportunity of dealing with him in detail. The country was thickly wooded, and the Federals still had the same difficulty of finding out where the enemy was and in what direction his entrenchments ran.

On the 9 May began what is called the battle of Spottsylvania — which was really a series of engagements lasting about nine days. The first two days were occupied mainly in reconnoitring. This work is usually done by cavalry, but they were of no use at all in such a country, and reconnaissances in force by brigades of infantry were therefore the only means by which Grant could find out anything about the enemy.

The skirmishers and sharp-shooters were very active on both sides during the day, and General Sedgwick was

---

[5] Four streams, drolly named by some early pioneer, the Mat, the Ta, the Po, and the Ny, unite to form the Mattapony River.

killed close to the entrenchments to the right of his line.
General Wright then took command of the Sixth Corps.

By this time it had been ascertained that the Confederate line ran from the Po, at a point 600 yards above the
crossing of the Shady Grove Church Road, to a point half
a mile south of the Fredericksburg Road, a distance of
more than four miles. It enclosed the Court House on
the northwest, north, and east, and covered the roads
southward toward Richmond. The most marked feature
of the line was a salient at the centre — a sort of loop a
half-mile wide from east to west, having a sharp apex
upon a high open point a quarter of a mile north by east
from the McCool house. At the salient, the line turned
southeast, for about 600 or 700 yards, with the woods
about the McCool house behind it, and fairly open
ground in front; then it ran in a southerly direction for
a mile and a half, with the ground in front partly broken
and wooded and partly open.

From left to right, the line was held in the following
order: Longstreet's corps, under Anderson; Ewell's,
around the loop in the centre; Hill's, except Anderson's
old division, now under Mahone, which was on the extreme left overlooking the Po. Early's old division, now
under Gordon, which was in reserve, was employed in
digging a trench at the base of the salient about 400 yards
south of the McCool house.

Hancock occupied the right of the Union line in an
entrenchment overlooking the Po; Warren was next, in
front of Anderson; Wright was on the left. Burnside,
with the Ninth Corps, was still near the Ny River on the
Fredericksburg Road. On arriving, Burnside had encountered a small force of dismounted Confederate cavalry, which he mistook for infantry. This led Grant to
believe that Lee was about to move against his line of
communications with Fredericksburg, and he ordered
Hancock to cross the Po and reconnoitre Lee's left.

By nine o'clock Hancock had passed the river with the
three divisions of Barlow, Gibbon, and Birney; his fourth
division (Mott), which came up late, had been sent to
the left to Wright's corps. During the night he had three

bridges built across the Po, to secure his retreat, and pushed on to the bridge of Shady Grove Road known as the Blockhouse, because of a house near it, built of squared logs. Here he found the Confederate line too strong to attack. About 10 A.M. on the 10th, Hancock received an order to leave one of his divisions to threaten the Confederate left, and return, with his two other divisions, to command an attack to be made at five o'clock with his own corps, and the corps of Warren and Wright.

After his departure, Barlow's division, which he left behind, was attacked by the Confederates, and finally driven back over the river. The enemy then prolonged his lines a mile upon the high ground, thus covering the approach by the Shady Grove Church Road.

During the day, Warren and Wright had been feeling out the lines in their front, and the former reported the opportunity was so favorable that he was ordered to attack at once, without awaiting Hancock's return. The assault was made about four o'clock by the Fifth and Sixth corps, and two divisions (Mott and Gibbon) of the Second. The troops reached the Confederate lines, but were all driven back with heavy loss.

At seven o'clock, Hancock made a second attack with Birney's and Gibbon's divisions, supported by part of the Fifth Corps, but this also was repulsed with heavy loss.

General Alexander thinks that Burnside's mistake, mentioned above, was most fortunate for Lee, as it led to Grant's sending Hancock prematurely across the Po and then withdrawing him. If he had remained upon that flank, and been reënforced by Warren, " it is hard to see how he could have failed . . . completely to turn Lee's flank, and get upon his communications which now ran to Louisa C. H." [6]

While these affairs were going on upon the Confederate left, Grant was preparing for an assault upon the weakest point of their line — the salient at the centre. The attack was made at five o'clock by three brigades under Colonel Upton. The works were carried, but the Federals were finally driven back, with a loss of about

---

[6] Alexander, 515.

1000 men, or 20 per cent. of the attacking column. The total Federal losses for the day were over 4000.

Upton's attack was to have been supported by Mott, but the division, when it attempted to advance, was broken up by a severe artillery fire, and fell back.

The next day, the 11th, was rainy and disagreeable, and no serious fighting took place. Grant thought that Upton's failure was due to lack of support, and he made his plans for a much more formidable assault on the salient by the whole of the Second and Ninth corps. The point of attack was to be the apex of the loop, afterwards known as the " Bloody Angle."

Owing to misleading reports of a Federal movement on his left, Lee believed that Grant was preparing for another flank march. He therefore ordered all of the guns withdrawn at sundown from the parts of his line nearest the enemy, so as to be ready to move quickly. Consequently, when the attack came, the guns had all been removed from the salient, which was untenable without artillery. This was a fatal mistake, as will soon appear.

There was no moon, and heavy rain was falling when the Federals began their movement. Hancock's arrangement is interesting, but it failed from errors in formation. As given by General Alexander it was as follows: [7]

BARLOW

BROOKS	MILES	BIRNEY
——————	——————	————————
——————	——————	
——————	——————	————————
——————	——————	

SMYTH	BROWN	MOTT
——————	——————	————————
——————	——————	
——————	——————	

GIBBON

——————————————————

(Advanced later)

[7] Alexander, 519.

Barlow's division was formed in two columns of two brigades each; Birney's, in two lines, and Mott's in one. Gibbon's division was deployed in the rear. The columns were 10 ranks (or 20 men) deep. All officers were dismounted, and the division and brigade commanders with their staffs marched in the centre between the lines. In Barlow's division there was so little distance between the ranks that soon after the advance began it was a solid mass.

The assault, which had been ordered for 4 A.M., was delayed 35 minutes by the fog. The distance to the Confederate works was about 1200 yards. Urgent calls had been sent for the return of the 22 Confederate guns, but only two arrived in time, and these only fired three rounds before they were captured with the rest. If these guns had been in place, the charge could not have succeeded. On no other occasion during the Civil War was such a target presented to so large a force of artillery.[8] The Federals came with such a rush that the Confederates were overwhelmed before they had a chance to fire more than two or three scattered volleys. Johnson was captured, with one of his brigadiers; in all, 4000 prisoners were taken, with 30 colors, and 20 guns.

The first assault had been a great success, but no further advantage was gained. Lee hurried up reënforcements from the right and left, and put in all his reserves. The Confederate line was reformed behind the trench at the south end of the salient. The Federals were much disorganized by their victory, and it was difficult to reform their lines within the salient.

It was reported to Grant that Hancock had been checked, and at eight o'clock eight brigades from the Sixth Corps were sent to his assistance. In the confined space, these reënforcements only added to the confusion.

In the meantime, at 5 A.M., Potter's division of the Ninth Corps had attacked the extreme right of the Confederate line, carried the works, and captured two guns; but the Federals were soon driven back and the guns retaken.

[8] Alexander, 520.

The Federals were finally driven out of the salient, but the combat there lasted all day, and till after midnight: it was perhaps the most desperate and the most sanguinary conflict of the whole war. At one time 24 Union brigades were engaged in assaulting a few hundred yards of the entrenchments. The men stood from twenty to forty deep outside the parapet. One tree, twenty-two inches in diameter, was literally cut down by the bullets.[9]

There was some fighting during the day by Warren on the right, and Burnside on the left of the Union line, but little was accomplished beyond preventing Lee from sending more reënforcements to his centre.

The Union losses in killed and wounded on the 12 May were about 6800; the Confederate casualties, between 4000 and 5000. Hancock suffered the most, his corps losing about 2500 men. The Federal generals Wright and Webb were wounded. On the Confederate side, two general officers were killed, four severely wounded, and two captured.

On the 11 May, General Grant sent his famous despatch, that he would "fight it out on this line if it takes all summer." On the 12th came the famous assault on the Bloody Angle, which failed because of over-concentration, as the charge of Pickett's division at Gettysburg had miscarried because of too light formation. "The military lesson to be learned from the failure of Hancock's assault," says General Alexander, . . . "is, that there is a maximum limit to the force which can be advantageously used in any locality, and a superfluity may paralyze all efforts." [10]

As explained by Colonel Henderson, however, the failure was not due so much to a superfluity of force, as to its unwise employment. "The principle is," he says, "that you mass opposite one point a great wedge which you intend to drive into the enemy's line, and that this wedge is composed of several lines one behind the other at such distance as may best suit the ground and the situation. . . . But it is a great point to remember that you should have a force behind this wedge in order to confirm

[9] The stump is still preserved in the National Museum at Washington.
[10] Alexander, 525.

success when you have broken in, for whatever may be the discipline of the troops it is impossible that confusion and intermingling of units can be avoided." [11]

In this case the distance between the lines should have been very much increased, and the second and third lines should not have closed in until they were needed to reenforce the first. This great attack was almost a complete success, "and the cause of its ultimate defeat was that in the excitement of the attack the second and third lines, instead of keeping their respective distances, closed in upon the first." [12]

The 13 May was comparatively a day of rest. Although the great assault had failed, it had come so near success that Grant was determined to make another effort. A movement by his left promised an opportunity of attacking Lee's right before it could be reënforced or its entrenchments extended.

The moon was young, the night foggy, rainy, and intensely dark. Warren and Wright were ordered to march by country roads, passing in the rear of Hancock and Burnside, cross the Ny, move through fields to the Fredericksburg Road, on it recross the Ny, form on Burnside's left, and attack the Confederate right flank at 4 A.M. on the 14th. Hancock and Burnside were to be ready, when ordered, to join in the attack.

Again Grant had the worst of luck. During the night the rain fell in torrents; the bonfires, and the torches of the signal men, were put out; and the troops, over roads knee-deep in mud, struggled wearily along at a very slow pace and with many halts. When day broke, only Warren with 4000 men had arrived at the appointed place. The other columns were so strung out in the rear and so scattered, the men so exhausted, that the attack had to be abandoned. "We doubtless had a narrow escape from serious trouble," writes General Alexander. "With ordinary weather the distance was not great, and both the Fifth and Sixth corps could have surprised our flank at dawn in the morning. Our entrenchments on that flank did not then extend much beyond the Court House." [13]

[11] Henderson 326.   [12] *Ibid.*, 325.   [13] Alexander, 526–527.

During the next three days, Grant remained in position opposite Lee's right, resting his men and receiving reënforcements. He ordered strong defensive lines built, which could be held by a reduced force, with the idea of concentrating again for another effort to carry the Confederate line at the salient where he had been checked on the 12th.

By the 17th, the works were strong enough to be held by Warren with the Fifth Corps; that night, Hancock and Wright were ordered to pass around Burnside, and the Second, Sixth, and Ninth corps to attack in conjunction at dawn, while the Fifth Corps (Warren) coöperated on the left.

The plan seemed to promise well, but the attack was an entire failure. The infantry was slow in finding its way through the woods, and it was eight o'clock before the troops came in sight of the Confederate lines. The divisions of Gibbon and Barlow, which had taken part in the assault on the 12th, led the way in lines of brigades, a much more effective formation than that employed before. This time the Confederate guns were in position, and their fire was concentrated on the infantry. Only a few men reached the enemy's line and none penetrated it. About ten o'clock, Meade ordered the attack discontinued, and the men withdrawn.

At noon on the 19th, Grant issued orders for Hancock to move that night on the road to Richmond. Lee had anticipated this movement, and had ordered Ewell to make a reconnaissance in force. By a circuitous route, Ewell took his men far around the enemy's flank, and got his entire corps of 6000 troops in the rear of the Federals. Here he occupied a very critical position. He succeeded, however, in holding off the enemy until darkness covered his withdrawal. In this venture he lost 900 men, or about 15 per cent. of his force.

This ended the battle of Spottsylvania, in which the losses on both sides were very heavy. Grant's casualties were 2725 killed and 13,416 wounded, a total of 16,141. His total loss since the beginning of the campaign had been in excess of 33,000. The Confederate losses, from the Wilderness to the close of the war, can never be accurately known, as few reports were made. Livermore estimates their losses for these two battles at 17,250, the missing not included.

Grant now tried a new manœuvre. On the night of the 20 May he started Hancock for Guinea Station, about ten miles east of Spottsylvania, with orders to march from that point south toward Hanover Court House. He hoped that Lee would move against this corps with the bulk of his army, and thus afford a chance of striking the Confederates in the open country before they had time to entrench.

At this time Sheridan was absent with most of the Union cavalry. After the battle of the Wilderness, Grant had sent him on a raid around the left of the Confederate army, with orders to attack Lee's cavalry, cut the Virginia Central and Fredericksburg railways, and do all the damage he could. Stuart followed him, as Grant had expected, and finally succeeded in placing his command across Sheridan's path at Yellow Tavern, only six miles north of Richmond. In the severe combat which followed, Stuart was mortally wounded, and his command defeated. Sheridan then passed close to the city, but was not strong enough to attack the works. He had a narrow escape from capture, but finally reached the James River, where he secured rations and forage from Butler. He then returned by way of White House, and rejoined the army on the 24 May, near Chesterfield, having ridden entirely around Lee's army.

This was only one more of those useless and perilous cavalry raids, so common during the Civil War. It had no material effect on the campaign, and deprived Grant of the " eyes and ears " of his army at a critical moment.

All of the cavalry that was left with the army was sent with Hancock under the command of Torbert. The Union movement was observed and hindered by the Confederate horsemen under Wade Hampton.

On the morning of the 21st, Warren started by the same route taken by Hancock, and was followed later by Burnside and Wright. Lee did not feel strong enough to assume the offensive, and therefore failed to fall into Grant's trap. As soon as he learned of the Federal movement he ordered Ewell to march directly for Hanover Junction, and followed with his whole army. Although Hancock had a start of twelve hours, on account of his long détour he did not arrive until after Lee. He found the Confederates drawn up behind the North Anna River, covering Richmond and the Virginia Central Railway. There were two bridges opposite their right, a ford in front of their centre, and another ford two and a half miles distant, beyond their left.

The line first held by Lee was dangerously extended, but he now executed a peculiar manœuvre; he shut up his line as one closes an umbrella. The line originally had been almost straight: it now assumed a triangular form, with the apex on the river. His whole army was then massed in a space not more than two and a half miles broad. He could reënforce any point attacked in much shorter time than Grant could concentrate at the same point.

At this time Lee was rejoined by Pickett's division, some 5000 strong, and he received other reënforcements aggregating about 4000 more, or a total of 9000 fresh troops.

Grant formed his line in front of Lee's position, with the Fifth and Sixth corps on the right, the Second and part of the Ninth on the left. The two wings were unable to communicate without crossing the river twice. Lee's position was so strong that it defeated its object, as Grant did not venture to attack. Lee was anxious to take advantage of his reënforcements to strike a blow, but the Federal entrenchments were very strong, and the flat, open country gave full play to their artillery. Besides, Lee, at this time, was confined to his tent by a temporary illness, so neither side made any serious attack. On the night of the 26th, Grant removed the temptation, ere Lee had recovered, by moving for the Pamunkey.

After dark on the 26th, Grant set his army in motion for Hanover Town, near which he crossed the Pamunkey

[14] See sketches.

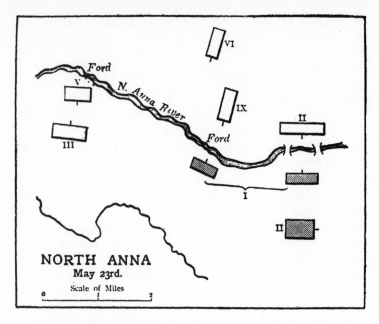

NORTH ANNA
May 23rd.
Scale of Miles
0   1   2

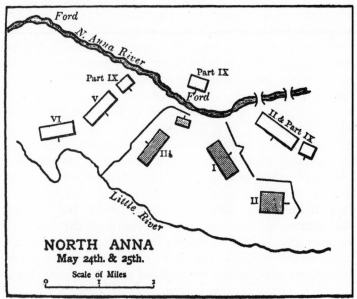

NORTH ANNA
May 24th. & 25th.
Scale of Miles
0   1   2

River. Sheridan's cavalry, which had just rejoined the army, led the way. At Haw's Shop, south of the river, it defeated the Confederate cavalry, under Wade Hampton, in a fierce combat which lasted all day.

As soon as Lee discovered, on the morning of the 27th, that the Federals had vanished, he marched by way of Half Sink to the Totopotomoy, which he reached the next day, in time to see the Union army just arriving on the opposite bank. As he moved by interior lines, about six miles shorter than the route taken by Grant, he won the race as usual. The Confederates immediately entrenched their position so strongly that Grant decided not to assault.

After leaving Spottsylvania Court House, the armies found themselves in a rich farming country, entirely different from the Wilderness. The farther south and east they marched, the broader and deeper they found the streams, the lower, flatter, and more marshy the land.

Grant once more moved by the left flank, Lee followed, and the two armies found themselves at Cold Harbor. In order to understand the strategic importance of this point, it is necessary to give a brief description of the country near it. Hanover Town, where the Union army was concentrated south of the Pamunkey, is about seventeen miles in a straight line northeast of Richmond. The theatre is traversed by two rivers, Totopotomoy Creek, running easterly into the Pamunkey, and the Chickahominy River, flowing southeasterly to the James. Between these, there are a number of smaller streams, with low banks, their borders swampy and covered with woods and thickets.

From Hanover Town three main roads lead to Richmond: the Shady Grove; the Mechanicsville; and the Cold Harbor, which runs via Old and New Cold Harbor, and Gaines's Mill. New Cold Harbor was little more than the intersection of cross-roads but Old Cold Harbor, a mile and a half east, and about midway between Hanover Town and Richmond, was an important strategic point, because it commanded the roads running south toward the James, and northeast toward White House, the present Union base.

SPOTTSYLVANIA AND COLD HARBOR

At Cold Harbor, Grant was joined by W. F. Smith with about 10,000 men of the Tenth and Eighteenth corps from Butler's army, and Lee was further reënforced by Hoke's division of 5000 men from Drewry's Bluff.

Lee immediately began to work southward, by extending his right flank, so as to secure Old Cold Harbor, and command the roads above described. On the 31 May, this important strategic point was seized by Sheridan's cavalry, which entrenched, and held the position until relieved by Wright's corps. Several desperate attacks by the Confederates on the following day were all successfully repelled. The Union losses were nearly 2000, and the enemy probably suffered to about the same extent.

On the 3 June, Grant assaulted Lee's strongly entrenched position, and in one hour lost nearly 6000 men, killed and wounded. On this occasion, Grant seems to have lost his head, and he regretted this useless slaughter to the last day of his life.[15] There was no manœuvring as there had been at Spottsylvania; there was no massing against any particular point. The order was given for the whole line to attack, and the army moved straight against the enemy's front.

Swinton is responsible for the statement, repeated by many other historians, that Grant ordered the attack renewed, but the men refused to advance: they knew that the position could not be taken. This is absolutely denied by General Alexander, who was present at the battle. He says, " No such silent defiance of orders occurred, or anything like it.[16]

Cold Harbor was only six miles from the outer works around Richmond, and the right of Lee's line was within three miles of those works. If Grant could have broken the Confederate centre at Cold Harbor, he might have

[15] See 2 Grant, 276.

[16] Alexander, 541. On the other hand, Wheeler (44) says that the same story was told him by General Titus, who was there. In his *Memoirs* (2, 143–145) Grant states that Swinton, " the historian," was warned for eavesdropping at Culpeper; and later, at Cold Harbor, was arrested by General Burnside, who ordered him shot for some " great offense," which Grant does not specify. Grant " promptly ordered the prisoner released, but that he must be expelled from the lines of the army."

destroyed Lee's army, captured Richmond, and ended the war at one stroke.

As early as the 26 May, Grant had taken steps to be prepared to cross the James, with a view of attacking Richmond and Petersburg from the south side. He ordered his engineers to collect material for making bridges, and telegraphed Halleck at Washington to forward to City Point all the pontoons on hand.

The Union army remained in front of Lee's position until the night of the 12 June, when Grant set his troops in motion to cross the James River. This ended the great campaign of the Wilderness.

The Union losses during the first twelve days of June totalled 1905 killed, and 10,570 wounded — in all 12,475. The Confederate losses are not known, but were certainly smaller. Grant began the campaign with 105,000 men, and received over 45,000 reënforcements. During the campaign he lost 55,000 men. Lee began with 62,000, and received about 14,000 reënforcements. His losses, as already stated, are unknown, but were probably under 20,000.[17]

The student will look in vain for anything brilliant in the way of strategy or tactics in Grant's campaign from the Rapidan to the James. His successive turning operations all failed of their object — to get between Lee's army and Richmond, and cut his communications. At every move he found Lee entrenched across his path. At the end of six weeks, he found himself on the James, where he might have transported his army in the first place, without losing a man.

Nor were his tactics any better. He seems to have had no plan of attack in any of his battles. At Spottsylvania he assaulted first one part of the Confederate lines and then another. He wore his troops out in marches and countermarches. Orders were issued and countermanded; corps were sent to places only to be recalled. The one outstanding feature of the campaign is Grant's tenacity of purpose — his determination " to fight it out on this line if it

---

[17] See 4 B. & L., 182–184.

takes all summer." He never seemed to know when he was getting the worse of it. The tenor of all his despatches was to the effect that the enemy was suffering more than his own army. To a deputation of influential politicians who recommended Grant's removal from command, President Lincoln replied, " I like that man — he fights! "

" If, as the mediæval chroniclers tell us," writes General Law, " Charles Martel [*the Hammerer*] gained that title by a seven days' continuous battle with the Saracens at Tours, General Grant certainly entitled himself to a like distinction by his thirty days' campaign from the Wilderness to Cold Harbor." [18]

In these words of General Law, we find outlined the great distinction between generals of the two definite types of McClellan and Grant: the former never could make up his mind to fight; the latter well deserved his appellation of " the hammerer ": like Napoleon, he never hesitated to make sacrifices, if necessary, in order to achieve victory.

Reference has already been made in these pages to the analogy between war and chess. Some commanders, like some chess-masters, never attain great success because, having too great a regard for their *matériel*, they refuse to part with it. It should always be remembered that men are only the pieces in the game, the means to an end, and as such they should be made subservient to the purpose in view, namely, victory; therefore, the great general, like the chess-master, must ever be prepared for sacrifices.

Napoleon is reported to have said, " What are a million men to me! " This remark, if ever made, was not so brutal as it sounds. All that he meant to convey was that, to achieve victory, he never hesitated to press home his attack, no matter how great his losses. [19]

" The *ardent desire* for the fight," writes Colonel Vachée, " was a *new and characteristic trait* of his genius, for how many generals-in-chief hesitate the moment they enter upon that terrible drama which is played at the cost

[18] 4 *B. & L.*, 143.
[19] Yorck de Wartenburg, 2 *Napoléon, chef d'armée*, 377.

of so many human lives, and on which there so often depends the fate of empires and nations! " [20]

At Saint Helena, Napoleon also remarked that it was rare to find generals who were in a hurry to give battle. They carefully took up their positions, and thought out their combinations, but they could not make up their minds to attack.[21]

The campaign was marked by the number of turning movements; the frequent night marches; and the changes of the base of supplies. As the army advanced, the base was shifted from the Orange and Alexandria Railway to Aquia Creek; then to Port Royal; next, to White House; and finally to the James River.

The most marked feature of the Wilderness Campaign, however, was the general use of entrenchments. As soon as the troops were halted, the men threw up shelter without waiting for the officers to give the order. In this wooded country it was an easy matter to construct entrenchments, and they were strong enough for the purpose. There were a great many expert axe-men in both armies, and trees were soon felled, or the fallen timber gathered. A pile of logs and branches made a good foundation, over these the men threw a little earth, and a breastwork was soon constructed that was bullet-proof at least. General Alexander says that the Confederate equipment with entrenching tools was very poor; the men habitually loosened the ground with bayonets, and scooped it up with tin cups. Their line was generally laid out by those who built it. The Federals, on the other hand, had a force of perhaps 2500 men, of engineer troops and heavy artillery regiments, habitually employed for this work under the direction of engineer officers.[22]

This use of entrenchments was copied by both the hostile armies during the Great War, and carried to an extent never before known.

In summing up his interesting and valuable study of the Wilderness Campaign, Colonel Henderson says:

[20] Vachée, *Napoleon at Work*, 266–267.
[21] *Mémorial de Sainte-Hélène*.
[22] Henderson, 319; Alexander, 513. See also Appendix G.

" For those who care to study the campaign closely, it is worth while noting with what skill Lee's positions were selected. His flanks at Spottsylvania, at the North Anna, and at Cold Harbor, were so secured by streams that it was very difficult indeed for his opponent to manœuvre without crossing one of these streams, and so dividing his army. It was not only the entrenchments, but the natural features of the ground also on which Lee relied in his defensive tactics. His eye for ground must have been extraordinary." [23]

[23] Henderson, 333.

CHAPTER EIGHTEEN

MAY — SEPTEMBER 1864

ATLANTA

Johnston Succeeds Bragg — Plans for a Winter Campaign — The Opportunity Lost — The Union Base — Measures to Secure the Communications — Sherman in Command — His Three Armies — Objects of the Campaign — Sherman's Turning Movements — Johnston's Defensive Policy — His Slow Retreat to Atlanta — He Is Relieved by Hood — The Battles around Atlanta — Defeats of the Confederates — Hood Evacuates the City — Numbers and Losses — Comments

THE Confederates were not actively pursued after the battle of Chattanooga. Bragg therefore halted at Dalton, only twenty-five miles from the field of his defeat, and entrenched his army. He was then relieved of the command, at his own request; but President Davis showed continued confidence in his ability by calling him to Richmond as chief-of-staff. He was ordered to turn over the command to the senior lieutenant-general, Hardee, who might have retained the position if he had not shrunk from the responsibility.

At this time there were but five officers of the full rank of general [1] in the Confederate service, of whom the only two available were Johnston and Beauregard. General Lee suggested the name of the latter for the chief command in the West, but Mr. Davis did not take kindly to the idea. While the matter was under discussion, General Polk wrote the President a strong letter urging the appointment of Joseph E. Johnston. Mr. Davis, who was not on very friendly terms with either Beauregard or Johnston, was placed in a very embarrassing position, but finally decided to appoint the latter. On the 16 December, Johnston was ordered to turn over the command of

---

[1] Cooper, Lee, Johnston, Beauregard, and Bragg. See Appendix B.

the Army of the Mississippi to Polk, and proceed to Dalton to take command of the Army of the Tennessee.

The Richmond authorities were in favor of a prompt renewal of the aggressive, with a view to the recovery of Tennessee. Both Mr. Seddon, the Secretary of War, and President Davis wrote Johnston, the last of December, urging him to assume the offensive as soon as the condition of his army would allow it.

In his reply, on the 2 January, Johnston presented the difficulties in the way of action. " I can see no other mode of taking the offensive here," he wrote Mr. Davis, " than to beat the enemy when he advances, and then move forward." [2] The correspondence continued throughout the winter, and Mr. Davis, by making it personal, evinced a desire to overlook former differences. But General Johnston's tone remained that of cold formality, and he showed no disposition to meet the views of the President. Finally, about the first of March, Mr. Davis dropped the correspondence, turning it over to General Bragg.

The situation was one which called for prompt action. During the winter, the Federal forces in the West were much dispersed, and a quick blow at Thomas, at Chattanooga, would have found him isolated. Schofield was at Knoxville, over 100 miles to the northeast; Logan, with part of Sherman's forces, was near Huntsville, an equal distance to the southwest; and the rest of Sherman's command was on the Meridian expedition or returning to Vicksburg. To wait for spring was to wait for the Federals to concentrate their now scattered armies, and be fully prepared for the campaign. It is no wonder that the Richmond Government lost patience with Johnston's attitude.

Lee, who had been in Richmond, was in full accord with this plan, and wrote Longstreet, who had not yet rejoined him after the Chattanooga Campaign, urging him to co-operate in influencing Johnston to adopt it. " If you and Johnston could unite and move into Middle Tennessee," he said, " it would cut the armies of Chattanooga and Knoxville in two, and draw them from those points, where either portion could be struck at as occasion offered."

[2] Johnston's *Narrative*, 275.

It cannot be denied, as General Cox states,[3] that this plan was based on sound strategy. Both Grant and Sherman were glad that they were allowed to complete their preparations, and were not called upon to meet the enemy before they were ready. Johnston's abilities are undoubted, and later he conducted his defensive campaign with great skill, but he lacked the audacity of Lee and Stonewall Jackson, which so often won victories for the Confederates.

Hood, who had been assigned to a corps in Johnston's army, wrote Mr. Davis on the 7 March that the army was well prepared, in high spirits, and anxious for battle. He strongly supported the plan of moving before Grant could concentrate.

As requested by Lee, Longstreet wrote Johnston on the 5 March, to the effect that he was ready to join in the movement. A week later, Bragg wrote from Richmond, outlining the plan of campaign mentioned above, and saying that on receiving the assurance of its immediate execution Johnston would be reënforced so as to have an army of at least 75,000 men. In his replies Johnston pronounced the plan impracticable, and again argued that it was better to let the enemy's forces advance, and fight them far from their base and near his own.[4] There were certainly very sound arguments in favor of his position.

The principal Union dépôt for operations in Alabama and Georgia was Nashville, centrally located as the capital of Tennessee, but 186 miles by rail south of the Ohio River. It was directly connected with Chattanooga by 150 miles of railroad, and indirectly by a line 35 miles longer by way of Decatur and Stevenson. It had the further advantage of water connection with the Ohio by the Cumberland River. A railroad had also recently been completed, some 70 miles in length, from Nashville to Johnsonville on the Tennessee, a much larger river, nearly parallel to the Cumberland in this part of its course. With these great lines of communication, the problem of supplying the army seemed to be solved.

[3] 2 Cox, 189.   [4] See Johnston, 291–297.

So much trouble had been experienced, however, in earlier campaigns, from the interruption of railway service by Confederate raids, that special means had been devised to protect the lines. Every wooden bridge across a stream was a vulnerable point, and a system of block-houses had been developed to guard all the bridges.

Ten tons made a load for the small freight cars of that day, and, with the iron rails and light locomotives, 20 to 30 cars made a full train. As Sherman estimated that he must receive at the front 150 car-loads daily, it is easy to understand the difficulty of supplying an army far from its base.

The work of the railways had also to be supplemented by the wagon-trains necessary in the field to carry the baggage of the army, its ammunition, and a few days' rations. The amount of food and forage required by a large army has already been referred to in connection with Grant's first advance on Vicksburg. It makes in the aggregate a bulk and weight astonishing to those who are not familiar with the subject. Great droves of beef cattle also accompanied the army, and the driving, feeding, and distributing of these, made, of itself, no small task.

After some further correspondence, the subject of the Confederate offensive in the West was dropped by the Richmond Government. It was now known that Grant would not personally lead the Western army, but would turn over his command to Sherman. Concentration on both sides was the order of the day, and Longstreet was directed to rejoin Lee. As Johnston had not accepted the aggressive plan suggested,[5] he was notified that he could not expect the reënforcement promised him on that condition. Polk was ordered to join him, and he also received about 4000 men from Mobile. All the troops that Beauregard could spare, and that could be withdrawn from the Atlantic coast, were sent to Lee.

"The very unsatisfactory relations between Mr. Davis and General Johnston," says General Cox, "cannot be

---

[5] It is only fair to state that Johnston expressly denies this. See *Narrative*, 298-301.

overlooked if we would judge intelligently the events of the Atlanta campaign." [6] Johnston may have been right in thinking a winter campaign impracticable, but he should have carried out the wishes of his government, or resigned in time to let another undertake the task.

Little had been done by the Federal forces in the West during the winter. Grant remained in command until March, when he went East to assume his position of lieutenant-general, and commander-in-chief of all the armies. He was succeeded by General Sherman in Tennessee.

It was impossible for Sherman to assume the offensive against Johnston before the first of May, due to the bad condition of the roads in the early spring, the necessity of accumulating supplies, and the depletion of his ranks through the so-called " veteran act." [7]

Prior to the opening of the campaign some changes were made in the organization of Sherman's army. The Twentieth Corps was formed by the consolidation of the Eleventh and Twelfth, and placed under the command of Hooker; and Howard replaced Gordon Granger in command of the Fourth Corps. The Army of the Tennessee, consisting of the Fifteenth, Seventeenth, and part of the Sixteenth corps, was assigned to McPherson. Burnside was succeeded by Schofield in command of the Army of the Ohio, consisting only of the Twenty-third Corps. Thomas remained in command of the Army of the Cumberland, made up of the Fourth, Fourteenth, and Twentieth corps. As will appear later, several changes were made in these commands during the campaign.

The returns for the 30 April 1864 show Sherman's strength to have been about 110,000 men. After making all deductions for the garrisons of Nashville and Chattanooga, and the numerous small posts and blockhouses, he was able to take the field with nearly 100,000 troops. At the opening of the campaign, his forces were distributed as follows:

[6] 2 Cox, 194.
[7] This act provided that all men who reënlisted for the period of the war should receive a month's furlough, transportation home, and a bounty of $400.

Army of the Ohio, Schofield, near Red Clay, on the railway thirteen miles north of Dalton, 13,559.

Army of the Tennessee, McPherson, at Lee and Gordon's Mill, twenty miles northwest of Dalton, 24,465.

Army of the Cumberland, Thomas, near Ringgold, on the railway twelve miles northwest of Dalton, 60,773.

The front from Red Clay to Lee and Gordon's Mill in Chickamauga Valley was twenty miles long.

Similar returns for Johnston's army at the end of April show that he had actually present at Dalton about 53,000 men.[8] He was soon reënforced by Polk with 14,000, and a few detachments amounting to some 5000 more, giving him an aggregate of 75,000 men soon after the opening of the campaign.

Grant's instructions to Sherman, given in his confidential letter of the 4 April, were, to move against Johnston's army, to break it up, and to get into the interior of the enemy's country as far as he could, inflicting all the damage possible against their war resources.

Sherman's first objective therefore was Johnston's army, and the second, his base at Atlanta, 85 miles from Dalton. In his *Memoirs*, General Sherman says, " Atlanta was known as the Gate-City of the South, was full of foundries, arsenals, and machine-shops, and I knew that its capture would be the death-knell of the Southern Confederacy." It was a large town, of great strategic importance, the junction of railways leading to Chattanooga, Richmond, the Atlantic coast, and Montgomery, Alabama.

The country between Chattanooga and Atlanta was generally rugged and hilly, and covered with forests. Johnston's position at Dalton was protected in front by a ridge running north and south, some thirty miles long, which could be crossed by an army at two places only — the gap traversed by the railway, and Snake Creek Gap, fourteen miles farther south.

Sherman's advance began on the 7 May. Finding Johnston's position too strong to attack in front, Sherman sent McPherson to turn it by way of Villanow and Snake

[8] Johnston (302) puts his "effectives" at 42,856.

Creek Gap. Thomas was ordered to support him by making a strong demonstration against Johnston's front.

McPherson encountered a Confederate cavalry brigade about to occupy Snake Creek Gap, and routed it. On the afternoon of the 9th he was in front of Resaca, but considered the position too strong to assault; he therefore returned to the southern end of the gap, and there took up a strong position.

Leaving Howard, with Stoneman's cavalry division, to guard his line of communications, Sherman now moved the rest of his army to Snake Creek Gap, where, on the 12th, he concentrated his forces at McPherson's position.

As Sherman's first objective was Johnston's army, he did not undertake these flanking movements merely to compel the enemy to retreat and yield more territory. His constant desire was to force conclusions as near his own base as possible; but, unlike Grant, he was too wise to wreck his army in frontal attacks against impregnable positions. " It was with an unwillingness growing at times into impatience that he found himself compelled to follow Johnston's slow and skillful retreat. It was not till the change of the Confederate commanders that aggressive tactics on the part of the enemy gave the opportunity for severe punishment and led to the speedy destruction of the hostile army. Herein lies the key of the whole campaign." [9]

On the morning of the 13 May, Johnston withdrew his army to Resaca, where he was joined by Polk's corps. He took up a strong position behind entrenchments on an irregular curve, covering the town, the bridges, and the railway. His right and left flanks were protected by the two rivers.

On the morning of the 14th, Sherman's advance was renewed, guided as before by the Army of the Tennessee on the right, and continuing the wheeling movement toward the east. The army was deployed in front of Resaca, and demonstrations were made against the enemy's front and right. At the same time, Sherman sent a division of infantry and Kilpatrick's cavalry to cross the

[9] 2 Cox, 207–208.

Oostanaula by pontoon-bridge at Lay's Ferry, five miles southwest of Resaca; and Garrard's cavalry division was despatched from Villanow by way of Rome to destroy the railroad between Calhoun and Kingston. These operations forced Johnston to withdraw from Resaca. Burning the railway bridge behind him, on the night of the 15th he began his retreat to Adairsville, where he arrived on the 17th. Here he was joined by a force of 3700 cavalry under W. H. Jackson.

On the 16th, Sherman took up the pursuit. The right under McPherson advanced by way of Lay's Ferry; Thomas, in the centre, followed the railway; the left, under Schofield, crossed the river a few miles east of Resaca. One division (Davis's) of the Fourteenth Corps was sent to the support of Garrard's cavalry in the capture of Rome. This town was important on account of the Confederate ironworks and machine-shops, as well as the large stores collected there.

The Union army was now in the most open district of northern Georgia, and Sherman was eager to bring the enemy to battle in this territory where his superior numbers would have a better chance of winning a decisive victory. He therefore pressed the advance of his columns.

On the afternoon of the 17th, Johnston selected a position for battle just north of Adairsville. Orders were given for the cavalry, strongly supported by infantry, to hold back Sherman's advance-guard until the deployment should be completed. The Confederate line was to be extended across the valley in which the railway ran, with the flanks upon the heights on either side. But, upon testing the position by a partial deployment, Johnston concluded that his army was not large enough to fill it, and he resumed his retreat on Cassville and Kingston. These two places were about seven miles apart. Johnston took the Kingston road with Hardee's corps, and the corps of Polk and Hood followed the route to Cassville. Johnston hoped that Sherman's columns would be so separated that he could concentrate upon one of them, and so fight his adversary in detail.[10] The two hostile armies were now

[10] Johnston, 319–320.

marching with wider fronts than at any time before, but the Federal flanks were farther apart than those of the Confederates.

The position on the hills behind the village of Cassville was so strong that Johnston decided to make a stand there and accept battle. He announced his purpose in an unusually formal manner by issuing a brief but stirring address to his troops. His plan was to have Polk's corps make a stand on the Cassville road, while Hardee guarded the flank toward Kingston, and Hood fell upon the left of Schofield, as the latter deployed to attack Polk. But when the Union left crossed Two Run Creek, and partly turned the right of the Confederate position, Hood and Polk became so uneasy that they protested against accepting battle there, and persuaded Johnston to continue his retreat through Cartersville across the Etowah River. Johnston always felt that he lost a great opportunity, and never ceased to regret it.[11]

The relations of General Johnston with the Richmond Government had been strained since the beginning of the campaign, and his continued retreat had brought matters almost to the breaking point. Even a defeat at this time would have been better than a sudden withdrawal in the night, after he had so loudly proclaimed his intention of leading his men to battle. " Either the order had been an error," says General Cox, " or the retreat was one." Nothing is more destructive of the *moral* of an army than vacillation.

On the 20 May, Johnston took up a position at Allatoona Pass, which Sherman decided not to attempt to assail in front. After giving his army three days of rest, Sherman therefore set out on the 23d to turn the position. As the army would be separated from the railway, supplies for twenty days were carried in the wagons. Three cavalry divisions covered the two flanks and the rear of the army, and the fourth cleared the front for the Union centre.

Sherman's general plan was to advance in several columns on Dallas, and from there on Marietta. Finding

[11] Johnston, 323, 324.

that his position at Allatoona was about to be turned, Johnston at once put his army in motion. His left under Hardee marched to Dallas, and took position south of the town, covering the main road to Atlanta and extending northeast toward New Hope Church. Hood held the right at the church, and Polk was in the centre upon the main road from Allatoona. Sherman's advance-column under Hooker vigorously attacked Hood's corps at New Hope Church, and the fighting lasted from about four o'clock in the afternoon until ended by the fall of night.

The Union army was now shifted to the left, and on the 6 June was again across the railroad at Acworth. In the new line the order of the armies was reversed, Schofield holding the right, and McPherson the left, with Thomas still in the centre. The base was moved to Allatoona.

In the meantime, Johnston had extended his line to the right until it reached from Lost Mountain to Brush Mountain, a distance of about twelve miles. Pine Mountain, an isolated hill in front of this line, was also occupied at first. Hardee's corps was still on the left, Polk's in the centre, and Hood's on the right. The cavalry, under Wheeler and Jackson, guarded the two flanks. The position covered Marietta, the railway back to Atlanta, and the bridges on Johnston's line of retreat.

On the 11th, the Union line was advanced close to that of the Confederates, and on the 14th Thomas deployed before Pine Mountain. On that day, while General Johnston, with Polk and Hardee, was reconnoitring on the mountain, Polk was struck and instantly killed by a shell from a Union battery. Loring succeeded to the command of his corps. That night the Confederate line was withdrawn from Pine Mountain.

Between the 16th and the 19th the Federals continued to press the Confederate lines, and Johnston drew in his forces nearer to Marietta. His line now extended along the crest of Kenesaw Mountain from end to end, and the Federals were close up to the Confederate trenches.

Since the first of June, it had rained continuously, and the whole country was a quagmire. There were only dirt roads in this region, and these were soon destroyed by the heavy army wagons. This greatly hindered the operations.

During the next few days there was considerable skirmishing between the two hostile lines, without any decisive result. Finally, on the 27 June, Sherman departed for the first time from his fixed policy and ordered an assault on Johnston's position on Kenesaw Mountain. The dense forest made any artillery preparation almost impossible, and the attack was one of infantry against unshaken earthworks. The assault was easily repulsed, with a Confederate loss of less than 500, while the Federal casualties are given as 2164 in the official reports.

The affairs at New Hope Church and Kenesaw Mountain convinced Sherman that it was impracticable to bring all his force to bear in this difficult country. He therefore resumed his advance by the tedious flanking movements, in the hope that the time would come when the enemy could no longer afford to retreat, and must resort to aggressive tactics.

Johnston continued to adhere to his patient and steady policy of defence, although he knew that his constant retreat was giving great dissatisfaction to the authorities at Richmond. He withdrew from one position to another, until he finally took up a line behind Peachtree Creek, to make a last stand for the defence of Atlanta. Meanwhile his relations with President Davis had reached a crisis, and on the evening of the 17 July he received a telegram from Richmond directing him to turn over the command of his army to Hood.

This step was taken by President Davis with great reluctance, and under strong popular and political pressure. It was claimed that Johnston intended to surrender Atlanta without giving battle. General Bragg was therefore sent from Richmond to interview him, and after spending two days at Atlanta telegraphed: " He has not sought my advice, and it was not volunteered. I cannot learn that he has any more plan in the future than he has had in the past."

Mr. Davis then telegraphed Johnston a direct inquiry: " I wish to hear from you as to present situation, and your plan of operations, so specifically as will enable me to anticipate events."

This was sent on the 16 July, and Johnston replied the same day as follows:

. . . As the enemy has double our numbers, we must be on the defensive. My plan of operations must therefore depend upon that of the enemy. It is mainly to watch for an opportunity to fight to advantage. We are trying to put Atlanta into condition to be held for a day or two by the Georgia militia, that army movements may be freer and wider.

This reply was certainly not specific, and was considered evasive. On the 17th, Adjutant-General Cooper telegraphed Johnston:

I am directed by the Secretary of War to inform you that as you have failed to arrest the advance of the enemy to the vicinity of Atlanta, far in the interior of Georgia, and express no confidence that you can defeat or repel him, you are hereby relieved from the command of the Army and the Department of the Tennessee, which you will immediately turn over to General Hood.

To this Johnston replied that the order had been received and obeyed, and added:

As to the alleged cause of my removal, I assert that Sherman's army is much stronger, compared with that of Tennessee, than Grant's compared with that of Northern Virginia. Yet the enemy has been compelled to advance much more slowly to the vicinity of Atlanta than to that of Richmond and Petersburg, and penetrated much deeper into Virginia than into Georgia. Confident language by a military commander is not usually regarded as evidence of competence.

It must be admitted that there was much truth in his statement, but it did not go to the heart of the matter. Between Lee and his government there was always a perfect frankness and a cordial understanding; so that in case of misfortune it was felt that he had done the best he could under the circumstances. Johnston's advice to Hood showed that he only needed to be equally frank with the Richmond authorities. Had he been so, it is quite safe to say that he would not have been removed.[12]

The removal of General Johnston at this time has been generally condemned, and the result was certainly disastrous to the Confederate cause. A more favorable view of the action of President Davis, however, is expressed by General Cox. " It cannot be denied," he says, " that there was a certain justification for Mr. Davis's conclusion that the circumstances foreboded the yielding of Atlanta without the desperate struggle which the importance of the position demanded. Had Johnston expressed any hopefulness, or said, what was the fact, that he was himself coming to the determination to try the effect of a bold attack whilst Sherman's army was in motion, he would probably have been left in command.[13]

Loring had already been succeeded by A. P. Stewart in command of Polk's old corps, and Cheatham now took the place of Hood.

John B. Hood, a native of Kentucky, was just entering upon his thirty-fourth year. After graduating at West Point in 1853, in the same class with McPherson, Schofield, and Sheridan, he had seen active service fighting the Indians on the frontier, after which he was for some time a cavalry instructor at the Military Academy. He entered the Confederate army at the outbreak of the Civil War, and fought in most of the Virginia battles during the first two years. He was severely wounded at Gettysburg, losing the use of one arm. Going West with Longstreet, he fought bravely at Chickamauga, where he lost a leg. From Dalton to Atlanta he commanded a corps with the rank of lieutenant-general, and now, on his promotion to the command of the army, he received the provisional grade of a full general. In his *Memoirs*, General Sherman says that " Hood, though not deemed much of a scholar, or of great mental capacity, was undoubtedly a brave, determined, and rash man." [14]

On the evening of the 19 July, the Union right under

[12] For a full discussion of Mr. Davis's relations with Johnston, see 2 Davis, 547; also Johnston, 349–370; and Maurice, 73.

[13] 2 Cox, 272.

[14] 2 Sherman, 75.

Thomas, and the centre under Schofield, were in the act of crossing Peachtree Creek at two different points, while the left under McPherson was near Decatur. The flanks of the army were fully ten miles apart, and there was a wide interval between Thomas and Schofield.

Johnston had expected to attack Sherman's army while it was divided in crossing this difficult stream, and he magnanimously explained his plans to Hood. In reading his statement, one cannot help thinking how unfortunate for him it was that he did not state his plans to Mr. Davis as fully as he gave them to Hood!

Pursuant to this plan, on the afternoon of the 20th Hood attacked Thomas in flank, while Cheatham held off Schofield and McPherson. The Confederate movement was well concealed by the dense woods up to the moment of the onset; but the assault was repulsed by Thomas. This was the battle of Peachtree Creek.

On the 22d, the second part of Johnston's plan was tried. While Cheatham advanced from the Atlanta lines and resumed the assaults upon McPherson and Schofield, Hardee's corps made a long night march to a position south of Decatur, and fell upon McPherson's flank. A great battle was fought along a front of five miles, but the Confederates were repulsed at every point, and forced to retire within the defences of the city. The brave McPherson was killed on this day, and Howard succeeded him in command of the Army of the Tennessee.

On the 28th, as Howard was marching from the left wing to the right, to extend the Union lines southward on the west side of Atlanta, Hood fiercely attacked the Federal flank at Ezra Church, but was again repulsed.

In these three battles around Atlanta the Confederate losses were about 15,000, while the Federal casualities were only 6000.[15] It was only a week since Johnston had been relieved, and the Confederate troops were so discouraged that for the first time in the Civil War they refused to continue the assaults.[16] It was generally understood on both sides that a change of commanders meant the adoption of an aggressive policy on the part of the

[15] Livermore, 122–124.   [16] 2 Cox, 280.

Confederates, but no one expected that it would so soon result in the ruin of their cause. At the time of his succession to the command Hood claimed that his army numbered less than 50,000 effectives; thus, in less than ten days, his tactics had resulted in the loss of thirty per cent. of his command.

At this time there were several more changes in the general officers of both armies. On the 26 July, Stephen D. Lee succeeded Cheatham in command of Hood's old corps. Hooker, who ranked Howard, resigned in disgust when the latter was promoted to succeed McPherson; and Slocum was assigned to the Twentieth Corps. Palmer also, a little later, took offense at being ordered to serve under Schofield, whom he claimed to rank, and gave up the command of the Fourteenth Corps. He was succeeded by Jeff. C. Davis.

At the end of July, Sherman was awaiting the result of several attempts with his cavalry to cut Hood's communications. These operations all failed, and he states in his *Memoirs:* " I now became satisfied that . . . nothing would suffice but for us to reach it [the railroad below Atlanta] with the main army."

In furtherance of this plan, during the first three weeks of August the Union line was extended to the west and south of Atlanta. In the meantime Wheeler had raided the Union communications as far back as Dalton, and done considerable damage. Taking advantage of Wheeler's absence, Sherman sent Kilpatrick to try once more to cut Hood's communications. The Union cavalry made a complete circuit of Atlanta, took some prisoners, and destroyed a few miles of railway, but in a day or two the damage was all repaired. Sherman therefore returned to his plan of a movement with his whole army.

Accordingly, rations for fifteen days were issued to the army, and the movement began on the 25 August. On the 31st, Hardee, with about half the Confederate army, made a fierce attack on the Union lines, but was repulsed. The following day, Hood evacuated Atlanta, and concentrated his army at Lovejoy Station. Sherman then occupied the city, to rest and prepare for further operations.

Thomas was stationed at Atlanta, Howard at East Point, and Schofield at Decatur. The cavalry covered the flanks and rear from Roswell to Sandtown. The Atlanta campaign was at an end.

According to the return of his army for the 30 April 1864, on file in the War Department, General Johnston had " present for duty " about 53,000 men. Between that date and the 10 June he received reënforcements to the number of 32,000 men. His army reached its maximum strength at New Hope Church, where he had about 75,-000 troops in line. At that same time General Sherman's army numbered about 93,000 men of all arms. The odds against Johnston, therefore, were not so great as frequently stated.

The losses on both sides during the campaign were approximately: [17]

	Federals	Confederates
Killed	4,423	3,044
Wounded	22,822	18,952
Missing	4,442	12,983
Totals	31,687	34,979

" High as was the National estimate of the importance of Sherman's campaign," says General Cox, " Southern men rated it and its consequences quite as high as we did. . . . When the city fell, the whole South as well as the North knew that a decisive step had been taken toward the defeat of the rebellion." [18]

The campaign began on the 7 May, and ended with Hood's evacuation of Atlanta. In less than four months, almost entirely by skillful manœuvres, Sherman had forced the Confederate army back about ninety miles, and reached his goal. In the same length of time, Grant had forced Lee back from the Rapidan to the lines in front of Petersburg, but he did not capture Richmond until the following April. In both campaigns the opposing forces were practically the same — 100,000 Federals and 60,000

[17] 4 B. & L., 289, 292.   [18] 2 Cox, 291.

Confederates. The difference between Grant's tactics of "hammering," and Sherman's of manœuvring, is shown by the list of casualties — Grant had lost over 50,000 men, while Sherman had lost less than 30,000. Both campaigns were made in very difficult country.

Sherman's campaign has been highly praised by both American and European critics, and little fault can be found with his strategy. His greatest mistake was the unnecessary and costly assault of Kenesaw Mountain. His excuse was, that the army was tired of marching over the muddy roads, and wanted to fight. The assault was tactically well made, but the position proved too strong.

Sherman seems to have missed a good opportunity to strike the Confederate army a decisive blow during Hood's withdrawal from Atlanta, when he had to make a flank march by the heads of the three Union armies. Hood himself expressed surprise that he was allowed to do so unmolested.[19]

If Johnston had not been relieved of command he might have held Atlanta for as many months as Lee kept Grant at bay in front of Petersburg.[20] But Hood, both by his natural disposition and the force of circumstances, was committed from the first to an aggressive policy, which speedily proved ruinous. He blamed his failure in the attacks of the 20th and 22d to one of his corps commanders, General Hardee. But General Alexander states that it was due largely to his own neglect " to supervise the execution of important orders — a sort of failure from which even the most eminent commanders have *never* been exempt." [21]

As in many other campaigns, the use of the cavalry in " raids " proved an amusement that was very costly to both sides. General Cox well remarks that, " the game was never worth the candle." [22]

Both armies in this campaign made constant use of field-

---

[19] 4 *B. & L.*, 344.

[20] John Russell Young reports Grant as saying: " I never ranked Lee as high as some other generals of the Confederate Army. I was more afraid of Joe Johnston." — 2 *Around the World with General Grant*, 459.

[21] Alexander, 577.

[22] 2 Cox, 290.

works. " Except in attacking the Kenesaw Mountain,"
says Hamley, " the character of Sherman's operations was,
throughout, the same. To protect his main line from a
counter-attack, he left a force entrenched across it. He
then reënforced his flanking wing to a strength sufficient
to cope with the whole army of the enemy, and directed
it, by a circuit off the main line, upon the Confederate
rear. In every case the operation was successful, obliging
Johnston forthwith to abandon his strongest positions,
and to retreat." [23]

" No officer or soldier who ever served under me,"
writes General Sherman," will question the generalship of
Joseph E. Johnston. His retreats were timely, in good
order, and he left nothing behind." [24]

[23] Cited, Steele, 548.
[24] 4 B. & L., 253. See also Johnston, 462–464.

CHAPTER NINETEEN

SEPTEMBER 1864 — APRIL 1865

NASHVILLE

Hood Moves Against the Union Line of Communications — Sherman Follows — Hood's Plans — Thomas at Nashville — Hood Invades Tennessee — Schofield Retreats to Columbia — His Narrow Escape at Spring Hill — Battle of Franklin — The Confederates Repulsed — Their Heavy Losses — Reasons for Their Failure — Hood Follows the Federals to Nashville — Thomas's Plans — Anxiety at Washington — Grant's Orders — The Unfavorable Weather — The *Terrain* — Battle of the 15 December — The Confederate Line Broken — Hood Occupies a New Position — Absence of Forrest — The Second Day's Battle — A Decisive Union Victory — Hood Retreats to Tupelo, and Resigns His Command — Numbers and Losses — Comments — Sherman's March to the Sea — Johnston's Surrender

FOLLOWING the occupation of Atlanta, there were no further military operations for a period of several weeks. Logan and Blair went home to look after politics, and many of the regiments claimed the discharge to which they were entitled by reason of the expiration of their terms of service. The whole army, officers and men alike, seemed to relax more or less, and desire a rest after the fatigue of the four months' campaign.[1]

Although Sherman had attained his goal, in taking Atlanta, he " had not accomplished all, for Hood's army, the chief objective, had escaped." [2] The " real trouble " had only begun. The Confederate army, composed of veterans inured to war, and still 40,000 strong, was only thirty miles away, at Lovejoy Station, on the railroad to Savannah. On the 21 September, Hood shifted his position to Palmetto Station, twenty-five miles southwest of Atlanta, and began preparations for an active campaign

---

[1] 2 Sherman, 130.   [2] 4 B. & L., 254.

against Sherman's line of communications, to compel him to abandon Atlanta. At this time, Hood was visited by President Davis, who made his celebrated speech in which he predicted that his army would make Sherman's retreat more disastrous than that of Napoleon from Moscow. Forewarned, Sherman took immediate steps to thwart Hood's plans. Newton's division of the Fourth Corps, and Morgan's of the Fourteenth, were sent back to Tennessee; and Corse's division of the Seventeenth Corps was ordered to Rome. Thomas was despatched to his headquarters at Nashville, and Schofield to his at Knoxville, while Sherman remained at Atlanta to await Hood's next move. Orders were given the Union commanders at Nashville, Decatur, and Chattanooga to take active measures to protect the railway.[3]

At this time, Grant had Lee's army invested at Petersburg; Canby at New Orleans was preparing for an expedition against Mobile, in conjunction with Farragut's fleet; and a combined land and naval expedition was contemplated against Fort Fisher at the mouth of Cape Fear River, in North Carolina. On the 12 September, General Grant wrote that he was in doubt as to the best plan for the use of the forces under Sherman's command. On the 20th, Sherman replied: " I should keep Hood employed, and put my army in fine order for a march on Augusta, Columbia, and Charleston; and start as soon as Wilmington is sealed to commerce, and the city of Savannah is in our possession." [4]

At this stage of the correspondence, Hood simplified the situation by taking the offensive, and threatening Sherman's long line of communications. On the 5 October he attacked the Union base at Allatoona, but was repulsed with heavy loss. Leaving one corps under Slocum to defend Atlanta, Sherman at once moved against Hood. A week later, Sherman was at Rome, while the Confederates captured Dalton, with its garrison of 1000 men. On the 15th, Sherman was back at Snake Creek Gap, where he had begun his campaign in May, and Hood was a few

[3] 2 Sherman, 140–145; 4 *B. & L.*, 254.
[4] 2 Sherman, 115.

miles south of Lafayette. Here Hood intended to select a position, and give battle, but he was deterred by his corps-commanders who advised against it. Therefore, after resting two days at Cross Roads, he directed his march on Gadsden, where he concentrated his army on the 22 October.

In the meantime, General Beauregard had been placed in command of the Military Division of the West, which included Hood's army, and Cheatham had been assigned to the old corps of Hardee, whom Hood blamed for his defeats around Atlanta. Hood's far-reaching plans at this time, according to his own account, were to capture Nashville, and make it a base for a victorious campaign in Kentucky; then to move east, through some of the gaps in the Cumberland Mountains, and fall upon Grant's rear at Petersburg. After this, his army, combined with Lee's, might turn and rend Sherman, or march north and capture Washington.[5]

Sherman followed Hood as far as Gaylesville, where he halted to see what the Confederates would do next. After a short pause, Hood crossed the mountains to Decatur, which he avoided attacking, as it was well defended, and finally halted at Tuscumbia, opposite Florence, Alabama, on the Tennessee River.

Sherman then sent two of his six corps by rail to Thomas at Nashville, and began his preparations for the march to the coast. Repairing the broken railroads, he collected at Atlanta all the supplies necessary for his expedition. On the 4 November, he had assembled four infantry corps, one cavalry division, and 65 field-guns, an aggregate of about 60,000 men.[6]

While at Gadsden, Hood received a visit from Beauregard, to whom he unfolded his plan of campaign, which was formally approved. Beauregard stipulated, however, that Wheeler's cavalry should be detached, to hang on Sherman's rear, but promised to send an order to Forrest to join Hood's army as soon as it crossed the Tennessee. Hood was detained three weeks at Tuscumbia, waiting for supplies, and for Forrest to come up. The cavalry was

[5] See 4 B. & L., 426–427. [6] 4 B. & L., 255.

much impeded in its march by muddy roads and high water, and did not join Hood until the 18 November. This delay proved to be the salvation of Nashville.

Notwithstanding all the efforts of the Union authorities to reënforce Thomas, there were only about 30,000 Federal troops within the whole District, when Hood reached the Tennessee River, the last of October. The Union forces were scattered in detachments all the way from Chattanooga to the Ohio River, guarding the lines of communication. As the success of Sherman's movement was bound up with Thomas's ability to defeat Hood's plans, it would have been more prudent to send another corps to Nashville, and make the march to the sea with a smaller force.[7]

The forces which Sherman left behind for Thomas comprised the Fourth Corps under Stanley, the Twenty-third under Schofield, and about 5000 cavalry under General Wilson, whom Grant had sent West from the Army of the Potomac, with the message, " I believe he will add fifty per cent. to the effectiveness of your cavalry." [8]

Thomas's force, of 22,000 infantry and 5000 cavalry, was entirely inadequate to cope with Hood's veteran army of 35,000 infantry, and 5000 cavalry led by the redoubtable Forrest, whose maxim was that " success lies in getting there first with the most men." But Sherman had sent to Missouri for an additional corps of 14,000 men, commanded by General Andrew J. Smith, an able officer. It was hoped that Smith could leave St. Louis by the 10 November, but he was busy driving Sterling Price out of the state, and this caused a delay of two weeks. He did not reach St. Louis until the 24th, and it was the last day of the month when he finally joined Thomas at Nashville. At the same time some 5000 men, belonging to different organizations, who had been belated in rejoining, were sent from Chattanooga, and formed into a provisional division under General Steedman. Other reënforcements

[7] On this point, see the masterly article of Mr. Ropes, in *Papers of the Military Historical Society of Massachusetts*, X, 144.

[8] For the detailed story of General Wilson's operations in the West, see his very interesting narrative, *Under the Old Flag.*

from different points also joined about the first of December, so that on that date Thomas found himself at the head of a motley array of between 50,000 and 55,000 men.

Hood's long delay at Tuscumbia — an accident upon which no one could have calculated — gave time for Thomas to concentrate his army, and saved the situation. This would seem to prove that Sherman was unwarranted in taking so large a part of his army for his " military promenade," and leaving so slender a force to oppose Hood. Everything finally turned out all right, but Thomas had an anxious four weeks at Nashville after Sherman cut loose from Atlanta.

Having finally obtained his supplies, and been joined by, the larger part of his cavalry, on the 19 November Hood crossed the river at Florence and began his northward march. Thomas was at Nashville, occupied with hurrying up his reënforcements, and the main body of the Union army, the Fourth and Twenty-third corps, was at Pulaski, under the command of Schofield.

Hood's army marched in three columns, Stewart's corps by the Lawrenceburg road, Cheatham's by the Waynesboro road, and Lee's by an intermediate road. Hood hoped to outflank Schofield's position at Pulaski, and cut off his retreat by seizing the bridge across Duck River at Columbia.

On the 22d, Stewart was at Lawrenceburg, sixteen miles west of Pulaski. Schofield now realized that he had no time to lose, and at once set his troops in motion. By a forced march he reached Columbia just in time to prevent Forrest from seizing the bridge, and cutting off his line of retreat. As fast as the troops arrived they were ordered to throw up earthworks to cover the approaches to the town from the south; the trains were sent across the river. There was a terrible storm of rain, turning to sleet and snow, and the roads were in such condition that Hood's army could make no more than ten miles a day. The last of his forces, therefore, did not arrive in front of Columbia until the 26th.

At Columbia, Schofield was joined by, one brigade of

infantry, and Wilson came forward from Nashville and took command of the cavalry, which had now been strengthened to 7000 horsemen. Wilson placed his force along the north bank of the river to observe the enemy's movements either to the right or the left.

As Thomas was anxious to preserve the railway bridge at Columbia for further use, he urged Schofield to hold his ground there. But Schofield became convinced that Hood intended to cross the river above the town and turn his position, so he withdrew his army to the north bank on the night of the 27th. The following night Forrest's cavalry forded the river; and early on the morning of the 29th, the corps of Cheatham and Stewart crossed by a pontoon-bridge three miles above the town, and marched to Spring Hill on the Franklin Pike, twelve miles in Schofield's rear. Lee's corps was left behind, with orders to make a strong demonstration in front of the Union position.

Information of these movements reached Schofield the morning of the 29th, and he immediately started Stanley for Spring Hill with two of his divisions, the trains and reserve artillery. When Hood's force of about 18,000 men reached Spring Hill at 3 P.M., the place was held only by one Union division, 4000 strong. Hood took Cheatham, with Cleburne, one of his division commanders, within sight of the pike, along which the enemy could now be seen retreating at double-quick, with wagons in a trot, and gave orders to attack at once and seize the pike. Similar orders were given to Stewart, and further commands were sent later by staff-officers. But no attack was made, and the Confederate troops bivouacked within gunshot of the pike, without making any effort to occupy it. After nightfall the Federal infantry all passed by, unmolested except for some random shots to which they made no reply.[9]

This failure to destroy the Union army has never been satisfactorily explained. In his book, Hood calls the opportunity "the best move in my career as a soldier." Nevertheless, as General Alexander says, it proved the

[9] Alexander, 578–579.

death-blow to Hood's army. " A single Confederate brigade . . . planted squarely across the pike, either north or south of Spring Hill, would have effectually prevented Schofield's retreat, and daylight would have found his whole force cut off from every avenue of escape by more than twice its numbers, to assault whom would have been madness, and to avoid whom would have been impossible." [10] General Alexander states that Cheatham and Stewart were both absent from their troops that evening, and the former subsequently frankly admitted his delinquency. In view of the distinguished records of the two officers, Hood magnanimously overlooked their failure.

Schofield had realized his dangerous position, and fully expected to find his route blocked, at least at Thompson's Station, three miles north of Spring Hill. He hoped that the corps of A. J. Smith might have reached Franklin, and despatched one of his staff-officers to hurry it forward. He also telegraphed General Thomas that he regarded his situation as extremely perilous. But he found the way clear, and his army reached Franklin without being seriously molested.

The river there was unfordable after the recent rains; the old wagon bridge was in bad condition, and the pontoon-train had been destroyed at Columbia, to prevent it from falling into the hands of the Confederates. As soon as Schofield arrived, therefore, his first care was to repair the wagon bridge, and plank the railway bridge. By noon this work was completed. In the meantime preparations were made to hold the south side of the river until the trains could be got across.

The little town of Franklin was located on the southern bank of the Harpeth River in a bend less than a mile across at its widest part. As fast as the troops came up, they entrenched a line upon rising ground, convex in shape, with both flanks resting upon the river, and completely covering the town.

The two main highways left the town by the same street, but forked at the southern edge, the Columbia Pike running south, and Carter's Creek Pike southwest. The

---

[10] Colonel Stone, of Thomas's staff, in 4 *B. & L.*, 446.

railway ran near the river, parallel to the road to Columbia. Just south of the town, and a quarter of a mile west of the river, the Carter house stood upon a low hill. To the east of the town, on the other side of the river, there was an earthwork, Fort Granger, where Federal batteries were placed, which commanded the open ground to the south and west.

The entire line of entrenchments was about a mile and a half long. The space between the river and the Columbia Pike, near the Carter house, was held by Cox's division; Ruger's division was between the two pikes; and Kimball's division carried the line to the river on the right. Wood was sent across to the north bank to protect the trains, and Wilson's cavalry was also on that side to guard against any turning movement of the enemy.

The Federal position was very strong, but it had one weak point which nearly proved fatal. On the arrival of Wagner's division of the Fourth Corps, which had served as rear-guard, the first brigade (Opdycke) took position within the lines, just west of the Columbia Pike, as a reserve; but the two other brigades (Lane and Conrad) made a halt on a knoll 500 yards in front of the lines. They were not entrenched, as there was no intention to have them remain in this position. Wagner had been ordered to occupy the point " in observation only till Hood should show a disposition to advance in force, and then to retire within the lines to Opdycke's position to act as a general reserve."

The head of Hood's column arrived between two and three o'clock on the afternoon of the 30th. Stewart's corps deployed to the east of the Columbia Pike, and Cheatham's to the west, with Cleburne's division on the right, partly astride the pike, Brown's next, and Bate's on the extreme left. Only Johnson's division of Lee's corps had come up, and it was held in reserve.

The impetuous Hood, anxious to make up for the opportunity that he had lost the previous night, ordered Cheatham to attack at once. The two divisions of Cleburne and Brown, charging at double-quick, fell like an avalanche upon Wagner's two brigades in their isolated position, and drove the men back in headlong flight. The Federal troops in the main line were obliged to withhold their fire in order to avoid killing their comrades, and the Confederates swept over the Union entrenchments on the heels of the fugitives. Over a thousand prisoners were taken, and a wide rent was made in the very centre of the Union line of battle.

For a moment it looked as though the day were lost, but Opdycke hurried up his brigade from its position in reserve, and he was supported by two regiments of Cox's division. In the hand-to-hand struggle which ensued the Confederates were finally driven out of the works. Just before nightfall Johnson's division went to Cheatham's support, but the Union line held fast. Simultaneous attacks were made by Stewart on the right, and Bate on the opposite flank, but no impression was made on the Federal lines. Though many of the Confederates succeeded in reaching the ditches, none crossed the parapets.

Franklin was one of the most fiercely fought battles of the Civil War, and the Confederates " went down to defeat in a blaze of glory." Over 10 per cent. of the force engaged were killed on the field, over 20 per cent. were severely wounded, and as many more were slightly wounded or captured. Their loss of general officers was unparalleled on either side in any action of the war: five were killed, five were wounded, and one was captured. Of the regimental commanders, fifty-three were killed, wounded, or captured.[11] Among the slain was Patrick Cleburne, the most brilliant Confederate division-commander in the West. He began his military career as corporal in the 41st Foot, and he himself attributed his rapid rise to the habits of efficiency he had acquired in the ranks of his old regiments in the British army.[12]

General Alexander attributes the Confederate failure to three causes: —

[11] Alexander, 579–580. Livermore (131) estimates the number of Confederates engaged at 22,000, and their losses at 5550.
[12] Henderson, *Science of War*, 239.

(1) Hood did not prepare his assault with any severe cannonade, because the village of Franklin was just in the rear of the Union line.

(2) The action did not begin until 4 P.M.; the sun set at 4:50, and there was no moon. Darkness therefore prevented Hood from getting in two of Lee's divisions.

(3) The presence on the field of Casement's Federal brigade with magazine breech-loaders, which did terrible execution.

The battle continued with violence until 9 P.M., and firing was kept up until 3 A.M., when the Federals withdrew from the field, leaving their dead and wounded.[13]

During the night the Union army continued its retreat to Nashville, taking with it the wagon-trains, more than 1000 prisoners, and 33 flags captured from the enemy.[14]

The forces of Schofield reached Nashville on the morning of the first of December, and took their place in the works. Wilson's cavalry, which had covered the flanks and rear of the retreating army, was sent to Edgefield on the north bank of the Cumberland.

Hood followed, and arrived the next day. He immediately took position in front of the Union works, and threw up entrenchments. Lee's corps occupied the centre of the line, astride the road to Franklin; Cheatham's the right, and Stewart's the left. Most of the Confederate cavalry was stationed on the left, between Stewart and the river. Hood's army was now reduced to about 25,000 men,[15] and he did not feel strong enough to assault the Union works. He hoped that Thomas would attack, and meet with a bloody repulse.

By this time, A. J. Smith's veteran Sixteenth Corps, 12,000 strong, had reached Nashville, and other reënforcements had brought Thomas's army up to about 55,000, including 12,000 cavalry.

The Union works ran on a line of hills around Nash-

---

[13] Alexander, 580. Livermore (131) puts the Union losses at 2300 out of 21,000 engaged.

[14] Fiske, 343.

[15] Livermore (133) estimates his effectives at only 23,000.

ville, extending from the river above to the river below the city. Steedman's division was on the left; next, the Twenty-third Corps under Schofield; then the Fourth Corps, now commanded by Wood,[16] and Smith's troops on the right.

Having finally, assembled an army, of good, though rather mixed elements, Thomas did not propose to fight an indecisive battle, like Shiloh or Gettysburg. He meant to make his victory a Waterloo, which should wipe the defeated army out of existence. He had a large force of cavalry, under a very able commander, and he intended to have it play an important part in the coming contest. He therefore proposed to give Wilson time to procure horses to replace the large number worn out during the campaign. He also needed time to prepare his trains and pontoons for a vigorous pursuit after the battle.

As usual, Mr. Stanton became impatient at once, and telegraphed General Grant that Thomas's course looked like " the McClellan and Rosecrans strategy of doing nothing." With Grant's own large experience of unavoidable delays, one would suppose that he would have shown a better appreciation of the situation, but he began bombarding Thomas with despatch after despatch, in which he displayed unusual anxiety and some irritation. On the 6th, he ordered Thomas to " attack Hood at once." But, in spite of this order, Thomas decided to give Wilson two days more.

On the 8 December, Thomas was entirely ready. Then there came a storm of sleet and snow which covered the ground with a sheet of ice, and made any movement impossible for several days. At last, on the 14th, a warm rain cleared the ice away, and orders were issued for an attack the next day.

In the meantime, Grant had prepared an order, which was never sent, appointing Schofield in place of Thomas; and on the 13th he directed Logan, who was still absent from his corps, to proceed to Nashville, and relieve Thomas. On the 15th, Grant himself reached Washing-

16 Stanley had been severely wounded at Franklin.

ton on his way to Nashville. Here he received news which satisfied him that neither he nor Logan was needed at Nashville.[17]

Nearly the entire space occupied by the Union army was inclosed by two small streams, Richland and Brown's creeks, rising near each other in the high Brentwood Hills, four or five miles south of Nashville, and flowing in divergent courses to the Cumberland. The Granny White Turnpike ran southward on the high ridge between the two creeks, and eight other pikes radiated southward from the city. The ground was broken and hilly, with knolls and ridges rising 200 to 300 feet above the river; but it was mostly open, with timber here and there.

Hood's main line, which was more than five miles long, stretched along a series of hills from the Chattanooga Railroad on the east to the Franklin Pike; thence it crossed the valley of Brown's Creek, passed over the ridge on which ran the Granny White Pike, and reached a high knoll near the Hillsboro Pike, where it made a sharp turn to the south, following a stone wall along the pike for about 1000 yards. In advance of the main line, a body of skirmishers was strongly posted on Montgomery Hill, at the Hillsboro Pike.[18]

Strong batteries were placed on three commanding points, and redoubts crowned two detached hills about a mile to the southwest, beyond a fork of Richland Creek. Hood's position was strong, but the line was too long to hold securely with his forces. The concave form was also an element of weakness.

Thomas's plan of battle was for Smith and Wood, supported by Wilson's cavalry on their right flank, to make the main attack on Hood's left wing. At the same time, Steedman was to make a vigorous demonstration against Cheatham, on the Confederate right. Schofield was to be kept in reserve.

The movement began at dawn on the 15 December. The early morning was foggy, but a hot sun burned off

[17] Grant's account of this affair in his *Memoirs* is not creditable to the writer: he displays a jealousy of Thomas, hard to understand.
[18] Cox, *Campaigns*, 110.

the mists before nine o'clock. The mud resulting from the thaw made the operations very slow. Wood's corps marched by the right flank until its left rested on the salient at Laurens Hill, which was the pivot upon which Wood and Smith were to wheel to the left. Smith formed on Wood's right, and Wilson's cavalry moved out to clear the Charlotte and Harden pikes of the enemy on the right.

Smith's corps and the cavalry advanced steadily, capturing the Confederate detached works one after another, until by noon they were well up to Hood's main line on the Hillsboro Pike. Wilson was then ordered to make a circuit to the right, with a view of gaining the Confederate rear, and Schofield was sent forward to take his place on Smith's right.

In the meantime, at eight o'clock, Steedman had advanced along the Murfreesboro Pike, and vigorously attacked Cheatham on the Confederate right. This demonstration not only occupied Cheatham all day, but it also neutralized Lee's corps and made it useless. Lee did not dare to send assistance either to Cheatham on his right, or Stewart on his left, for fear that the Federals would charge straight down the Franklin Pike and pierce the thin Confederate centre.

In the afternoon, Smith continued his advance against the Confederate left, and drove away the defenders behind the stone wall on the Hillsboro Pike. A division of the Fourth Corps had already taken the strong Confederate outpost position on Montgomery Hill, and Thomas now ordered Wood to carry the salient on the hill in front of his line. This was done in brilliant fashion, and the whole Confederate left was now shattered and falling back. The broken line did not rally until it had withdrawn behind the Granny White Pike. Here darkness ended the fighting.

After nightfall, Hood formed a new line about two miles farther south, and entrenched it. He also changed the arrangement of his corps: Cheatham was moved over to the left flank, Stewart was placed in the centre, and Lee, who had taken little part in the action, was stationed on the right. The line, which was about two miles long, covered the two main roads to the south. The right rested on Overton Hill, just east of the Franklin Pike; the left, on two hills west of the Granny White Pike; the centre was on lower ground which was broken by several branches of Brown's Creek. The cavalry, under Chalmers, was on the extreme left of the new line.

Forrest's cavalry, except Chalmers's division, was absent during the battle. A detachment of some 8000 Federals had been stationed at Murfreesboro to guard the Nashville and Chattanooga Railroad. On the 2 December Hood sent Bate's division, reënforced by two infantry brigades, to coöperate with Forrest in a raid against the railway and Rousseau's command at Murfreesboro. The expedition was successful in capturing a railway train and destroying several bridges and blockhouses, but Bate was defeated by Rousseau, and then recalled. The absence of Forrest, as General Cox states, " made the opportunity which resulted so gloriously for our arms." [19]

On the morning of the 16th, the Federals advanced against the new Confederate line. The alignment was practically the same as on the previous day: Steedman on the extreme left; Wood next; then Smith and Schofield, with Wilson's cavalry on the extreme right.

After a preliminary reconnaissance in force, to feel out the Confederate line, soon after noon Wood's corps, supported by Steedman's division, assaulted the right of the enemy's position, but was repulsed with severe loss. Meanwhile Wilson's cavalry had reached a position in the rear of the Confederate left. About four o'clock Schofield and Smith attacked this part of the line in front and flank, while Wilson's dismounted troopers assailed it from the rear. Under the fire of artillery, which prevented the Confederates from raising their heads above the breastworks, the Federals made a sudden and gallant charge up to and over the entrenchments. The line, thus pierced, gave way, and soon afterward broke at all points. General Hood says: " I beheld for the first and only time a Confederate army abandon the field in confusion." All hope of rallying the troops proved vain.[20]

[19] Cox, *Campaigns*, 135.   [20] 4 *B. & L.*, 437.

Wilson's dismounted men, when the break came, were widely separated from their horses. This delayed their pursuit, which was also impeded by a drenching rain which set in after nightfall. Two miles from the battle-field they found Chalmers's cavalry division strongly posted across the Granny White Pike behind a barricade of fence-rails. This checked the Federal cavalry long enough to enable the fleeing Confederate infantry to pass the danger point, organize a rear-guard, and make good their escape the next day.[21]

On the morning of the 17th, Smith and Schofield were ordered to follow Wilson along the Granny White Pike, while Wood's corps pursued the mass of the fugitives, who took the Franklin Pike. The cavalry caught up with Hood's rear-guard four miles north of Franklin, and captured 400 prisoners. Forrest rejoined the army at Columbia, and covered the retreat to the Tennessee River. There the pursuit was abandoned. On the 10 January 1865, the remnant of the Confederate army was at Tupelo, Mississippi. Three days later, Hood asked to be relieved from his command.[22]

It is difficult to give an exact statement of the numbers and losses during the Nashville Campaign. At Franklin, Schofield had about 30,000 men of all arms; and at Nashville, Thomas had some 55,000. The Union losses at Franklin are reported as 2326, and at Nashville, as 3057, or less than 6000 for the whole campaign.

At the end of the Atlanta Campaign, Hood had about 35,000 infantry, and he was joined at Tuscumbia by Forrest with perhaps 5000 horsemen. He states that he lost 7500 men at Franklin, and that his effective strength at Nashville was only 23,000. As he had sent Forrest, with part of his cavalry, and Bate, with his division, reënforced by two infantry brigades, or an expedition against Murfreesboro, this estimate is probably correct. Van Horne puts his losses at Franklin at 5252, Livermore at 6252, and Alexander at 7550. Hood made no estimate of his losses at Nashville, except to state that they were " very

21 4 B. & L., 469.   22 4 B. & L., 437.

small." Thomas reported 4462 prisoners, and Hood puts his " missing " at about 4500. At Tupelo, after the campaign, the Confederate army was reduced to about 18,000 men of all arms.[23]

At Nashville, the Confederate army in the West was virtually annihilated. It was the most decisive victory gained by either side during the Civil War, and one of the most brilliant.[24]

The campaign of Franklin and Nashville is one of the most interesting and instructive of the war. Hood's operations during the first month, from the time he left Lovejoy on the 20 September until he arrived at Gadsden, were bold in conception and brilliant in execution. He drew Sherman with his army all the way back to Resaca, seventy miles, and from there to Gaylesville, over forty miles farther, and away from his line of communications. At this point, however, Sherman occupied a very, strong strategic position, which left no course open to Hood except to cross the Tennessee at a point beyond Sherman's reach, and move northward. This is precisely what Hood did.[25]

Major Steele thinks that General Thomas ought to have stopped Hood's army south of Duck River, and General Cox says that Thomas's right policy was to concentrate all his available forces promptly and meet Hood as near the Tennessee River as practicable.[26] But with all deference to these authorities, it is doubtful whether the final outcome of the campaign would have been so decisive if Thomas had advanced from Nashville.

Hood really lost the campaign through his stay of three weeks at Florence, while awaiting his supplies and the arrival of Forrest. This gave time for Sherman to transfer the Fourth and Twenty-third corps from Georgia to Tennessee; for Smith to bring the Sixteenth Corps from Missouri; for Thomas to concentrate the scattered Fed-

[23] *Cf.* Alexander; Livermore; Van Horne; 4 *B. & L.*; 93 O. R., 40; 94 O. R., 699.
[24] Fiske, 359.
[25] Steele, 577.
[26] *Cf.* Steele, 578, and Cox, 132.

eral detachments; and finally, for Wilson to mount his cavalry. Up to about the 10 November, Stanley's corps and a few regiments of cavalry were the only Union troops between Hood's army and Nashville.

Hood's delay at Florence, however, came near turning out a strategic advantage for him, as it afforded an opportunity of outflanking Schofield at Pulaski. Later, at Spring Hill, he failed to cut off and destroy the Union army only through the negligence of two of his corps commanders, which has never been satisfactorily explained. With victory almost in his grasp, like Hooker at Chancellorsville, Hood let the opportunity slip away. Although Cheatham was primarily to blame, Hood was on the ground, and cannot shift the responsibility.

After his failure at Franklin, Hood's advance to Nashville was a great mistake: it simply invited disaster. His final blunder was sending Forrest on a raid toward Murfreesboro. The absence of the bulk of the Confederate horsemen made possible the turning movement of the Federals which gained the victory on the second day. It was only one more instance of the general misuse of the cavalry during the Civil War.

Although Thomas was very slow in getting ready to attack Hood, his final operations were nearly perfect in plan and execution. His cavalry did more actual fighting than was done on any other battle-field of the Civil War, but it fought dismounted. " Considering the disorder and rout in which Hood's beaten army quitted the battle-field," says Major Steele, " it might seem that they ought to have been cut off and blocked by Wilson's horsemen, 12,000 strong, and captured or destroyed by the pursuing infantry. But the earthen by-roads over which the cavalry had to march were in such deplorable condition, the streams with their bridges destroyed were so high, and forage for animals was so scarce in the country, that Wilson, in spite of great exertion, was unable to check the fugitive column before it was safe across the Tennessee River." [27]

* * * * * * * * * * *

[27] Steele, 585. See also 4 *B. & L.*, 470–471; 2 Cox, *Reminiscences*, 371.

On the 2 November Sherman finally secured Grant's permission to undertake the " March to the Sea," on the understanding that Thomas was to be left strong enough to deal with Hood. Sherman began his preparations by burning every building in Atlanta — " not a single one was spared, not even a church." This was excused on the ground that " War is Hell." As General Alexander tersely remarks: " It depends somewhat upon the warrior. The conduct of Lee's army in Pennsylvania presents a pleasing contrast." [28]

On the 15th Sherman started, taking with him four infantry corps, 63,000 strong, besides 5000 cavalry under Kilpatrick. The wagon-trains carried rations for twenty days, but he proposed to have his army live largely off the country. The Confederate authorities had hoped that the Georgia militia, aided by the few troops which could be gathered in the state, and by thirteen brigades of cavalry under Wheeler, might impede the march, but such expectations proved vain.

The march is notable mainly as an example of an army's cutting loose from its base and communications. The main purpose was to destroy the resources of the Confederacy, and this was done over a wide area. " There is no question," says General Alexander, " that the moral effect of this march, upon the country at large, both at the North and at the South, and also upon foreign nations, was greater than would have been the most decided victory." [29]

The march through Georgia met with no serious opposition. On the 10 December, Sherman was in front of the works about Savannah; on the 20th, Hardee evacuated the city, and withdrew to Charleston with the garrison of 18,000 men. On the 23d, Sherman occupied the place,

[28] Alexander, 581. Lee's orders, when he invaded the North, were to spare private property. " The strictness of his orders in regard to pillage during his invasions of the North is well known; but they were not only strict in form, they were carried out in fact, as is proved by the testimony of his enemies, to the lasting glory of both army and commander. Violation of these orders provoked Lee's wrath more than anything except brutality, and when he himself detected one soldier in theft, he ordered him shot at once." (*Atlantic Monthly*, July, 1911, page 85 — " Lee and his Army.")

[29] Alexander, 581.

and sent President Lincoln a telegram stating that he made Uncle Sam a Christmas present of the city, with 150 heavy guns, and 25,000 bales of cotton.

From this point began the far more arduous march northward through the Carolinas. Fort Fisher was captured by General Terry about the middle of January 1865, and toward the end of that month Sherman started by way of Columbia, South Carolina, to join General Grant in front of Petersburg.

In February the Confederate Government made Lee general-in-chief, and he appointed Johnston to the command of such forces as could be assembled to oppose Sherman. Only about 30,000 men could be found to contend against the Union army of 90,000 veterans.

There was an action at Averysboro on the 16 March, and engagements from the 19th to the 21st at Bentonville. The Confederates were defeated at both places. Sherman then concentrated his army at Goldsboro for a further movement to the north.

On the 14 April, near Raleigh, North Carolina, General Sherman received from General Johnston a message requesting a cessation of hostilities with a view of negotiating terms of surrender. Arrangements were at once made for a personal interview on the 17th. As Sherman was starting for the meeting, he received a despatch from Secretary Stanton, announcing the assassination of President Lincoln by John Wilkes Booth at Ford's Theatre in Washington on the night of Friday, the 14th. After an interview with Johnston, another meeting was arranged for the following day, the 18 April, when a conditional treaty was signed, subject to the ratification of President Johnson. The terms were not approved by the President, as they covered matters of a political nature, and on the 26 April General Johnston surrendered his army upon the same terms that General Lee had received. There was never the slightest justification for the criticisms showered upon Sherman for his course in this matter.[30]

[30] See 4 *B. & L.*, 755–757; also Johnston, 401–420.

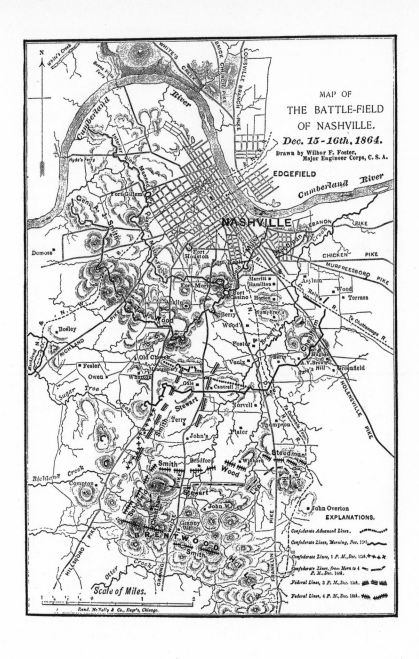

MAP OF
THE BATTLE-FIELD
OF NASHVILLE,
Dec. 15-16th, 1864.

Drawn by Wilbur F. Foster,
Major Engineer Corps, C. S. A.

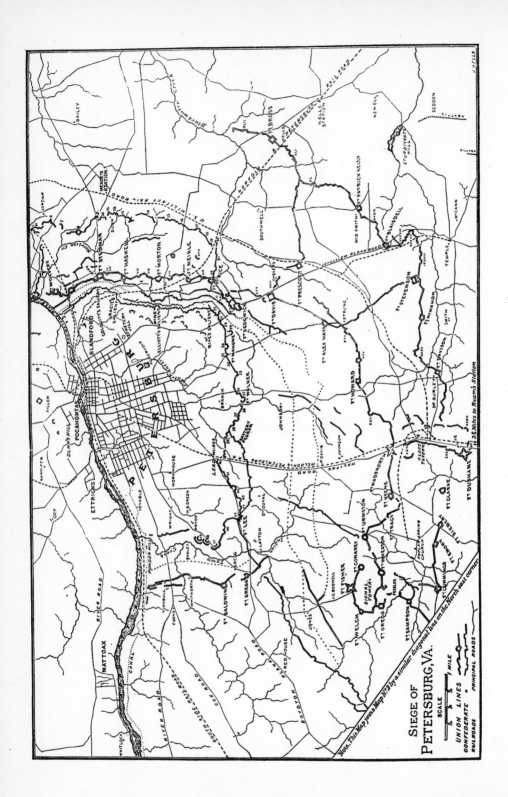

SIEGE OF
PETERSBURG, VA.

CHAPTER TWENTY

JUNE 1864 — APRIL 1865

PETERSBURG

Depression at the North — Grant Decides to Cross the James — Success of the Operation — Difficulty of the Task — Beauregard's Defence of Petersburg — Lee Finally Moves — The Trevilian Raid — Early Threatens Washington — Sheridan in the Shenandoah — The Petersburg Mine — Its Failure — Grant's Operations — The Attack on Fort Stedman — Grant Moves to the Left — Five Forks — Lee Abandons Richmond — Grant's Pursuit — His Correspondence with Lee — The Surrender at Appomattox — Lee's Remarkable Record — Numbers and Losses — Final Meeting of Grant and Lee — Comments — Grant's Fine Strategy — Hancock's Delay on the 15 June — Reasons for the Length of the Siege

A T no other period during the Civil War was there such depression in all circles throughout the North as after Grant's bloody repulse at Cold Harbor. The expenses of the war were nearly four million dollars a day. Gold was at a high premium and advancing rapidly: it went from 168 in May 1864 to 285 in July. The terrible casualty lists of the Wilderness Campaign had brought mourning to every hamlet in the country. Although stimulated by enormous bounties, enlistment had almost ceased. It was under these circumstances that Grant, after a week of indecision, decided to transfer his army to the south side of the James, and thence move directly upon Petersburg. It was the supreme Crisis of the War![1]

Grant's movement, says General Alexander, " involved the performance of a feat in transportation which had never been equalled, and might well be considered impossible, without days of delay." [2] His object was to capture Petersburg, then to turn Beauregard's entrenchments in front of Butler at Bermuda Hundred, and move on

[1] See Alexander, 545–546.   [2] *Ibid.*, 547.

[403]

Richmond. The capture of Petersburg would cut off Lee's lines of supply by the Weldon and the Southside (Lynchburg) railways, and would leave no unbroken line entering the capital except the Richmond and Danville. This road Grant purposed seizing later, thus compelling Lee to abandon Richmond and retreat toward Danville or Lynchburg to avoid investment.

Grant's movement was accomplished without mishap, and in such incredibly short time that Lee for three days refused to believe it. During this period, from the 15 to the 17 June, Grant's whole army crossed the James, and assaulted Petersburg, which at first was defended only by Beauregard with 2500 men. In the meantime, Lee, with the corps of Longstreet and Hill, lay idle in the woods on the north side of the James.

On Saturday, 11 June, the Fifth Corps (Warren) was moved down the Chickahominy about ten miles, to the vicinity of Bottom's Bridge. The next night it crossed on two pontoon bridges, and took position east of Riddle's Shop, where it entrenched to cover the passage of the other corps. The Second Corps (Hancock) crossed on the same bridge; the Sixth (Wright) and the Ninth (Burnside), at Jones's Bridge; and all marched to Wilcox's Landing on the James. The Eighteenth Corps (Smith) was sent back to White House, where it took transports for City Point, and was landed there the night of the 14th. Here it was joined by Kautz's cavalry, 2400 strong, and Hink's colored division, 3700, making in all about 16,000 men. This force was ordered to move at dawn on the 15th, and attack Petersburg, which was only eight miles distant. Here we shall leave them for the moment.

Hancock reached the James on the night of the 13th, and the three other corps during the course of the following day. Pending the construction of the bridge, on the 14th Hancock's corps was ferried across the river by the transports which had brought Smith to City Point. By the morning of the 15th the whole corps was across, and at 10:30 set out for Petersburg to join Smith, who had marched at sunrise. Hancock had 20,000 men, and only sixteen miles to go. All the complicated details of this movement had been thought out with remarkable care, and fully covered in the orders and instructions — *with a single exception,* and this oversight postponed the fall of Petersburg for over nine months!

The whole trouble came from the supposed " political necessity " of keeping Butler in command of the Army of the James. As Smith's corps was a part of that army, it was necessary to have his orders issued from headquarters, and on the 14th Grant visited Butler for that purpose. On his return Grant neglected to notify Meade of the details of the orders to Smith, and Meade, of course, could not inform Hancock. It thus resulted that Hancock did not march until 10:30, when he could just as well have started five hours earlier, and, furthermore, he was not directed by the shortest route. He therefore arrived in front of Petersburg after dark — too late to assist in Smith's attack.

Meanwhile the three other corps of the Army of the Potomac awaited on the north side of the James the construction of the " greatest bridge which the world has seen since the days of Xerxes." [3] At the point selected, the river was 700 yards wide, ninety feet deep, and had a rise and fall of tide of four feet, causing very strong currents. The construction was begun simultaneously at both ends at four o'clock on the afternoon of the 14 June, and finished at midnight. The artillery and trains immediately began to cross, and the Ninth, Fifth, and Sixth corps followed in the order named. At midnight of the 16th, Grant's entire army was south of the James. Considering the size of the river, it was as great a feat as Napoleon's passage of the Danube in the face of the enemy with his army of 150,000 men in July 1809.

To return now to Smith's column of 16,000 men, which began its march on Petersburg at sunrise on the 15 June. Beauregard, who was in command there, to gain time, sent forward a battery, and a regiment of cavalry, which delayed the march of the Federals for about three hours. But about nine o'clock the head of Smith's column came in sight of the Confederate works. The lines of Peters-

[3] Alexander, 549.

burg, then some ten miles in length, encircled the city, about two miles out, from the river above to the river below. The entrenchments consisted only of a small outside ditch and a parapet, with platforms and embrasures for guns at suitable intervals. There were no obstructions in front, but the forest had been felled within the zone of fire.[4]

Beauregard had a good supply of guns and ammunition, which he used freely, to delay the placing of the Federal batteries and the deployment of their troops. Smith took time for a long and careful reconnaissance of the Confederate position, which convinced him that the entrenchments were held only by a very thin line of infantry. He therefore decided to attack, not with a column, but with clouds of skirmishers. It was now five o'clock, and another hour was taken to form the troops. When all was ready, it was found that the artillery horses had been sent to water, and it took another hour to get them back. That hour saved Petersburg. " By such small and accidental happenings does Fate decide battles! "[5]

At seven o'clock, the Union guns opened fire, and the cloud of skirmishers advanced to the attack. They carried about a mile and a half of the entrenchments, capturing twenty guns, and taking many prisoners. About nine o'clock Hancock came up with his corps, and relieved Smith's troops. Smith had heard of the arrival of Confederate reënforcements, and he thought it wiser to hold what he had gained, rather than to venture more and risk disaster.

During the night, Beauregard's engineer laid out, and began work on, a better located permanent line about a half-mile in the rear. At the same time, he was reënforced by the arrival of Hoke's division from Drewry's Bluff, and by part of Johnson's division, which gave him in the morning about 14,000 infantry. Before the arrival of these troops the whole force at Petersburg consisted of one brigade of infantry, not more than 1200 strong; two small regiments of cavalry, and a few artillery men.[6]

[4] Alexander, 552.　　　[6] 2 Roman's *Beauregard*, 229.
[5] Alexander, 553.

On the 16th, the Ninth Corps arrived, and Hancock, who was now in command, had about 48,000 men. He attacked each flank of the broken Confederate line, and during the day succeeded in capturing one redan on the left, and three on the right.

On the 17th, the fighting began at 3 A.M. and was continued until 11 P.M. The first attack, made by Potter's division of the Ninth Corps, was a complete surprise to the exhausted Confederates. Another redan was captured, with four guns, and 600 prisoners; but no advantage was gained elsewhere. In a final assault, late in the afternoon, the Federals obtained temporary possession of one more redan, but were driven out, with the loss of over 1000 prisoners. After the fighting ceased, the Confederate troops were withdrawn to the new line which had been prepared.

At 4 A.M. on the 18th, a general assault was made by the Second, Fifth, and Ninth corps, with the Sixth and Eighteenth in reserve. Information had been obtained from the prisoners and a few deserters that the Confederate lines were held by a very slim force, and the corps commanders were ordered to press the attack. The whole Union army was now at hand, and no further Confederate reënforcements had arrived, but practically nothing was accomplished during the whole day. This, as General Alexander remarks, " is striking evidence of the condition to which the Federal army had now been reduced." [7]

General Lee did not discover until the morning of the 13th that the enemy was gone, and then, for several days, he was completely deceived regarding Grant's plans. Thinking that it was Grant's intention to advance on the north side of the James, so as to draw nearer to Butler, he moved his army across the Chickahominy and took position between White Oak Swamp and Malvern Hill. Hoke's division alone went on to Drewry's Bluff, and later was sent to Petersburg, as we have seen. No other change was made in Lee's position until the morning of the 16th, when Pickett's and Field's divisions of Longstreet's corps were sent to the lines at Bermuda Hundred to take the

[7] Alexander, 555.

place of Johnson's division, withdrawn by Beauregard the night of the 15th for the defence of Petersburg. Kershaw's division followed only as far as Drewry's Bluff, and was halted there.

Meanwhile Beauregard had repeatedly reported to Lee the arrival of Grant's army in front of Petersburg, and begged for reënforcements. Lee replied on the morning of the 16th that he did not know the position of Grant's army, and could not strip the north bank of troops. At noon on the 17th he again said, " Until I can get more definite information of Grant's movements, I do not think it prudent to draw more troops to this side of the river."

At 6:40 P.M. on the 17th, Beauregard telegraphed Lee that unless reënforced he might be compelled to evacuate the city very shortly. Upon receipt of this despatch, Kershaw's division was started for Petersburg. As soon as the fighting ceased, at about midnight, Beauregard took more radical measures to convince Lee of the situation. During the night, within two hours, he sent three members of his staff, one after another, to report to Lee. The first officer, who arrived about 2 A.M. on the 18th, could not convince Lee, and the second was not allowed to see him, as he was sleeping. The third, who came at 3 A.M., insisted on an interview, and succeeded in convincing Lee, from the statements of prisoners, that Grant's entire army had been across the James for over forty-eight hours. Lee immediately set his army in motion for Petersburg.

As a part of his general plan of operations, on the 5 June Grant had started Sheridan westward with his cavalry to break up the Virginia Central and Fredericksburg railways. Sheridan also had orders to form a junction at Charlottesville with Hunter, who had succeeded Sigel in command in the Shenandoah Valley. Hunter had defeated the Confederates in that region, and was then moving toward Lynchburg. This part of his task Sheridan was unable to carry out, as he found the Confederate cavalry under Wade Hampton across his path, and could not shake them off. He therefore returned to White House on the 21 June. This expedition, known as Sheridan's Trevilian Raid, thus ended in failure, like so many others.

PETERSBURG

In the meantime an even more famous raid was in progress. On account of ill health, Ewell had been succeeded in command of the Second Corps by Early, who was sent by Lee on the 13 June to the Shenandoah. He drove Hunter over the mountains into West Virginia, then marched down the Valley, crossed the Potomac, and on the 11 July reached the outskirts of Washington. There was great alarm throughout the North, and Grant sent Wright from Virginia with two divisions of the Sixth Corps. He arrived on the 12th, at the same time as General Emory, from New Orleans, with part of the Nineteenth Corps. There were enough troops in Washington to defend the city, but these reënforcements made the situation doubly sure. Early, pursued by Wright, retreated to Virginia.

As a result of this last Confederate invasion of the North, Grant sent Sheridan to command the Union forces in the Shenandoah. He expelled Early from the Valley, and so thoroughly devastated that granary of the Confederacy that, to use his own words, "a crow would have had to carry its rations if it had flown across the Valley."

On the 7 August 1864, Sheridan assumed command of the forces for the protection of the Valley, subsequently known as the Army of the Shenandoah. His appointment was opposed by Secretary Stanton, who thought that Sheridan was too young for such important responsibility. Grant had decided that the Valley must be rendered useless to the Confederacy for future aggressive operations, and Sheridan was ordered to devastate it in a way as little injurious to the people as possible.

On the morning of the 10 August Sheridan, who had massed his army at Halltown, in front of Harper's Ferry, moved against Early's line of communications. On the 12th, his cavalry came up with the enemy's rear-guard at Cedar Creek. Here Early was reënforced, and Sheridan made preparations to retire to a position better suited for defence. After an engagement at Winchester, he fell back to Halltown.

Then the pressure of Grant's army at Petersburg caused the recall of Early's reënforcements, and Sheridan moved forward once more. About this time Grant visited the Valley, and found everything to his satisfaction.

At 2 A.M. on the 19 September, Sheridan's army advanced to attack Early in front of Winchester. After a hot engagement, which lasted all day, the enemy was driven in disorder from the field, and only darkness saved Early's army from capture.

The Federals pursued the following day, and found the enemy in a strong position at Fisher's Hill. After a careful reconnaissance, Sheridan decided to turn the Confederate position. The movement was entirely successful, and the enemy was driven from the field in confusion. Early refused to fight again, and retired up the Valley to Port Republic. Staunton was captured by the Union cavalry, and all the army stores destroyed. Kershaw, who was at Culpeper on his march to Lee, was ordered to rejoin Early.

Sheridan was opposed to the Government plan of operating against Central Virginia from his base in the Valley, on account of the difficulty of protecting his long line of communications; and he was finally ordered to withdraw, destroying on his return march everything which could be of value to the enemy. It was a severe measure, but excused, like Sherman's burning of Atlanta, as a necessity of war.

Sheridan placed his army on Cedar Creek, north of the Shenandoah. On the 15 October, he was called to Washington for a consultation with Secretary Stanton and General Halleck. During his absence, at early dawn on the 19th, Early surprised the Union troops in their beds, and the left and centre, under Crook and Emory, were driven from their positions. Wright's men, who were in reserve, made only a short resistance. The whole army fled in disorder toward Winchester.

Stopping over night at Winchester on the 18th, on his return from Washington, Sheridan heard the noise of battle the following morning, and hurried to the field. His coming restored confidence; he readjusted the lines, and then ordered an advance. It took less time to drive the enemy from the field than it had required for him to gain it. Night ended the pursuit at Fisher's Hill. Early lost three battle-flags, and almost all his artillery and trains.

The battle of Cedar Creek has been immortalized in song and story. It was one of the most spectacular victories of the Civil War.

This practically ended the operations in the Valley. Sheridan's command passed the winter at Kernstown. Toward spring, most of the infantry, and all of the cavalry, rejoined Grant's army, in front of Petersburg.

Sheridan had about 43,000 men in the Valley, and his total losses were 17,000. Early never had over 20,000; his losses are unknown.[9]

Grant did not renew his assaults on Petersburg on the 19 June. Orders were given to entrench the positions gained by the several corps, and the two opposing lines in this part of the ground remained practically unchanged until the end of the siege.[10]

The Federal losses from the 13 to the 18 June were over 10,000 men, killed, wounded, and missing. Since the opening of the campaign, on the 5 May, the casualties had been in excess of 62,000. No returns exist for Beauregard's losses at Petersburg, but they have been estimated at a total of 4700. The losses of general officers on both sides were very severe: Federals, 6 killed, 8 wounded, 2 captured, total 16; Confederates, 8 killed, 15 wounded, 2 captured, total 25.[11]

The most interesting episode in the long and tedious siege of Petersburg was the affair of the Mine. This promised to be a great success, but through the neglect and cowardice of some of the principal actors it turned out a dismal failure.[12]

Running approximately parallel to the general line of the Confederate works was the deep valley of Poor Creek,

[9] 4 B. & L., 500–532.
[10] Humphreys, *Campaigns*, 224.
[11] Alexander, 559.
[12] For a full detailed account of this attempt, see General Alexander's interesting narrative in Chapter XXII. Also 4 B. & L., 545, *et seq.*

the western edge of which was only 400 feet from a point in their front called Elliott's Salient. The salient was held by Pegram's battery, and Elliott's brigade occupied the adjacent lines. By the assaults of the 17 and 18 June, the Ninth Corps (Burnside) had gained an advanced position in front of the salient. Along the farther edge of the valley the Union troops built strong rifle-pits, with elaborate head-logs and loopholes, from which a constant fire was kept up on the enemy's works. In the valley behind, there was ample room to collect and mass a large force, out of view of the Confederates.

Lieutenant-Colonel Pleasants, who had been a mining engineer and who belonged to the 48th Pennsylvania, composed for the most part of miners from the upper Schuylkill coal region, suggested to his division commander, General Robert Potter, the possibility of running a mine under the salient in front of this point. The plan was approved by General Burnside, and work was begun on the 25 June. A gallery was successfully extended over 500 feet, with two branches at the end, to the right and left, each 37 feet long. These branch galleries were charged with gunpowder in eight parcels of 1000 pounds each, connected by open troughs of powder to be fired by safety fuses coming through the tamping and along the gallery. All the preparations were finished on the 28 July.

The last of June, General Alexander became convinced that the enemy was preparing to mine the position at the salient, and warned General Lee, who ordered his engineers to start countermines. The shafts, however, were located on the right and left flanks of the battery, and the countermines did not meet the Federal gallery, which was so silently built that the Confederates did not know of its proximity.

The morning of the 30 July was chosen for the explosion of the mine, and all preliminary arrangements were made, such as massing the troops, removing parapets and abattis to make passage for the assaulting columns, and so on. No possible precaution was overlooked by General Meade, and very explicit orders were issued.

On the morning of the 30th, Lee had in the lines about

Petersburg only the three divisions of Hoke, Johnson, and Mahone, about 18,000 men, most of the balance of his army being twenty miles away. Three of the Union corps, and parts of two others, with two divisions of Sheridan's cavalry, 16 divisions in all, some 60,000 men, were concentrated to follow up the surprise to be given by the explosion.

Everything had been so carefully prepared, that it is difficult to explain how the attack failed so completely. One cause was the same which on the 12 May nullified the Federal surprise at the Bloody Angle at Spottsylvania [13] — too many troops had been concentrated, and they were in each other's way. The main reasons, however, were the cowardice of two of the Union division-commanders, Ledlie and Ferrero, and the negligence of one of the corps-commanders, Burnside. These three officers, with two others, Willcox and Bliss, were subsequently censured by a Military Court, and Burnside resigned from the service.

The assault was to be led by Ledlie's division of the Ninth Corps, followed by the colored division under Ferrero, but both these commanders took shelter in a bomb-proof, where they remained during the entire action.

The mine was fired at 4:40, ten minutes before sunrise, and the explosion made a crater 150 feet long, 97 feet wide, and 30 feet deep. The parapets were partially destroyed and largely buried by the falling earth. Two guns, 22 cannoneers, and perhaps 250 infantry were carried up in the air.

The assaulting columns literally swarmed into this crater, until it was packed so full the men could hardly move. Considering the surprise, and the novelty of the occasion, the Confederates rallied very quickly. The decided lack of energy on the part of the assailants permitted the defenders to form barricades, which were successfully held to the last. The attacking column, instead of spreading out, remained massed in the crater, and made no further advance; the reënforcements in the rear were prevented from coming up. Finally Meade ordered all

[13] *Cf.* Maurice, 261.

offensive operations to cease, and the men were withdrawn. The Federal casualties for the day were in excess of 4000, while the Confederates lost less than 1500 men.[14]

Between this period and the month of March 1865 several movements of the Union armies were made to the left and the right, which resulted in the extension of the entrenchments in both directions, and a corresponding prolongation of the Confederate lines.[15] As these operations possess but little interest, no attempt will be made to narrate them in detail.

Each of Grant's movements, at the time, had some special object beyond extending his lines. Toward the end of July, for example, Hancock was sent to the north bank of the James with his own corps (Second) and the Tenth (Birney). Grant's thought was to prevent Lee from sending more reënforcements to Early in the Valley. Hancock remained there until the 20 August, when he was recalled.

On the 18 August, Warren was sent on an expedition against the Weldon Railway with the same object in view: to force Lee to withdraw some of his troops from the Shenandoah. While he was tearing up the track, Warren was attacked by Hill, and lost nearly 3000 men. He then withdrew to open ground about a mile back and entrenched. No further attacks were made, and the Union lines were then extended by the Ninth Corps from the Jerusalem Plank Road to connect with Warren's lines on the Weldon Railway.

The last week in October, Grant made another movement to the left with the view of turning Lee's right, and seizing the Southside Railway. The operation was not a success, and the Union troops were withdrawn to their former positions.

In December, Warren was again sent on an expedition against the Weldon Railway, and destroyed some twenty miles of track. This increased the difficulty of supplying the Confederate army.

At the beginning of February another ineffectual attempt was made to turn the Confederate right and seize the Southside Railway. This movement, made by the

---

[14] Alexander, 572–573.   [15] Humphreys, 267.

Second and Fifth corps, was met by Lee's right, and check-
mated. The Union line had now been extended to
Hatcher's Run near the crossing of the Vaughan Road,
and the Confederate entrenchments reached across the
Run at the Crow farm, and from Burgess's Mill along
White Oak Road, and west of the Claiborne Road.

The winter was unusually severe, and the Confederate
troops, with their insufficient clothing and meagre food,
suffered terribly. They had no coffee or tea or sugar,
except in the hospitals, and only a little meat, mostly im-
ported from abroad. The condition of affairs throughout
the South was truly deplorable. The loss to the army by
desertion averaged a hundred men a day, the soldiers leaving in response to frantic appeals from their families at
home.[16]

In March 1865 the Confederate lines were so extended
that it was thirty-seven miles by the shortest route from
the extreme left on White Oak Swamp below Richmond
to the extreme right beyond Petersburg. At this time
Lee's army was reduced to about 50,000 men, and Grant
had 124,000.[17]

Early in March, Sherman had advanced into North
Carolina, where he was confronted by General Joseph E.
Johnston, who had been placed in command of a small
Confederate force composed of the garrisons of Savannah
and Charleston, and the remnants of Hood's army which
had been brought over from Tupelo, Mississippi. It was
evident that Lee would soon be forced to abandon Richmond and Petersburg, and endeavor to join Johnston, to
crush Sherman before he could unite with Grant. But
prior to undertaking this " almost impossible task," General Lee " determined upon one last effort to break up
Grant in his immediate front." [18] On the 25 March, he
gave orders to Gordon, now in command of Early's corps,
which had rejoined, to assault Fort Stedman, which was
only 200 yards in front of his line. The Union troops

[16] See Humphreys, 311; also Taylor's *Four Years with Lee.*
[17] Alexander, 585.
[18] Alexander, 588. See also Long, 404–405, and *Lee's Confidential
Despatches to Davis,* 342, *et seq.*

were taken by surprise, and the fort captured, but the assailants were soon driven out, with very heavy losses.

Fearing that the object of Lee's assault was to induce him to transfer troops from his left to his right, which would make it easier for Lee to withdraw his army, and begin his retreat, Grant decided to take the initiative at once, and move around Lee's right flank. Leaving only one division (Devens) north of the James, and two divisions under Weitzel in the Bermuda Hundred lines, Grant began to transfer all the rest of his infantry, about 90,000 men, and all of his cavalry, to his extreme left.

On this occasion, Grant narrowly avoided the mistake made by Hooker in May 1863, by Lee in June 1863, and by himself in May 1864, of sending his cavalry off on a raid against the railways. He countermanded such an order, issued on the 28th, and kept his cavalry with the infantry.[19]

On the 31 March, Lee sent the two divisions of Pickett and Johnson, about 6600 strong, and two of Fitz Lee's divisions of cavalry, 5800 men, on an expedition against Sheridan, who was driven back in much confusion nearly to Dinwiddie Court House. During the night, Pickett, who was far in advance, was nearly cut off by Warren's corps; but he succeeded in withdrawing to Five Forks, four miles from Lee's right flank. Here he made the mistake of halting and entrenching, assuming that he would be reënforced. The following morning he was attacked by Sheridan's cavalry, and Warren's corps, and routed; 3244 of his men were captured, with eleven colors, and four guns, while the Federals lost only 634 men. The whole action was fought in the absence of Pickett and Fitz Lee, who were only a mile away, but heard no sound of the battle, owing to the same peculiar conditions of the atmosphere noted at Perryville and Chancellorsville.

After the action was over, Sheridan removed Warren from the command of the Fifth Corps, under charges of which he was afterwards fully acquitted by a Court of Inquiry.

On the 2 April, Grant renewed his attacks on the Con-

[19] Alexander, 590.

federate right, breaking their line, and forcing it back. The Federals then gained possession of the Southside Railroad, and pursued the enemy toward Petersburg, until stopped by the fire of Fort Gregg. In this last day's battle, General A. P. Hill was killed. He had borne a conspicuous part in every action fought by the Army of Northern Virginia, except Spottsylvania, where he was ill.

That night Lee abandoned Richmond and Petersburg, and started his army westward, in the hope of reaching either Danville or Lynchburg ahead of Grant. He had expected to find rations at Amelia Court House, but by some blunder the supplies had gone on to Richmond. This caused a delay of twenty-four hours, to collect supplies from the country.

In the last phase of the campaign, Grant, for the first time, used his cavalry to the best possible advantage. Instead of sending Sheridan off on some useless raid, he kept the cavalry with the main army, and it did most effective work. But for the Union horsemen, Lee might have reached the mountains of Virginia, and prolonged the struggle for several months.

After the evacuation of Petersburg and Richmond, Grant followed Lee on the south side of the Appomattox River. Weitzel was sent to take possession of Richmond, which surrendered at 8:15 the following morning.

Sheridan's cavalry and the Second and Sixth corps led in the pursuit. Both armies were trying to reach the junction at Burke's Station, and the Federals won in the race. At Sailor's Creek, on the 6 April, Ewell's corps, which formed the rear-guard, was cut off, surrounded, and captured, some 8000 men, with six general officers, including Ewell himself, and Kershaw.

After sundown on the 7th, Lee received the first letter from Grant, proposing a surrender: —

April 7, 1865.

GENERAL: The result of the last week must convince you of the hopelessness of further resistance on the part of the Army of Northern Virginia in this struggle. I feel that it is so, and regard it as my duty to shift from myself the responsibility of any further effusion of blood, by asking of you the surrender of that portion of the Confederate army known as the Army of Northern Virginia.

U. S. GRANT, *Lieutenant-General.*

Within an hour, General Lee sent back the following reply: —

April 7, 1865.

GENERAL: I have received your note of this date. Though not entertaining the opinion you express on the hopelessness of further resistance on the part of the Army of Northern Virginia, I reciprocate your desire to avoid useless effusion of blood, and therefore, before considering your proposition, ask the terms you will offer on condition of its surrender.

R. E. LEE, *General.*

During the afternoon of the 8th Lee received Grant's reply to his inquiry as to the terms proposed. Grant said that, peace being his great desire, there was but one condition upon which he should insist, namely, " that the officers and men surrendered shall be disqualified from taking up arms again against the government of the United States until properly exchanged." He concluded by saying that he was ready to meet Lee for the purpose of arranging the terms.

Lee immediately prepared his answer, and sent it to Grant the same evening. He said that he did not intend, in his previous note, to propose the surrender of his army, but to ask Grant's terms. He added: " I cannot therefore meet you with a view to surrender the Army of Northern Virginia, but as far as your proposal may affect the Confederate States' forces under my command, and tend to the restoration of peace, I should be pleased to meet you at 10 A.M. to-morrow on the stage road to Richmond between the picket-lines of the two armies."

Some time before the fall of Richmond, Grant had received a letter from Mr. Lincoln prohibiting him from embracing anything of a political nature in any negotiations that he might have with General Lee. As Lee's letter seemed to imply such a discussion, Grant decided to avoid the proposed meeting. He accordingly replied, on the morning of the 9th, that he had no authority to treat on the subject, and that the proposed meeting could do no good.

Meanwhile the Confederate army had arrived within two miles of Appomattox Court House, only to find the road barred by Sheridan and Ord. Lee sent orders to Gordon and Fitz Lee to clear the way, but they could make no progress against the large forces already in their front. On receiving Gordon's report, General Lee exclaimed, " Then there is nothing left me but to go and see General Grant, and I would rather die a thousand deaths! " [20]

Lee accordingly wrote Grant, asking an interview in accordance with the offer contained in his letter of the 8th, and rode to the rear, hoping soon to meet Grant and be able to make the surrender.

That morning Meade had taken the responsibility of granting a truce, pending the negotiations for a surrender. When this was arranged, Lee returned to his front and stopped in an apple orchard a hundred yards or so in advance of the line, where General Alexander had some fence-rails piled under a tree to make him a seat. Within two days this tree was cut down for souvenirs by the Confederate and Federal soldiers.[21]

Here, while talking with General Longstreet, Lee received Grant's final letter, sent by Colonel Babcock of his staff. It read: —

April 9, 1865.

GENERAL R. E. LEE, Commanding C. S. A.: —

Your note of this date is but this moment, 11:50 A.M., received. . . . I am at this writing four miles west of Walker's Church, and will push forward for the purpose of meeting you. . . .

> Very respectfully,
> Your obedient servant,
> U. S. GRANT
> *Lieutenant-General.*

[20] Alexander, 603.

[21] Alexander, 609. This seems to have been the only basis for the legend about " Appomattox and its famous apple-tree," used with so much dramatic effect by Senator Conkling in nominating Grant for a third term at the Chicago Convention in 1880. See 4 *B. & L.*, 734; also Long, 422.

The meeting, by a strange coincidence, took place in the house of Major Wilmer McLean, who had owned the farm on Bull Run on which had occurred the first collision between the two armies at Blackburn's Ford on the 18 July 1861. His house there was used for a time as the headquarters of General Beauregard. To avoid the active theatre of the war he moved to the quiet village of Appomattox. Thus the first and the last scenes of the war in Virginia took place upon his property.[22]

The house was a plain two-story wooden structure, standing a little distance back from the street, with a yard in front. A wooden porch, reached by seven steps, ran the length of the house. On each side of the hall, there was a single square room, entered by two doors, and having two windows, one in front and one in rear.

General Lee was accompanied only by his military secretary, Colonel Marshall, and a single courier, who held the horses during the meeting. Lee reached the house first, and entered the room on the left to await the arrival of General Grant, who came about one-thirty. It was Sunday, the 9 April 1865.

General Grant had in his party Generals Sheridan, Ord, and Ingalls, and nine members of his staff, including General (then Colonel) Horace Porter, who has given us a very interesting account of the interview.[23]

General Grant sat at a marble-topped table in the centre of the room; Lee, at a small oval table near the front window, and facing Grant. Some of the party found seats on the sofa and the few chairs in the room, but most of them stood.

"The contrast between the two commanders," says General Porter, "was striking and could not fail to attract marked attention." Grant, then nearly forty-three years of age, was five feet eight inches in height, with shoulders slightly stooped. His hair and full beard were a nut-brown, without a trace of gray in them. He wore a plain blouse of dark-blue flannel, an ordinary pair of top-boots, with his trousers inside, and was without spurs. His boots

[22] Alexander, 23, 610; 4 *B. & L.*, 743.
[23] See Porter's *Campaigning with Grant*; also his article in 4 *B. & L.*, 735–744.

and uniform were spattered with mud. He had no sword; and, apart from the shoulder-straps which designated his rank, his uniform was that of a private soldier.

Lee, on the other hand, was fully six feet in height, and erect for one of his age, for he was Grant's senior by sixteen years. His thick hair and full beard were a silver gray. He wore a new uniform of Confederate gray, and carried at his side a long sword of very fine workmanship, the hilt studded with jewels. He wore top-boots, with handsome spurs. Like his uniform, his boots were remarkably clean. A felt hat, the color of his uniform, and a pair of long buckskin gauntlets, lay beside him on the table.

After a few words of general conversation, General Lee suggested that Grant should put his terms in writing. Whereupon Grant called for his manifold order-book, and wrote his well-known letter, which he handed to General Lee to read. Lee laid it on the table beside him while he drew from his pocket a pair of steel-rimmed spectacles and wiped the glasses carefully with his handkerchief. Then he adjusted the spectacles very deliberately, and read the letter carefully. When he came to the sentence about the officers being allowed to retain their side-arms, horses, and baggage, he said, with considerable warmth of manner, " This will have a very happy effect upon my army."

In answer to a question from Grant, as to whether he had any suggestions to make regarding the terms, Lee said, after a little hesitation, that the men in his cavalry and artillery owned their own horses. Grant replied that the subject was new to him; then he added that, without altering the draft as written, he would instruct the officers appointed to receive the paroles " to let all the men who claim to own a horse or mule take the animals home with them to work their little farms." Lee showed a very lively appreciation of this concession, which, he said, would have the best possible effect upon the men, and would do much toward conciliating his people.

Grant then ordered one of his staff to copy his letter

in ink, and while this was being done, Lee had Colonel Marshall draw up for his signature a letter of acceptance of the terms of surrender.

After the letters had been copied and signed, Lee spoke of his lack of provisions for his men, and Grant offered to send him at once 25,000 rations.

At a little before four o'clock General Lee shook hands with General Grant, bowed to the other officers, and with Colonel Marshall left the room. As soon as the horses were saddled, he mounted, saluted the Union officers by raising his hat, and rode slowly away. General Grant and his staff then mounted and started for the headquarters camp, which was now pitched near by. Firing of salutes had already begun, but Grant ordered these stopped at once, saying that the war was over, and the rebels fellow-countrymen once more.

On his way to headquarters, Grant was reminded that he had not yet announced the important event to the Government. He dismounted, sat down on a large stone by the roadside, and wrote the following despatch to Secretary Stanton, dated 4:30 P.M.: —

General Lee surrendered the Army of Northern Virginia this afternoon on terms proposed by myself. The accompanying additional correspondence will show the conditions fully.

U. S. GRANT
Lieut.-General.

Lee was appointed to the command of the Army of Northern Virginia on the first day of June 1862. In the brief period of two years, ten months, and nine days, with an army always inferior in numbers, poorly equipped, and badly supplied with food and clothing, he had fought seven great campaigns, against six picked generals of the Union. With a force which never exceeded 80,000 men, he had put *hors de combat* 262,000 Federals. There is no parallel in history to this record except Napoleon's twelve major campaigns, covering a period of nineteen years. [25]

The effective strength of the Union army at the begin-

[25] Alexander, 618–619. *Cf.* Roosevelt's *Thomas H. Benton*, 38.

ning of the final operations was 120,000, and the losses
up to the day of the surrender were 10,515. Grant's entire losses since crossing the Rapidan were 124,000 — a
number about double the maximum strength of Lee's
army. At the time Lee evacuated Richmond, he had about
50,000 men; his losses during the retreat are unknown.
There were 28,231 men paroled at Appomattox; but Lee
had lost large numbers by capture or desertion since leaving Petersburg.

Grant did not enter the Confederate lines after the surrender. He designated General Joshua Chamberlain to
command the parade on the day that the Confederate
soldiers marched out to lay down their arms and colors.[26]

On the morning after the surrender, the 10 April,
General Grant rode out about nine o'clock, and had a
final interview with General Lee between the lines of the
two armies. Their conversation was entirely private; but,
as afterwards reported by Grant, it was mainly on the
subject of peace, and reconciliation between the two Sections. Grant urged Lee to use his great influence to bring
about this happy result. Lee, however, was averse to
stepping beyond his duties as a soldier, and said the
authorities would doubtless soon arrive at the same conclusion without his interference. There is no foundation
for the statement that Grant asked Lee to see President
Lincoln regarding the terms of reconstruction.[27]

After this interview, which lasted about half an hour,
Lee rode back to his camp to take a final farewell of his
men,[28] and Grant returned to the McLean house to await
the hour of his departure. Some of his officers, who had
been visiting the enemy's camp, now returned, with
Wilcox, who had been groomsman when he was married;
Longstreet, who had also been at his wedding; Heth,
who had been with him in Mexico; Gordon, Pickett, and
several others.

[26] This is the only basis for the statement frequently made that Grant
delegated to Chamberlain " the honor of receiving Lee's surrender." (See
Mitchell, *Memoirs*, 31.) This officer was not even present when Lee surrendered to Grant. The story that Lee offered his sword to Grant is equally
erroneous. (See 2 Grant, 344–346.)

[27] See Porter's article, 4 *B. & L.*, 746.

[28] The text of his order is given in 4 *B. & L.*, 747.

At noon, Grant mounted his horse, and with his staff started for the station to take the train for Washington. Lee set out for Richmond, the same day.

For the first time in four long, bloody years, the Army of the Potomac and the Army of Northern Virginia turned their backs upon each other!

"Grant's movement from Cold Harbor to the south bank of the James," says Major Steele, "belongs to a class of strategical operations which are considered among the most hazardous and difficult in warfare. It was a flank movement involving the crossing of close and wooded country by narrow roads, and the passage of two difficult streams, the Chickahominy and the James, over which pontoon bridges had to be laid." [29]

Grant, and his efficient staff, are entitled to great credit for the skill with which the operation was carried out. The Union army had over fifty miles to march; Lee held nearly all the bridges across the Chickahominy, and had better roads, as well as fuller knowledge of the country, to aid him in attacking the right flank of Grant's columns. The Union army was withdrawn from a position only "a few hundred yards from the enemy in the widest place"; and the movement was so effectively screened that Lee was kept in ignorance of Grant's plans from the time he started, the night of the 12 June, until the morning of the 18th, when Grant had his army concentrated in front of Petersburg. Taken as a whole, the operation must be considered one of the finest achievements of strategy in military history. [30]

Then came the fatal mistake of the campaign —Hancock's waiting for his rations on the morning of the 15 June. This delay of six hours probably prolonged the life of the Confederacy nine months. Yet no blame attaches to Hancock's fine record; the fault was entirely General Grant's, and the explanation of it is very plainly intimated by General Alexander, [31] although he attributes the neglect to give Hancock proper orders mainly to "the political necessity of placing Butler in command of

[29] Steele, 528.
[30] Steele, 529.
[31] See Alexander, 557.

the Army of the James," [32] which was really only a secondary cause.

As the primary object of Grant's campaign in front of Petersburg was to get possession of the two railways leading into Richmond from the south and southwest, it is not easy to understand why he could not succeed in less than nine months. Major Steele's explanation is, that Lee's army was never really invested; that he was so favored by the relative positions of Richmond and Petersburg, and the conformation of the two rivers, that Grant could not leave a small force in front of Petersburg, to detain Lee, while he moved with his main army against the railways, without thereby giving Lee an opportunity to seize the Union base on the James. [33]

"Knowing as much as we do now about trench warfare," writes General Maurice, "it is easy to see that, without a far greater preponderance of artillery than he possessed, Grant had at no time much chance of carrying the Confederate lines. The rifles of 1864 were precise enough and could be fired sufficiently rapidly to make assault a dangerous expedient unless the defences had been flattened out and the defenders driven from them by accurate bombardment, or unless the attack could be made in overwhelming numbers and regardless of loss. Throughout the siege Grant's superiority in numbers was rarely more and often less than two to one, while Lee's watchfulness was such, and his handling of his reserves so masterly, that, though Grant was always free to choose his point of attack on a very lengthy front of defence, he was never able to accumulate sufficient strength to crash through the defences. The battle of the 'Crater' ended in a similar failure to that of the 'Bloody Angle' of Spottsylvania and for much the same reasons. Grant would indeed have been much better advised to have avoided a direct attack and relied earlier upon the policy into which he was forced by events of continually ex-

[32] *Ibid.*, 548. For "the secret of the hold which General Butler had on General Grant," see Macartney, 60–61; also George F. Hoar's *Autobiography*, 1, 361–363, and 4 Rhodes, 493, 495.
[33] Steele, 533.

tending his left and so gradually cutting off Lee's lines of supply. But his plan of keeping Lee tied to the defences of Richmond and Petersburg, while elsewhere the Federal forces steadily reduced the area from which the troops in those defences could draw men, food, and munitions, was the best possible. Lee's great weapon was manœuvre, and Grant had taken it from him; events proved that no plan was better calculated to undermine the *moral* of the people of the South." [34]

In further explanation of Grant's inability to accomplish his object, we give below the official returns of the two armies for the seven months from June to December 1864.[35]

	Federals	*Confederates*
June	107,000	55,000
July	77,000	57,000
August	59,000	35,000
September	77,000	35,000
October	85,000	47,000
November	87,000	56,000
December	110,000	67,000

In the five months, June to October inclusive, Grant's casualties were over 47,000, and his forces were further reduced by detachments sent to Washington and the Shenandoah, so that he was not strong enough, compared to Lee, to assume a more aggressive policy.

[34] Maurice, *Robert E. Lee*, 260–262.
[35] 4 *B. & L.*, 593, 594.

CHAPTER TWENTY-ONE

1861 — 1865

CONCLUSION

The Military Situation of the South at the Outbreak of the Civil War — How the Confederacy Armed Its Men — Unpreparedness of the North — Reasons for the Early Confederate Victories — The Military Policies of the Two Governments — General Superiority of the Southern Commanders — Strategy and Tactics of the War — Numbers and Losses — Gross Exaggerations of the Northern Authorities — Final Comments — Cause of the Confederate Failure

THE story that John B. Floyd, while Secretary of War in the cabinet of Mr. Buchanan, transferred guns from Northern to Southern arsenals, in order to arm the South for the Civil War, has been told and retold so often that it is still believed by many Northerners. It is not so generally known that this charge was investigated by a committee of Congress, which, in February 1861, made a report showing it to be groundless. The chairman of that committee was Mr. Stanton, afterwards Secretary of War, who was one of the most prominent Republicans in the House.

The facts are, that in 1859 the Armory at Springfield, Massachusetts, had become so crowded that it was necessary to remove some of the arms stored there. Accordingly, in December 1859, nearly a year before the election of Mr. Lincoln, the War Department ordered about one-fifth of the guns at Springfield distributed among five Southern arsenals. The total number of arms thus transferred was 125,000, of which all were obsolete patterns except 10,000 rifled muskets. About 400,000 of the old guns, and all of the new and improved ones, were kept in the North.[1]

[1] Article on John B. Floyd, in *The Americana*; Johnston's *Narrative*, 426–428; 6 Channing's *United States*, 285.

In reality, the South, at the outbreak of the Civil War, was poorly supplied with arms and ammunition. According to Mr. Davis, in the *Rise and Fall of the Confederate Government*, the six arsenals in the South, which were only storehouses, contained just 15,000 rifles, and 120,000 muskets, the latter mostly of antiquated patterns. Another authority states that the South had about 150,000 small-arms, of which only about 20,000 were modern rifles.

In a memorandum to Mr. Davis, General Gorgas, chief of ordnance of the Confederate army, writes: " We began in April 1861 without arsenal, or laboratory, or powder-mill of any capacity, and with no foundry or rolling-mill except in Richmond; and before the close of 1863 . . . we supplied them." With no stock on hand even of such necessary articles as copper, leather, and iron, in that short period, the South created, almost literally out of the ground, foundries and rolling-mills at Richmond, Selma, Atlanta, and Macon; smelting works at Petersburg; chemical works at Charlotte; a powder-mill at Augusta, equal to any in the United States; and a chain of arsenals, armories, and laboratories stretching from Virginia to Alabama.

Without any previous industrial organization; shut off by the blockade from the commerce of the world; crippled by a depreciated currency; obliged to send nearly every able-bodied man to the field; unable to use slave labor except in the most unskilled departments of production, such an achievement of industrial organization has never been surpassed in the history of the world.

At the outbreak of the war, General Rains, of North Carolina, who had been professor of chemistry at West Point, left a prosperous engineering business at New York to enter the service of the Confederacy. He was almost at once put in charge of the proposed powder-mill at Augusta. He immediately set parties at work to explore the caves of the mountains of Virginia and Tennessee for saltpetre; cellars and old tobacco works were searched for nitre, and immense beds were developed at Columbia, Charleston, Savannah, Augusta, and Mobile. All the material obtained in this way was sent to Augusta, where,

CONCLUSION

under the direction of General Rains, the powder-mill became the most famous example of Southern industrial efficiency.

When the Union troops evacuated Harper's Ferry, after setting fire to the arsenal, civilians rushed in, and saved a large part of the machinery. By the end of 1861, this machinery, set up at Richmond and Fayetteville, was turning out thousands of muskets, and firearms of every description. Prior to that time, the Southern arsenals had hardly a machine above the complexity of a foot-lathe.

The South had no skilled laborers to speak of; but a few men, like Ball, who literally died of over-work, trained the hundreds who were willing.

Lead at the rate of nearly 80,000 pounds a month came in from the mines near Wytheville, Virginia, to be smelted in the new plant at Petersburg. Every Confederate victory brought large supplies of arms and ammunition;[2] the battle-fields were literally combed for guns and bullets, with excellent results.[3]

Within the Southern Confederacy, at the outbreak of the war, there were no arsenals at which guns were manufactured, except a small plant at Fayetteville, and the United States Arsenal at Harper's Ferry. The story of how the South armed its soldiers is an interesting one; and the way in which the emergency was met is a matter of which all Americans to-day may be proud.

There were but six sources of supply:

(1) The weapons already on hand.
(2) Conversion of old sporting arms to military use.
(3) Manufacture of new arms.
(4) Purchase in the North.
(5) Purchase in Europe.
(6) Capture from the enemy.

The first has already been mentioned; and the supplies obtained from the next three sources were so small as almost to be negligible. At first, every gunsmith in the

[2] In two campaigns, the Seven Days and Second Manassas, the Confederates captured 82 guns and 58,000 small-arms. (Alexander, 218.)

[3] Article in the *Springfield Republican,* quoted in the *Confederate Veteran,* January 1922.

South was kept busy altering and repairing private arms, but the results were not satisfactory. There was not much more success with the manufacture of new arms. The machinery for making the long rifled musket, saved at Harper's Ferry, was set up at Richmond, but the output never exceeded 1000 guns a month. The machinery for making the short Harper's Ferry rifles was sent to Fayetteville, where, in April 1862, it began to turn out about 400 rifles a month. There were also a number of private gun factories in the Confederacy, but it is difficult to obtain definite data about them, and their output seems to have been small.

At the beginning of the war, the South found little difficulty in making contracts with a number of Northern manufacturers to supply arms, but this matter became such a scandal that the Government put a stop to it by a strict embargo on all shipments to the South.

When the Confederacy found the factories of the North closed to it, the authorities turned to Europe. In May 1861, Major Huse was sent to England, where he succeeded in buying 12,000 Enfield rifles. He also contracted for a lot of 100,000 Austrian rifles from the Imperial Arsenal at Vienna. There was little trouble in running these guns through the blockade. In February 1863, General Gorgas reported that Major Huse had shipped over 131,000 guns, of which about 81,000 were long and short Enfield rifles, and carbines. At the same date, 23,000 rifles at London, and 30,000 at Vienna, were awaiting shipment. The long Enfield rifle, a splendidly made weapon, was the official arm of the British infantry, and proved the most popular gun with the Confederate army. It was about the same size and weight as the Springfield rifle, used by the Union troops, and would take the same cartridge.

It has already been stated that the South armed and equipped itself at the expense of the enemy, and it is certain that a large proportion of the arms used by the Confederates was captured from the Federals. General Gorgas reports that during the four years of the war 320,000 small-arms were issued from the main arsenal at Richmond. Probably one-half of these were captured guns. Richmond was the great arms clearing-house for the East, and guns gathered on the Virginia battle-fields were sent there to be put in order and reissued. Many of the finest patterns, however, like the Spencer carbines, were useless, because the Confederates could not get the cartridges. During the last months of the war, a machine was devised for turning out the cartridges, but it was too late to be of service.[4]

The beginning of the Civil War found the North almost as unprepared as the South. Of the 198 companies in the regular army, 183 were guarding 79 posts on the Western frontier, while the remaining 15 garrisoned the Canadian border, the Atlantic coast, and 23 arsenals. Few posts had even so much as a battalion, and in many cases a small company was split up into detachments. To hold in security three million square miles of territory, the United States had less than 13,000 men!

When South Carolina seceded there were few regular officers who had commanded as much as an assembled battalion. Their military life had been passed in the scattered forts along the Indian frontier, where, as expressed by General Ewell, a veteran of nearly twenty years' service, they " had learned all about commanding fifty United States dragoons and had forgotten everything else." The militia of the several States had had no training in field-service, and were of little value for national defence.

A breech-loading rifle, the first of the successful repeaters, was invented this year (1860) by Christopher Spencer, and was destined to have considerable influence on some of the later battle-fields of the war.[5] Only a few of them, however, could be manufactured in time to be of service, and nearly all the troops were armed with old-fashioned muzzle-loading muskets.

The Springfield arsenal was the only service manufactory of small-arms in the United States, and its output

---

[4] Most of the above facts are taken from an article in the *Confederate Veteran*, for May 1924.

[5] It was a seven-shot rifle, loading brass shells through a magazine in the butt, and was a great advance in rapidity over the muzzle-loader.

did not exceed 2500 a month. As above stated, the Secretary of War, Mr. Floyd, had sent a part of the supply of small-arms to the Southern arsenals, which immediately fell into the hands of the seceding States. At first the Federal troops were so ill-provided that even flintlocks were issued. The markets of Europe were scoured by Federal agents, and every kind of weapon available was purchased at a high price. The calibres were as varied as during the Revolution, and few soldiers could use the ammunition of their comrades, even in the same company.

Although Parrott and Rodman had produced the best types of rifled cannon, none had been adopted by the Government; but there was an abundant supply on hand of smooth-bore guns of iron and brass of all calibres. Since the Government had no foundries of its own, the new cannon were hurriedly manufactured and poorly tested: the consequence was that many burst when they were first fired. The guns used were of many sizes and patterns, and on one battle-field of the war 36 different kinds of balls were picked up from the ground!

Immediately after the secession of the Southern States, nearly one-third of the 900 officers in the Old Army resigned their commissions, and 65 of the cadets at West Point resigned or were discharged. With the exception of 26 men, however, the rank and file remained in the service of the North.

No effort was made by the Union to utilize the experience of regular officers with the volunteers. The men of the local regiments were allowed to elect their officers. Many of the former officers who offered their services were ignored. Grant, who was in business, wrote the War Department, but was not even honored with a reply. Many graduates of West Point served throughout the war in minor capacities, while regiments were commanded by men with no military training or experience. The records show what the North lost by this remarkable procedure: 51 major-generals, 91 brigadiers, and 106 colonels came from the officers of the Old Army; but as against these 248, there were 308 former officers who were kept in subordinate positions.

CONCLUSION

The South, on the other hand, made early provision to accept the services of officers of the United States army, and to give them their original relative rank. Of the 250 who went with the South, 182 rose to the rank of general officer, including such men as Lee, Jackson, Longstreet, and the two Johnstons. In addition, as already stated, the Confederacy created ranks suitable to the units commanded; whereas, on the Union side, armies, corps, and divisions were commanded, indifferently, by major-generals.

The South organized early; it took the utmost advantage of every trained soldier among its adherents; it quickly concentrated in main armies; it gave confidence and stability to the troops by placing recruits beside old soldiers in the ranks; it clung to its leaders in the face of defeat and did not harass them; it built up *moral* in every possible way.

The primary organization of the North, on the other hand, was chaos. It did not seem to know how to make use of the few trained soldiers it had. It put excellent leaders in untenable positions, failed to support them properly, and promptly relieved them when they failed. By its ignorance of military affairs it destroyed the *moral* of as brave troops as ever marched. The result was that the war was dragged out for four long years, with an inordinate loss of life and public treasure.[6]

"I am of the opinion," writes Colonel Henderson, "that in order to discover the secret of the Confederate successes there is no need either to search for nice distinctions in races closely akin, or to appeal to the fact that Lee and his great lieutenant, Jackson, were a head and shoulders above any Union leaders who had as yet appeared. It was not only the genius of its commanders that won the laurels of the Virginia army. Many of its victories were achieved by sheer hard fighting: they were the work of the soldiers themselves; and that the Confederates were able to wrest success from opponents of equal vigor

[6] Ganoe, *The United States Army*, 244–297. See also 2 Barton, 161–163, and 6 Channing, 398 *et seq.*

was due to their superior organization, more accurate shooting, and above all to their stronger discipline.

" As to the first, the Federal Government allowed the pernicious principle of the election of the officers by the rank and file to flourish without restraint; and, secondly, the strength of the army was kept up, not by a constant stream of recruits to the seasoned battalions, but by the formation of new regiments. . . .

" The Southerners, on the other hand, early adopted the conscription; the superior officers were appointed by the Government, and the recruits sent to fill the vacancies in the ranks. . . . Few ' political regiments ' existed in the South; men commanded because they were competent to command, and not because they could influence votes.

" Secondly, a great advantage in favor of the Confederate troops was their skill as marksmen. . . .

" Lastly, as to discipline, . . . the rich planter, possessing many slaves dependent on him . . . acquired habits of command and organization highly useful to the officers of an army." [7]

President Davis was a graduate of West Point; he had served with distinction in Mexico, and afterwards as Secretary of War. He had thus had many opportunities of learning the capabilities of the officers of the Old Army, and this knowledge he turned to good account. His selections for command were very judicious. All the regular officers who joined the Confederacy were given high commands, and no civilians were placed in positions of responsibility until they had demonstrated their fitness by handling troops in the field. Taught by military experience, Mr. Davis did not remove a commander because he had been unfortunate. Both his greatest generals, Lee and Jackson, met with reverses, but retained his confidence. He refused to accept the resignation which Lee tendered after Gettysburg. The only great mistake he made was in relieving Johnston in 1864.

In the North, on the other hand, the military policy was very different. Commander succeeded commander with startling rapidity. The Army of the Potomac was com-

[7] Henderson, *Science of War*, 198–199.

manded by no less than six different officers, each one of whom except the last, Grant, was degraded for ill success. Neither President Lincoln, nor his Secretary of War, Mr. Stanton, had had any previous knowledge of military affairs; but, notwithstanding, they attempted to dictate to their generals in the field. Many of their selections for high command were unfortunate, and in too many cases were dictated by political, rather than military, considerations. The appointment, and the retention in positions of responsibility, of such men as Butler, Banks, Fremont, and Sigel, is hard to excuse. It was not until the last year of the war that the President and his advisers learned wisdom, and forbore to interfere with Grant and Sherman.[8]

" It is a significant fact," says Colonel Henderson, " that, during the war of Secession, for the three years the control of the armies of the North remained in the hands of the Cabinet, the balance of success lay with the Confederates. But, in March 1864, Grant was appointed Commander-in-Chief; Lincoln abdicated his military functions in his favor, and the Secretary of War had nothing more to do than to comply with his requisitions. Then, for the first time, the enormous armies of the Union were manœuvred in harmonious combination, and the superior force was exerted to its full effect." [9]

" Lincoln, when the army he had so zealously toiled to organize, reeled back in confusion from Virginia, set himself to learn the art of war. He collected, says his biographer, a great library of military books; and, if it were not pathetic, it would be almost ludicrous, to read of the great President . . . poring night after night, while his capital was asleep, over the pages of Jomini and Clausewitz. And what was the result? In 1864, when Grant was appointed to the command of the Union armies, he said: ' I neither ask nor desire to know anything of your plans. Take the responsibility and act, and call on me for assistance.' He had learned at last that no man is a born strategist." [10]

---

[8] Cf. Henderson, *Science of War*, 239–240.   [10] *Ibid.*, 500–501.
[9] 1 Henderson, *Stonewall Jackson*, 255.

The first year of the war was one of unpreparedness; the second, of mismanagement; the third, of alternate success and failure. The fourth year marked the end of the political mismanagement of the forces: a trained soldier, for the first time, took full control of military operations. It had required three years of war to teach the Union authorities that trained professional soldiers should run armies, just as much as educated surgeons should manage hospitals.

" In war," said Napoleon, " men are nothing; it is the *man* who is everything. The general is the head, the whole of an army. It was not the Roman army that conquered Gaul, but Cæsar; it was not the Carthaginian army that made Rome tremble in her gates, but Hannibal; it was not the Macedonian army that reached the Indus, but Alexander; it was not the French army that carried the war to the Weser and the Inn, but Turenne; it was not the Prussian army which, for seven years, defended Prussia against the three greatest Powers of Europe, but Frederick the Great."

" The history of famous armies," writes Henderson, " is the history of great generals; for no army has ever achieved great things unless it has been well commanded." [11]

The history of the Army of the Potomac well illustrates this point. Between the soldiers of the North and the South there was little difference in martial qualities. Both were equally strong in defence, and displayed that stubborn resolve to maintain their ground which is characteristic of the Anglo-Saxon race. " My men," said Stonewall Jackson, " sometimes fail to drive the enemy from his position, but to hold one, never! " The Federal generals might have made the same assertion with equal truth.

But, if the armies were well matched in defence, it must be conceded that the Confederates were more vigorous in the attack. At Antietam, McClellan had twice as many men as Lee; at the Second Manassas, on the first day, Pope outnumbered Jackson two to one; yet on both

[11] 2 Henderson, 417.

occasions the smaller force was victorious. Except at Borodino, where he held his Old Guard in reserve, and probably wisely, Napoleon never hesitated to put in his last man. Just before the battle of Chancellorsville, Lincoln warned Hooker " to put in all his men "; and the final defeat of the Union army was due mainly to the commander's failure to follow this advice. The Federal generals invariably kept large masses in reserve, and these masses were never used.

Again, the Federal soldiers in the East fought under the terrible disadvantage of having no confidence in their leaders. McClellan won the affection of his men, but it is doubtful whether they ever gave him credit for dash or resolution. The other commanders of the Army of the Potomac did not succeed in inspiring either love or confidence.

In the West, the Union armies were more successful, because they were better commanded, while the Confederates were led by men of inferior ability, as compared with Lee, Jackson, and Longstreet. Yet the Western armies of the Confederacy were fully as brave and as well disciplined as those of Virginia.

Without in any degree disparaging the high reputation of the Confederate soldiers, we may say, then, that it was not the Army of Northern Virginia which for three years kept the Federals at bay in front of Richmond, but Lee; not the Army of the Valley which paralyzed the Washington Government in 1862, but Jackson.[12]

Strategy is defined as the art of bringing the enemy to battle, while *tactics* are the method by which a commander seeks to overwhelm him when battle is joined.

Grand tactics, the art of generalship, include those strategems, manœuvres, and devices, by which victories are won, and concern only those officers who may find themselves in independent command. *Minor tactics* include the formation and disposition of the three arms for attack and defence, and concern officers of every rank.

Defeat is far more often due to bad strategy than to

---

[12] 2 Henderson, 416–460.

bad tactics. So the Confederates, despite their numerous successes, were beaten in the end through strategical faults: the failure to concentrate in sufficient numbers to reap the fruits of victory; the unnecessary dispersion of the troops; the deliberate disregard of the great end of strategy, namely, the annihilation of the enemy's fighting men, and the destruction of his material resources. To bring a stubborn enemy to his knees, the war, like that of Rome against Carthage, " must be carried into Africa."

Stonewall Jackson constantly advocated the invasion of the North, but in the councils of the South political expediency over-rode military considerations. Mr. Davis, always trusting that sooner or later the European Powers would intervene, chose *defence*, not *defiance*, as his motto.[13]

Whenever he could seize the initiative, Napoleon never hesitated to invade the enemy's territory, even when he was inferior in strength to the mass of the opposing forces. The wisdom of an offensive policy is shown by the campaign of Gettysburg, where the Confederacy was " within a stone's throw of independence."

But the South, having deliberately chosen a defensive policy, made good use of its opportunities. Strategical points which lay at a distance from the main field of operations were garrisoned with the very smallest force compatible with security, while the two main armies, in Virginia and in the West, were always maintained at the greatest possible strength. There was one notable and fatal exception to this rule: after the loss of the Mississippi, by the fall of Vicksburg and Port Hudson, no less than 55,000 men were retained west of the river where they were absolutely useless to the Confederacy. These troops, transferred either to Virginia or to Tennessee, might have turned the almost evenly balanced scale.[14] The explanation probably is that many of the Southern soldiers objected to serving outside their own States. The strong feeling of States' rights is shown by the fact that Lee

---

[13] *Cf.* Henderson, *Science of War*, 38, 168, 45, and 253.

[14] Even before the fall of Vicksburg, General J. E. Johnston recommended this course to President Davis, but no action was taken. See Johnston's *Narrative*, 149–153.

always preferred Virginians, both officers and men, for his own army.

Throughout the war, the Confederates possessed the great advantage of interior lines, of which they availed themselves on many occasions. Thus, in 1863, after Gettysburg, Longstreet was sent West with 16,000 men from Lee's army, and enabled Bragg to gain the important victory of Chickamauga, which prolonged the life of the Confederacy for many months.

It must be said, however, that this shifting of strength from one wing to the other was made feasible by the errors of the Federals. It was not until Grant took command in 1864 that the Union forces operated in combination. Grant seems to have been the first to recognize the fact that the true objective of a campaign is the defeat of the enemy's main army. Before he took command, as Sherman well expressed it, " the trouble was that the commanders never went out to lick anybody, but always thought first of keeping from getting licked." Grant was always ready to force the fight, and his policy of constant " hammering," although terribly and unnecessarily expensive, was in the end successful.[15]

Some of the most remarkable victories in the war — such as the first and second Manassas, and Chancellorsville — were won by two distinct forces, approaching the field of battle from different directions, and crushing the enemy between them. Moltke has laid it down that the junction of two previously separated forces on the field of battle is the highest triumph of generalship; but Napoleon, although on more than one occasion he availed himself of the expedient, was never weary of pointing out the risk.[16]

In all ages the power of intellect has asserted itself in war. It was not courage and experience only that made Hannibal, Alexander, and Cæsar, the greatest names of antiquity. Napoleon, Wellington, and Archduke Charles, were certainly the best educated soldiers of their time; while Lee, Jackson, and Sherman, probably knew more

[15] Henderson, *Science of War,* 253–256.
[16] *Ibid.,* 75.

of war before they waged it than any one else in the United States.[17]

Surprise has been the foundation of almost all the grand strategical combinations of the past, as it will be of those to come. To what Federal soldier did it occur, on the morning of Chancellorsville, that Lee, confronted by 90,000 Federals, would detach the half of his own small force of 50,000 to attack the enemy in flank and rear? The heaven-born strategist "takes no counsel of his fears." Knowing that success is seldom to be won without incurring risks, he is always greatly daring; and by the skill with which he overcomes all obstacles he shows his superiority to the common herd.[18]

The enlistments in the Union army during the Civil War aggregated 2,562,611. This does not include 105,000 seamen and marines, or some 230,000 militia and "emergency men," who served for short terms. Many of the enlistments, however, were for terms of only three to nine months, and the number, reduced to a term of three years, was 1,556,678.

It is not so easy to give exact figures for the Confederate army. Colonel Livermore says: "It is most disappointing that the mass of records published by the War Department contains no summary of the numbers who were under arms on the Confederate side. General Cooper, the adjutant-general of the Confederate army, stated soon after the war that no such summary existed. (7 *So. Hist. Society Papers,* 209)." [19]

On the contrary, General Cooper stated (2 *So. Hist. Society Papers,* 20): "The files of this office which could best afford this information [as to numbers] were carefully boxed up and taken on our retreat from Richmond to Charlotte, N. C., where they were unfortunately captured, and, as I learn, are now in Washington."

There is no doubt as to the fact that the files referred to by General Cooper were in the archives of the War Department as late as 1867, and why they have never been published officially is a mystery.

[17] *Ibid.,* 3.
[18] *Ibid.,* 35, 36.
[19] Livermore, 1–2.

CONCLUSION

The New York *Tribune* of the 26 June 1867 printed, from " Our Special Correspondent," an article on this subject which, for a long time, was supposed to have been the work of Swinton,[20] but later was attributed to Whitelaw Reid. It read:

" Amongst the documents which fell into our hands at the downfall of the Confederacy are the returns, very nearly complete, of the Confederate armies from their organization in the summer of 1861 down to the spring of 1865. These returns have been carefully analyzed, and I am enabled to furnish the returns in every department and for almost every month, from these official sources. *We judge, in all, 600,000 different men were in the Confederate ranks during the war.*"[21]

In the absence of official records, this is certainly good secondary evidence; and further confirmation is to be found in the fact that the *American Cyclopedia* (1875), edited by Charles A. Dana, late Assistant Secretary of War, quotes General Cooper's statement as to numbers, without comment.

Vice-President Stephens, Generals Cooper, Early, Wright, and Preston, Dr. Jones, and Dr. Bledsoe, — in fact, all of the Confederate authorities, who were familiar with the facts, agree that the total number of men in the army was about 600,000.

Their estimates are based upon the following figures:

Killed, or died of wounds		74,508
Deaths from all other causes		125,836
		200,344
Discharged	57,411	
Deserted	83,372	
Prisoners (1865)	90,000	
Surrendered (1865)	174,223	405,006
		605,350

[20] Swinton was connected with the *Times* — not the *Tribune*.

[21] The italics are ours. The tables are omitted here, but can be found in full in Gardner's *Acts of the Republican Party as Seen by History*. See also 6 Channing, 430–436, where the potential military strength of the South is estimated at 900,000, and the number who served, " at one time or another," at 800,000.

A very instructive report to the Confederate Secretary of War, in January 1864, covering only six states east of the Mississippi, gives the following statistics regarding those not in the service:

Deducted for disloyalty	44,000
Unaccounted for (skulkers)	70,000
Exempt for all causes	96,000
Liable, but not enrolled	126,000
	336,000

Adding this total to the number of men actually enrolled (605,000) we have an aggregate of 941,000, which accounts for all but five per cent. of the men of military age in the Southern States, as shown by the Census of 1860.

During the first year of the war the Confederate ranks were filled entirely by volunteers. Then the act of the Confederate Congress of the 16 April 1862 authorized the President to call out for three years all white men resident in the Confederacy between the ages of 18 and 35. An act approved 27 September the same year enlarged the conscription to include all white males, not exempt, between 18 and 45; and the act of 17 February 1864 made all white males between 17 and 50 liable for service.

The only reliable basis, therefore, for estimating the potential military strength of the Confederacy is the United States Census of 1860. This gives in the eleven Confederate States a total of 984,475 white males between the ages of 18 and 45. It is thus demonstrated that the maximum possible strength of the Southern forces was less than a million men.

In the issue of *Current History* for August 1923, there is a labored article by A. B. Cassellman, in which he endeavors to prove that there were 1,650,000 men in the Confederate army! This, by the way, is an increase of 10 per cent., or 150,000 men, from his previous estimate of 1,500,000 in *The Century* for March 1892.

Based upon the Census, Livermore estimates the number at 1,239,000; and based upon the average strength of regiments, at 1,228,000 to 1,406,000.

On the usual assumption that one in five of a total population is of age for military service, the Census of 1860, which showed in the Southern States a white population of about 5,500,000, would give an aggregate of 1,100,000 men of military age, but the actual figures were 984,000. Deducting the disloyal, the skulkers, the sick and unfit, and those legally exempt, we find that the actual military strength of the Confederacy could not have much exceeded 600,000 men.

The "estimates" of Colonel Livermore, and other Northern authorities, that there were from 1,200,000 to 1,650,000 men in the Confederate service are therefore manifestly absurd. The maximum man-power was less than a million, and no nation can possibly mobilize more than 60 per cent. of its entire male population. Granted that there were three and a half millions of slaves, to do the domestic work, and furnish the manual labor, for raising the crops, and working on roads and fortifications, there must have been a large proportion of the adult white male population engaged in non-combatant work, such as making arms, ammunition, and supplies of every kind for the army, as well as employed in clerical and other positions.

In arriving at his figure of 1,239,000, for the number of men who came within the conscription acts, Colonel Livermore takes the census figures of 1860, then adds about 25 per cent. for the boys who reached the age of military service during the war, and assumes that *they were all in the ranks!* But this increase was fully counterbalanced by the number of men who passed the age of service; by deaths from natural causes, and by losses in battle. Moreover, fully 40 per cent. of the million adult white population of the Confederacy was in the four states of Tennessee, Arkansas, Louisiana, and Texas, from which comparatively few recruits were obtained during the last two years of the war.

In the letters of General Lee to his Government we find constant complaints of the unsatisfactory results from the conscription. For example, on the 11 February 1863, he writes the Secretary of War that only 421 new men have joined and 287 deserters returned, an aggregate of 708; while his losses by deaths, discharges, and desertions, amount to 1878. He begs the Secretary to use every means in his power to fill up the ranks.

Colonel Livermore, in another place, estimates the total Confederate levies, reduced to a three years' term of service, at 1,082,119, as compared with a similar figure of 1,556,678 for the Union army. This would give the Confederates about 70 per cent. of the Union strength; but a comparison of the Confederate and Union rolls, on the first days of January 1863, 1864, and 1865, gives them only 50 per cent. approximately of the Union totals. No adequate explanation of this discrepancy is offered.[22]

The total number of men in the five main armies of the Union and the Confederacy, in service at any one period during the last year of the war, was approximately as follows:[23]

	Federals	Confederates
Arkansas	30,000	20,000
Tennessee	70,000	40,000
Shenandoah	40,000	20,000
Carolinas	60,000	30,000
Virginia	100,000	60,000
	300,000	170,000

The same authority estimates the largest number of men in the Confederate army at any one time, the beginning of 1864, as 472,000; and, assuming that the deaths *prior to that date* were 250,000, arrives at an aggregate of over 700,000.[24]

As the Confederate deaths, *during the entire war*, were about 200,000, these figures practically confirm the Confederate estimates.

The total deaths in the Union army during the Civil

[22] See Livermore, 1–22, 47–50.
[23] 4 B. & L., 367, 472, 530, 696, 590.
[24] 4 B. & L., 767–768.

CONCLUSION

War, as shown by the Official Records, and in the Confederate army, as estimated bv General Cooper, were:

	Federals	Confederates
Killed, or died of wounds	110,000	75,000
Deaths from other causes	250,000	125,000
	360,000	200,000

These statistics show that, in the Union army, 25 men died from disease to 11 who were killed or died from their wounds, while in the Confederate army the ratio was 25 to 15 — the average accepted ratio being 25 to 10. Taking into consideration the meagre hospital equipment of the South, the comparatively small proportion of deaths from disease is difficult to explain; but there is no doubt of the fact that the Southerners proved themselves able to withstand the strain of war better than their Northern opponents.[25]

A whole volume might be written on the subject of numbers and losses, but we think that enough has been said to show that the Southern figures are substantially correct, and the Northern estimates grossly exaggerated.

The history of the Civil War conclusively proves the truth of Napoleon's adage, that Fortune always favors the heaviest battalions. There was but little difference in the fighting qualities of the two opposing armies. The South, on the whole, had abler commanders, a superior staff, and a more efficient intelligence department. The Confederate soldiers were better disciplined, more expert marksmen, finer horsemen, and more enduring marchers. Finally, the South had the enormous advantage of interior lines, and of acting generally on the defensive.

The North finally won, when it brought all its strength to bear, because it had far greater numbers, and enormous superiority in physical resources, such as arms, munitions of war, transportation, food, clothing, and hospital supplies. These advantages were, to a certain extent, counterbalanced by the fact that the Union armies were

[25] See 6 Channing, 24.

generally acting on the offensive, in the enemy's country, far from their base, thus making necessary large detachments to guard their lines of communication. Many Federal troops also were employed in non-combatant work, such as was done by negroes for the Southern army. Moreover, during the first three years of the war, the Union generals were constantly hampered by interference from their Government, and by lack of confidence on the part of their troops. " The success of our army," writes General Palfrey, " was undoubtedly greatly lessened by jealousy, distrust, and general want of *entente cordiale.*"

It is not necessary, therefore, to imagine that the South had twice as many soldiers as it really had, in order to explain why it took the North four long years to subdue a nation of a quarter its size.

Opinions have always differed, and probably always will, as to the reasons for the failure of the Southern States to achieve their independence. Northern writers generally assume that it was due to the larger population and greater resources of the Union; Southern authorities ascribe it to a want of perseverance, unanimity, and even of loyalty, on the part of the South.

The main cause, however, seems to have been the bad financial policy adopted by the Confederate Government. Mr. Davis and his Cabinet must have realized that a full treasury was necessary to defray the expenses of a great war; but they deliberately rejected the best means of raising money: the sale of the large and valuable cotton crop.

Statistics show that the cotton crop of 1860 amounted to nearly four million bales, and it is estimated that the South had on hand at the outbreak of the war about five million bales. During the war, " the price of cotton reached almost fabulous figures " in England. The mill-owners were finally forced to shut down entirely, and two million people were reduced to great distress. This cotton, if stored abroad at that time, could have been sold for at least $500,000,000, and probably for much more. The blockade of the Southern ports was proclaimed in May 1861, but it was not at all effective until the following spring. There was thus a period of nearly twelve months during which shipments could easily have been made. "The sum raised in that way," writes General Johnston, "would have enabled the War Department to procure at once arms enough for half a million of men, and after that expenditure the Confederate treasury would have been much richer than that of the United States." [26]

Not only could the forces of the Confederacy have been completely armed and equipped, but the men could have been well fed, well paid, and the sick and wounded properly cared for. The Government, however, rejected this means of filling the treasury, and limited its financial efforts to printing bank-notes, which soon became practically worthless. During the last year of the war the monthly pay of a soldier would scarcely buy one meal for his family. Many men, thus compelled to choose between their loyalty to the State and their duties to their wives and children, left the army, or took every means to avoid military service, in order to support their families.

The proposition, that the Confederate Government should acquire all the cotton in the South, and ship it to Europe to be sold, was made when the problem of financing the war was seriously discussed at the outbreak of hostilities. The owners were ready to accept any fair terms that might be offered; and at that time, as above stated, there would have been no difficulty in putting the plan into operation. But this wise policy was rejected by Mr. Davis and his advisers, in the expectation that the distress caused by the lack of cotton in England and France would lead these two Powers to intervene, and force the United States to raise the blockade. Instead of relying on their own ample resources to win their independence, the Confederate States thus threw away their only means of financing the war. It was one of the worst political blunders in history, and it resulted in the loss of the struggle. With a full treasury, the success of the Confederacy would probably have been assured.

[26] Johnston's *Narrative*, 422. See Appendix H.

[447]

BIBLIOGRAPHY

THE principal source for the history of the Civil War is the *War of the Rebellion Official Records of the Union and Confederate Armies*, in 128 volumes, published by the Government, 1880–1901. In citing the Records the serial number only of the volume is given.

The list of books on the war is so long that it is possible to mention here only a few of the more important titles. For a fuller bibliography, see the *Cambridge Modern History*, vol. VII; also J. N. Larned, *Literature of American History*, in which about 300 of the more important works up to 1902 are considered. A guide to the thousands of articles published in magazines will be found in Poole's *Index*.

In addition to the special works listed below, the reader is referred to the general histories of McMaster, Rhodes, and Schouler.

WORKS CITED

ALEXANDER, GENERAL E. P. *Military Memoirs of a Confederate*. New York, 1907.

BATTLES AND LEADERS OF THE CIVIL WAR. 4 vols. New York, 1887.

BUCHAN, JOHN. *Two Ordeals of Democracy*. New York, 1925.

CAMPAIGNS OF THE CIVIL WAR. 12 vols. New York, 1882–1883.

    1. NICOLAY. *The Outbreak of Rebellion.*

    2. FORCE. *From Fort Henry to Corinth.*

    3. WEBB. *The Peninsula.*

    4. ROPES. *The Army Under Pope.*

    5. PALFREY. *The Antietam and Fredericksburg.*

    6. DOUBLEDAY. *Chancellorsville and Gettysburg.*

    7. CIST. *The Army of the Cumberland.*

    8. GREENE. *The Mississippi.*

    9. COX. *Atlanta.*

    10. COX. *Franklin and Nashville.*

    11. POND. *The Shenandoah Valley.*

    12. HUMPHREYS. *The Virginia Campaign of 1864 and 1865.*

BIBLIOGRAPHY

CHANNING, EDWARD. *History of the United States.* Vol. VI. 1925.

COX, GENERAL J. D. *Military Reminiscences.* 2 vols. New York, 1900.

DAVIS, JEFFERSON. *Rise and Fall of the Confederate Government.* 2 vols. New York, 1881.

FISKE, JOHN. *The Mississippi Valley in the Civil War.* Boston, 1900.

GANOE, MAJOR WILLIAM A. *History of the United States Army.* New York, 1924.

GRACIE, ARCHIBALD. *The Truth about Chickamauga.* Boston, 1911.

GRANT, GENERAL U. S. *Personal Memoirs.* 2 vols. New York, 1885.

HENDERSON, COLONEL G. F. R. *Stonewall Jackson.* 2 vols. London, 1898. Also, *The Science of War.* London, 1919.

JOHNSTON, GENERAL J. E. *Narrative of Military Operations.* New York, 1874.

LIVERMORE, COLONEL T. L. *Numbers and Losses in the Civil War.* Boston, 1901.

LONG, A. L. *Memoirs of Robert E. Lee.* Philadelphia, 1887.

LONGSTREET, GENERAL JAMES. *From Manassas to Appomattox.* Philadelphia, 1896.

MACARTNEY, C. E. *Lincoln and His Generals. Philadelphia,* 1925.

MAURICE, SIR FREDERICK. *Robert E. Lee.* New York, 1925.

RHODES, JAMES F. *History of the Civil War.* New York, 1917.

ROPES, JOHN G. *Story of the Civil War.* 2 vols. New York, 1894–1898. Also the continuation by Colonel W. R. Livermore, 4 vols. New York, 1913.

SHERIDAN, GENERAL P. H. *Personal Memoirs.* 2 vols. New York, 1888.

SHERMAN, GENERAL W. T. *Memoirs.* 2 vols. New York, 1875.

SMITH, THEODORE C. *Life and Letters of James A. Garfield.* New Haven, 1925.

STEELE, MAJOR M. F. *American Campaigns.* 1 vol. and atlas. Washington, 1922.

UPTON, GENERAL EMORY. *Military Policy of the United States.* Washington, 1912.

VAN HORNE, THOMAS B. *History of the Army of the Cumberland.* 2 vols. and atlas. Cincinnati, 1875.

INDEX

INDEX

Ball's Bluff, battle of, 85

Banks, General N. P., in the Shenandoah Valley, 92 *ff*; in campaign of Second Manassas, 125–148; in Vicksburg campaign, 276

Barlow, General F. C., at Gettysburg, 229–263; at Spottsylvania, 344–365; at Petersburg, 403–426

Barnes, General S. M., at Chickamauga, 283–310

Barry, General, at Manassas, 31–45

Bartow, General, at Manassas, 31–45

Bate, General W. B., in Nashville campaign, 384–400

"Battle above the Clouds," 321; the legend of, 454

Beauregard, General P. G. T., sent to Fort Sumter, 8; demands surrender of Fort Sumter, 9; in Manassas campaign, 27–45; at Shiloh, 64–82; gives up Western command, 193; placed in command in the West, 386; approves Hood's plans, 386; his defence of Petersburg, 405 *ff*; his reports to Lee, 408

Beatty, General Samuel, in Nashville campaign, 384–400

Beaver Dam Creek, battle of, 106–108; losses, 108

Bee, General B. E., at Manassas, 31–45

Big Black, engagement at, 279

Birney, General D. B., at Chancellorsville, 226; at Gettysburg, 229–263; at Spottsylvania, 344–365; at Petersburg, 403–426

Blair, General F. P., Jr., in Atlanta campaign, 366–383; goes home for politics, 384

Blenker, General, at Manassas, 29–45

"Bloody Angle," at Gettysburg, 253; at Spottsylvania, 351–354

Bonham, General, at Manassas, 31–45

Bragg, General Braxton, at Shiloh, 64–82; at Murfreesboro, 191–206; succeeds Beauregard, 193; his advance into Kentucky,

196 *ff*; return to Chattanooga, 198; occupies Murfreesboro, 199; at Chickamauga, 283–310; at Chattanooga, 311–326; sent to Atlanta, 376; report to Davis, 376

Brandy Station, cavalry battle at, 235

Brannan, General J. M., at Chickamauga, 283–310

Breckinridge, General J. C., at Shiloh, 64–82; at Murfreesboro, 191–206; at Chickamauga, 283–310; at Chattanooga, 311–326

Brockenbrough, General J. M., at Gettysburg, 229–263

Buchanan, President, decides to reenforce Sumter, 6

Buckner, General S. B., at Fort Donelson, 55 *ff*; at Chickamauga, 283–310

Buell, General Don Carlos, sent to Major Anderson, 5; in Donelson campaign, 49–62; in Shiloh campaign, 64–82; on pursuit at Shiloh, 78; his march on Chattanooga, 192 *ff*; withdraws to Louisville, 195–197; is relieved of command, 198; sketch of, 198; Mr. Ropes's opinion of, 198

Buford, General John, at Gettysburg, 229–263

Bull Run, *see* Manassas

Burnside, General A. E., at Manassas, 29–45; at Antietam, 149–172; at Fredericksburg, 173–190; his plan of campaign, 180; his orders at Fredericksburg, 184; relieved of command, 189; at The Wilderness, 327–343; at Spottsylvania, 344–365; at Petersburg, 403–426; his neglect in the affair of the Mine, 413; his resignation from the service, 413

Butler, General B. F., commands Massachusetts brigade, 25; his rôle in the Petersburg campaign, 405 *ff*; his hold on Grant, 425, note

Butterfield, General Daniel, at Fredericksburg, 173–190

INDEX

INDEX

INDEX

INDEX

INDEX

scription of the field, 28; battle of, 31–45; numbers and losses, 39; comments, 40–45

Manassas, Second, Campaign of, 125–148: — theatre of the campaign, 128; battle of the 29 August, 136 *ff*; repulse of the Federals, 139; arrival of Longstreet, 139; comments, 145–148; battle of the 30 August, 142 *ff*; defeat of the Federals, 143; losses, 144; general comments, 467–469

Mansfield, General, in Antietam campaign, 149–172; killed at Antietam, 165

March to the Sea, *see* Nashville Campaign

Maurice, General, on the siege of Petersburg, 425–426

McClellan, General G. B., appointed commander-in-chief, 46; plan of operations, 47; in command of Army of the Potomac, 83; sketch of, 83–84; the Peninsula campaign, 83–104; description of situation at Washington, 84; powers of organization, 84; plan of campaign, 85; ill with typhoid fever, 85; the Seven Days, 105–124; criticisms of his campaign in the Peninsula, 119 *ff*; despatches to the Government, 122–123; recall from the Peninsula, 124; his army leaves Harrison's Landing, 130; Antietam campaign, 149–172; reinstated in command, 151; his army recrosses the Potomac, 175; he is relieved of the command, 176; estimate of, 176–179; compared with Grant, 363 *ff*; General Upton on the criticisms of, 463 *ff*

McClernand, General J. A., at Donelson, 52 *ff*; in Vicksburg campaign, 264–282

McCook, General A. McD., at Shiloh, 64–82; at Murfreesboro, 191–206; at Chickamauga, 283–310

McCook, General Daniel, at Chickamauga, 283–310

McDowell, battle of, 94

McDowell, General Irwin, at Manassas, 27–45; in Peninsula campaign, 91 *ff*; at Second Manassas, 125–148

McLaws, General Lafayette, at Antietam, 149–172; at Fredericksburg, 173–190; at Chancellorsville, 207–228; at Gettysburg, 229–263; at Chickamauga, 283–310

McPherson, General J. B., in Vicksburg campaign, 264–282; in Atlanta campaign, 366–383; killed at Atlanta, 379

Meade, General G. G., at Antietam, 149–172; at Fredericksburg, 173–190; at Chancellorsville, 207–228; at Gettysburg, 229–263; appointed to command, 237; decides to stand at Gettysburg, 245; calls a council of war, 249; decision not to withdraw, 249; his manoeuvres against Lee in autumn of 1863, 327 *ff*; at The Wilderness, 327–343; at Spottsylvania, 344–365; at Petersburg, 403–426

Means of Transit, 11, 48

Mechanicsville, battle of, *see* Beaver Dam Creek

Merrimac, 87, 90

Merrit, General Wesley, at Spottsylvania, 344–365; at Petersburg, 403–426

Miles, General D. S., at Manassas, 29–45

Mill Springs, battle of, 51

Mine, the Petersburg, 411–414

Minty, General R. H. G., at Chickamauga, 283–310

Missionary Ridge, battle of, 322–324

Mississippi River, 266 *ff*

Mitchell, General J. G., at Chickamauga, 283–310

Monitor, 87

Monroe, Fort, 87 *ff*

Morell, General G. W., at Antietam, 149–172

Morgan, General John, destroys tunnel at Gallatin, 194

Mott, General Gershom, at Spottsylvania, 344–365; at Petersburg, 403–426

INDEX

INDEX

344 *ff*; Henderson's comments, 344–345, 364–365; Grant's determination to win, 345; ovation from his men, 346; battle of Spottsylvania, 349–356; the "bloody angle," 351–354; reasons for Union failure, 354–355; Sheridan's raid, 357; death of Stuart, 357; Lee's position at North Anna, 358; Grant's assault at Cold Harbor, 360–361; numbers and losses, 362; comments, 362–365; Grant, the "Hammerer," 363–364; entrenchments, 364

Spring Hill, Hood's failure at, 389

Stanley, General D. S., in Atlanta campaign, 366–383

Stanley, General T. R., at Chickamauga, 283–310

Stanton, Secretary, his impatience over Thomas's delay, 394; opposes Sheridan's appointment, 409

Stedman, Fort, Lee's assault on, 415–416

Steedman, General J. B., at Chickamauga, 283–310; in Nashville campaign, 384–400; commands provisional division, 387

Steele, Major, comments on Fort Donelson, 61; comments on Peninsula campaign, 124

Steinwehr, General Adolph von, at Chancellorsville, 207–228; at Gettysburg, 229–263

Stephens, Alexander H., elected Vice-President of Confederate States, 8

Stevens, General I. I., at Second Manassas, 125–148; killed at Chantilly, 144

Stevenson, General T. G., at The Wilderness, 327–343; at Spottsylvania, 344–365

Stewart, General A. P., at Chickamauga, 283–310; at Chattanooga, 311–326; in Atlanta campaign, 366–383; succeeds Loring, 378; in Nashville campaign, 384–400; his negligence at Spring Hill, 389

Stoneman, General George, absent at Chancellorsville, 224; in Atlanta campaign, 366–383

Stones River, *see* Murfreesboro

Strategy, at Manassas, 40–42; general, in the West, 60; of the Change of Base, 120; Lee's at Fredericksburg, 190; in Vicksburg campaign, 282; in Wilderness campaign, 362 *ff*; Thomas's in Nashville campaign, 400; definition of, 437; of the South, 438–439

Stuart, General David, at Shiloh, 64–82

Stuart, General J. E. B., at Manassas, 36–45; in the Peninsula, 83–104; his first cavalry raid, 103; at Second Manassas, 125–148; at Antietam, 149–172; raid in October 1862, 173; at Fredericksburg, 173–190; at Chancellorsville, 207–228; in command of Jackson's corps, 220 *ff*; in Gettysburg campaign, 229–263; failure of his raid, 263; at The Wilderness, 327–343; at Spottsylvania, 344–365; killed at Yellow Tavern, 357

Sumter, Fort, siege of, 3–10

Sumner, General E. V., the Seven Days, 105–124; at Antietam, 149–172; at Fredericksburg, 173–190; relieved from duty, 189

Sykes, General George, at Manassas, 30–45; at Antietam, 149–172; at Chancellorsville, 207–228; at Gettysburg, 229–263

Tactics, at Manassas, 42–44; at Shiloh, 73, 79, 81; Confederate at Gaines's Mill, 111; at Antietam, 171; at Murfreesboro, 206; Colonel Henderson's comments on Lee's, 228; in Wilderness campaign, 343, 362 *ff*; in Atlanta campaign, 382–383; Thomas's in Nashville campaign, 400; definition of, 437

Theatre of the Civil War, 10–13

Thomas, General G. H., at Mill Springs, 51; sketch of, 51; in Murfreesboro campaign, 191–206; at Chickamauga, 283–310;

INDEX